I COULD BE ANYONE

*The cover photograph - showing from left to right: Matthew Scurfield, Pete Glass and
Ian Owen Moore, alias Emo, on Garret Hostel Bridge in Cambridge during the early
60s - was taken by an American tourist, who told us we would be arrested if we went
around looking like that back in the States.*

Monticello
18 Saint Peters Street
Gharb, Gozo
Malta GRB 1503

Note

From vagrant actor to full time scriber, it has taken the good part of ten years to write this book. No great shakes you might think, but for someone who could hardly put one word in front of another, during his schooling and for much of his adult life, this is a massive achievement.

To the so called standard eye the style of writing may reflect grammatical shortcomings and the author makes no apologies for this. Over the first two thirds of this story he has deliberately tried to write as age and circumstance dictated, without any mention of dyslexia – in educational establishments, during the fifties and early sixties, the word for the most part just didn't exist. Within the circle of the scholarly classes, such as the Cambridge family he pertained to, this could only mean one thing, abject failure. If the author had written this book without the computer and speech recognition he would have been unable to bypass the major hurdle of spelling and grammar, the text would have been so illegible that any potential reader would have given up in despair before they'd even turned the first page.

The belief in an external world independent of the perceiving subject is the basis of all natural science. Since, however, sense perception only gives information of this external world or of "physical reality" indirectly, we can only grasp the latter by speculative means. It follows from this that our notions of physical reality can never be final. We must always be ready to change these notions - that is to say, the axiomatic basis of physics - in order to do justice to perceived facts in the most perfect way logically.

Albert Einstein

I COULD BE ANYONE

MATTHEW SCURFIELD

For Cecilia

Last Curtain

I know that the day will come
when my sight of this earth shall be lost,
and life will take its leave in silence,
drawing the last curtain over my eyes.

Yet stars will watch at night,
and morning rise as before,
and hours heave like sea waves casting up pleasures and pains.

When I think of this end of my moments,
the barrier of the moments breaks
and I see by the light of death
thy world with its careless treasures.
Rare is its lowliest seat,
rare is its meanest of lives.

Things that I longed for in vain
and things that I got
—let them pass.
Let me but truly possess
the things that I ever spurned
and overlooked.

Rabindranath Tagore

Preface

During a heavy rain storm the shelter of a crumbling gateway brings together a woodcutter, a priest and a peasant. As they begin to talk we find out that the woodcutter was a central witness to a terrible crime. We are shown this horrifying event from the view point of different characters that make up the story. Each character has their own truth and is convinced by what they've seen, but to anyone watching, the truth of what really happened is by no means clear.

Very broadly speaking, this is the narrative of Akira Kurosawa's deceptively ambiguous film about truth, *Rashomon*.

I was fourteen when I first saw this classic motion picture and even then it had a huge impact, but I never really understood why. I remember struggling to piece the narrative together and after a lot of careful consideration left it behind, with the rationale that it was a bleak story about how the imagination can deceive us. But the other day, lounging in front of the television, I inadvertently started watching it again. I felt a little tired and simply allowed the film to wash over me without judgement. I began to realise that my previous attempts at trying to figure out how the truth can lie had been far too intense.

Once I accepted each witness's account as being different, it became clear that Kurosawa's masterpiece isn't about working out what happened and neither is it about guilt, innocence, or verdict; I now think it draws us into something far more challenging: the inability of any one person to realise another person's truth, particularly of a past event, regardless of how clearly he or she thinks they see it.

The convolution of a family truth is such that there are often many different angles from which to view an event, especially when it is viewed from under the canopy of the past – and this is why *Rashomon* is such a good illustration of how complex a simple truth can become.

No matter how we look at it, the overall truth of any event is different, depending on where and how we are in relation to it.

What I went through and the situations that make up my story may be alike, but they are not necessarily the same as anyone else's within the circle of my family and friends. There may be similarities and our paths might cross at many points, but this obviously doesn't mean that we experience the story of what happened in the same way.

Is it possible to see the past as individual and unique? Why should someone else's truth, particularly someone you love, become such a huge threat? How do we see another person's difference without judgment and condemnation, when it is so far away from our own?

If I remain buried in my childhood needs, locked up in a private dungeon with wishes and regrets, I will continue to condemn the differences between us; I will do everything in my power to make you see the world the way I do in order to get what I want. This, as I realise to my emotional cost, is a truly destructive path; a path which, if fulfilled, can at best build a grand facade with foundations made of sand.

It wasn't just my brother's suicide, all those years ago, that rang the alarm bells; there were other major factors that drew me into wanting to write this book. I could no longer avoid the responsibility for my volatility. For the simple fact of my own sanity I needed to get a handle on how to hold the reins; putting words to paper seemed to work; though being around long enough to know I wasn't alone was perhaps the mainstay. It always helped when someone shared their truth and I wanted to give something back by sharing mine. But why should this matter and who really cares?

When I began unravelling the trials of my own life I started to see that many families have a wounded heart, even if it isn't obvious, it's usually somewhere there, tucked out of the way in the attic of the psyche. I have come to believe that it is this very private and personal pain that really fuels the forward motion of our lives. However good our intentions, I think it is this deep rooted suffering that directly, or indirectly, is pushing the planet in the direction of a toxic demise.

Isn't it so, that with all our science and our expertise, we are closer than ever before to a man-made global crisis of monumental proportion. There can certainly be little doubt that we have reached an impasse. It is generally thought, even within the scientific community, that the earth is already in the midst of an ecological meltdown. This oncoming disaster, we are told, has been brought about by man's insatiable need, which to some is seen simply as greed.

Unless we are directly affected by these severe changes, it seems we are too busy with day to day living to heed them much attention. It's not, as we see it, a personal issue.

In western society cynicism has reached epic proportions. It is almost as if it has become so much a part of our upbringing that it's seen as completely abnormal to be otherwise. I believe this basically means we are geared up and all too ready to make those who can't work the system into the enemy, or at best the outsider, a one off quirk of nature who doesn't fit the regular market place.

With or without our scepticism, most of us see the enemy as someone, or something, which comes from elsewhere. In this impulsive world it's certainly important to remain vigilant and extremely cautious when dealing with a malicious force, especially in the short term; but I think in the long term the only enemy really worth considering, is the enemy within us. By enemy, I mean the part of our self that becomes convinced that our lives cannot be other than what they are.

I would like to consider how the destructive side of our nature actually comes about; how this enemy, called by some the devil, ends up lodged like a hidden nemesis inside so many of us.

We are told in no uncertain terms that the acquisition of more knowledge is the answer to all our problems and yet we are closer than ever to blowing ourselves out of the water. Education today is so convinced by the linear formulaic mindset that thousands upon thousands of people, who have a lack of skill in the conventional sense, end up in prison, on drugs, or at worst going to a premature death in someone else's war. Whichever way we look at it, this outcome is a huge burden on society.

By dismissing the man, woman, boy and girl, whose apparent academic worth is nonexistent, are we brushing aside the very pill which might, if it isn't too late, be able to turn this hell bent ride around? By ignoring the person who is seen by many to live in the slow lane, are we in danger of severing a vital life saving link in the chain? This may seem, to many of the experts, as an absurd hypothesis, a ridiculous ideal, but I think that by looking at the problem in a nonlinear way, there is a distinct possibility of an extraordinary shift.

Let's be honest, until the junky, the rapist, or the terrorist climb in through our window, we don't really care what they do, or who they are. Unless the floods come in through our back door, the apparent ozone disintegration is not something we pay much mind to; as long as the war is in another country, what do we really care about who's selling what arms to which leader, or for that matter who gets killed. Until the misfit is one of us and it's up close and in our face, we basically have no time for any of these horrors.

As someone who was to have one foot well and truly rooted in the bottom of the lowest class and the other firmly centred in the excellence of the academic stage, I had what I believe now to be a unique insight into a great divide. From the springboard of my upbringing I found myself at the centre of a fulcrum, where the opposite ends of a dominant society seemed to be spinning further and further out of reach. Sitting at the very heart of this split, I came to see how our global predicaments are born out of a very private and extremely personal place and not something that just emerges from thin air. Our guilt, the wages of our misdemeanours and even our felonies are not born out of original sin, as much of the media and many of our statesmen would like us to believe.

The sting in this tale confronts the fickle agility of our minds, the part of our brain that deceives us into thinking we're walking forwards when we're not. By digging that bit deeper the story goes to the centre of those buried insecurities where an innocent journey is turned into a path of fear, full of mistrust, misdeeds and self destruction.

In the academic heady atmosphere I was born into, it was very hard to accept that our way of life may not be what it seems, as the crème de la crème of our social circles, how could it possibly be otherwise?

Prologue

When I first heard the news of my brother's death, a part of me shut down inside. I guess I went into what is commonly known in therapeutic circles as denial. And although I had been expecting to get the phone call for years, I still wasn't really prepared for it.

Once the flustered funeral had been dealt with, a time for reflection came and instead of grieving, I just went further into the mire of chastising the Cambridge fraternity from which I had evolved.

I wish I'd been less afraid to flow with Ponji's beliefs back then, he was after all my big brother and I looked up to him, but I just didn't feel comfortable with the way he was advocating physical detachment. I am ashamed to say I felt threatened by what he was saying.

Over the many years before he died he would try to explain again and again that the body was just a prison holding back the journey of the soul. I had no idea that what he was really talking about was the pain in his life. If only I'd been more aware of this, I might have been able to stand with him, but I was a million miles away.

I believe that what happened to my brother came about because of his need to feel on top in any situation, particularly when he was around our relations and Cambridge friends. Like me he had always been encouraged to show off; a continuation of the theme that had been prominent in our upbringing.

Nothing could possibly be amiss with such a liberal family! The higher above the ground we danced, the more delighted the audience! Our way of surviving was to not let the side down at any cost. Taking on any task basically meant being the best at it and if we weren't the best then we weren't going to play. When it came to the spiritual wall we had to be the first to climb it and when he jumped off, it was who could jump the furthest.

All I can do now is look back and learn from the lessons that have been racked across my back for all this time. Even without the insight that the practise of yoga was to bring to my life, I could see then that the body was no more an illusion than anything else. I felt quite clearly that our physical existence is made up of the same substance as everything else in the universe and in this sense there is no separation between the body and the soul.

Ponji's conviction in the renunciation of the physical self, in the hope of reaching divine heights, continued to stoke my confusion. His beliefs, or at least the way he put them across, could at times bring me to a standstill and occasionally my temper would erupt.

The worst it ever got was when I took out a knife from the kitchen drawer in the house where I was staying when I was studying acting in north London. I pinned him up against the wall with the point of the sharp blade at his throat and said, "If your body is such an illusion, tell me about it now." He blasted out at me not to be so stupid and to put the knife down. I hit back by saying, "If the body is an illusion why are you so upset about having a knife put to it in this way?"

I was hardly aware of my brother's self-depreciation when I was staying with him in South Kensington in the sixties, but it was there, as it always was, right from the beginning. Most of the time of course, he was able to rise above his feelings and there was no doubt that he was charming and entertaining to be with. When everything was in its place, Ponji would be out and about with our mates and so smooth was he that they would rarely be aware of the downbeats. His meticulous timing and the way he looked could often lead him to a place of tight distraction, especially if he was going out with one of his friends. Like me, he may have put it across differently, but what I really remember of Ponji at that time was of someone caught up in the unending treadmill of what other people thought of his character.

Unlike my brother's previous digs, his room in this London flat was light and airy, but the same neatness cut across the four walls. I can picture myself sitting in the one and only chair there, the same chair which had followed Ponji's lead from his bedroom in our childhood home in Cambridge. Staring down at the pair of Levi jeans, neatly folded across his bed, I'm reminded of how coming across to others was so important in his sweet life. The crease in his cavalry twills was forever present in his personality.

In 1966, on the first day of my visiting this new home, Ponji didn't get back until the evening. He greeted me with his customary calm reserve and warm heart and welcomed me into his room where I stayed the night. He told me in his usual considerate way about his weekly psychotherapy sessions, which involved his taking LSD as a way of getting back to his childhood. There was an air of mystery and intrigue about this; LSD was hardly something I or anyone else for that matter knew much about then. As far as I know Ponji never took LSD for recreational purposes. Very occasionally he smoked marijuana but these times were few and far between.

In my brother's case, LSD opened the door to the nursery. How it was dealt with is uncertain; but the infamous hallucinogen shouldn't be confused with the room itself. It is my belief now that Ponji began to reveal, through opening the door in this way, what was there all along, and when the baby emerged the therapist hadn't got a clue what to do with it. In the aftermath of the sixties, the letters LSD became a very handy hook, on which numerous families hung many of the psychotic and schizophrenic ailments that came pouring forth when these doors of repression were opened.

Lying there on the floor next to his bed reminded me of when I used to hang out with him and his mates from school, in an underground shelter he'd made in the garden at our Aunt Alice's house in Cambridge. Inside this turf covered cave everything was just so, right down to the candle-lit shelving, the glass window and the little wood-burning stove. It was perfectly normal, if it was decided that I could stay the night, for me to share his sleeping bag. I found the warmth and smells of his body comforting.

One of Mozart's symphonies was playing on the Dansette and Ponji was adamant that I should listen, as this was the music of the soul. I don't think he really felt comfortable with sounds that were too popular; this didn't mean he didn't like the cooler vibe. As far as the upbeat tempo went, Miles Davis did it for him and so did the incredible Jimmy Smith. How can I forget the first time I heard Oscar Brown Junior's immortal lines; 'I've always lived by this golden rule / whatever you do don't blow your cool.' The way in which those lyrics hit my parched ears tipped the balance. This primitive rap, about a man whose woman has walked out on him, ends with him shooting his hound dog dead and declaiming at the last minute 'but I was cool'. How Ponji loved that wicked contradiction.

About a year after moving to his flat in South Kensington, my brother graduated from The London Film School and took a job as an editor with a film company in Soho. Soon after this, he attended his first Satsang in Earl's Court: he was blown sideways. Within days he decided to take the trip to India where he became initiated by a spiritual teacher, the Maharaj Charan Singh of Radha Soami Satsang, Beas.

On his return from India, Ponji sat amidst many of his companions and shone like a very bright star. Those that gathered before him talked of a palpable spirit and untold love emanating in radiant form from his face and eyes. Despite his obvious ascent I remained sceptical. Full of bliss my brother moved back to Cambridge, where he was fervent in his practice, spending hours sitting in meditation. To earn money he took on a humble job as an attendant on the punts down by the river.

Ponji went out of his way to share the harmony he had discovered with his friends and relatives. Very gradually he started to turn to his siblings, trying to convince each one of us of his newly found path. We showed some tentative interest, but couldn't really acknowledge this science of the soul that he advocated. None of us took any pleasure in the fact that he had discovered something very special for himself and we ultimately shut the door on any dialogue. He went to our parents with his pearls, but their atheist leanings just couldn't budge, they too weren't able to build any bridges.

After a couple of years things gradually began to wear him down and he got disheartened. He collapsed in on himself and went back to the place of his origin; he went to see our Aunt Alice at Number Nine. The misery streak had won and like a defeated fugitive he confided in her. Unbelievably, her response to being entrusted with his truth was to use her powers as a psychiatrist and have him certified. Barely noticed by his family and friends, Ponji ended up in the mental hospital that is Fullborn just outside Cambridge, where he was given several sessions of electric shock treatment.

With his brain frazzled, my brother came back to London and started doing the rounds; the way he was feeling would dictate where he ended up staying the night. He had a number of close friends who were always happy to put him up.

Ponji wasn't to be thwarted. Like a knight of the grail, he continued trying to bring those closest to him into the fold. It almost seemed at times as if he were testing his faith, using us as a sounding board, digging deeper into our beliefs so as to clarify his own. It wasn't long before the progression of his convictions had him tied like a slave to the helm of a spiritual ship - a self-denigrating soothsayer.

With increasing regularity he would tell us how he was just a hobo and that his body meant nothing in the cosmic and spiritual sense. To get his point across he would occasionally spend all night walking the streets. He started standing for prolonged periods of the day at bus stops and in railway stations whilst repeating his mantra and marshalling his demons. Even in these circumstances there was a meticulous air about his slight body. With his luxuriant hair, bright eyes and ready smile, he still cut a dashing figure. As far as the inquisitive passer-by was concerned he was just another person on the street, but on closer inspection his tired, frayed mac and smart worn shoes told a different story.

By the time the early eighties had crept up on us, I was well into yoga; in fact I was somewhat fanatical. Sometimes three or four hours could go by and I would still be struggling with the heart of an asana; but my practice would become even more intense if Ponji came around. He would often visit my apartment in Fulham, usually when he was at his lowest ebb. Troubled and wound up, he'd sit on the stairs proclaiming that he was a tramp and that his body was just an illusion, a mere prison, a temporary holding place for his soul. Gradually I kind of accepted that this pouring forth was a pattern he'd fall into each time he came to visit; but like they say in the tabloids, 'I didn't think he'd really go and do it.'

There were a couple of witnesses at Victoria Station who saw Ponji just before he died and when they spoke at the tribunal, it was said that he shouted out, as he was running across the platform towards the oncoming train, "I refuse to be a coward for the rest of my life."

And then he jumped.

1

My mother's first husband, Dr. John Robinson, became one of the many to be sacrificed in the bleak whirlpool of World War II. His untimely death meant she was left with two young children, my half sister Elizabeth and my half brother John Paul, whose nickname, from a play on his initials, became Ponji.

Just after the war, our mother and her second husband, my blood father, chose to live in the small village of Shepreth, situated some fourteen miles outside Cambridge. At this time Ponji and Elizabeth were still being looked after by all and sundry at my mother's sister Alice's house in that distinguished city. This meant I only saw them during the school holidays and at the weekends. Of the two of them I saw much more of Ponji, because Elizabeth, for the most part, chose to stay over in Cambridge when she had time off from school.

Ponji, six years my senior, was gregarious to say the least. He loved the spirit of the world and his energy held no bounds in catching up with it. He was practical, charming and loved by everyone. He had artistic hands, with lithe agile fingers that were there for being creative and when he put them to use with his mind, the outcome could be exhilarating. He was well on his way to becoming a Queen Scout. At school, he threw the javelin and discus with aplomb, became a champion high-diver, and a head prefect who knew how to turn a blind eye. He could have fitted with ease into the shoes of head boy, but with definite wisdom chose to steer away from the trappings of such accolades. In the areas he felt lacking, he still strove for excellence. He was forever building superb underground shelters or small well-designed camps to hang out in with his mates. He took to climbing the tallest tree without hesitation, and when we all lived in Cambridge, he sought out the highest steeples among the colleges and ascended their peaks too. He did all this with fearless abandonment, but never compromised his style. And did Ponji have style! He could spin on a sixpence and still be cool. If there was any chink in his armour it was hard to see. He bent the rules when it suited him and usually we were none the wiser.

He strove for perfection in everything he did. When this precision wasn't forthcoming, as on the scholastic side, he would castigate himself rather than blame anyone else, as when, unlike Elizabeth, he failed the eleven plus. Later, this would prove to be his Achilles' heel.

Some few years after I came into the world, Ponji began life as a pupil at the Chesterton School for Boys in Cambridge, where street credibility ruled, whilst Elizabeth was well-established at the County Girls' School, which had, if you like, a more refined curriculum. Continuing the true Edwardian educational tradition meant that coeducation in those days was not yet on the agenda.

Chesterton was a place of learning, full of boys coming from some of the roughest homes in Cambridge. And believe me, I mean rough! Ponji had to learn basic street survival quickly, for his own self-protection. He was a nimble fighter and his tactical skills were such that if the punch-up became too one-sided, he was always able to find a more diplomatic way out of being beaten up. His popularity knew no bounds both at the school and at home. When he and Elizabeth lived together at our Aunt Alice's house in Cambridge, it was Ponji who could do no wrong. This was the persistent theme throughout their life and in this sense, Elizabeth was somewhat overshadowed by her younger brother and at times it became fiercely tiresome for her.

Like Ponji, Elizabeth was highly talented. She was at home in many areas of art and music and found, unlike Ponji, that academic work came her way with ease. She could have gone to university, but chose instead to pursue a career as a dancer. Throughout most of our time in Cambridge Elizabeth seemed to be away and chose only to return during the holidays. As soon as she left school, she began studying ballet at a college in Germany.

Living abroad was to become her specialty. When I was young, her life seemed full of exotic expectation. I loved the idea of her return, because she would bring unusual gifts and tell glamorous stories about where she had been and how well she was doing.

The house filled with excitement and peppery anticipation a few days before she was due back and on her arrival there was a great feeling of camaraderie, where love and warmth spun in all directions.

Then after a few days, when the reality of living with the family kicked in, life started to slip back into a domestic routine and the moods in the house began to change. Gradually Elizabeth's pleasure at being home would evaporate into inevitable wrangling with our mother Cecilia, which increased with intensity as we got older.

When Elizabeth was home for any length of time and Ponji was around, all hell could break loose. Other than petty domestic differences, it was never clear to me why they came to blows, but they did and it always seemed to be my father, rather than my mother, caught in the middle of their ferocious fights. During the years in Shepreth and for a short time in Cambridge he was physically strong enough to keep them apart, but separating them seemed a short-term solution. Like the poles of two strong magnets crashing together, you could almost guarantee, as soon as my father's back was turned they'd be at each other's throats again. I can see him now, in over his head.

Like any child I suppose, I don't remember anything being right or wrong as such. There was no normal or abnormal, just varying degrees of temperament. Mood swings were how I gauged the world I was in. These early memories were very different to the post war optimism my parents must have felt. As far as I was concerned my parents were living the way that suited them; the best way they knew how. I may not have particularly enjoyed Ponji and Elizabeth fighting; or the way my father went about the practicalities around the house; nor for that matter the distance between myself and my mother - but these familial idiosyncrasies were as normal as any other part of my life. It was how I came to live with them that dictated my path into the new world.

Even now I can be caught off guard by a particular environment. This stirring of panic in a grown man may seem completely irrational, but the substance of these memories lights up my mind's eye like the beam of a torch exploring a dark world. The recall makes it as real to me now as it was then, except I have a vague notion of something earlier. I can't be sure, was it dreams of snuggling in my mother's ample breast? There is a clearly defined vision of my mother and another person silhouetted in the doorway of the nursery, when I was no more than a year old. My mother had brought someone to see me in my cot. I found this stranger extremely disturbing and began to cry out. They left abruptly, quietly shutting the door behind them, leaving me in the dark with disquiet for company. The distress finally subsided when my father George came and picked me up.

2

During the first five years of my life, when ration-books were still needed for much of the basic edibles, my parents and I, along with my younger sister Sarah, lived in a 17th century manor house called Docwra`s Manor, situated in the centre of the village. For me there was much darkness, especially inside the house, and as far as I can remember I never moved from my father's side. I clung to his corduroy trousers as if they were my life blood and everywhere they went, I went too. During these tender years we did everything together, from changing my nappies, to being a postman, typing, driving and feeding the pigs.

Docwra`s came with approximately one-and-a-half acres of land, situated mainly to the back of the house. Leaning towards self-sufficiency, my mother and father began to grow their own vegetables and even took to having some livestock about the place. Pigs screaming blue murder from a pig-sty seemed to know when it was their turn for the skip. Chickens, who should have known better, roosting in the trees, laying their eggs in obscure places, made breakfast a daily game of hide and seek. Ferocious geese, given free range, took to attacking anything that moved, particularly humans. When they started attacking me, my father decided they were too much to handle and got rid of them. In the midst of this barnyard fusion, my parents started turning the garden surrounding the house into a botanic haven fit for a queen.

A little over a year after I was born, my mother Cecilia was busy with my sister Sarah, the fourth of the seven children that she was to bring into the world. This vital preoccupation made my longing for my mother even more intense.

Sarah had a fair complexion, with fine blonde hair, giving her a delicate, innocent aura, much like an angel. I loved having a younger sister and came to feel extremely protective toward her. I would take it upon myself to hold her hand whenever we were out-and-about together venturing forth into the unknown.

Outside, hazy days and long afternoons of silence, disturbed only by the insistent hum of a bumble-bee, or the song of a curlew high in the azure sky, made playing an essential pastime. On the inside meanwhile, darkness closed in as I became more aware of my limitations. Gradually I began to get an inkling of a mirage and my surrounding world started to take on an uneasy quietness, which seemed at times to be overwhelming in its power.

The unending silence was occasionally ruffled by the chimes of a fish-and-chip van, or the weekly deliveries of the groceries and the Tizer fizzy drink lorry. Once or twice a year, the suit-and-tie salesman would visit us, with his brown leather suitcase full of handcrafted brushes of all sizes and types, convincing my unsuspecting mother they were the best she could ever have. Sometimes the onion man would come on his special bicycle, all the way from France, peddling into our world like a character from a Jacques Tati movie. He would bring fresh garlic and onion to a welcoming household, and was duly invited in for tea, so whoever was staying in the house could practise their French.

As far as the adults were concerned, fear was something confidently left behind with the war and certainly not to be associated with the immediate neighbourhood of this English family. The celebration of peace was still very much a priority for my parent's generation and for these fortunate survivors of the war, any signs of apprehension were consigned to a recently horrific past. The freedom to allow their children space and time in a quiet traffic-free environment was a welcome relief for both parties; the children had somewhere where they could play, whilst mummy and daddy were free to get on with the bliss of tying up their apron strings.

One of the many entrepreneurial ventures my mother and father undertook in those post-war years was to bake large quantities of bread in the AGA at Docwra's. My father would load the freshly baked loaves into the back of the Jowett van, which he had to start amidst much frustration, with a crank handle, and drive to Cambridge, making deliveries to a few select families in the Adams Road area. This wasn't your usual run-of-the-mill white sliced. This was wholemeal bread, the sort you might buy from a whole-food shop today, but back then it was a rare phenomenon. As word caught on, their bread became highly sought-after, by friends and acquaintances who, in post-war Britain, wanted their toast and sandwiches to be a little more substantial. The taste of their bread was so successful that they wrote a book about it called *Home-Baked*, which I am proud to say, is still highly sought after by eager bakers, even today.

It was during one of these deliveries with my father that I made my first visit to Cambridge, memorable because the door of the van slammed shut on the forefinger of my left hand. George had to take me to have it bandaged by Aunty Alice at Number Nine Adams Road. It was then that Alice started calling me Mitty. I clearly remember standing in a pool of tears in the kitchen and Alice wrapping the sticky-backed Elastoplast round my finger. She made two little ears with the corners of the bandage at the top, then drew a matching face on the plaster and said, "There Mitty, a little rabbit to keep you company".

A trip to France was taken in the Jowett, with my parents in the front, and me, Sarah, Ponji, Elizabeth and her close friend, our cousin, Margaret Alice, all packed together with the camping equipment in the back.

This excursion was unforgettable because it was the first time I had experienced the full on inhalation and exhalation of the sea. I remember running along a beach, hand-in-hand with Sarah, thinking the waves were going to catch us and then daring to stand still a few feet from the water's edge, feeling overwhelmed by the power of the upsurge. I thought we would be sucked into the cavernous, dark blue underbelly of the wave, with its torrid foaming mouth, and disappear forever, when the voice of my dad calling from a distance brought us out of our trance.

We camped in the grounds of a beautiful Chateau, absorbing an evening of whispering trees and fairytale castles interlaced with the sweet smell of a warm French breeze. This was disturbed, only as the evening drew in by what was to become the habitual routine of Ponji and Elizabeth in the midst of a violent quarrel. For the first time I started to take in the terrible struggle that my dad was having as he tried to calm them down.

~

George and Cecilia got married immediately after the war. They had been introduced to each other at a party at Number Nine by George's close friend Jack Goody, a fellow English student and budding anthropologist. They were all up at Cambridge together.

As with many others of their age group, my parents' utopia was to create an environment, for bringing up a family, in a house based on collective principles.

Within months of being in Shepreth, George was writing profusely but wasn't earning enough money for us to live on, so both he and Cecilia sought other creative ways for my father to make some. Becoming the village postman was one, baking bread another.

He proudly and regularly had short stories and poems printed in several anthologies including Tambimuttu's *Poetry in Wartime*. I can sense him now shut away at his desk where he rigorously and silently immersed himself in the unfathomable darkness of the war, writing copiously in that private space. He also wrote about his life in the village. For as long as I can remember he continued producing literary works of art from his typewriter; two of his early novels, set during the war, were published to some acclaim. When I was little and if I was allowed to, I sat on the floor quietly absorbing his soothing presence, as the tac tac tac of his fore-fingers tapping the keys seemed to take him elsewhere. Occasionally he would disappear up to London for the day, to Broadcasting House. In the late afternoon, those of us at home would wait excitedly in the sitting room, then listen intently to the sound of his voice emanating with warm reassurance, telling his stories, from the wooden polished box next to the crackling fire-place.

I was hardly aware of what the polished box was, or how it had come about, but it wasn't long before I became infatuated, particularly at that time with *Listen with Mother*. This program became a daily fix for me. No matter where we were, or what was going on, it was imperative to be sitting comfortably on Daddy's knee and then tune into the sounds of those comforting voices after the music stopped.

Smoking had yet to be directly linked to lung cancer, so both George and Cecilia took to fervent social and political examination whilst puffing on Woodbine cigarettes. George's passions were writing, politics and Cecilia. If any of these came to the forefront during a family debate and he felt the need to speak, his commanding presence became like an emotional barometer. The blood in his veins would rise in temperature as his speech became more animated and the hair on the sides of his head, wired with gentle electrocution, seemed to lift sideways as if in harmony with his verbal delivery.

George took to wearing sandals for the majority of the year and grew a beard whilst on our trip to France, wearing it proudly when it was unfashionable to do so. During the chilly season he felt most comfortable in faded corduroy trousers, soft desert boots and thick oversized handmade pullovers, which Cecilia knitted from intricate Celtic patterns. On smart occasions he wore a tweed jacket with leather patches on the elbows, but with the same well-worn trousers.

My parents gave the impression of not being too concerned about outward appearances. This isn't to say that they weren't aware of what they looked like; in fact George could be fastidious, particularly if he was taken up with grooming his beard. Most evenings they enjoyed sharing the bathroom, and indeed the bath water, before going to bed, so you could never accuse them of being unclean.

Their bedroom was a very private place and the only time I felt it was permissible to disturb their sleeping was if I felt sick, or when I had the need to share the distress of a bad dream. My troubled equilibrium always seemed to agitate my mother, so I felt reluctant to enter the quiet of their bed chamber unless it was absolutely necessary.

I sometimes caught sight of my mother sitting in front of the dressing table looking for the entire world like Rapunzel brushing her long hair, which during the day was tied up in a no-nonsense bun at the back of her head. I was always amazed at just how much hair she could manoeuvre into such a compact space.

If I could sneak into their bedroom during the day I would fondle with care a special brush-and-comb set composed of two brushes, one filled with pale soft bristles, the other looking a bit like the back of a hedgehog, with spine like nails. I would sit there in a timeless state, running my fingers through the soft brush, pulling out traces of my mother's dark hair with a large brown comb and wondering longingly about love.

~

My mother had a passion for theatre and the celebration enshrined in its many guises. Like George she'd been up at Cambridge before the war, but reading English there was as much as she'd tasted of the freedom given to some young ladies of her ilk, whose parents were unencumbered enough to allow them to tread the boards. Nevertheless, she loved getting stuck into any dramas passing her way, and whenever possible her theatrical desires would spew forth into the muck and courage of putting on plays.

My earliest realisation of my mother's theatrical passion is clearly emblazoned in my mind's eye as if it were yesterday. She produced/directed a production of *Beauty and the Beast* at the village hall in Shepreth, and I could not help but become drawn into the emotional roller-coaster of the following weeks. For some reason it was thought of as inappropriate for me to see the play, but the drama acted out at home was enough to give me an idea of that spectacular event. The ride began as I feasted my eyes on a frightening mask made of cloth and papier-mâché, emerging like an apparition from the sitting-room floor. I am sure that when my dad wore that great and terrifying mask it brought the whole village to a standstill. Certainly the house seemed to vibrate with excitement during the mounting of this dramatic event, and the enthusiasm created was to resonate throughout the entire neighbourhood for ages afterwards.

The ride continues to this day, with the echoes of seeing my father transformed into the Beast by that fateful mask.

~

George and Cecilia both came from large families; my father was the last of eight. I am told my grandfather on his side, Harold Scurfield, was a conservative, no-nonsense, well-to-do Yorkshire man who had reached his fifty-seventh year when my father was born. My grandfather was a doctor who became Professor of Medicine and Director of Public Health in Sheffield and sounded as if he could be brazen company. According to George, my grandmother Mary was a gentler person to be with. She taught my father to read and write, and through constant lively debate planted the seeds of socialism in him.

George was eventually sent away to be schooled at Oundle, which he loathed, but almost by accident he found his love for poetry there. It was the writing of poets, he said, that spoke to him of an everyday life, in the language of the people. But it wasn't until he was up at Cambridge, that the fire of socialism really flared up. During his first term at St John's, he joined the Communist Party, which he said was mainly a sentimental and altruistic move on his part.

He slipped from Communism into the Territorial Army and eventually wound up as a Major, in command of a small troop of Ghurkhas during the Second World War, searching out the Japanese, in the Chindwin Hills in Burma. He was awarded the Military Cross for his bravery and twice mentioned in dispatches. Like many of his age group, he found little escape from the nightmares which continued to plague him throughout his life. It wasn't until I read the memoirs of his war years, which he wrote at the latter end of his life, that I began to see the enormity of what he had carried tight to his chest. One thing that leapt out from those pages above all else was his admission to killing two of his own men in Burma. He'd found himself in the terrible and impossible position of having to shoot them dead so they wouldn't give anything away if they were captured.

I shall never forget. I shall never forgive myself. Surely I should have made some kind of effort to get those men home to Imphal. Or I should have made them comfortable and left them with food to last until they were found. But they never would have been found except by tigers; rats and ants; shitehawks and vultures. They asked to be shot. They were noble in their deaths, just as they had been good and true in their lives.
"We must die, sahib, you must kill us." I shall never forget.

George Scurfield

He wrote relentlessly to rid himself of these dark shadows, but he could still be caught out by the horrors at the most unexpected of times.

"One night, a few years ago, Cecilia and I thought, the weather being so fine, we'd go for walk on Holkham Beach. We parked the car in Lady Ann Drive and strolled toward the Gap and the sands. The moonlight was so bright, so pearly, so phosphorescent, it made me think immediately of Burma. Holkham sands became those paddy fields near the Chindwin, shining, glowing under the moon, and I found myself sweating and trembling."

George Scurfield 1988

3

The one and only school in Shepreth served a diversity of children of various ages from around the extended area. I was a little over four years old and it was thought that I might enjoy going to this educational establishment. Indeed, in my innocence I certainly wanted to go.

When I walked hand in hand with my father through those wide school gates, I was determined to show him how strong I was. I wanted nothing more than to cut loose from his leg and make him the proud father of a strong boy.

As we stood on the threshold together, the overwhelming reality of this monumental occasion took control of my senses. My dad's corduroys had become like a centreboard to my body, a body which however was about to turn into a rudderless sailing boat, launching on a premature journey out to sea.

On letting go, disorientation prevailed. Outside the classroom, there was sunshine and a clear blue sky, yet within the walls a storm was brewing and dark clouds were beginning to drift in from faraway horizons.

The last thing I remember was turning away from the silhouette of my dad, who had been standing with the teacher in the doorway, and staring into the many faces locked behind rows of desks stretching back into infinity. I looked back anxiously for daddy, but he had gone. Time closed in on me and the doors to the outside world resolutely shut.

As the bright light from the outside began to spin away with increasing speed, gravity seemed to draw me down into a centre of calm at the heart of this turbulence, where a sense of detachment allowed me to see the extreme beauty of who and what I really was. But just as time had tricked me into this sealed vacuum of security timelessness seemed to burst out of nowhere, and everything disappeared.

The next thing I knew I was pulling myself out of a dark pit, into a haze of nausea and cool air.

As the reality of passing out became clearer, I found to my embarrassment that I was sprawled diagonally across the lid of a desk, at the front of the class, looking up into a sea of eyes staring down with disbelief at this awkward new boy who had, for no apparent reason, keeled over in an ungainly heap. It became evident very quickly that I was in a classroom of much older children and because of my pride I became mortified at what they might think. I tried to straighten up my body by sliding it from the top of the desk with as much dexterity as I could muster, at the same time fixing my gaze with such intensity on the floor that I could see a tunnel to hide in. As I began to convince myself that I was inside a warren and invisible to the outside world, my brain relaxed enough, to begin thinking that my conundrum would be seen merely as a trifle, a superfluous mishap. In this moment of vain hope I felt the warmth inside my shorts. This was insult upon injury and what was left of my pride disappeared through the floor.

I tried to conceal my apprehension, in the hope that no one had noticed this appalling slight, when a cloak of darkness seemed to creep over me, bringing a feeling of cold into the very heart of my existence. I froze in terror as a human slug from behind the desk I had collapsed on, slowly reached out towards my hapless body. Then as quick as he was slow, he took hold of my throat like a python seizing its prey and proceeded to squeeze the last remaining crap out of me.

The teacher, who must have left for a moment with my father, finally came back into the room and to my rescue. On her return, the slug, like a retracting snail, withdrew into his shell and worked it like nothing had happened.

The teacher was nice enough, but the seeds of mistrust had been sown and my initiation into the fear of institution had begun.

Ponji got wind of this episode and gave the boy a bloody nose! I was elated and wanted to tell my dad of his heroics, but at my brother's behest this incident was to remain between us and was never mentioned again. I loved and respected my brother for doing what he did, but somehow I always felt a sense of guilt about the whole business. I remained adamant that I owed him one and standing guard in front of the pigsty, whilst he and his mates took to smoking cigarettes inside, was the least I could do.

My parents were considerate of my new fears and after a great deal of crying on my part they asked me what I wanted. They suggested that perhaps I could attend the school for a couple of hours in the mornings to start with, hoping that I would gradually become more familiar and confident with this daunting procedure. I found the whole business intensely difficult. The last thing I wanted to do was to upset them by letting them down, but the suggestion of going near that building again filled me with dreadful queasiness, and I refused categorically to participate in any idea of going back. They agreed to give me a few weeks to think about it, which I was immensely grateful for, because in that time a change in their circumstance came to my rescue.

~

George and Cecilia had a combined zeal for good food and had become fascinated with how we go about our culinary lives. They saw cooking in terms of an art form, with a hint of science thrown in. They particularly loved French cuisine and were very aware of how the French took for granted the importance of having the right cooking utensils for the best results. They absorbed how the Italians adored eating and like the French took seriously how they cooked their food and what they cooked it in.

In England at this time it was problematic if you wanted to take a more, shall we say, continental approach to the kitchen. Quite simply, it was hard to get hold of the right kitchen paraphernalia, which is common today with shops like Habitat and the ever popular food programmes on television.

My parents saw an opening in this gastronomic area and decided after careful deliberation to sell Docwra's Manor, free up some capital and move to Cambridge, with the idea of starting a small kitchen shop. This came as a huge relief to me, because it meant I didn't have to grapple with my feelings of letting them down, by not attending the village school. Maybe my feelings even played some part in their decision to move, after all there was a better selection of schools in Cambridge. Whether I had anything to do with it or not, seemed in the final decision to be superfluous. There were more children appearing by the minute and what with Ponji and Elizabeth still being looked after by those at Number Nine, and already at school in that revered city, moving to Cambridge seemed like the most practical thing to do.

At the tail end of 1953, with some strong encouragement from Aunty Alice and after nearly seven years of living in Shepreth, my parents found a new home for us, right next door to Alice's in Adams Road.

By the time we arrived in Cambridge I was settling into my sixth year and along with my brother Ponji I had three sisters: Elizabeth, Sarah and the newest arrival, Lucy. But my mum and dad hadn't finished yet; Polly and Sophie were still around the corner.

"I didn't understand much. I didn't think that mattered. I still don't. There was this mysterious empathy. They spoke the language of 1936, and if they were like Day Lewis and Spender their politics were the same as mine, too".

George Scurfield

4

Meat, butter, margarine and bananas were finally released from the ways of rationing, and the thoughts of the war were disappearing into the annals of time faster than the introduction of the jet aircraft into the uncharted skies. The telephone sat at the end of the hall, used only for emergencies and the occasional incoming call. In spite of the advent of television, which had recently gained domestic notoriety with the Queen's coronation, congregating around the wireless was still a popular pastime. Such shows as *Educating Archie, Journey into Space, The Goon Show* and *Ray's a Laugh* graced the airways and stole the hearts and minds of many families in the UK.

Finding a good hiding place may on the surface have started as a simple game, but it eventually became about securing a safe haven, away from the accoutrements of the adult world. Disappearing in our new home however, didn't come that easy. Large and detached as it was, number eight Adams Road had a light, open ambiance. There were few secret corners and no unused rooms tucked out of the way. Even the attic had been converted into two airy bedrooms. The only place secret enough for a hide-and-seek specialist like me, was a slight cupboard directly under the stairs at the centre of the house. But this bolthole always felt a little too conspicuous for comfort, because the entrance was clearly visible from the dining area of the kitchen, unless of course the door to the hall was closed, which was highly unusual.

It soon became clear that number eight was the complete antithesis of Number Nine which was filled with a great many darkened nooks and crannies, made perfect for a small person to disappear in.

For a prominent and informative time in my life, Number Nine became the house of intrigue next door and that's just what we called it, my sisters and me – 'Next door'. For most though, it was affectionately known as Number Nine and it was home to the world of Dr Alice Roughton and her unwieldy powers.

Alice was the oldest and my mother the youngest of seven girls and like some strange quirk, the costume of these houses seemed to fit their relationship like a glove.

Before long, George and Cecilia began to establish their creative mark in Cambridge, and an organic relationship of opposites between number eight and Number Nine began to emerge.

Like the house, the garden at number eight was large and simple in design - luscious flowerbeds, shrubs, roses, fruit trees, a neat vegetable garden complete with asparagus bed and the compulsory compost heap. While along the back of Number Nine, through the remains of formal majestic flowering, was a forlorn pond, once the elegant home for large gracious goldfish, which over time had disintegrated into a mushy abode for duckweed and lucky frogs. By way of rambling paths, the hilly remains of a bomb shelter, well worn chicken runs, efficient vegetable plots and rickety gates surrounded by overgrown foliage was a deep paddock with a small orchard, more vegetable plots, a couple of cows, pigs, substantial sheds and some rusty farm machinery.

From the first day we moved into number eight there seemed to be a lot of toing-and-froing between the two houses. For many guests the relative tranquillity of our new home, with its well groomed beds and neatly mown lawns, became a blissful respite from the wilder garden next door.

I guess it can sometimes seem mawkish to start talking about houses as having character and personality, as it can give the impression they are more alive than the people who live inside them. But when you're six years old, as I was when we first moved to Cambridge, the makeup of these two houses was enormously significant.

If I am to swallow my pride and dig that little bit deeper into my heart, I can easily transport myself to a world where cars were toys with faces, and trains were personalities from a storybook in the playroom. Allowing for this kind of dramatic licence, you might say that by conventional standards, number eight was quite a large dwelling, but built as it was, in the shadow of Number Nine, it gave the impression of being like a little sister to an older brother.

Like Alice, my mother Cecilia veered towards the practical, but enjoyed her feminine attributions a lot more than her older sister. It was very rare to see Aunty Alice in anything other than her blue boiler suit, whereas my mother primarily wore skirts and wasn't adverse to face cream and a little make-up, maybe even some lipstick if she was going out of an evening, unlike Alice who for the most part saw make-up as something to be frowned on.

Cecilia's cooking was lighter, more decorative, and a lot more palatable than Alice's, whose war habit, of throwing things together from whatever was available and making do, marched ever onwards. One irony that never ceased to amaze us was the fact that Auntie Alice taught my mum how to cook.

There were obviously a few exceptions to this rule of opposites, one of them being that they both had their hair in a particular way so as to be practical. They grew it very long, but always kept it tied up behind their heads in a neat tight bun. If they got together in the kitchen at Number Nine, an electric charge between them could produce howls of laughter, which could be heard a considerable distance from the house.

Alice and Cecilia may have had their differences, but the one thing they shared, above everything else, was the accumulative ability to store copious amounts of useless and useful knowledge in their collective brains. If you needed information about absolutely anything, they always seemed to have an answer or an explanation ready and waiting for the gullible recipient.

~

One of my preoccupations in Shepreth, had been to go round to various doors or cupboards, not just in our house, but in other people's as well, and fix their locks with a screwdriver, a small hammer or any other tool that would fit into my young hands. I was getting a flavour for what it was like to do a proper job in a professional manner. I was completely intrigued by how workmen worked - it may not have been going anywhere in grown-up terms, but it was unquestionably well motivated.

So it came as a welcome surprise when we first moved into number eight, to find that my mum and dad had made arrangements for a local building firm to come and make fascinating alterations to the house.

Len and Archie were the decorators, Mr. Bird a bricklayer cum carpenter, and they came to work in our house for quite some time. Len was a handsome man with slicked back hair, who used to have a charming way with the girls. He wasn't shy about flirting with Elizabeth when she was at home, or with any other attractive nymphets who happened to be at number eight at the time, like Elizabeth's vivacious friend, one of the many cousins on our mother's side, Margaret-Alice, who came to stay with us for a few years to help George run the shop. Unlike Len, Archie always seemed reserved. He arrived in the morning, immaculately turned out in gleaming white overalls and black shiny work boots, polished to a grand shine, as if he were in the Grenadier Guards.

I was quietly delighted to be in their company and they were nice enough to me, but it was Mr Bird, who took my fascination with building works seriously. I loved spending time with him, particularly when he decided it was time for tea and a rollup. I think he liked working at our house. He certainly felt very relaxing to be with and I am sure he shared the relish I had for the mixture of tastes and smells, which came with the combination, of rollup tobacco, new plaster, freshly sawn wood, paint, mugs of strong tea and anything else brought together in the builder's bag. He would ask my advice as to what my mum and dad might think if he did a job in a particular way, making me feel that his insecurity about how something should be done was at one with mine. There was never a feeling of being talked down to. He would sit with upright purpose, in his chippy's overalls, sown with pockets to hold every conceivable tool and discuss with me what we should do next.

In the middle of the downstairs hallway, which ran from the kitchen through to the sitting-room, was a lavatory and adjoining room, which was to be made into a small washroom. Mr. Bird was wondering if it wouldn't be a good idea to convert this room into a place for taking showers and proceeded to ask me what I thought. Perhaps my mum and dad had already told him how they wanted this small, utilitarian room to be, but it was certainly never ever discussed with me, so this was the first time I knew about it. He approached the shower room project as if it were our idea, allowing me to feel that I would be an intricate part of how it would turn out. My trust in him began to grow and in this way Mr. Bird could have taught me absolutely anything.

A little later on I developed a similar relationship with Ron, the milkman, who used to come straight to our house on his milk float, pick me up and treat me as if I were just another milkman. I was allowed to hop into the cart and help with the delivery of fresh milk, eggs and orange juice to the neighbouring houses. He too, seemed to show a kind of trust towards me. He would confide in me, telling me about his life at home, his marriage, what he wanted for his daughter and other such personal matters. I really believed he saw me as an equal, a confidant. I was always too thrilled to speak back and anyway, I would certainly never have questioned what he said to me, in case it jeopardised my position on the round.

As the two floors of the house began to take shape, I became uncomfortably aware of my father's gentle, but firm reminder that at some point, I would have to go to school in Cambridge. I was terrified of this proposition, which made me want to hold onto the coat tails of his reality with ever more determination.

The sounds emanating from my father going through the ritual of his early morning chores were extremely comforting. He took on these household tasks with rhythm in his stride; stoking the Aga, emptying the ash, filling it with coal. Once or twice a week he would remove molten hot clinkers from the bottom of the boiler and refill the hopper, always accompanied by a sound he made, that was somewhere between humming and whistling. On Sundays he would roll out the croissant dough, carefully prepared the night before, into the crescent shapes we now know so well, and when the rooster brought in the dawn, pop them in the oven for the morning fortunate.

No matter how hard I tried, these reassuring realities couldn't stop the world from forging a path to the school gates.

"When I very first went to the school it was run by Mrs. Berry. She and her sister, Miss Johnson, lived not far away and they were sisters of the poet Lionel Johnson. This was unknown to me at the time and would have meant nothing to me if I'd been told. Tennyson's name I knew but not Johnson's. "The Brook" was my favourite poem so Tennyson was the poet - not the poet - just the poet. There was no other".

Cecilia Scurfield

5

'With much trepidation I started Newnham Croft primary school when I was six years old, in the second year, when they were already well into the techniques of basic maths and English.

Mrs Gibson was the name of my teacher, and she was nearing retirement and gave the impression that she just wanted to get the job at hand, over and done with. She seemed unsympathetically determined to get all the children in her class learning words and sums with no nonsense and as quickly as possible. And God help anyone or anything which got in the way.

She came across to me as one of the grouchiest old ladies I had ever encountered, she reminded me of my grandmother. Things weren't right between me and Mrs Gibson from day one.

My physiological and psychological functions were all over the place when I started in her class. The way the school worked made me feel nauseous and claustrophobic. My academic faculties just weren't ready to roll in the way they were supposed to. During inappropriate moments, I would become unbelievably terrified, particularly if put on the spot by a seemingly logical question, as is the normal procedure in the classroom.

When asked to stand for any length of time, as we all were during the school assembly, I'd resign myself to the conclusion of passing out. The stifling air, in which we were made to stand, for what seemed like an eternity during these morning prayers, became heavy with anticipation. If it wasn't me, you could almost guarantee that some other unfortunate soul would fall to the floor, a dense sack of pale wasted skin.

One of the main causes for my disintegrating into nausea was, I now suspect, largely due to my inability to get sufficient oxygen to my lungs and brain. My incapacity to control my sinuses and breathe properly was so excruciatingly embarrassing, that I wanted to be anywhere other than in the company of adults, or anyone else for that matter, who had misgivings about snotty nosed kids. I so wanted to look right and show them with distinction that I could breathe through my nose with ease. I would find the overwhelming experience of being in another's company, mind boggling, then jaw dropping, and once my chin had well and truly hit the top of my chest, it became inevitable that my nasal passages would block up and my face would begin to stream with phlegm.

In the playground, a chubby, red faced boy bursting with energy, called Steven Bagley became my timepiece. He would set off in his imaginary heavy goods lorry clocking his way up through the gears. Just from the sounds emanating like squashed farts from the side of his mouth, I knew how fast he was going. His timing was so good I could have set my watch by him if I'd had one. He would start shuffling his feet over the asphalt, slowly at first and then gradually begin increasing his forward motion. Having gone round the circuit a couple of times, hooting madly at any stray pedestrians in his way, he reached the optimum speed, then I knew it was almost time to go back into the classroom.

So where I played at my first school in Cambridge was always with Steven Bagley within earshot. This was usually under the safety of a bush, on the periphery of the recreational area, near the wire fence. Sprawled stomach down on the ground, with a dinky toy or two making major roadways in the dust, I'd wonder at the dandelions pushing their way up through the almighty weight of the tarmac and dream about a key; a golden key that might unlock the door to a freer world. I noticed early on that if Steven was in first or second gear I felt kind of alright, but as his dynamism increased (along with his blood pressure) I became ever more anxious about my return to the constriction of ink-stained desk lids and angry teachers.

It seemed as if every cell of the surrounding walls, of every book, the desks and even the pupils, were exploding with life, making any writing coming from the hand of the teacher like a small speck of a boat, breaking waves, far away on the horizon of a tempestuous sea.

I would have got more sense from looking at particles of coal, scattered randomly in the snow, than looking at the letters of the alphabet in a book. Like a sunny day in the Alps, I was overwhelmingly dazzled by the white mass of paper surrounding the words. Any amount of focus that I could gather would continually pull out and disappear into the vast and busy concoction, surrounding the tiny piece of chalk drawing illogical patterns on the blackboard.

It was common back then for anyone who couldn't manage simple school work to be called a dunce. It may not have been normal teaching procedure elsewhere, but it was certainly a ploy used by Mrs Gibson to intimidate credulous pupils, who were unable to get to grips with their basic reading and maths. During my introduction to primary school, it was not unusual to be told to stand in the corner with your back to the class if you couldn't give a satisfactory answer to her sharp questioning. Wracked with bewilderment and guilt, we would occasionally be told to wear a pointed hat, which had a capital D emblazoned on its circumference. I cannot over emphasise how humiliating and intimidating this means to an end was. I found the whole business excruciatingly painful to say the least. It was unbearably demoralising and I wanted with all my heart not to be there.

The summer holidays just couldn't come along soon enough.

"Perhaps it wasn't surprising that I felt that everything good had happened before I was born or could remember – before Uncle Cecil died, before Daddy died, before the accident, before the war. The family and national disasters seem to overlap and become the same; old ways were vanishing; old Customs falling out of use".

Cecilia Scurfield

6

There were times during those early years in Cambridge when I'd meander out from a tree-lined darkness into Adams Road, the street in which we now lived, and find myself standing in a natural cathedral full to the brim with rays of magnificent sunlight.

With the warm tar-black speckled pavement beneath my feet stretching out before me and school a million miles away, my confidence would emerge from the self conscious depths and resume play. Amid this welcome release my mind became super agile; a pathway stone could be a mountain cast from diamonds, the sky a liquid sea playing with its clouds of tall ships sailing towards the shore of their island earth.

If there wasn't a pressing need to get home, time wasn't a consideration, and the place I was in would become all encompassing. Ungoverned by familiarity, the road and its surroundings revealed a multilayered fairy tale space.

Perhaps it wasn't always like this and romantically reminiscent it may be, but as I look into this anamnesis of past times, there definitely seemed to be more sunshine at this end of Adams Road.

When the vague notion of home began to prick my conscience, I had a tendency to leap in the opposite direction and find myself on the other side of the road, hidden behind a long squat broken hedge in an immaculately kept playing field, which called out for me to run all over its virgin expanse. If I felt daring, I would jump back and forth through the hedge, playing leapfrog with the gaps, whilst keeping a wary eye on the hut in the lower right hand corner of the field for the grounds-man, who, I knew, on seeing this crazy boy bounding around and messing with his chaste turf, would begin walking furiously in my direction. Then I'd have to leg it post-haste back to the road and, in a more subdued manner, continue on my journey.

If the need to get home became a pressing matter the distance to my house seemed to increase a hundred fold. To deal with this vast extending of space, I'd divert my mind by musing over the other houses on either side of the road. These large detached mansions, of various proportion and character, were the living quarters for some of the most successful, and often eccentric, scholastic personages living in this acclaimed city. All around lived and breathed first-class degrees with honours, the highest echelons of the country's learned: archaeologists, economists, anthropologists, scientists, professors of law, of English literature, of history and languages of all sorts - Greek, Latin and every other tongue.

I'd go next door and play with Russell, sit on Leavis's knee, swap cards with Keynes, climb trees with Wittgenstein and have tea with Bragg.

To the passerby, each house separated from the road by a large brick wall or even larger garden hedge seemed overtly neat, but seen out of the corner of my auspicious eye they could quite easily become ominously dark and rather foreboding. The fortresses were guarded and locked, and kept within their impregnable walls were unseen kings and queens of mysterious unfathomable learnings. In actual fact they were a front for the knowledge mafia, people whose lives were mostly held together by sad, complex academic one-upmanship.

The inaccessibility and unfriendliness of these castles could make the walk home seem a long and laborious journey. To bring relief to this interminable expedition, I would summon up the trickster, a mischievous internal imp who lured me with dark rewards, ever onwards to the seductive caverns of Number Nine. Unlike most of the other houses in Adams Road, Number Nine always seemed to preserve a somewhat bedraggled exterior. I could never work out why this was. Even with a fresh coat of paint, it still managed to retain a feeling of dowdiness.

As age took its turn, – aside from the afore mentioned fact that it was our house next door – Number Nine stood out not because of its rambling architecture or its dishevelled appearance, but because of its accessibility, and what went on within the confines of its motley walls. The overwhelming pull could become so alluring, that I would often find myself walking, with an air of single-minded determination, directly past my own home straight to the driveway of the house next door.

Approaching the front door of Number Nine, with its message of 'PLEASE COME IN' written boldly across its chest, was always enticing, for within this house was a labyrinth of humankind; you never knew into whose world you could fall.

To the left of the entrance, were the remains of a red hitching-post, which was used not that long ago by my cousin, Auntie Alice's daughter

Rosemary, who rode to school in a pony and trap. It must have been handy to tie up the horse here on her return home.

Oddly, if I approached Number Nine too slowly, heavy contradictory feelings of loneliness and excitement could envelop me; this often became more intense if I lingered for any length of time by the front door, which was for the most part never closed.

If you were unlucky and found the front door locked, as it was on odd occasions during the winter months, you had to go in via the back door, which meant the kitchen run.

The kitchen was often packed to the gills with inquisitive grown-ups, making it uncomfortable to get through if you were feeling private, or in a hurry. Most of the time though, getting ensnared didn't present itself as a problem, because the front door was pushed back, wide open, against the right hand side of a comparatively small, dimly lit porch. In more recent times, if you were to cast your eyes down towards the dusty pale red tiled floor below, a mat would shout up 'Step in and Welcome'. I could be anyone.

"........It is best not to let you have details now except the following which have been told me. Jack was leading. Then came the sisters. Then father. He was found with his hands still gripping the unbroken rope in the act of trying to save the others. Jack was found with his hands on his head and by him a loose stone. And considering the place, these facts give much probability to the supposition that the stone hit Jack and caused the whole disaster. That death was instantaneous is almost certain." Ellen Ewing to her brother Bertram Hopkinson (my maternal grandfather), on the death of their father and siblings in the Swiss Alps.

7

With the beat of widespread industrial changes at the latter part of the 19th century beginning to forge and throttle its way across the globe, my great grandfather on my mother's side, Alexander Siemens, came over to England as a young man to join his uncle, Karl Wilhelm Siemens, in the English branch of the family firm of electrical engineers. Alexander's family had lived in Hanover and fled from the tyrannical Bismarck. I am led to believe that they were steeped in class and not without royal connections, as their grandmother, Generalin von Hartmann, was lady-in-waiting to the last Queen of Hanover.

Alexander and his brother were instrumental in bringing electricity to The British Isles and during the 1870's they laid the first fully working telegraph cable across the Atlantic.

As part of the Anglo-German electrical engineering dynasty, Sir Alexander Siemens, as he became known, was once enormously wealthy, but I am told he lost a lot of his money to Germany and the Great War. But prior to this, in 1897 he had Westover Hall built at great cost. This sprawling house, which today stands as a high-class hotel on the edge of The New Forest, commanding spectacular views of Christchurch Bay and the Isle of Wight, was considered in its day to be the most luxurious residence on the South Coast of England, and it was here that my mother and her sisters spent a great deal of their childhood.

But like all true fairy tales there was a dark side to all this opulence. My mother always maintained that if it hadn't been for the brooding presence of Granny Siemens, Westover Hall and the grounds would have been marvellous. She said "Your great-grandmother was like a black cloud moving slowly and silently over everything there. There was always a threat that she might suddenly appear out of nowhere and wither us up with a biting sarcastic remark".

When they weren't somewhere within the bountiful ramblings of Westover Hall, Cecilia, Alice and their other sisters could be found with their parents in the equally posh Ten Adams Road in Cambridge; an affluent family home their father, Bertram Hopkinson and their mother, Mariana, had specially built for the family in 1903.

Mariana Siemens met Bertram through her father's close association with another brilliant engineer of that industrious time, John Hopkinson. A fatal accident befell John Hopkinson whilst he was in the prime of his career as Professor of Electrical Engineering at King's College London. He set out with his son and two of his three daughters, to climb a mountain in Switzerland and the party never returned. All four bodies were found the next morning roped together in a valley five hundred feet below the summit. One of the two remaining sons, Bertram Hopkinson, was to become my grandfather when he married Alexander's daughter, Mariana Siemens. Forging ahead at home and in the field, this illustrious pair gave birth to seven, strong, versatile girls, the youngest being my mother.

Bertram Hopkinson's life story, like his father's, was also to end in heroic tragedy during his distinguished career, as Professor of Mechanism and Applied Mechanics University of Cambridge. Bertram, my grandfather, took on the mantle of flight engineer. He learned to fly, although he was twice as old as the average pilot, because he felt this would help our understanding of what was required by pilots. He worked on the problems of flying at night, in bad weather, and on navigating in clouds and was one of the first to fly into chronic electrical storms, to see what effect, if any, they had on aeroplanes. Paradoxically two years after he had opened an experimental centre for his research in Suffolk, my grandfather was flying a Bristol Fighter (which he had been instrumental in designing for the army) from Martlesham Heath to London; the plane fell foul to bad weather, crashed and killed him instantly. It was to be a fateful accident; my mother was 18 months old.

Bertram, like many fathers, dreamed of having a son. In fact it is thought by some of the older members of my extended family that so extreme was this need, the flying accident, in which he died, was no accident at all: I was told he desperately wanted to carry the family name into the next generation. Not for want of trying, my mother was the last of the seven girls: could she have been the final straw?

It seems Cecilia was on a losing wicket before she even set foot on the green. She once told me, that as a baby and young child she appeared to have given no joy to her mother, who, because of Bertram's sudden death seemed to lose any parental motivation she might have had for bringing up her children. The die is cast. Over those vital but arid years, the young Cecilia developed a sharp intellect to woo her mother's love, the strain of which started to harden Cecilia's heart toward any childhood vulnerability.

My mother took what love and support she could get from Dawson, the kindly family chauffeur. On rainy days she cut out paper dolls with her polite Victorian nanny. She said 'I was often smacked by Nanny - never by Mother as far as I can remember - yet I loved Nanny more than Mother which I once confessed to one of my sister's, who gave me a sound scolding - of course one loved one's mother more than anyone else in the world!"

There was a fourteen-year age gap between Cecilia and Alice and Alice's every word became my mother's guide; parental decisions were made and the choice of which path should be taken in Cecilia's life were decided by her eldest sister.

My great-grandmother on the Hopkinson side, who sounded as if she gave off an air of foreboding just as intense the Siemens one, purchased Number Nine Adams Road, so she could live out the rest of her days next to her son Bertram and her seven granddaughters. Before Great Granny Hopkinson died in 1933, she planned to leave Number Nine to her sister Ellen. Great Aunt Nellie, as she was called, didn't want such responsibility and this was when the Roughtons stepped in.

My mother's eldest sister Alice married Jack Roughton junior. Through this intervention Alice came to spend the rest of her life at Nine Adams Road. Alice and Jack's relationship was such that Jack chose to spend most of his time during the Second World War in America where he was put to use for his expertise in colloid science, the stuff and biochemistry of blood, which basically left his wife, to do as she pleased with the house. Under Auntie Alice's supervision Number Nine was given over to the war effort and the trend for how she lived out the rest of her years was set.

Alice, by the time I came to know her, was a regular GP, a psychiatrist, and, like my mother, highly cerebral.

I don't think you could have called her house a boarding house in the conventional sense, but it did become home for an awful lot of people from across the globe. Of the many diverse personalities and members of the immediate and extended family that ended up living there, some paid their way or helped out domestically, whilst others would visit for a few days and wind up staying forever.

By the time we came to live in Cambridge, Alice in a sense was past her heyday, but she was still a force to be reckoned with. She continued to deal out help to her surrounding world, with the same energy and commitment, as if the war had never ended.

When we moved into number eight in the early part of 1954, Ponji and Elizabeth emerged from their years at Number Nine like two young refugees from a halfway house. As we settled into a way of life in this sedate road, their presence having been minimal in Shepreth, now loomed large. My parents made sure that they were given two of the biggest rooms in our new home. This was to make up for the years they'd spent in the ever communal house next door, where having any space of their own had been virtually impossible. I had a vague idea of the hardships they had endured during and after the war, but I was far too young to really realise the gravitas. I had for instance, no idea of their being evacuated to Switzerland, as they had been, or what this meant, or come to that anything about the tragic consequence of losing their father at such a formative age and how it could affect their lives.

I wasn't aware of any jealousy, but there must have been some, for I was conscious of the fact that I wanted the same kind of attention that Ponji and Elizabeth seemed to get when we started living together. I somehow thought this special treatment had to do with their years of living at Number Nine and came to wonder how I might infiltrate the labyrinths next door. This way I might have a chance to discover for myself some of their magic formula.

Friends, relatives and overspills from Aunty Alice, often came to stay for prolonged periods at our house, which meant number eight never seemed empty of hungry mouths to feed. Like many mothers of the time, my mum's culinary magic was put to the test. She found a permanent place for herself in the kitchen, serving up meals to all and sundry and as far as I remember she rarely missed a beat. She did this with amazing fortitude and skill, but as time slipped by, I think the idea of this altruistic lifestyle that she and George had advocated, began to wear a bit thin.

The kitchen and dining room in our house were modernised into one big room, separated by a long wide wooden counter, fixed so that the cupboard space underneath was accessible from both sides of the room. Two benches were set into the walls on the dining side, making an L-shape seating arrangement coming out from the corner of the room. With the table and chairs in place, it wasn't unusual to see a dozen or more persons at a meal sitting.

As the reality of running a prominent house, like number eight, and the certainty of no escape sunk in, Cecilia became increasingly temperamental particularly around the kitchen and in the mornings.

In addition to the cooking, my mother insisted that the mammoth task of organising and cleaning the house was easier if done on her own. You can begin to see how her time was all used up.

George's ability to pacify her became paramount to the smooth running of the Scurfield household, and in some ways a remarkable lesson in diplomacy. He must have been keenly aware that by keeping Cecilia happy the ship was far less likely to capsize. He quickly got into the routine of coaxing her into the new day with a cup of coffee, often taken whilst she was still in bed, after which mummy seemed better equipped to come downstairs.

Over the years it became progressively harder for her to make it down for breakfast. I guess she felt too wretched to face the hordes. If on the rare occasion she did come down too soon, it was imperative to allow her the space for a second coffee and a cigarette before entering into any kind of discourse. All too often I would stumble into the quagmire of her moods, where it was difficult for me to understand what was going on - to know how and why her temperament was so earth shatteringly difficult to deal with.

I desperately wanted her to be happy, hoping that if she felt good about herself, she would then feel good about me. When she was peaceful it was a truly delightful experience to be in her company, but alas, these moments were far and few between. Like a lemming leaping into the void, my vulnerability would propel me towards the comfort of her bosom, only to be greeted by inexplicable outbursts.

In later years, like Ponji and Elizabeth before me, I developed cunning and manipulative ways for keeping my mum sweet, but when these plans to appease her went wrong, I got into the unfortunate habit of lashing out verbally before she had a chance to belittle me.

It became more and more important for me to keep my mother occupied; good or bad measures, either way it didn't matter, as long she was taken in by my antics she would, it seemed, be able to give me some sort of attention. To paint a clearer picture of how I later became such a convincing liar (actor), it is somehow reassuring, to remind myself of how and where I got my training.

Cecilia had the perfect body for childbirth and in some ways was ideally suited for rearing a family, but the idea of having children is one thing and the reality is another. At this essential time in my life, mothering for her seemed to be more of an ordeal than a pleasure. My disquiet may have seemed childish in my mother's eyes, but I had no other means at my disposal, except being the child that I was, to get what I felt I wanted, or indeed needed. For her part I don't believe that there was ever a deliberately malicious thought and I'm sure there was always the idea of love. As she knew all too well from her own upbringing, for a child the idea of love is one thing, but the reality is very much another. If you don't feel it, nothing else will ever really have the resonance needed to make you feel truly secure. I realise now after years of change and discovery that my mother was trying to give something she'd never really known herself. She was in a sense as out of her depth as we were, and therefore it was ridiculous to expect her to manage otherwise, but at the time we weren't to know that and neither it seems was she.

~

Meanwhile, as the school holidays were grinding down, I was feeling to all intents and purposes like I was losing a father. Working full on to establish a winning seam in the retail trade meant he was away from number eight until late in the evening. In my father's eyes he may just have been setting up the new kitchen shop, but as far as I was concerned he was miles away. As my dad was elected to be the breadwinner, I suppose he had the perfect get out clause, some breathing space away from the domestic wrangling of running the house. My mother did her best to steer the raft away from the rapids, but when daddy wasn't there, the emotional centre of the family seemed at times to destabilise almost to breaking, and I began to miss him desperately.

Then, before I could get the hang of it, the sickening reality of another school year came round again.

It had taken me the several months of the long summer holidays cajoling, pleading, pretending and really being ill to eventually persuade my father that it was essentially non-productive for me to attend school at this time. Since it was deemed necessary for me to keep out of my mother's skirt tails, it was thought best that I should spend this hard won time off school next door.

Maybe George and Cecilia entrusted me to Alice because of my ongoing dilemmas with the classroom, after all she was a psychiatrist. Whether this was the case or not, I was now free of going to school, at least for one term and possibly longer. But in order to prolong this state of affairs, I knew I would have to keep as low a profile as possible.

Egged on by my desire to discover their intrepid blueprint, I followed in Ponji and Elizabeth's footsteps and spent a great deal of time during my seventh year submerged in the assorted dimensions of Number Nine, which I can only describe as being like a dreamscape. Of the countless characters that passed through, some had names and a life, but most were just faces to me, with no beginning middle or end.

"Understandably perhaps, Granny Hopkinson had an impatience with lesser, weaker mortals, an often domineering way of behaving which made her a frightening figure to a little girl like me. Her face with its jutting chin and grim mouth showed that side of her character. Her eyes looked straight at me in a disconcerting way. She was getting deaf and used her ear trumpet like a weapon of war directed at a retreating enemy."

Cecilia Scurfield

8

To begin with Auntie Alice's house seemed overwhelmingly scary, particularly around the oak room and the dark unknown upstairs. It wasn't going to be long however, before Number Nine was to become the perfect sprawling warren I needed to escape the hawk-eye of scholarly excellence, that seemed to be scrutinising my backyard in ever increasing circles.

Any grownup supervision I was allocated often drifted away, which meant many along hour was spent alone in the kitchen at Number Nine. Once the idea of my being around had become acceptable, I was pretty much left to my own devices. I lifted my confidence by creating heroic scenarios with imaginary friends. These imaginings would take on a theme, in which I was usually the heroic explorer going into the brave new world. My adventures were certainly inspired by the current bedtime story my father had been reading to us. This could be anything from *Swallows and Amazons* through to *Lord Jim*. George's love of the story and relaying thereof, unlocked the great sense of adventure found in books that would never otherwise have entered my life.

During this escape from my troubles at school, Auntie Alice sometimes took me on her doctor's rounds, which I saw as a treat because it meant we would hurtle around Cambridge in her Jeep. However, it was a Londoner, a genuine cockney called Frances Walls, who really took me in hand.

Frances, who came to Cambridge whilst in the Land Army, was brought into Number Nine as staff, in order to help out with the war effort, and gradually over the years she became a major player in the family and household. Before I knew it I was standing close behind her, as she went about her various duties, which ranged from milking the cows to polishing the furniture. Despite the cosmopolitan nature of the address, she lived very much alone in a little room in an apex of the house, which she shared with a special Alsatian, a German Shepherd called Lassie. Under Frances's command Lassie could do just about anything, from leaping high fences to playing the piano. For a small person, unused to the presence of such commanding domestic beasts, it was always a little nerve-wracking coming into Lassie's presence, but once the chemistry of being together settled down, she became an enormously friendly and exciting dog to be with.

Frances was separated from family and guests by the upstairs-downstairs role she felt most comfortable with. Notwithstanding all the liberal small talk that went down, she knew her place. Within a mutual understanding of what was right for her and Alice, This this is what really suited the running of the house.

She had been married in the past, but by the time I came along this was shrouded in mystery, something that was never mentioned. I don't really know why this was, but it became clear as time went on how uncomfortable Frances seemed around the male of the species. When we were little this apparent complexity with the opposite sex never really presented itself as a problem, but as I grew more in understanding than in age, a sharp reprimand was often needed on her part to bring the nose of the inquisitor out of her business. I once asked her where her husband went during the day and she spat fire and brimstone at me. Other than her being very religious, I wasn't sure why my curiosity should have had such an effect, but I surely watched my P's and Q's in her presence after that.

Frances had two nephews, Jimmy and Alfi, who occasionally came to stay for the summer holidays. Hailing from the north of England, endowed with broad Yorkshire accents, they were equally angelic and mischievous. Usually adorned in nothing more than string vests, PE shorts, no socks and well worn black plimsolls – they were like two ragamuffins who had fallen on the house by accident from a cross-country run. I once watched Ponji entice them up a drainpipe to an outside window so they could spy on one of the au pairs changing her underwear. Frances caught them in mid flow. She laid into Ponji verbally, but reprimanded the two boys, by pulling on their ears, at the same time clipping them round the head with a mighty telling off, the likes of which I'd never heard or seen before.

Inside the main hallway of Number Nine, directly opposite the front entrance was an ornate dresser with an old mirror above it which had lost its ability to reflect clearly. On this polished cabinet, neatly laid out in sequential order, were attention-grabbing envelopes. These letters, which were often covered with exotic stamps, provided my limited time as a stamp-collector with the temptation to steal. It was the job of Frances Walls to organize where and how the mail ended up, and as I knew only too well how terribly strict she could be, I felt it best to leave well alone.

Complete collection of the various letters or parcels, which had come from all over the world, was a somewhat difficult task, for the intended recipient would often survive their stay with no mention of a forwarding address. Without France's intervention, the mail would have built into a small forgotten stockpile. I can only guess at what she did with the undelivered mail, but I can understand now why she had a stamp collection coveted by the few professional philatelists of the day.

Around about the time of the Queen's coronation and presumably as part of her work deal, Frances stipulated that she be given a television. Alice then, and throughout the rest of her life, made it abundantly clear that she disliked anything to do with this new media, which she thought to be full of trashy American propaganda, so it came as a surprise when she gave way to the demand. Any feeling of separation from humanity that Frances might have harboured was now, along with Lassie, lessened by a new kid on the block called Television. How intriguing, like the wireless but with moving pictures! For a while the small screen was the only thing my contemporaries at school ever seemed to talk about. As I had never seen or heard one, Frances's television very quickly became a desirable enigma. As far as I knew it was the only set for miles around, so it became imperative to keep on her good side. If we were good, we could, along with Lassie, all pile together on the single bed in Frances's room, which, shrouded in warm dog smells, was full of souvenirs commemorating the Queen's Coronation. Huddled together like sardines we'd watch very specific programmes that Frances thought suitable; *Dixon Of Dock Green*, *The Billy Cotton Band Show*, *Sunday Night At The London Palladium* and anything about the Royal family. She loved and approved of westerns too, so we got to watch a lot of them. Among my favourites were *Hopalong Cassidy*, *Roy Rogers* and *The Lone Ranger*.

Frances, I am sure at her convenience, was a little hard of hearing and liked to have her TV volume on the loud side. Unfortunately, a spindly grey-haired lady from Germany called Mimi, lived in a small room directly next to Frances's and found the sounds annoying to the point of cataclysmic distraction.

Mimi seemed prematurely aged by the misfortunes of time. She came over to England from Germany before the war, with Kurt and Aino Jooss, as the nanny to their daughter and was one of those faces who ended up living at Number Nine forever. She never complained directly to Frances about the blaring noise coming through her bedroom wall, because she knew her place, which meant Mimi kept her grievances forever in pent-up misery. When she could bear it no longer, she would break down in the kitchen in front of Alice, who would offer her help by way of sleeping pills rather than broach the complaint to Frances Walls, lest it upset the careful balance Frances brought to the running of the house.

One afternoon exploring the upstairs boundaries, I found myself having to hide in the linen cupboard to avoid Mimi who was hovering unexpectedly nearby. She had a nervous tendency which made her approach seem sharp, so it felt best if she was around to nip off elsewhere. I dove in amongst the shelves of neatly folded sheets and towels, which were distinctly dull in colour from years of washing. Buried deep in the darkness all ears and eyes, I overheard muffled sounds of Mimi sobbing, out on the landing, onto the broad shoulders of a tall dark Turkish immigrant called Dr Ikin.

From a small person's perspective both Mimi and Dr. Ikin were some of those familiar faces who ended up at Number Nine with not much more than a name to their story. Of course the cultural difference didn't mean it wasn't possible for the ear of an inquisitive mind to catch on to some of their goings on.

Dr. Ikin stayed at Alice's whilst researching some deeply important something or other in Cambridge. He slept in another larger room next to Mimi's on the top floor, which looked out over Adams Road. He had, as far as I could gather from my eavesdropping, taken on a polite and helpful stance towards Mimi's tearful complaints. At least this is what it sounded like. I sensed, however, that he was only showing impartial courtesy to Mimi, and indeed any of the other ladies in the house, because I had seen firsthand how his keener interests in the female lay elsewhere.

During his prolonged stays at Number Nine, he became infatuated with my sister Polly, from when she was four years old. We of course never paid much mind to Dr. Ikin's passions for Polly; in fact we encouraged her to be committed to his advances, because we would benefit from the leftovers of his generosity. To us he was just a mysterious dark stranger with a bushy moustache, who came over to our house and showered Polly, who would shy away from his approaches, with gifts and affection.

Polly was to me always the angelic nymph, more at home with her flowering aspirations than my other sisters, and I totally understand now why Dr. Ikin became so besotted with her. I can't help thinking now how a kind of Lolita-ish infatuation started to infuse their relationship. After all, he was a grown man who was trying to entice her, as she blossomed through the years at number eight, into going back with him to his native country.

The walk-in linen cupboard, next to Dr. Ikin's room was big enough for me to disappear in, but it was, as I'd discovered, not secluded enough to feel really safe. The slightest noise could bring me to the attention of the prying eyes of any grownups camping out on this floor. Worst of all, there was the possibility of Frances Walls or Mimi heaving me out of this hiding place, with a great deal of reprimanding and threats of turning me into Auntie Alice or my cousin Rosemary. This pressure pushed me into finding a more foolproof solution to my need for seclusion.

The bathroom on this top floor was, like other washrooms in the house, a practical utilitarian space, with the usual well worn linoleum floor and scrubbed wooden shelving. But unlike the other bathrooms, this had a door which led to a cupboard-like room, a back attic used sporadically for the hanging of wet towels, ladies underwear and other such personal smalls.

During an afternoon of exploration, I discovered low down in the corner of this back attic, behind a sheet of old fibreboard, a hidden entrance big enough for a small body to clamber through. On the other side of this tight opening was a loft, made up of dirty redwood beams and old cobwebs, which was home to a few pigeons, a scatty barn owl and two enormous disgruntled water tanks, that seemed to gurgle and groan every time someone ran a bath or flushed the loo.

A shaft of dusty light came in from the far end, where some battered grey pinewood was hung in such a way as to leave a hole big enough to allow the birds their freedom. This old planking was, I soon discovered, covering a large opening to the outside. With a bit of careful manoeuvring I managed to adapt the piece of wood so that I had a secret vantage point onto the outside world.

For a time this loft became a special place, where my rattled brain felt unencumbered enough for reflection on what I was beginning to see as the trappings of the adult world. The grown-ups, like a spiders-web of emotional inducement, could on occasion be extremely difficult to steer through. If and when I managed to shimmy through the downstairs rooms and came on guard up here, I was the lighthouse keeper, the main man in the control tower. There could be a lot of coming and going during any one day and I had the bird's eye view of it all from up here. From here I could watch the ships come and go from the harbour and spy the survivors unloading the captain's orders onto the dock.

On this, the kitchen, side of the house there was a slight incline of tarmac from the road to a large garage, which was home to a grand old convertible Rolls Royce, and the varied array of tools needed to keep such a machine in trim.

Above the garage was a small apartment, originally built as a residence for Dawson the chauffeur and his family, but for me it will always be the home of Gabor Cossa.

If Alice's jeep or Gabor's bike weren't parked in front of the garage, it meant that the coast was clear for me to step up, into the majestic cockpit of the Rolls, and feast my hungry eyes over the innumerable switches and levers needed to make this rocket fly.

Bald, with loud tufts of grey hair, often a little unshaven, along with his brusque manner, Gabor was a vast powerhouse that would pick me up without a moment's hesitation and smother me with hugs and kisses. I was, "Darling Cecilia's son!"

His love and kindness, along with his enthusiasm for his latest dramatic or intellectual endeavour, were so loud they could very easily make a young boy like me feel completely helpless. When he spoke, his broad Hungarian accent made it very hard for me to understand. I would nod anxiously in agreement, hoping the nods came in the right place.

As and when time took its course I got to know Gabor very well, and although he always remained a commanding figure, it turned out that he wasn't really that tall.

The story goes that he came from a line of prominent Jewish bankers in Budapest and rather than continue in his family tradition, he set off to pursue his dream of becoming a dancer. Before the Second World War started, he found his way to working with The Ballet Jooss, a radical dance company founded by Kurt Jooss.

Jooss had worked closely with the great movement theorist and dancer Rudolf Laban and emerged in the 1930's to win plaudits all over the world, with his satirical ballet on the futility of war called *The Green Table*.

According to my mother, Gabor, became infatuated with Kurt and in 1935 like Mimi, he moved to England with the company when they fled Germany to escape Nazi persecution.

Just before the outbreak of war The Ballet Jooss was invited to set up in residency at Dartington Hall in Devon. Once they became well established in the UK, the company began a tour of America, by which time I am told Gabor had found a more suitable role as company manager and sometime stage director.

Kurt with his wife and collaborator Aino Simola (Aino's official job was that of Stage Designer) had, through various Cambridge connections, become good friends of Alice's. They chose not to go to

America with the rest of the company. Instead they stepped headlong into the open arms of Number Nine. Kurt's country of origin was Germany which meant at the beginning of the war he was interned on the Isle of Man. This was short lived and he soon returned to Cambridge and Nine Adams Road, where he was to settle with Aino and their daughter Anna in the flat above the garage.

Meanwhile because of the political circumstances the rest of the troupe found that they were stuck in America. Back in England however, the economist Maynard Keynes, whose love for ballet had made headline news when he married the Russian ballerina Lydia Lopokova in the 1920's, found a way to bring the company back across the Atlantic and to Cambridge. Passage was found on different boats and Gabor was one of the last over. The ship he was on dropped anchor in the docks of Belfast where he was held in custody for some weeks by the Irish authorities. The police, who were convinced that Gabor was the enemy, thought that the music manuscripts for the company, which Gabor had in his possession, were secret German codes.

Through his connection with King's College, Keynes secured a university apartment for some of the company on King's Parade in Cambridge, while the rest were to be put up at Alice's house in Adams Road. Eventually Gabor was released from prison and found his way back to England, Kurt and Number Nine, where he was to put down roots and start a lifelong friendship with Alice and Cecilia.

After some respite in Cambridge the company set off, dancing their way round the British Isles, taking ballet to the masses. It was when they had finished with this excursion that Cecilia, who had recently lost her first husband, decided to take a job with the Jooss Company as Gabor's secretary. She went on a lengthy tour of Europe, leaving Ponji and Elizabeth, who were barely out of the nursery, to fend for themselves at Number Nine.

After the war Kurt and Aino moved out of the apartment above the garage and Gabor moved in, bringing with him his relentless character, with its loud aroma of exotic pipe tobacco, antiques, masculine perfume and love for young men.

For the many graduates wanting a way out from the mechanistic highways of university life, Gabor's theatrical know-how was a much needed antidote, and an essential step into the precarious world of show business.

He ran a small antique shop directly opposite the Fitzwilliam Museum in Cambridge, and the revenue from this small business provided him the freedom to indulge his passion for mounting plays.

My mother often intimated that he wasn't a particularly good director; nevertheless Gabor's productions were a useful sounding board for any aspiring undergraduates wanting to make a platform for themselves in one of the main theatre venues in Cambridge.

His apartment was often full to the brim with lively social occasions. Gabor's love for young men made him a soft touch and it was they, who more often than not, would be seen coming and going up and down the stairs, which were placed at an uncertain angle on the exterior of the garage. These wooden steps led straight up to Gabor's front door and they were a treacherous climb, particularly on rainy days, when the algae came to life and made them slimy and slippery. It was a wonder that no one ever fell down them in the excited rush.

Instantly inside Gabor's separate and distinctly private domain, was a small functional kitchen. Immediately to the left, directly opposite an Edwardian gas stove, was a secluded bathtub, boxed in by faded ornately painted wood and veiled from the eye by the fold-down lid, which was covered with antique biscuit tins, ornate crockery and kitchen utensils. This certainly made the kitchen a practical place, but I used to wonder how a bath, if ever, was taken.

Directly adjacent to this compact kitchen, was an elegant living room, full of lush antique furniture, exquisite knickknacks, tasteful prints and small figurines. All was impregnated with the rich smell of pipe tobacco and gentleman's aftershave. It was here that we met up for what was for me the first ever read-through of a play, after which Gabor insisted on throwing a small party so that the cast might get to know each other a little better.

At that age I had no idea, or really cared about anyone's sexual orientation. Even so, it wasn't hard to notice a loaded, if not ambiguous relationship between Alice and Gabor not dissimilar to that of Alice's with Frances Walls; in other words it was confusing.

My ability to disappear into the background, when they were together, allowed me to become a voyeur to Alice and Gabor's domestic persuasions. As far as my young eyes could see, Alice for her part would take on the role of the male, and Gabor that of the opposite sex. If either of them didn't get what they essentially needed from each other, a matrimonial like tiff could break out.

There was no doubt Alice was in charge, but domestically Gabor always seemed to get what he wanted. He had a love of good food, but apart from breakfast he rarely ate many main meals in the kitchen. As I saw it, Gabor was a reliable barometer for what was good or bad to eat at Number Nine.

Getting to and from my secret watchtower was a bit like a military manoeuvre in a nudist camp, because Frances and guests in this area of the house used the upstairs bathroom a lot. I worked out pretty quickly that the best time to sneak in unnoticed was mid-afternoon, when everyone was going about their worldly business and Frances was having her afternoon nap.

Occasionally my planning would get shot to pieces; like the time I was coming out of hiding and became transfixed by what I was seeing through a crack in the doorway. Brigitte Schenk, one of the German girls staying at Number Nine to learn English, in the stark naked process of bathing.

Waiting patiently for the soapsuds to subside I started to drift off. I had all but lost consciousness, when she stood up in the tub and started looking round for a towel, which she had forgotten to place nearby for convenience. I remember feeling seriously rooted to the spot, as she and her undeniable beauty stepped out of the bath and began walking with casual purpose towards the door I was hiding behind. With some essential dexterity I managed to roll backwards, like a quiet trapeze artist, onto a pile of blankets behind the door so as to be hidden from her sight. She grabbed a towel and returned to her bathing pleasures, pulling the door between us firmly shut. The decisiveness, with which she shut the door, made me feel as if she knew of my whereabouts. Stock still, I crouched for what seemed like an eternity, until everything was definitely quiet in the bathroom, then took the bull by the horns, threw open the door and fell smack into the arms of Frances Walls, who was without teeth, in her underwear and covered in hair curlers. This terrible collision put a stop to any further escapes to my watchtower. As far as Mrs Walls was concerned, this planted the seeds of suspicion between us for as long as I care to remember.

For a while, after the bathroom incident, I was back under adult supervision tagging along in the company of either Frances or Alice as they went about their various duties. This never felt like a punishment, but I'm sure I was in a place where one of them could keep an eye on my whereabouts. Sometimes I ended up with both of them together. This was mostly in the kitchen, where again I found I would become invisible while they argued, the same as when I was with Gabor and Alice, reminiscent of rows between married couples.

Both in dress and certainly at times in manner Alice and Frances leant in the direction of being quite masculine. Their favourite costume about the house was the humble blue boiler suit, making them resemble two butch car mechanics. They were in a sense totally dependent on each other, both practically and emotionally. No matter how entangled their affiliation, Frances always seemed to keep to the formalities of calling Alice 'Doctor' or 'Doc'. Was the servant, or the master, running the house, was a question that seemed to increase in size as the years rolled by. Apart from the occasional emotional clash, I always felt they both ran the house with equal command but by the same token in equally different ways.

Leaving the garage, en route to the back door of the kitchen, you would be confronted by a large red gate, in width and height approximately six feet. Opening the gate revealed a courtyard, where Alice spent a lot of her domestic time, stirring buckets of putrid smelling pigswill. Like a witch's concoction these brews were slow-cooking on gas rings placed at the end of snakelike coils of rubber tubing, stretched out from a dusty outbuilding, into the perimeter of the yard. This adverse mixture for the pigs, dutifully collected whilst on her doctor's rounds from the back doors of schools and colleges, often looked to her good and edible. Pulling out the bits deemed fit for human consumption she'd throw them into a clean stainless-steel bucket, and serve them to the unsuspecting guests and residents at the next appropriate mealtime.

Just inside the kitchen porch opposite an antiquated boiler room was an old dairy, with the requisite churns, sinks and butter-making equipment. The sweet smell of freshly milked cows always greeted anyone entering the house from this side.

Alice kept most of her shoes here, which were divided into two camps in the porch. There were the ones that were worn down on the right heel and the ones that were worn down on the left. When she decided it was necessary she would swap them around on her feet so that the soles wore out evenly, which at times made her feet look like that of a duck-billed platypus.

Directly inside the kitchen was the smaller of two Edwardian dressers, where Alice kept a mixture of medical supplies and domestic apparatus. Papers, stethoscopes, crockery, plasters, bandages, blank prescriptions and medicine of all kinds, were forever spilling out into the kitchen. Search hard enough and you would find uppers and downers – opium compound, black bombers, Phenobarbitone, (which my mother maintained were prescribed to her by Alice to stop her being beastly to the children,) Purple Hearts, Dexedrine and other such substances; a speed freak's dream!

As I spent more time with Alice I started to see how the kitchen was her main province. It was here that she held court and generally tried to fix life for those whose paths strayed her way.

It was common knowledge, for anyone staying at Number Nine for any length of time, to know that one of Alice's regular jobs was to prepare the bread dough last thing at night, ready for baking in the morning.

She would light a cigarette and place it in the corner of her mouth, where it would stay until it went out. She didn't seem to inhale and her face would contort all over the place, as she tried to keep the smoke from her eyes, still managing to have a squinting-like conversation, with her hands tied up in the kneading process. Precariously drooping from the corner of her mouth, the ash from the cigarette always seemed to partner a silvery dewdrop, emerging at the same time from the end of her nose. As the conversation and kneading became more intense, gravity deemed to pull unnoticed, except by children like me, the snotty drop along with the ash, into the rotund earthenware bowl of dough.

If I refrained from thinking too precisely on what had gone into the bread and put lashings of marmalade and homemade butter on the thickset toast, as Gabor liked to do, this, along with the freshly laid eggs, made breakfast a reasonably safe bet.

Despite mine or Gabor's misgivings, meal times were usually packed with people from all walks of life. At such times Alice presided over a dominant kitchen table, which had been scrubbed so ferociously over the years that the hardest of the grain rose away from the soft, leaving a surface of smooth bleached undulations. At any one sitting some of the most sought-after brains in Cambridge could be in place, eagerly conversing and posturing. I suspect another part of the attraction for these eminent few was the diverse and plentiful personalities; including refugees, Alice's patients, her intellect, beautiful au-pairs, hungry students and other international strays staying in the house at the time; not to mention the constant squeezing in of resident family members.

Increasingly I started to feel hemmed in by any questions that such loud occasions might engender and began to stand in the shadows, always a few paces back from the table.

During any meal time the black Bakelite phone isolated in the right-hand corner on the long narrow windowsill was bound to ring. The phone-calls from her patients were often of a very personal and private nature, but this didn't really matter to anyone in the kitchen much, as they were always pretty hard to decipher. "Cambridge 53890 Doctor Roughton speaking....... yes.......yes.......yes........"

The conversation would begin and end as it had gone along, with the occasional 'No' thrown in for good measure and the alarming afterthought that perhaps she hadn't actually spoken to anyone at all, but was just making it up for show.

On rare occasions Uncle Jack would appear, usually passing by way of the kitchen, but I don't think I ever saw him eat a meal there, at least not when other people were present.

He was always the stranger and a rare sighting at the best of times. If you held on long enough, you might catch sight of him, gliding slowly down the middle stairs of the house and walking toward the front door, hovering by the cabinet in the hall to see if there was any post.

He had a methodical deliberate air about him and once outside he would mount his traditional black bicycle, as if in slow motion and set off down the road toward the city centre, his long legs pedalling with simple purpose.

Uncle Jack, or to give him his full name Francis John Worsley Roughton, was a biochemist, a distinguished expert on respiratory physiology. He and Alice had separate rooms in a large functional apartment located at the centre of the house. In the mornings, when he was at home, Alice took a soiled wooden breakfast tray of boiled eggs and toast to his room punctually and without fail.

If I bumped into Uncle Jack when I was little, it was usually accidentally. He came across to me as a carefully spoken gigantic man with a gentle imposing presence, who would lean down from on high and just when I thought he was going to tell me off, whisper into my ear how he had found a building, or another person named Matthew, whilst going about his hobby of researching his family tree.

It wasn't unusual to hear long term guests in the kitchen asking Alice who the strange man was lingering in the hall, and a typical throwaway reply would be, "oh, that's just my husband, can you get the boiled ham from the larder?"

The larder had a particular smell which came from the combination of cold meats, sacks of pulses, flour and extensive quantities of the dutifully retrieved second-hand food - anything from boxes of rotten bananas swarming with fruit flies, through to cheese crawling with sensible penicillin.

Next to the larder door opposite a grand old AGA, covering the wall from floor to ceiling was the other much larger dresser. Built into the fabric of the room, faded and off white, this shelving and cupboard space accommodated other assorted bits and pieces for this unusual kitchen. Unnoticed, except by someone with a keen eye, was the butt end of a twelve-bore shotgun tucked away at the back of the highest shelf. This double-barrel gun was used to shoot occasional unsuspecting pigeon or pheasant, which were then hung up to bleed, in a shed under a very tall yew tree in the garden. It was never clear who stood in charge of this firearm; the only time I ever saw it used, was when Ponji fired it off accidentally in the Oak Room.

Winding up alone at the kitchen table was often a latter day pastime for any lost souls procrastinating, waiting and deciding on their next move.

When the kitchen's activity died away, the warmth from the cooker and the glow from the dignified goldfish tank were all that remained in this timeless place. Intertwined with an intense loneliness, the clock above the entrance to the larder, always fifteen minutes fast, seemed to enter this mood of seclusion with its ceaseless ticking.

Number Nine in more recent years ...out of frame left is the garage and Gabor's apartment; out of frame right The Oak Room and beyond that number eight.

9

They may have bitten off more children than they could chew, but my parents weren't for a millisecond going to let a little thing like that overwhelm their designated time in Cambridge.

With the family growing upwards and outwards at number eight, my mother became increasingly preoccupied by her domestic challenge. I continued to seek out a place of dreams where everything worked to my order. Whenever the weather permitted I spent more and more time kitted out as the hero, a lonesome cowboy, bringing law and order to the garden next door.

It was at such a time, lost and buried in adventure, that I heard an upbeat kind of music coming from the Oak Room. My curiosity found these sounds intriguing and like a fish to bait, the jumping melodies enticed me through the wide open French windows towards the side of a grand piano in this grandiose room.

It was Joe, the compelling lawyer from Ghana, who when staying at Number Nine relaxed by smoking a cigarette and playing the piano. I snuck in as quietly as I could and stood as close as possible, trying not to disturb his warm mysterious world. With my eye-line just above the height of the keyboard, I watched with wonder as his long black elegant fingers danced out rounds of startling jazz! Few words passed between us; he would occasionally gaze down with eyes as deep as a soul can go and throw a smile nonchalantly in my direction. As if detached from the stillness of his laid-back body, his lower arms seemed to fly about from one end of the keyboard to the other, whilst the music just simply poured out with natural ease from his agile fingertips.

I don't know what happened to Joe; certainly my sister Elizabeth was smitten and bitten by his alluring ways and it broke her heart when at the last minute he decided not to marry her. For me he was just a fantastically charismatic figure who played the piano. A true jazz man; someone who could on rare unforgettable occasions, coax the Oak Room into a smoky lair full of beguiling sound.

The Oak Room, had been built and commissioned by my great grandmother in the late eighteen hundreds and was very much a part of the house on the inside, but the exterior, with its rectangular shape and flat sunken roof, was big enough to make it seem like a distinctly separate and relatively modern annexe.

A change in its construction was made by my grandmother Mariana, when a large dance floor of polished oak planking was laid for midsummer balls and lavish parties. The floor was refurbished with a small amount of give in it, to accommodate any nimble skip or jump that might come down a little too hard during one of the many hallowed festive events. I am told these grand parties were thrown to introduce my mother's sisters into the social circles of the academic select, in the hope that they would all be married off to men of fine scholarly worth.

To get to the foremost part of this illustrious room from the house, one would have to go through a dimly lit antechamber known as the Front Oak Room. Invariably, on passing through the presence of over loaded bookcases, heavy curtains and tired carpets, it was wise to be as quiet as possible, in case someone was sleeping, either in one of the beds, or under one of the many piles of clothes, cushions or blankets, that littered this part of the room in an apparently organized manner.

Every Sunday, without exception, Alice would arrange and preside over open house and the Oak Room became host to all and sundry, including of course the usual peppering of Cambridge brains. The idea was that anyone who had a connection with Number Nine could invite friends or acquaintances for leftover food and dialogue of international standing. There was always the possibility of meeting someone new, or catching up with undisclosed affairs left behind in the giddy mix of the past; all of-course under the confines of Alice's communal umbrella. A slight unease seemed to dominate the room on these occasions. As long as there was distance then everything worked well, but if I got too close I became engulfed by a blanket of discomfort, as any real warmth had a tendency to disappear up the highbrow scale.

For special parties, the many sofas and armchairs would be pushed back to the side of the room and the carpets rolled up. Then if we children were lucky we would take turns to sit in a blanket, and get Ponji or Alice's visiting son, my grown-up cousin Geoffrey, to hold the ends of the four corners, twirling us at ever increasing speeds, until abruptly letting go, shooting the excited child out across the vast polished space - a bundle of terrified fun.

On winter nights the fireplace, which seemed disproportionately small to the rest of the room, gave out little or no warmth – it was more likely to throw smoke back into the room rather than up the chimney. To put out extra heat, Alice would sometimes insist on bringing a tree trunk or two in from the garden, which were often so big that they stuck out well beyond the hearth into the bulk of the room. Tattooed around the skirting of this large well-worn hearth were battered remnants of attractive Edwardian tiles, which in better days came together and told a romantic story of horses and carriages.

The whole room seemed to luxuriate in a mixture of dark wood and cloth. Over the years, the off-white curtains, which covered most areas in the room from floor to ceiling, became musty from the smoke. So enveloping were these lavish drapes that it made real the possibility of a small body disappearing forever in the endless sea of cloth.

Along with the grand piano, taking pride of place, toward the centre of the Oak Room, was a full size professional billiard table, where young men who were staying in the house posed and played tournaments. As I remember, the group often consisted of Geoffrey when he was home, Ponji and his good friend Jan Bredsdorff.

We were all besotted with Jan, all of us, especially my Mother, my Father and Elizabeth. He was like another member of the family. As far as I could see he was cool before the word was invented. He knew about the demons and the tragedies they could cause. The mixture of low self-esteem and academic pressures, found his brother hanging dead from a rope in his collage rooms at the beginning of his first term up at Cambridge.

Jan came from a family of eminent Danish scholars who lived in Cambridge. He was very tall, wildly handsome and emanated charm. He stayed in China for a while before it was acceptable in the West to do so and wrote extensively about the people there and his love for the country.

Sometimes there were other familiar bodies at the billiard table, like Jean Simone an impressionable energetic young man from France, who also liked to jive the cue to the ball. And of course there was me. Well, I was only allowed to watch and wonder from down below the green, which suited me just fine.

It was said that Jean Simone had deserted the national service in France and fled to England. For his protection he sought help from the Labour minister Frank Allaun, who one way or another, found him secure accommodation at Number Nine. My only real connection with Jean was when he tried to clamber unannounced into my tree house, which as far as I was concerned at the time was absolutely not on. My tree house, which I constructed sometime during my twelfth year at the top of a large beautiful copper beach tree in the heart of the garden, was the last remaining hiding place where I still felt free of any adult intervention.

When not being used for a game, the billiard-table was covered with three large sheets of polished wood and used as a buffet table for special occasions and the Sunday nights. It eventually came to a sad demise and was broken up for the slate. The legs were burnt, and the wooden cover sooner or later, was put to exemplary use as roofing for the tree house, under which I had my first close encounter with true love.

Frances Schuster lived at number ten Adams Road, the house where my mother and her sisters were brought up. She was a year younger than me. I became besotted with her mysterious eyes, dark hair and glowing looks. It was as if the space separating us said it all. She definitely liked me, but I kind of knew deep down that she wasn't as star struck as I was. Hardly a word ever passed between us. We always met separated by this polite distance, apart from one distinct time when I managed to persuade her to clamber into my tree house. After proudly showing her the fully working kitchenette, candle lighting and the bird's eye view of Number Nine from the small fully functioning window, we sat opposite each other on the carpeted floor in an awkward silence, unable to move, for what seemed like an eternity. Climbing back down, I saw my best chance slip out of reach.

Any mention of my infatuation at home just saw me swallowed up in a shameful bubble. My sister Elizabeth and my mother may have seen their teasing as playful jibing, as it no doubt was, but I couldn't help feeling entrenched in a mixture of guilt and embarrassment, if I showed any signs of these stirrings of love for Frances in front of them.

Frances's family was of German Jewish origin and in truth a little out of my league. Compared with us they were very tidy and extremely precise. Her grandfather Paul Hirsch escaped to England and took up residency at ten Adams road, which he purchased from my grandmother just before the war, bringing with him one of the finest personal collections of musical manuscripts in the world. This library of classical works was smuggled out of Germany at great risk by the train load right from under the nose of the Nazis, and today sits safely in the British Library. Frances had a younger sister who giggled a lot. When she and her sister were together, I couldn't resist a compulsive need to be a little daring in their company. One evening I found myself in their bedroom just before bedtime. I started with a miniscule amount of showing off, (playing aeroplanes if I remember rightly) when I heard their mother coming up the stairs. Their mother had these bulbous eyes that were scary and she was very strict, especially after hours. I hid behind an armchair, but it wasn't secure enough and she caught me out when she came into the room. As I saw it I hadn't done anything untoward, but she assumed differently and smacked my head accordingly, at the same time telling me never to come back to the house. After that I don't remember seeing so much of Frances. A million years later I was to meet up with her after a play I was in, where she introduced me to her husband who was a vicar; quite understandable; but even then I couldn't stop wondering what might have happened if we'd fallen headlong into a kiss.

The black shadow of school continued in its own insidious way to creep across these salad days like a terrible plague.

When I was a child, I resented my father. Whenever his name was mentioned my mother's eyes filled with tears. He was an intrusion a cause of jealousy and frustration. I felt inferior to my sisters because I was the one who couldn't remember him"

Cecilia Scurfield

10

After nearly a year's absence I was back at Newnham Croft primary school. This time in Mrs Lingwood's class and you might say with a little more confidence than when I started in Mrs Gibson's. But my desktop capabilities were as pathetic as ever. Whenever the technical aspect of words and sums presented themselves I still lost all sense and meaning. Under pressure what little word vision I had mastered, became completely impaired.

Learning how to overcome shyness and be at ease in the body is what I desperately needed to master at this time, especially if I was to have any chance at all of taking in school work. I am still incensed and it is incredulous to me that the only real reason for being in school is, increasingly it seems, for academic purposes only.

Mrs Lingwood was a petite, attractive lady, but she didn't quite have the self-confidence to enjoy her beauty, or delight in the feast of children wanting above everything else to enjoy her company. Instead, she took to reprimanding and scolding anyone who showed the slightest sign of joy.

She often got us to sit in an open circle, where the boys' shorts had a tendency to ride up the leg when sitting on the chairs, leaving naked flesh vulnerably exposed. If we were seen to be out of line, her meanness would culminate with her slapping one of us sharply across the thigh, just below the hemline of our shorts. The smack of her hand left a red indentation embedded in the skin, which seemed to disappear soon after while the shock lingered around for days.

The fear of her sharp reproach terrified me and yet again made me feel in the wrong, a pattern that was to continue throughout most of my time in educational establishments.

I felt I could survive if my mind became constantly occupied with looking forward. Forward to the end of the school day and further still towards the holidays. So I turned my dreams away from the present and entertained thoughts of a lighter easier way of life in a make believe world, where creating havens was the main past time and I added up to something really worthwhile.

One of the essential elements that brought some breathing space to my difficulties at school was a love for being in water. I taught myself to swim in a paddling pool not far from Newham Croft, where my dad promised me a shilling if I'd go from the paddling pool into a deeper more defined swimming hole called The Snobs.

The Snobs was a narrow estuary which branched off from the River Cam, ideal for the likes of those who had just started to manage the water. Here I could duck and dive with the fish. I discovered a way of survival, a way of being contradicting everything I was going through at school. The silky feeling, the soft hues enveloping my body made the world I was in absolute. I was submerged in life and nothing else came close. I spent hours, sometimes days, swimming in and out of the depths of the Cam. Water became the absolute respite I needed, to remain in contact with the earth, which at times felt as if it was being pulled away from under my feet.

The teachers, it turned out, weren't all bad eggs. In contrast to Mrs Lingwood, Mrs Coe was a delight. In my last year at primary school I was fortunate to find myself in her class and by this time hormonal changes were beginning to kick in. Simply to be in her presence would lift the temperature in my body.

Mrs Coe was an attractive, voluptuous, well crafted dark haired lady, who, unaware of our sexual motivations, sat in front of the class, always it seemed with a somewhat preoccupied air about her person. She would lean her elbows on the desk, clasp her hands together in front of her chin and with the brightly painted nail, of her protruding forefinger gently prod the centre part of her delectable upper lip. Bewitching us with every slight movement, she would stare out of the window into the middle distance and pine, pine for her knight in stardust armour, who could ride in and carry her off to a richer world. I remember being overcome with jealousy, as I became aware that her desire for a new life was seen to be outside mine.

A prefabricated building called the hut was the classroom in which Mrs Coe presided, and she shared this space with the lively comings and goings at lunchtime.

The staff room was at the end of a long corridor next to the head teacher Mrs Thompson's office. I used to stand at the end of this long corridor, just outside the doors to the playground and wait for Mrs Coe to leave the staff room. She always seemed to be late and had to hurry to get to the hut. When she ran her ample breasts would be practically falling over themselves to please and I couldn't help but gaze wantonly at their natural beauty.

During the summer, if it was hot and sunny, she insisted on teaching us outside. Seemingly oblivious to our drooling, she would unbutton the top of her blouse and tuck the lapels down the sides of her breasts. Whilst she bathed the tops of her abundant bosom in the sunshine, we sat at her feet on the grass, tongue-tied, gazing up with wide-eyed wonder at her gorgeous figure, and taking in every word of her softly spoken voice.

At the end of my last year at Newnham Croft, I took a spelling test in a class taken by the head teacher, the austere Mrs Thompson, and as usual I miss-spelt all the words. When the test was finished, she came over to my desk and as if making an announcement to the world said, "Never mind Matthew we need dustmen". In my innocence I didn't think this sounded so bad, however my peers weren't so naive and it wasn't long before playground jibes brought home the reality and the profound disgrace caught up with me.

I needn't have worried. That afternoon the sun pushed aside the growing stone weight of failure at school, when Alice came and picked me up. The weather allowed the canvas top to be removed, leaving the loosely fitted jet-black four-wheel-drive open to the elements. I had no idea where we were going, but sitting next to Alice in her Jeep with the rush of air brushing and pulling against my face, seemed to whisk any self-effacing thoughts far away for the day.

When we arrived at the airfield I was still none the wiser.

Marshalls was a family run firm which made motor vehicles and aeroplanes for the rich and famous. The firm's sprawling complex comprised numerous spacious hangers, workshops and an airport, which was home to the Cambridge gliding club, of which Auntie Alice was a member.

Today it had somehow been decided that Alice, being the expert flyer, would take this young boy for the ride of his life. It was all out of my hands and I became overwhelmed by a paralysing mixture of panic and excitement.

I clambered up some rickety steps into the back seat of a simple two-seater open cockpit. To anything Alice might have said I could only nod, with open mouthed approval.

Up to this point I knew nothing about Alice's experience with wings, which I later learnt, after she had nearly killed herself in a gliding accident, was limited to say the least. I have a vague memory of her excitement, or was it nervousness, as the actuality of flying this giant bird took over.

Waiting for the tow rope to take the strain, I began to realize how I had all but disappeared into a remote part of Alice's subconscious. I sat behind her, with the angst rising steadily along with the anticipation. Here was the young girl who was out to show the world that she meant ferocious business.

Of course like many boys I'd flown paper aeroplanes and even been with Ponji when he flew a model spitfire in the garden at number eight, but my knowledge of flying a real glider amounted to zilch. So as the steel rope, which stretched from the nose of the cockpit into a small cranking shed way off at the end of the field, began to tighten I was wondering if I should scream or not. As we moved forwards with increasing speed, thumping and bumping on the grassy floor below, I squeezed the seat of my pants tight, hoping nothing untoward would happen down there. Then the rough ride came to a sudden stop, leaving me to guess, from the relative quiet, that we had lost contact with the ground and were then heading for the open sky.

The feeling of sitting on the back of this great bird, as it began to ascend the heights, was just sensational.

Amidst a rushing of wind, we started to reach a peak, at which point Alice managed to turn back to me and shout out something about the tow line. Within a few seconds of her unheard instructions, I felt the release of the rope. My stomach whooshed up to my head as the plane plunged downwards like a dead weight and then stopped somewhat abruptly when the underbelly reached its designated cushion of air.

Once the extreme shock of being released from the umbilical cord began to wear away so did my fears. We started to glide forwards, an airborne boat at one with the air currents, and as I looked downwards toward the ground below, I saw what I had somehow known all along; the roads, cars and the houses were toys inhabited by tiny ants, and not the great big giants that they thought they were.

"I was a little ashamed of my origins, of having been at Oundle, of having had a father who'd become a doctor and a mother with a somewhat aristocratic background. I longed to be a man of the people, a Leslie Halward or a Bill Naughton."

George Scurfield

11

Although our home was like a beacon of repose, where I could eat like a pig and sleep as sound as a log, my sense of worth was starting to feel exposed there. It seemed for all the good intent as if I were being spellbound in a powerful spotlight of optimism, a place of brilliance that was becoming too bright to see behind the lens. There was no escaping the plain fact – I was starting to stand out like a new car in a knacker's yard. Even my intricate hiding places in Number Nine were beginning to feel uncovered.

Imperceptibly the thought of being caught out got the better of me. The feeling of not being good enough, crept into my relationship with the grownups, like a dark night stealing the reflections along an evening river bank. At times it seemed like I could never be still. I started running, ricocheting between the two houses like a rubber bullet fired from a shotgun in a confined space.

There was no doubt that Auntie Alice could be kind, but her judgmental attitude seemed to get more acute as I got older. This made it difficult not to feel increasingly off centre when in her company. No matter which way I tried to pitch it, I would lose. The escape route slowly and unwittingly took its course. If she or any other adults were in the kitchen at Number Nine, I went through the front door and likewise, if she was in the hall or the Oak Room, I'd do my best to shimmy through the kitchen.

Proving to her father, that she was as worthwhile to him as any man meant Alice became a very powerful woman; someone who strove to completely dominate the world in which she lived. I am convinced now that this was the backbone of her energy and brought about her whole philosophy and way of life, which for a lot of visitors to Number Nine made enormous amounts of sense. But like the captain of a ship, whose destiny becomes a blind imperative refusing to acknowledge that there can ever be anything wrong, she proudly hides her deepest fears from the crew and for the sake of the passengers, carries on regardless.

Contrary to the, *I know best* syndrome, buzzing about her persona, Alice, like my mother, did have a seam of gullibility tied to her sleeve and visitors who tapped into this, could if they so desired get away with an awful lot. This apparent freedom was accomplished by making sure their allotted domestic chores were fulfilled and their opinions kept to themselves. For those guests who ended up staying forever, it just seemed inevitable that they would become permanent pillars of her iron clad convictions.

As I grew through the years I became increasingly aware that Alice had to have people around her who propped up her way of life. Any doubt in the equation was always categorically thrown out with the bath water. Like my mother she needed to have the last word, to be right at any cost, which from my view point seemed to become more excessive with time. Unless you had the wherewithal for manipulating her otherwise, as Ponji seemed to have when he was a boy, it was easier not to enter into the arena.

In the end avoidance seemed like the most diplomatic course to take. Even when Alice wasn't around, the house was difficult to steer through without bumping into one of the many inquisitive visitors who often seemed to take up all the available air, leaving me constantly manoeuvring to avoid being squeezed into a claustrophobic space. With Alice in charge, Number Nine was and always had been a house predominantly overrun with lost grownups and enthusiastic intellectuals, a house where children were at best seen but not heard.

On the right of the cabinet where the mail was kept, in the front hall at Number Nine, is now a huge bedroom, which in the days of bourgeois convention was the dining room. Here, staff dressed in tails and pinafores would have served elegant meals. This is hard to believe with the house under Alice's prominent reign, as it was now thought large enough to become home for many a hapless family of refugees, or visiting scholars washed in from other shores. And indeed, for them to retain their dignity along with their independence, it was often thought best that they should be allowed their own kettle and a small cooker. It wasn't unusual then, whilst passing in the garden, to peep in through the open French windows and see a family of down at heel academics, or a party of exiles partaking in high tea.

To the right of this room, was an overcast central lobby known as the hall, home to the main stairway. There were two bedrooms leading into this hall used by the usual global persons in uncertain transit. If the door from the hall into the front hallway was open, it blocked access to a scrubbed self-conscious bathroom, which resounded with an unfortunate echo. For a paranoid schizophrenic sleeping downstairs, the possibility of getting out of bed and not colliding with a strange passer-by could make brushing their teeth, or using the lavatory here, like a game of Russian roulette.

When the main police station in town became overly full, they would often phone Alice to see if she had any room at Number Nine. The answer was usually, "Yes of course, carry on." Being a prominent psychiatrist she had the same arrangement with Fulbourn, a large mental hospital in the village of the same name situated on the outskirts of Cambridge.

Squeezed between this downstairs bathroom and the kitchen, there was and as far I know still is, a walk-in cupboard. This small overgrown rectangular room groaned with the upheaval of languid silver platters, old candlesticks, cranky coffee grinders, dishevelled pots and pans, knives, forks and all manner of aging utensils that might accompany the dining of bygone days. During the time of the war and while we lived in Shepreth a shelf was made up, among the clutter at the far end, with some cloth draped over it for Ponji's bed. Alice, until the last years of her life, continued to call this utility cupboard 'Ponji's Room', in the same way as she insisted on calling me 'Mitty'.

I never did find out where Elizabeth slept, or how she really managed in those early years. If it wasn't another store room, she was constantly moved from pillar to post to make room for the incoming guests.

They tell me it was because he was the younger that Ponji was given his own space, albeit a large cupboard filled with kitchen junk, but I think this was probably more to do with his unlimited charm than his age. For one of Ponji's endearing qualities was to see him on parade, playing the high ground. When he was really on form, it was extremely entertaining to be in his company. It became a habit, almost unconsciously, particularly for the family and his closest friends, to egg him on. Elizabeth hated this. Franticly jealous, she would use every available resource to get her own back.

From as far back as I can remember I wanted to be, or even own, a part of my brother's buoyant life. This desire came to a head on numerous occasions, but there is one event which kind of sums it up, when he caught me stealing from his plentiful and neatly arranged stamp collection.

Compared with Ponji's, my album of penny blacks seemed to be a long way from a decent array. I never did find out how Ponji knew I was stealing his stamps, but he did. I thought I was being discreet in only taking two or three at a time. When he came to me about this pilfering he didn't show malice or anger, just perplexity, which made the whole thing much worse. Strangely, despite my guilt and his disbelief, it initiated a greater love and respect between us. Perhaps it showed that he could speak his truth without my running away. This isn't to say that he couldn't be antagonistic. At times his charming forgiveness seemed to go hand-in-hand with a kind of pedantic arrogance, which I found extremely taxing. I remember on several occasions sitting in the lavatory, with him on the other side of the locked door, asking me how many sheets of loo paper I used and if I said six or more, he would say "I use far less, just two or three".

Another example of his swaggering came about when I was in the bath one evening. He entered the bathroom with such a high and mighty stance that I thought he was going to take off. Oozing with smugness, he told me how he was going to see the most frightening film ever made and that one day, if my age permitted, I might be able to go on such an outing with him. When he came on like this, he really did make me feel as if he was the only one who had ever set foot in the brave new world. The film was Hitchcock's *Psycho* and the following morning he was found to be cowering under the sheets in the bedroom of one of the au-pair's.

My last remaining respite, before I grew away from Number Nine, was to be in the company of my second cousins once removed, Francis and Johnny. Francis and Johnny were younger than me and lived in an apartment on the second floor of the house with their mother, Alice's daughter Rosemary, and their father Frank. For most of my childhood years all I wanted to do was to play with them, but unless they came over to our house, getting to them became more and more like an escalating game of chance.

Once inside the front door of Number Nine I had a quick decision to make, do I tiptoe surreptitiously up the squeaky naked staircase, or do I do the polite thing and say hello to Auntie Alice in the kitchen? Oh sod it! I'd throw caution to the wind and bolt up the stairs.

On getting to the middle landing, gasping for air, I'd make sure all was clear on the grown-up front. Whilst getting my breath back, a self-conscious eye seemed to cut into the back of my neck. It was as if the aging full-length mirror that stood opposite the door to Francis and Johnny's apartment was scrutinizing me. I suspect this was largely due to the fact that this window to the underworld was right next to another apartment, that of Alice and Jack. Their fortified dark wooden door sat tight in its carcass and told me these living quarters were a no go area. Quite honestly the thought of being trapped in there on my own, was enough to put me off. But occasionally, curiosity got the better of me and I would find my hands turning the shiny doorknob and pushing the large oak door to its uncomfortable opening.

Upon entering I'd be confronted by a long fading central corridor, the smell of carbolic soap and old books. The overwhelming aroma of carbolic came from a bathroom a few feet down on the left. This was a purely practical place for ablutions, with no feminine attributions whatsoever. It was dusty clean, in a scrubbed wood sort of way. Not a place where physical gentleness or feminine worth, presented itself.

Opposite this bathroom, with its door always ajar, was a large room overflowing with boring textbooks. There were however a couple of shelves in here, which were home to the many thank you presents that had been left by visitors who had come and gone over the years. Alice would keep these presents and give them out at any forgotten birthday that might happen to spring on her by surprise.

Strewn all over the floor and a grand old table, which took central position in the room, were piles of half empty boxes, papers, letters and more books. This clutter obscured the view to Alice's bed. A thin horsehair mattress laid out on the floor, next to the ever-open French windows, from which, in her old age, she was once carried, wrapped in one of those silver foil blankets, suffering from extreme hypothermia.

Down the hall from Alice's room were Uncle Jacks living quarters. If ever I got this far down the corridor I would try to sneak a look into his study, but lose my nerve at the last minute. The weight of awkwardness and my pounding chest soon saw me rushing back to the relative safety of the landing, where the bell to Johnny and Francis's apartment was finally rung.

Alice's daughter, my cousin Rosemary, would usually be the one who answered. To my asking if her sons Francis or Johnny could play, she would call out to the boys, with her usual shy reserve, at the same time allowing me to slip quietly inside. This apartment was equally as big as Alice and Jacks, but felt more lived in, cosy even and exuded more light.

Rosemary's husband Frank Summers was a quietly spoken man from a Glaswegian mining family, who had left school when he was fourteen and like his forefathers ended up six days a week down the pit. But unlike his mates, on his days off he worked hard academically and eventually secured himself a scholarship at Ruskin's Collage in Oxford.

During his time at Ruskin's Frank entered an essay for a competition. On the back of this essay E M Forster, who was one of judges, told the governing board at Kings in Cambridge that they should without hesitation grant him a place.

One way or another he ended up living at Number Nine, where he was to meet and subsequently fall in love with Rosemary, who he was to marry, following their graduation in the summer of 1952.

Although Rosemary's background couldn't have been more different to Frank's, there were similarities as to how she gained her place at Cambridge.

Having been sent to the state run County Girls School in Cambridge, Rosemary was expected to help Alice with the running of the house, so like Frank she continued her education as best she could, off her own back. Remarkably, she set up a secluded workspace in the small cowshed at the bottom of the garden and whenever she had spare time she could be found studying there. Despite the lack of support, she secured a place at Girton College, and at the end of her time there she came away with a first class degree in archaeology and anthropology. Later she went on to get a doctorate in medicine.

For the few years their parents tried to stitch it together, 'Afraid of Virginia Wolf', in the flat at Number Nine, Frances and Johnny became a shelter for me at the end, of a disquieting human assault course. Placed at the very heart of the house, it was to them that I'd look for companionship, for they were more like brothers than second cousins once removed.

Francis was the older brother to Johnny and only a couple years younger than me. It was with Francis that I spent most of my time. He was unbelievably bright. By the time of his tenth year he had read many of the classics. His great love was *Lord of the Rings*, which he knew pretty much by heart by the time he was nine years of age, and this was before the sixties. When he was sixteen he started to learn Chinese. But absorbing literature and languages was not where his heart lay, for deep down he had a shaman's understanding of how the earth worked. This led him away from the formalities of learning in a classroom, towards the deeper mysteries of the universe. On a clear frosty night, it could seem as if the Holy Spirit were emanating through his body into everything around us. Along with his light blonde hair and poetic manner, this could make him seem tantalisingly beautiful.

Johnny was more of a loner than Francis, but was equally exquisite to behold. John, as he now likes to be called, had his feet firmly on the ground and took delight in conjuring up the trickster, which helped me a lot when frustration came yapping at my heels. Was it Johnny who set the cowshed on fire? It was Johnny who kept me company on a tractor driven from the Rothschild's farm, out into the vast desert of a nearby cornfield and then abandoned, through lack of driving skill. When we were little Johnny could go to sleep at the drop of a hat. Once when we were playing hide and seek, he hid and we really couldn't find him. With mounting exasperation from our parents, hours went by. In the end, they called the police who found him fast asleep inside a cardboard box, in the cupboard, behind the garden door at number eight.

I was often accompanied on my comings and goings next-door by my sister Lucy, this was particularly so during the holidays. Like Sarah, Lucy had blonde hair. She was both wilful and endearing. Unlike Sarah, who by now had given up with any of my playing suggestions, she was up for anything, particularly getting stuck into adventure games. She had the dearest face which was highlighted by the National Health spectacles of the day. These thin, pink plastic covered glasses seemed to magnify her weak eye giving the impression that only one was really focused. It wasn't until later that she became concerned about her appearance and increasingly annoyed if anyone, usually me, started to tease her about her looks.

Like many children we were always on the cusp of change, torn between interest and boredom, the doll or the cowboy suit, the dream and the light.

When we played time didn't really exist. It was only the thought of school looming over the horizon of the holidays that brought the notion of chronology into our endless worlds. My father would say later that it was when I started secondary school that a rougher element began to creep into our games.

What started off as galloping across the wild prairies, or thrashing our way through thick African jungle, eventually moved on to war, smashing panes of glass on the building sites across the road, sticking fireworks in cowpats, cowering in anticipation of the explosions, driving Alice's jeep, clambering on the roofs, dropping water filled grenades on the unfortunates below, smoking my mother's woodbines...

And Number Nine?

Well the encumbered house just went on reeling from one story to another, until Alice, a few years before she died, with much reluctance, released the wilting baton to her daughter.

Hanging on the wall to the right in the front hallway, was a large unremarkable picture of my grandfather. Below the picture was a fireplace, which with time became blocked off by an outsized heavy table covered with domestic debris. Alice, with all the enthusiasm of a nine year old, collected this bric-a-brac for some starving third world country. The build-up of these undistinguished bits and pieces seemed to increase as the years rolled by, and the phone on the table, when it rang, became progressively harder to find. It was as if the very fabric of her good work was literally smothering the heart of the house. This may sound uncharitable, but along with Alice's need to always be right, her warlike obsession with helping others, seemed to leave her immediate family forever on the backburner.

Ponji's cupboard at Number Nine: the shelf for his bed was where the freezer chest is below the window on the left; apparently not much else had changed.

12

Failing the compulsory eleven plus, cast a shameful and humiliating shadow. The marking of a measly exam was it seems, going to decide the outcome of my future. I ended up, as my brother had done, going to a school for lesser mortals somewhere in the nether regions of the city.

In the early part of 1959, shortly after my eleventh birthday, I went with my dad to an open day at The Manor secondary modern school for boys, which was situated on the eastern edge of Arbury council estate. This estate was typical of a lot of post-war housing, built with little or no thought for packing a lot of people into an isolated area with few amenities. But the impending social impact didn't deter my dad from being delighted at the prospect of what lay ahead for his son in this school, all newly built and paid for as it should be by the tax payer.

Any romantic notions I might have picked up from George were immediately shattered by the sheer brutality of the place. I entered this raw and seething atmosphere totally unprepared, without any understanding of the armour and weaponry necessary to survive.

The top class was A the bottom D and below D there was Removed, the class where I was to start my first term. Along with myself there were around nineteen other boys who were barely able to speak let alone read or write.

As far as the school authorities were concerned, here was this boy from the right end of town in the same class as a bunch of oiks. Some teachers seemed perplexed, but most went out of their way to put what they saw as a boy of privilege well and truly out of joint.

I discovered pretty quickly that The Manor was more like a boot camp than a place of love and learning. The seeds of apprehension that had been planted at primary school came to fruition here and eventually began to choke the remaining clarity from my path.

As the stark reality of total unease unfolded at this school, I became unbearable to myself and my family. By the end of the second term, I had started provoking my sisters into disliking me as much as I had now begun to dislike myself. I became secretive. I needed to constantly test the ground to see if what was happening to me was true. I think the love in me became embarrassed, I started to feel heavy and uncomfortable with the ones I held dear. Teasing my sisters and aggravating my parents became like an addiction, the deeper I got stuck in the harder it was to stop.

My mother and father's response to my educational difficulties started in a place of heartfelt concern, but ended up in a place of anger and frustration. For them it became a terrible muddle all round. They continued to blame the school and themselves. Their understanding of the system meant they felt disempowered to do anything. With their hand on their heart they'd tell me how they had no choice. As time went on the problems and relentless anguish became more and more about my inabilities and less and less about the school's. Any discussion always seemed to be teetering on the brink of an explosion from both sides.

"You're not stupid Matthew of course you can read and write!" But the school and the distinctly academic environment in which we lived was telling me otherwise. The fear of how my parents and the teachers would react, when I tried to convey my terrible lack of ability, meant I started to dabble with ways of blanking and numbing out their world. The word failure, like a broken record began pounding around as a permanent fixture inside my head.

The first year was about survival, not just in terms of school work, but learning to grapple with the other boys. It became perfectly normal during a break to see at least one fight where blood was spilt. It was quite common for the older boys to use flick knives, or knuckledusters, particularly if the punch-up took place outside the gates after school.

By the time of my second year I'd seen a boy impaled and killed with a javelin, another shot and paralysed with an airgun and many horrific fist fights. If ever the fire of a fight caught up with me, which it increasingly did, I'd inevitability become blind with rage and usually wound up beaten into the submission and tears of a snotty, toffee nosed wanker. This pool of violence, which was my school, came to dictate my way of operating in the world; if it wasn't for learning a lot about how to escape the horrors and how to face up to them, I just wouldn't have survived.

~

Occasionally, I would cycle into the city centre after school, leaving my bicycle at the end of a small road called Senate House Passage, which was situated between Gonville and Caius College and The Senate House.

Because I lived a stone throw from the eastern side of the city centre, leaving my bike here presented me with a quick and relatively, traffic free way to get home. Taking this route, I would cycle down Garret Hostel Lane, which runs between Trinity and Trinity Hall, then over Garret Hostel Bridge, down Burrell's walk, past Clare College and the University Library, on to Grange Road and then across Grange Road to Adams Road and up to number eight. Although it was a longer way back from school, it offered up a more picturesque journey back from school and the opportunity of checking out the shops.

One afternoon during one of those early terms at The Manor, some workmen were cleaning the stonework of The Senate House and because it was covered in scaffolding, I parked my bike on the opposite wall and set off on foot to the town centre.

By the time I got back it was after five o'clock. Everyone had finished work, the streaming water used for cleaning the masonry had been turned off and all was quiet in this road of inflexible stone, or so I thought.

There was a boy in my class called Roy Wellford, who at the time had a gang that was mostly made up from mates who lived in his street. On this particular evening, unbeknownst to me, they hid themselves up on the scaffolding behind some tarpaulin and waited for my return.

When I came to collect my two wheeled friend, they suddenly swung down from all directions, giving the impression that they were trying to ambush me. They nearly succeeded, but I just managed to make a head start at the get-away. The only damage taken, as I made the heroic leap across my saddle, like a cowboy jump starting a run-away horse, was when one of the gang members caught up with me and punched me with such a hard thwack between the shoulder blades, it sent a shockwave down my spine forcing the air from my lungs, like a blow-out on a juggernaut lorry.

Swerving between the adrenalin and the tears, I took off for Adams Road. By the time I got to where Burrell's Walk crosses over Queens Road, I slowed down enough to glance over my shoulder and was relieved to see they were no longer in pursuit. In between catching my breath and slowing down, I saw a policeman standing by the zebra crossing and in the heat of the moment, I took it upon myself to go and tell him what had happened. He listened intently and with an air of professional kindness tinted with disbelief, he told me he would look into it. I waited for a moment, expecting something else. After a few seconds silence, I realised it was time to be on my way.

Initially I think Roy Wellford saw me as a potential twat, and his manner of stalking and hanging out at The Manor made me feel uneasy. I became aware of the danger from observing him, early on in the first year, making a pair of knuckledusters during metalwork in full view of the class, without a god damn as to what the teacher or anyone else thought. It became my undivided intention from the start to give him a wide berth. I went out of my way to avoid his eyes during classroom activity and if physically possible kept out of his way between lessons and at the end of a school day.

Before the Senate House incident, I had no idea just how much animosity Wellford really held towards me. It began to dawn on me that if I was to survive my time at this school, it was essential to win him and others like him over, and I really had nothing but my wit to do this with. It was a matter of great urgency and my determination to appease them became an absolute priority.

From the beginning the only common ground Wellford and I had was a mutual mistrust of the teachers. I was terrified of being caned, so my approach in trying to deal with any classroom complications was to be emotionally manipulative. I quickly learnt to use comedy and tragedy as a way of diverting the teacher's attention away from the hot seat. When I was being reprimanded, I became ingratiating and even at times turned on the tears. When it came to this breaking point, I had to convince the teachers to take me seriously, and to do it in such a way that let the other boys know it was just an act. This meant I won my classmates approval, but survived any serious threat of a beating.

I soon began to realise that Wellford's needs were basically the same as mine, but his whole approach was the opposite. The way he worked it was to give the impression that nothing in the way of physical punishment could harm him. And this infuriated the teachers.

Underneath it may have been a different story, but on the surface, he seemed to have a sense of daring fearlessness. Captivated by his bottle, I was determined to get him on my side.

~

My usual desperate ploy to get off school was to feign illness. Although they came to me with weary arguments as to why I should attend, my parents could, for the most part, be taken in by my stories.

The way it would work was to start first thing, during breakfast, with refusing to eat, complaining miserably about an acute pain coming from the stomach. Getting this excruciating act across was always easier when combining the pretence with bleary morning grogginess. As the morning progressed, I'd start to feel a little better and by lunchtime there could be a complete recovery, but I had to time it, to make resuming school in the afternoon a senseless proposition.

It was in such a fashion that I decided to take the day off, sometime during that summer term. Early one morning, I found myself doubled over with extremely bad stomach ache, which had me curled up on the floor like a clenched fist next to my bed. Miraculously, a couple of hours later, I felt well enough to set up a deckchair just outside the French windows leading from kitchen into the garden. I had decided, because it was such a glorious day to sit there with nothing on but a bathrobe. Undisturbed I began to soak up the warmth of the sun.

In a state of semi consciousness I had started to drift off, when the shrill sound of my mother's voice from behind my head, pelted me back into the bright light of day. "Matthew" she said, with a loud you can only be guilty tone to her voice, "what have you done?!"

Like a human cannon ball I shot out of the deckchair onto the lawn and found myself in a crumpled heap of nakedness and towelling, staring up at the dark blue, wool worsted trouser leg of a very tall policeman.

"Hanslow!" he yelled in a deep gruff voice, "come ere!"

The sound of feet shuffling through the gravel brought my friend Trevor Hanslow into the garden and to heel. With his head just above a well buckled leather belt he looked up at the policeman's face, with an obliging Cheshire cat grin.

"Is this him?" said the officer nodding in my direction, "I think so" Trevor replied a little hesitantly.

I gave Trevor a quizzical look, he shrugged his shoulders. None the wiser I threw a glance toward my mother's disapproving eyes, then looked up to the policeman and by the time I got round to Trevor again, the penny had dropped.

A couple of days previously, Alan Willis, Trevor Hanslow and I had climbed over the Number Nine paddock wall and got into the university O.T.C. rifle range, which was infrequently used for battle and shooting practice by the cadets. Tucked into the side of a grass hillock, was a wooden door, with a padlock dangling unlocked from a rusty catch. After some easy prying we had managed to gain entrance to a small ammunitions hut. For three young boys in search of a thrill this was a goldmine. We couldn't resist taking some shells and cartridges, but the main attraction was the rather bigger catch, and after careful deliberation we decided that one mortar bomb each, wouldn't go amiss.

We climbed back over the wall, into one of the paddocks at Number Nine, playing an excited game of catch with our find. In full view of my house my conscience got the better of me and I hid the treasure under one of the many shrubs in the garden. But Trevor did no such thing. He took his to school in his satchel and pulled out what now seemed a relatively large mortar bomb in the presence of the science class, thinking that his classmates would be impressed. The master became concerned and took him and the device to the head-teacher, who immediately called the police.

With a hint of dismay, I told the policeman that my mortar bomb was hidden under the laburnum bush at the bottom of the garden. He and another officer removed the bomb, which they held with two sticks at the end of their outstretched arms, with extreme caution.

After I got dressed, Hanslow and I were put in one of the two police cars parked outside my house, only to find our friend Alan Willis, who had been sitting there all along, looking like a confused puppy. The policeman told us to wait there while he went back to ask my mother a few questions. I noticed that there was a hand grenade next to me on the back seat. I managed to get Hanslow's attention away from his fiddling with the walkie-talkie, by waving it around in his face. At the same time the policeman came back to the car. Caught out again, or so I thought. But after a quizzical look he told me it was no longer an active grenade. "The bomb squad has dealt with it," he said with pride. He told us it had been taken off an old lady's front door; apparently she had been using it as a door knocker since the war and it was only discovered recently and subsequently removed.

We were taken down to the police station, where we met up with my mum and Alan and Trevor's parents. My guilt was paramount. I tried to conceal it by putting on a brave front, but I found this hard particularly when we arrived and I saw my mother scowling with concern in the sergeant's office.

The station sergeant seemed polite and respectful, which was a huge relief. After a few phone calls he put our misdemeanour down to careless army considerations and let us off with a heavy warning. He then told us to go off and enjoy the midsummer fair, which we kept telling everyone we were going to go to if we didn't go to prison.

By this time my mother had calmed down, mainly I suspect because Alan's parents were completely unflustered by the whole event. Trevor's parents were a different matter though. They were hard with anger and his father slapped him viciously round the head a few times as we were leaving the police station.

In terms of how our lives panned out this bomb squad charade was quite telling. Shortly after he left school Trevor Hanslow became ill with addiction for many years, Alan Willis built up a very successful Hi-Tec engineering company in Cambridge, whilst yours truly managed to slip through as a work in progress.

~

Things were beginning to turn out well for my father at number two Jesus Lane. Scurfield's, as it was called, was becoming a Cambridge name, an unusual store for those who had a love for cookery. Over those few years, George and Cecilia built this culinary escapade into a respected and well-established business for the now familiar kitchen utensils, made common by shops like Heals and Habitat. Their pioneering spirit paid off; the shop became hugely successful, establishing itself as a place of inspiration for people like Terence Conran and Elizabeth David. I remember a terribly enthusiastic lady called Laura Ashley trying to persuade my father to sell her dresses alongside her tea towels and kitchen aprons, which were already popular with the customers. He didn't really see the need to stock the dresses, but was too nice to say so; he consequently put them in a bottom drawer and only brought them out if a keen punter showed some interest.

George was decidedly conscientious and in some ways gullible to the ways of the retail world. He never encroached on the buyers, but there was always plenty of time to discuss the latest cast-iron pots from France, or award winning earthenware from Finland if they so desired. He would constantly tell cash stretched students to go to Woolworths for the cheaper pan, if he thought it better suited their needs.

It was by no means a regular occurrence, but as I became familiar with helping out around the shop, I would occasionally see some undergraduates walk furtively round the small showrooms, filling up the odd carrier bag and stepping into the street without paying. Whenever I brought this uneasy sting up with my dad, he would say "I wouldn't worry about that, we can put those kinds of losses down to the insurance company."

I did take it upon myself once, to follow one young man who had been shoplifting, out and on to the streets. His lead took me round the corner to a coffee bar called the El Patio. I remember being intrigued at what I saw through the doorway of this smoky den full of soft hair, leather jackets, black polo necks and jeans. I felt far too intimidated to go inside and left it at that. I had no idea at the time that I would end up becoming close to many of the writers, poets and guitar strumming persons sitting amidst the bustle of that illustrious cappuccino dive.

On my way back I found a roll of one pound notes on the pavement opposite the shop in Jesus Lane. I showed it to my dad and because it was nearly one hundred pounds, a lot of money then by anyone's standards, he thought we should take the wad to the police station where they were to keep it for three months. After such time, if nobody made a claim, the money was mine. It was with this windfall that I bought my first bike with straight handle bars and a secret pair of winkle-picker shoes, which I hid in my bicycle saddlebag and only put on when I was nearing the vicinity of school.

Eventually the shop grew in size and expanded in all directions. George had discovered a gold mine, but he had an ingrained twitch around earning too much money and the success story was to be cut short in its prime. Later, after so many years in the shop, he'd say how he wanted something else, a simpler life with poetry and books.

Socialism became like a religion for my parents, particularly for my dad. I think he felt it was a spirit if you like, that could overcome the forces of greedy materialism and western propaganda.

George's work with The Labour Party in Cambridge culminated in him standing in a by-election, which for the Prime Minister Harold Wilson, was an important one for him to win. Fortunately for my mother George lost by a close shave. If my father had taken this seat, he would have disappeared from the family home for days at a time and my mother categorically did not want this to happen. She gave the appearance of supporting him and although nothing to the contrary was said to us, it came across loud and clear that she didn't want him to win at any cost.

Whichever way their dialogue blew, there were many meals that became the focal point for huge heated debates. They dictated, deliberated and argued amongst themselves and anyone else who frequented our ever moving house. Their ideals were put across with such passion, that we were just simply convinced. With the best of intentions their persuasive doctrines overruled us. We were swept along on a tidal wave of answers; as children we found ourselves drowning in a sea of absolutes, arguing and shouting for our end of the story, but rarely being heard.

It didn't happen often, but in those early years my father's temper could erupt with fury, often at something my mother said. On rare occasions, a ferocious force, that would have built up over a few days, culminated in him throwing an inanimate object at the floor or wall. Then he would storm out of the house, leaving Cecilia to tell us how he'll be all right when he comes back; "He just needs to go round the block and walk it off."

The pride was such that for the most part our father gently but firmly brushed these thorns aside and got on with his life. Sometimes, if we got near to pressing his wrong buttons, he resorted to scolding us. But he was uncomfortable around the idea of punishment and the resolve to spank his children dwindled into the understanding we came to know so well – the understanding of a loaded silence where nothing more is said.

Even at the beginning of my second year at The Manor I still had great difficulty doing up my shoelaces. I would squat on the floor in the mornings with George, crouching over my back, trying to teach me this fidgety task. With mounting intensity he'd grab each hand and spell out, between clenched teeth and with as much patience as he could muster, "Left over right and right over left, through and over, left over right and right over left". The more impatient he became, the more the knot seemed destined to elude me.

I may have had a twisted time trying to do up my shoelaces in front of my dad, but I could show him, with some muted pride, that I'd learnt to spell the whole of my own name. Then as if something clicked into place, he seemed to take on a more relaxed attitude to my difficulties; no doubt this had a lot to do with his business venture gaining notoriety and his oncoming popularity within the Cambridge Labour Party.

As the shop blossomed, George became more entrenched in local politics and about a year after the difficulties I had with Wellford's gang in Senate House Passage, my dad became a Labour councillor for the Petersfield Ward. He was extremely conscientious about his responsibilities and got to know, as well as he could, the householders in his constituency. One of the families, living in the area he represented, was the Wellford's and it happened, that my father's political intervention, brought him into their home, I think to help them with some kind of housing difficulty. But whatever it was, this must have had some effect on turning things around at school, because to my relief, it was soon after this that Roy Wellford started to treat me with less scorn and a little more respect.

My grandfather, Bertram Hopkinson
Professor of Mechanism and Applied Mechanics

13

For I have known her wake an hundred nights, When all the pillow where she laid her head Was brine-wet with her tears. I am to complain to you, sir; I 'll tell you how they have us'd her now she 's dead: They wrapp'd her in a cruel fold of lead, And would not let me kiss her.

John Webster, *The White Devil*

As the oncoming terms took their toll at primary school the fantasies of making my mother happy, by acting in the school play, became more and more elaborate. When the teachers drew up a list of candidates for the cast, I waited with baited breath, but I was never chosen as anything more than chorus. I imagined myself as the main actor, and my mother sitting alongside all the other parents, looking up at her boy on the stage with a proud smile written across her face. It wasn't until my third year at The Manor that I was able to really get near to this lasting desire.

One evening after school my mother approached me with the idea of meeting up with Gabor in order to be in his play of the year.

I couldn't believe it; this was the real thing, better than anything my school might have conjured up.

I was told by Cecilia that I would have to read aloud the part of the young Prince in the *White Devil* by John Webster, as a kind of audition. This was to be a monumental challenge. The thought of putting the few lines of dialogue across to such venerated company, brought on a feeling of dread which was to be almost uncontrollable.

My mother seemed so completely won over with the idea. It was a great delight to see her in Gabor's company, because he made her laugh so much and of course anything to do with theatre excited her. I painstakingly braved the waters to please her, but mainly to prove to myself that I could amount to more than the stone weight of failure strewn around my neck at The Manor.

It was Cecilia's absolute conviction that gave me the strength to go the extra excruciating mile. So sure was she that after a lot of reading and rereading with her, the few scenes I was in began to click into a kind of coherent slot. She then felt I was confident enough to go next door for the meeting with the maestro, which had been setup in the Oak Room. My mother stayed for every turn of the page, if she hadn't, I just don't think I would have found the courage to go on.

Because she and Gabor seemed to me to be so highly accomplished with words, it was impossible not to feel that I was entering a place where I wanted to be, but couldn't for the life of me handle; a fearful paradox that was to haunt me.

After some awkward fumbling on my part and a great deal of encouragement from Cecilia, I began to get the lines across. The mood swing in the room started to change. As the acceptance fell into place, any doubts I might have had were simply brushed aside by my mother and to a lesser extent by Gabor, who remained a stickler for hitting the mark, right up until the first performance. He fussed and fluffed over the staging, like a jackdaw over a prised gem. "No, no, noo Marttew" he would say with his thick Hungarian drawl, pushing and prodding me into the right place, emphasising a word I hadn't pitched to his liking from the classical text.

When the days of rehearsal started for real, he was, regardless of his obsession for the staging, sensitive to my being a novice. In front of the other members of the cast, made up mostly of undergraduates, I was relieved to find he treated me with great respect.

Gabor was a passionate, larger than life director, whose artistic nature was always arguing for his vision of the play. His undoubted enthusiasm could, when it came in too close, push some of the students into a heated quandary. Trying to defend their corner, they occasionally resorted to shouting him down; this ruckus was usually just a glitch brought about by the pressure of getting the curtain up on time. On the whole everyone was deferential of Gabor's directorial prowess. There was however one bright young man who slugged it out until the bitter end, calling Gabor a lily-livered whore and threatening to take him to court over some damning defamation of character. I wasn't sure what happened there, but they must have extinguished the quarrel because the actor in question hit the opening night intact.

The White Devil was put on at the ADC Theatre in Cambridge and had in it such luminaries as John Shrapnel, Michael Pennington, Tony Palmer and Richard Eyre; all of whom went on to become eminently successful on their varied artistic journeys.

I remember thinking how most of the cast of male graduates seemed so self-assured, like a race apart. They were certainly far too preoccupied to take much notice of me, which I was grateful for as this meant there was less likelihood of my being found wanting.

Here I was allowed to hold the reins and ride the horse without having to know the ins and outs of how the carriage worked. There was no testing for verbs or doing words, no need to understand adjectives, or to be put in one's place for smudging the copybook. Once I was away from the possibility of being tumbled in rehearsals and in front of an audience, I found my nerve and a home away from home. After this release, even Gabor made it clear that he was pleased with my input.

I certainly felt much protected by John Shrapnel, who played my uncle. I can remember Michael Pennington looking a little pale, and clearly I remember how his jeans had holes in the knees and thinking how they needed mending. I also remember Richard Eyre as someone apart, a young man with bigger fish to fry, always busy after rehearsals, looking quite spivy with his James Dean hairdo and blue suede shoes. But the main thing I remember was my mother being thrilled at the way my first proper appearance on the stage had worked out and this, above everything else, fulfilled a dream.

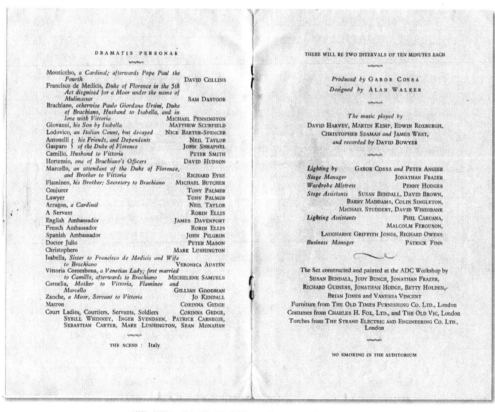

"The White Divel" ADC Theatre January – February 1962

14

Being in Gabor's play brought with it some badly needed confidence for my third year at The Manor. I even found nibbles of enjoyment within the school's heartless regime. The scholastic side of the bench may have remained befuddled, but I was beginning to find placating the teachers and keeping my contemporaries sweet a lot easier. I discovered that if I pushed my accent toward the Cambridge London drawl, by indiscernibly dropping my T's and slurring the H's, I began to blend in pretty well. The gods had even seen fit to put me in a couple of classes above Removed.

I had become better friends with Alan Willis and Trevor Hanslow and although it had taken me the better part of two years to do so, Roy Wellford.

Wellford wore his jet black hair in such a fashion that from a distance he looked like Elvis Presley. He kept it laden with dollops of Brylcream and had a proud quiff out front with a DA down the back. A DA, or to give it it's correct name, Ducks Arse, is where the two sides of the hair are slicked backwards from the front of the head. The sides meet to give the impression of a v-shaped groove coming down from the crown of the head to the nape of the neck, where, if the hair is long enough, it turns up over the collar to give the impression of a little feathered tail.

Much to the chagrin of the teachers, Wellford thought nothing of combing his hair at the most inappropriate times. In the middle of a lesson, with the class staring on in disbelief, he would put his feet up on the desk and nonchalantly take out his comb with his right hand, stroke it smoothly through his hair several times, whilst carefully arranging the quiff with his left hand. He finished this considered grooming, which left a residue of dandruff, hairs and white grease, between the teeth of the comb, by wiping the comb on the blazer of the boy in front, who expected and accepted this without fuss.

Occasionally Wellford took to wearing sharp pointed winkle pickers to school, but mostly his feet were ensconced in a huge pair of hob nail boots, well worn, with two small patches of shiny steel glinting through from behind the scuffed black leather toecaps. How he wore them made them intimidating to the casual observer. If you caught his eye line the wrong way, it left a sinking feeling in the pit of the stomach.

The more he came to trust me, the more comfortable I felt sitting closer to him in class. Because we had both given up with any hope of pleasing the school authorities, or ever succeeding with any academic work, a mixture of trust and coercion grew between us. We were there for each other when the anarchy of our separate ploys took flight. We set out to try and get to the teachers through our class mates, by ways of making them laugh.

It was pretty much an everyday occurrence for Wellford to be singled out during the school assembly for letting the school image down. Wearing winkle pickers, greasy tight jeans and a bootlace tie, did not go down well. Yet even after numerous canings to try and correct his dress sense, he continued his unruliness and with even more gusto.

The only concession he made to these demands, was the school blazer, but even this was stamped with his own inimitable brand. His mother had replaced the school badge on the breast pocket, with an emblem of an eagle, which I think he must have got from the US air force. At this time there was still a heavy influx of US military in Cambridge, because of the huge American airbase at Lakenheath.

~

The school terms passed insufferably slowly and education, as it was being put across to most of us, became painfully boring and utterly pointless. It was only when the teacher managed to implant enough terror in me that I knuckled down to what was on the blackboard and my desk. What was the point of trying; I was convinced I would never be good at it. When I did make an effort to achieve something, it was always, either torn down personally by the masters, or belittled by the school's obsession with results. And as this was the whole point of being there, it very quickly became utterly futile. To survive, I became as many of us do, the school idiot, clown, buffoon, or if you like, total arsehole.

3B. saw a mixture of boys torn between loyalties. At the front of the class sat a small minority, who believed that if they worked hard their future was assured. This left the majority of the desks to be taken up by boys who felt they were being ground down by the mechanical, relentless repetition of what they were being taught. This indoctrination was largely put across by sadistic teachers and naive parents, who felt that humiliation and punishment, given in uncompromising doses, was the road to character building and academic success. This may have been seen as a way to preparing us for the highs and lows of the outside world, but this certain ideology was backfiring, instilling in us a desperate need to survive at any cost.

For any teacher it basically became a question of keeping tighter control. Most of them did this by trying to intimidate us by way of tactical fear. There were as ever a few teachers who couldn't draw the line and to a bunch of hungry falcons like us, they came across as weak, easy prey.

One such teacher we called Mr Pettigrew, a name borrowed from a radio show of the time called *Whacko*. Our Mr Pettigrew was a tall, thin, emaciated man whose face was a sad mask of broken veins. He wore a pale tweed jacket with sleeves too short and wool trousers that sat at half-mast above his standard issue shoes. His shirts were always frayed and encrusted with grey around the collar.

The rumour was that he had a number tattooed on his left arm, given to him by the Japanese when he had been as a prisoner of war. This made sense, because he seemed to get the shakes very easily and any slight bang, if it didn't make him jump, made him extremely twitchy.

During the winter mornings Wellford used to sit at the back of Mr Pettigrew's class with his feet up on his desk. After a while of acute boredom, he would carefully remove his sandwiches from the crisp paper packaging, take out the bacon from between the white sliced and with a great deal of precision, lay the meat in neat rows on the cast iron radiator next to his desk. "Wellford what are you doing?" shouted an exasperated teacher. "I'm keeping my bacon warm till break sir" said the boy with an air of nonchalance.

Hanslow and I used to chew up pieces of white blotting paper, soak them in saliva, and when Mr Pettigrew had his back to the class we threw them at the blackboard, which they hit with a satisfying splatter. On one occasion, 'a bumbly' as we called them, hit the back of his neck. He turned round in a terrible fluster and knocked one of the white ceramic ink jars, which had just been filled up with dark blue ink, down the front of his trousers. Prompted by a cataclysm of nerves he rushed out of the classroom to clean himself up. On his return he demanded a culprit, but was greeted with a wall of silence.

At the end of the school term he found his old Austin on the roof of the bicycle shed, compliments of the hard boys. Nothing as far I know was ever mentioned about this, or any of the other numerous incidents that this unfortunate teacher was the victim of.

My take on the school and who Mr Pettigrew really was, changed on one of those palpable, long hot summer days, where you no longer care about how you or anyone else is dressed.

The main objective was about keeping cool, as the sleepy afternoon dragged on into thoughts of swimming at the end of the day.

Sat at the back of the class, caught in the grip of this sticky malaise, I was struggling to occupy my mind and somewhere between the sweat, monotony, doodling away, I began toying with words, trying to dissect them into packets of sense. I needed a rubber; so in a daze I raised my arm to get attention. When Mr Pettigrew asked me what I wanted, I let the words slip out from under my breath. "rub…her" Those in the class who heard sniggered appropriately. He became annoyed and wanted to know exactly what I'd said, and out of sheer boredom, I repeated with enough volume, "**Rub…..Her**". This time I had everyone's attention, meaning the class caught the meat of what I'd said like a bunch of crazy hyenas. When everyone calmed down, I was told to come up and stand to attention by his desk, with my back to the class for the rest of the afternoon.

At close quarters Mr. Pettigrew's shyness seemed magnified to such extent I just assumed he would suffer the sweltering. Then, as if it were beyond his control, the heat took over and he pulled his jacket from his meagre frame and placed it neatly on the back of his chair. Realising my astonishment at what he had done, he took another brave step toward cooling down; he rolled up his shirt sleeves.

After a while, having got used to my presence, he started to turn his full attention to the rest of the class. From the sideline I started to explore his drawn and sad complexion. My prying eyes wandered in the direction of his thin arms and I was thinking how they were like bone wrapped with a very thin layer of delicate skin, when I noticed a faint grey outline of numbers, ingrained just above the wrist on the inside of his left arm.

As it sunk in, I became overwhelmed with a great sense of sadness at just how tortuous his life must have been. I felt ashamed and confused about the system. I couldn't understand how he was allowed to be put in a classroom where he was so obviously out of his depth. It seemed to me to be adding insult to his injury and to ours.

Here was a sad and pathetic man, who had obviously been tortured to the extreme and instead of being held up as a hero, he was being humiliated on a daily basis by a group of boys, who through no fault of his or theirs, didn't want to be in the same building, let alone in the same room.

15

There were times at home when my frustrations would erupt into rages beyond anyone's control, unnerving my sisters and creating a wider rift between us. Apart from fist-fights at school where I always lost, this was the only place I felt able to let off steam. When I calmed down, my parents just kept saying they loved me and that school didn't matter. This made me feel even more confused and a thousand times worse. I wanted with all my heart to be integrated, especially with my family, but I was beginning to feel like a rank outsider and intuitively began looking for solace elsewhere.

I wasn't completely out of synch with how the journey to London worked. Frances Walls had taken me, when I was in my ninth year, to visit her nephew, who lived above a fish and chip shop in the East End. Soon after this my dad felt obliged to accompany me there after I'd won two tickets for Bertram Mills Circus, from entering a competition in a comic called *The Swift*. The big tent had found a home for itself at Olympia in Earls Court. Part of the prize meant meeting Coco the Clown in his caravan after the show. He was so miserable though, that any excitement we may have enjoyed in the ring immediately fell flat in the wings along with the elephant dung. George seemed terribly disheartened by this slight, but Coco's lack lustre ways didn't really dampen my spirits, as any outing with my dad at this time was such a pleasure.

My father may have fed me the idea that money was a tight, if not a downright dirty commodity, but he didn't let his financial grip stop any outlay for further visits to London. The great capital held a special place in his heart as somewhere he had gone to catch up with the movie stars he loved, visiting the picture houses, when he passed through on his way home from boarding school. He was never forthright about it, but he gave the distinct impression he wanted to share this unique time with me. So I was overjoyed when he suggested we go again. This time to see *The Crazy Gang* who were coming to the tail end of their irreverent lives at the Victoria Palace. I loved the Egyptian sand shuffling and slapstick antics of Eddie Gray and my virgin perspective gulped with glee at Flanagan and Allen causing riots of laughter from an entrance through the stalls, not more than a yard from where we sat; my dad was thrilled too. For my twelfth birthday he got tickets for the musical *Oliver*, which was having its first run in the West End. We were both absolutely captivated by the singing, the raw energy and the innovative setting. It's hard to believe now, but what we saw on that night seemed totally new; it breathed space, inspiration and even revolution into me. This was the first time theatre had really dug into my heart.

On one of these special outings we had lunch on the second floor in a Lyons Corner House, which was home to art deco, the aspidistra and the grand piano; a very elegant affair. Maybe the tail end of the war had something to do with it, where everyone had to muddle in, or perhaps it was because of its grand scale that these multi-storeyed restaurants were somehow accessible to every class and background. Not that they let any old riffraff in, it was essential to be dressed for the occasion, even if it wasn't the full skirt or a suit and tie.

A polite waiter spilt tomato sauce down the front of George's tweed jacket. The manager, who was beside himself with apologies, took the aforementioned clothing away to be cleaned. By the time we had finished the meal he returned it, pressed and spotless. I couldn't help thinking that my father, having been embarrassed by the fuss, quite liked the commotion it caused.

It was clear then that I knew something of how the sprawling metropolis spun around, but I hadn't in any way trod the city pavements on my own. In spite of my hard insights into the rough side of the street at The Manor, the plan of going to London alone remained a distinctly daunting prospect.

So it was, with a mixture of trepidation and excitement that I would brave a visit, during the holidays of my fourteenth year, to stay with my brother and be initiated into the byways of the big smoke. As far as I was able to see Ponji was at the head of the queue. I felt unequivocally that if I spent time with him my life would be on course, particularly as I'd given up all hope of pinning the tail on the donkey at home.

Upon arrival at Kings Cross I made my way into the caverns and tunnels of the underground, and systematically followed my nose to Piccadilly tube station. I finally ascended the stairs leading to daylight.

From previous excursions with my dad, many of the buildings and streets seemed recognizable, even the street hustle had a ring of familiarity, but the truth is I had absolutely no idea where I was. The only instruction given by my brother was to ask for directions to Shaftsbury Avenue at the newsagents opposite the cinema, which wasn't as easy as it appeared. The poor man selling newspapers had a nose that looked like it had been eaten away by some kind of terrible disease and this made it very difficult to discern the instructions. He kept standing his ground and shouting, and I kept standing mine and listening; "Hround da wvooddy former; the wvooddy corner!!?" Much to my embarrassment his muffled ranting brought in a crowd of onlookers from the flowing throng, but with their help, I quickly established that Shaftsbury Avenue was 'around the bloody corner!'

Having left the news vendor in a wake of commotion and finding the front door in easy reach, I rang the bell. My brother stuck his head out of a top floor window like a jack-in-the-box. Pleased as punch he threw the keys down bundled in a gentleman's handkerchief, and I let myself in.

Don Levy was an expatriate Australian, who had met his wife while she was working as an au-pair at our house in Cambridge. He had recently finished directing a highly acclaimed documentary about time called *Time Is*. On the back of this film Don later went on to direct what would become his sole feature, *Herostratus*. Meanwhile he had been given a fellowship in The States – meaning he had started to spend most of his time over there. This left their top floor flat in Shaftsbury Avenue vacant and it was felt that Ponji, who was working for Auntie Alice's son Geoffrey at his market research company at the time, could look after it while they were away.

Dominating the living room of this tiny but blindingly stylish apartment, was a state of the art sound system; we are talking the best of equipment Hi Fi wise, the dog's bollocks. This was when most hipsters, popsters and music lovers used a Dansette for their listening needs and speakers were people who stood up to be heard at Speakers Corner in Hyde Park.

Ponji could never listen to music without a great deal of settling down beforehand. During one of these attempts to bring the sound up to the mark, it became too difficult for him not to fiddle with the delicate mechanics holding His Masters Voice in place, and the worst happened. He broke the needle arm on the turntable.

Ponji's fanaticism for getting things right, meant my first ever assignment in the capital, was to collect a new turntable arm, from a warehouse somewhere way-out in the suburbs on the District line. To save money, my brother carefully instructed my green ears to buy two of the cheapest underground tickets; "One for getting through the gates at

Piccadilly and the other for disembarking on my return at Leicester Square". In those days they never used to check the tickets in the middle of the day at those far flung stations. He continued; "What you have to do, if they do happen to stop you at the other end, is to say you got on at the last but one station and they'll ask..."

As I was listening to the way Ponji was relaying his precise instructions, the usual noise of unease began to pull at my sleeve and I lost track of what he was saying.

Something must have gone in though, because I followed my brother's directions and my footsteps down the stairs. Like a tentative swimmer dipping his toe into water, I set foot outside the front door. The buzz on the street was so seductive that any initial anxiety, I might have laboured with, seemed to evaporate into the flurry of citizens scurrying to and fro in all directions.

I passed the first barrier with my nerves just about intact, then the journey unfolded in slow motion, one step at a time. Tickets in hand I managed to pursue the outline of my brother's voice to the letter, It was as if I were being shown how the physical reality of doing something new might require some risk, but if I tuned into my surroundings, the time and place could map out the way, with the details taking care of themselves.

By convincing me to traverse a major urban environment on my own, and take on what was for me the distinctly ambiguous task of cheating London transport, Ponji had inadvertently opened my eyes to a keener sense. Like my mother had done with Gabor's play, he had been so convinced in my ability that I pulled it off, just as he said I would. I completed the mission with a self-belief, which up until then, I could only dream of.

The needle was replaced with some quick dexterity and once again the room filled with an air of jazzy tightness. I was never quite sure if my brother listened to the music he liked, or the music he thought he should like. The choice of which album to play may have been confusing for him, but I didn't care, whichever score was agreed upon, it seemed to go along with my mood.

Over those next few days Ponji invited me to be in his company when he went out with his friends, which occasionally involved scenes of a very personal nature, as in meeting girlfriends from the office. When sitting in their company I was beginning to realise a twinkle in my own eyes, but I also began to see glimmers of a sadder picture in his. Even with the obvious infatuation many of Ponji's companions seemed to show him, he still couldn't stop his meticulousness from continuously pushing his self-belief into an unworthy corner.

In spite of the misgivings he had about himself, his engaging spirit couldn't help but shine through. He went out of his way to show me a broader view. What may seem today like some minor events, became representative of an enormous leap in my life. One way or another and without too much intervention on his part, my brother gave me the space I needed to shift up a gear and inherit an inner resolve that I hadn't known before.

When I wasn't with Ponji, I spent my time wandering the streets within the vicinity of Shaftsbury Avenue. Around the corner from the flat, in China Town, was a road filled from beginning to end with electrical shops. Most of these retail outlets had small stalls outside overflowing with all sorts of complex electronic equipment, some of it useful for bringing miniature theatres, or ancient crystal sets to life.

The other thing I did was to find cheap places to eat, where I would sit for hours, finding courage for my next move and fantasising about revenge for what I saw as terrible wrongdoings at school. After some serious reflection I began to see that if I really wanted to stay above the bulwark, I would have to fight back, and when the time came to return to Cambridge and The Manor I was ready to go to the wire.

When I was little we lived in 10 Adams Rd, the last house before the open fields began – well and truly on the right side of the tracks. Far away lay Romsey town, unknown territory around Mill Road and the railway station. It was still sometimes called Little Russia when George and I were living in Cambridge in the 1950s and it was then, so many years later, we saw Palme Dutt, the old left wing activists, being interviewed on television."Why did you become a socialist?" asked the interviewer. "My father was a doctor in Romsey town in Cambridge," Dutt replied. "We knew all about the criminal classes in Adams Road with their maids and their polished floors.

Cecilia Scurfield

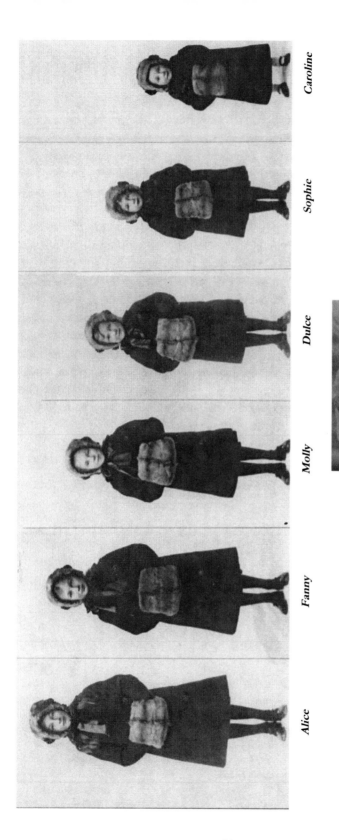

Alice Fanny Molly Dulce Sophie Caroline

Cecilia with her sisters above

My great grandmother Evelyn
Hopkinson in hat with relations in the
garden at Number Nine

Right: Docwras Manor, Shepreth

*Below: The garden at Number Nine
showing the pond and vista going on
forever, taken in the early 30's*

*Matthew, Sarah, Polly and George in
the kitchen at Number Nine, early 50's*

My cousin Rosemary, Francis, My Grandmother Mariana and Auntie Alice, early 50's

Alice in the bottom of the garden at Number Nine, late 70's

*My sister
Elizabeth
early 50's*

*Cecilia
sometime in
the 50's*

Alice, in her heyday being fed by Lady Taylor, with Erica Bousch a German Jewish refugee and Hans Zullig making bread. 1942

Elizabeth and Ponji, evacuees in Switzerland

Frances and Lassie

*Gabor Cossa outside his shop
Cambridge, early 50's*

Sitting at the front, my mother Cecilia with pigtails, my great-grandmother Evelyn in the middle, my great aunt Ellen to her left with husband SirAlfred Ewing behind and to the right my grandmother Mariana hidden from view by child, they are surrounded by my mother's sisters, their children and various husbands.

99

*Waiting in my high chair, Shepreth
1949 give or take a few months*

Lost in a flower, Cambridge early 50's

*Sarah, Cousin Johnny, Lucy, Matthew (Robert Mitcham), Sophie, and Polly, outside
the kitchen at number eight, late 50's.*

Georges sister Frances, Sarah, Elizabeth, Matthew & George –
Shepreth, before the trip to France

Ponji sticking his neck out and me holding back in the Jowett van, Shepreth, early 50's

Elizabeth

Ponji

A small part of my extended family from my mother's side, taken in the latter half of the fifties in Gestingthorp and not a tie in sight

Emo aged fifteen centre, with friends in the coal yard

Matthew and Emo working it out in The Mad Bugger: late sixties

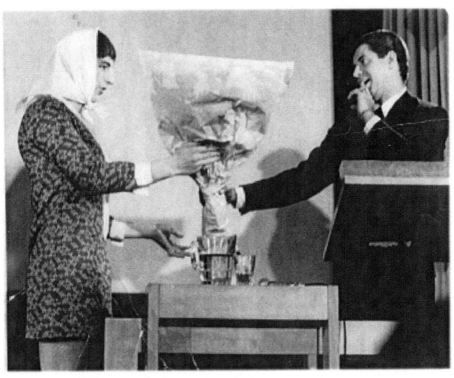

The collage mascot presenting flowers to Jerry Lewis 1967   Photo courtesy Chris Morphet

Emo, on the left, with his older brother

Ponji at Emo's flat a few days before he died

16

How shall the summer arise in joy,
Or the summer's fruits appear?
Or how shall we gather what griefs destroy,
Or bless the mellowing year,
When the blasts of winter appear?

William Blake

At my primary school the cane was a straight red stick, positioned for all to see, above a replica of a Vincent van Gogh painting of some fishing boats in Mrs Thompson's office, but it was rarely used. Nevertheless, it still induced dread into the imagination of a small child. At The Manor it turned out to be a good deal different. Caning was an everyday way of life.

The most common material used for corporal punishment when I was at school in the fifties was rattan. Not even a home grown plant. It was brought into England, through the growth of Britain's world trade, from the Far East, during the latter part of the nineteenth century. Apparently the stem of this lean bendy cane took over from the birch, as the preferred instrument of chastisement, because it was said that it fitted in with Victorian ideals of modesty.

During one of my first assemblies at The Manor we were given a lecture about stepping out of line, and how the cane would be administered to any boy who was not behaving according to the school rules. We were told that this diabolical form of torture would only be used if it fitted the magnitude of the crime, but we were never told what constituted a crime worthy of such treatment.

Mr Maxwell took severe delight in telling the assembled school that even through two or three layers of clothing the cane could impart a considerable sting. "Of course", he whispered with a hint of secrecy in his voice, "The pain is even more intense if applied to the bare buttocks".

It was mainly through conspiratorial talk between classmates in the playground that the fear of a beating really took off. "Jesus it really hurts!" a wide eyed boy would say. "I put a comic down the seat of my pants, so when the cane hits it don't hurt at all". "Liar!" snarls his friend "How many did you get?" "I got six, burns like a line of fire". Again and again these horrendous anecdotes, shared in anticipation for the next poor sucker to suffer this hideous pain, kept teasing our deepest fears. If this fiery gossip wasn't enough to push you off your stride, hearing 'Nobby's Dick' thrashing its target through the thin walls of that prefabricated prison certainly did.

I may have had inklings of what a sham it all was, but my life at this time was beginning to be alarmingly disproportionate at its centre. The disturbing muddle, which had built up over the years as a way of defending my nervous system against the perpetual feeling of failure, had become like tangled string. But unlike string when it's knotted and jumbled, there was no getting rid of it; this stuff just seemed to stick with me like shit to a blanket. I felt weighted down and tied in, like a straitjacket full of jelly.

The time-consuming process of disentanglement seemed to me and everyone else in my family to be a laborious and improvident process. We learned to shove most of these complications deep down in a bottom drawer, hoping that over time, like an unfortunate phase, they would miraculously resolve and disappear.

By now I was thought of as nothing much more than a troublemaker at The Manor. Perhaps my behaviour, as seen from the teacher's point of view was excessively belligerent, but to me and many of my friends it was quite simply a matter of survival.

As the screw began to tighten my behaviour became more and more erratic. One day during a math's class I catapulted out of my seat and asked where numbers came from and what gives them their rite. I was hauled out from behind my desk and told, in no uncertain terms, to explain myself.

Tightening my nerves, I tried to put across why a zero is the starting point of any given numerical quest. With my contemporaries looking on in opened-mouthed amazement, I expressed my fascination for this void, this space between the numbers. I was making it up as I went along and I could sense the teacher and my classmates clutching their desks with gleeful anticipation as I waded deeper into the quagmire. Unfazed by their fateful expectancy I continued, boldly I thought, by trying to give the down trodden zero a run for its money. I pronounced with as much elocution as I could muster that if a naught is really nothingness, a void from which all the other numbers are measured, then being in this class room was a waste of time. After an awkward silence, there was a great deal of frenzied shouting and cheering. I thought the better of carrying on and tried to get out gracefully by taking a courteous bow, which lifted the atmosphere to a new level. With complete anarchy setting in, Mr Ferno began losing his grip. To take control, he screamed out that I was nothing more than a performing monkey, but this just seemed to fan the flames, the class erupted with a cacophony of animal noises. I stood there somewhat bemused at what I'd started, whilst Mr Ferno, in a pot-boiling rage, rushed out of the classroom and within seconds was back with the head of the English department, the undeniably top heavy Mr Pendlebury.

I was hot-footed out of the classroom, arm in arm, by the teachers, like two military policemen with a drunken private. Down two flights of stairs, through the assembly hall, to the headmaster's office, and since he wasn't there, I was pinned up against the wall and told to wait outside in the corridor for the summoning.

I stood there behind a glazed face of repressed tears. Bizarrely, the more upset I felt, the more philosophical my thinking became. Like a prisoner of war before torture, I tried to justify my beliefs quietly and quickly to myself. In desperation I called on some higher power to help me. Somehow if I could sow together what had happened with the Christian belief that God had created the world in seven days from 'nothing', I would be let off! I cried out from within myself, NOTHINGNESS IS THE WOMB OF GOD.

The walls of this neat, suburban corridor grew smaller. As my time in retrospect diminished it became clear that no amount of praying would bring God to my rescue. So my frantic brain, turned to the scientific and with logical expectation, raced to find an explanation from my thimbleful of cosmological knowledge. Whether we are atheist or religious believers, it is a commonly held belief that from the space between, from this void, from this blank light, was born the creation! So what is this everything, if it is not born of nothing? What are these words if not for the page? There is no painting without a canvas! Without a...

Mr Lewin was like a caricature of a head teacher from a comic book. A cold blooded reptile, with very short back and sides and a waspish, pale moustache, who insisted on wearing a long black University gown, often partnered with a large mortarboard, which looked like it had been stapled to his head. He had, it seemed, very little time for anyone, including the teachers. When not in his office, he would stride hurriedly about the school, like Batman looking for Robin.

The truth is, I had been hauled in for questioning so many times now and gave up to the inevitable, as he came hurtling round the corner less like a cape crusader, more like Dracula in search of a neck.

He used the thin bendy cane, which we knew by now was the standard issue of its day. It was common knowledge that his caning was very precise. Although I admired other boys, who could take punishment without tears, I had no shame in showing mine. One of the things I could do with apparent ease, when things became threatening in the extreme, was to cry with uninhibited abandonment. He ushered me quietly into his office and sat down behind his desk. As if in defiance he crossed his arms and began to rock back and forth on his swish office chair, bringing an arrogant, threatening air to the proceedings. After scrutinizing me for several seconds, he began to lecture me on how I should behave and how important the school image was and how he couldn't understand with my parents being who they were, why I had ended up as such an imbecile. This made me feel awkward and really hemmed in. I blurted out something about how I didn't care about them and what business was it of his anyway. This made him seethe.

After a magnified silence, he broke the ice and mumbled something about how he didn't like doing it, how he had no alternative, but to make an example of me.

He asked me to take down my trousers and bend over his desk, which I proceeded to do with my tear ducts on the brink of explosion.

Having humiliated me with words and no trousers, he stood up and went over to get the cane from a utility cupboard in the right-hand corner of the room. Before he came round behind me, I turned on the taps and the dam burst open with a crescendo of unadulterated sobbing, which I tried to orchestrate so that it overshadowed the oncoming pain.

I think I must have got through to him, because he stopped whipping my behind after two. Either that or it was the pool of water my head was lying in, that had begun to turn the papers on his retentive desk into an inky mess, which stopped him.

I left his office like a wounded animal, with the rage and bitter resentment hot on my heels. There was a pattern of purplish-red welts across my backside for a few days. I wasn't sure whether they were a mark of pride, or a slash of shame.

Lessons were brought home with the seriousness of World War Three. The teacher's absolute conviction allowed for no shifting of ideas to take place. And if I had held to their beliefs it would have built a ship, which would undoubtedly have collided on the rocks of psychotic hatred years ago. At the time this was excruciating territory to manoeuvre, but as it turned out, it wasn't entirely negative. Learning to observe and let go of enforced institutionalised structures, has helped me to hone a profoundly positive space from which to live.

Now, I hear you say, if it wasn't for these character-building scenarios in my life, I wouldn't be what I am today. But to me that's like saying you have to start banging someone's head against a brick wall, to know what it's like when it stops. I see now how much time I wasted pulling away from the true centre of my life. What came across to me all those years ago as all important truths, often in the guise 'For your own good', were in fact untruths coming from the heart of the adult's misplaced fears. This constant energy pouring into my being, manifested into diversions, pulling me away from the core of my being, towards a commonly held belief that life is not to be joyous, but to be feared, frightful and full of dread.

In my more charitable moments, I will begrudgingly allow for one small saving grace at The Manor. The school plays. These token productions may have been written and directed by Mr Lewin, but they brought with them some time off from the constraints being slammed home at the desk. Of course it went without saying we weren't bright enough, or worthy enough, to tackle the classics; however, Mr Lewin's theatrical endeavours did give me a chance to parade my aptitude for turning heads, which was so often berated in the classroom. I was selected along with a couple of other boys to play female roles. I didn't mind the constant sniggers in the wings, because here I found a place, worthy of attention from the school, resembling some value.

Over those too few weeks I made new friends, among them Stuart Limpus. We often saw Stuart, who was the son of a local butcher, teased beyond his limits in the playground because of his weight. Even when he was heaving his bulbous body over the horse in the gym, he had a wonderful capacity to laugh at the dark side of his life. I wouldn't say we were the greatest of companions, but his impersonations of the comic actor Oliver Hardy and of many of the teachers, which he managed to do right up behind their backs, saw me cracked sideways in fits of giggles.

Acting was so obviously a great way of giving our so called limited brains a chance to engage and blossom, but these showcases were only seen to be worth mounting once a year, with most of the work being done after school hours. The thought that we might actually benefit from that kind of creative release in the classroom, was closed down before we had a chance to gain any solid ground. From a personal standpoint I suppose it was some kind of acknowledgment, as they gave me a drama prize for my acting, but it was never enough! The teachers were not going to let me off the hook that easily.

The Manor Secondary School for boys first opened as a brand new shiny school in 1959, my first year, with all the hope in the world attached to its image. Woodwork and metalwork classrooms with lots of crisp sharp tools hung up in neat rows, ready for the new and eager to get their hands on. Science laboratories ready for every experiment in the world. Immaculate playing fields, partnered a fully equipped gymnasium, with each facility crying out for energetic fresh faced boys to play on. And classrooms, oh the classrooms, all with brand new desks, pens, paper, books and fresh ink, patiently waiting for the new boys to celebrate their literary and mathematical skills.

What a load of old bollocks that turned out to be! We were actually drowned in poisoned deceit.

The deputy headmaster Mr Maxwell was a short, podgy, high-blood pressure man, whose face looked like it was always about to explode. He had come to The Manor from Chesterton Secondary Modern, bringing with him the toughest boys of that year.

I was warned by Ponji that Maxwell was a tyrant before I started. And during most of the three years of being at this appalling excuse for a school, I managed to avoid getting caught up in his hooks. But as time went on, my self-esteem began to slip and I became careless with my behaviour.

"SCURFIELD, HANSLOW and WELLFORD", he yelled out our names with vitriolic hatred steaming from his lips, see me after assembly! We had been falling about with laughter, whilst the rest of the school was singing God Save Our Gracious Queen. To Mr Maxwell this was a red rag to a bull and he hauled us out in front of the whole school and told everyone we would be caned for being disobedient not only to the image of the school, but also to the Queen.

I was beaten severely. I had just about perfected my act of indifference and almost found the strength to hold on, but the tears couldn't help but burst forth. Please sir, I'm sorry sir, WHAT ARE

YOU? I'm good for nothing. WHAT DID YOU SAY? Good for nothing sir. GOOD! NOW GET OUT OF MY SIGHT!

My parents were very keen that I should become an actor and to this end wanted me to be involved in the theatre at any level.

The man who ran the Arts Theatre in Cambridge at this time was known as Commander Blackwood. He was a very forthright gentleman who looked more like an old fashioned bank manager, rather than someone who might run a theatre. During my third year at The Manor, through my mum's involvement with the theatre at a local level, I got to meet The Commander. Much to my surprise he agreed to give me a job as a stagehand and general dogs-body throughout the holidays.

I got to know the back stage staff quite well and they treated me pretty much as an equal. This was the first time in my life that I had been extended proper responsibility by any grownups. So it wasn't surprising that I learnt a damned sight more than I ever would have, given the same amount of time at school.

The stage director was a man called Cliff who had a slight tic. He would tell the crew what to do, whilst his right arm made involuntary jerky movements, which he would try to suppress by tugging at the crutch of his trousers. He was a nice man who was constantly making sure that I didn't sit on the concrete steps backstage. "Maffew", he'd say with that flat Cambridge London accent, "I wouldn't sit dare you'll get piles my son". He told me loads of jokes, all of which went in one ear and out the other, but the very fact of him telling them made me smile.

I spent a lot of time with Cliff in the workshop where they made scenery and kept the costumes, in a disused theatre called the Festival, which was situated somewhere up the Newmarket Road. I used to love ferreting about in this old-fashioned space. The Festival was a fully equipped late Georgian theatre, built in its time with some of most up-to-date machinery for putting on plays in Europe. It still had a hand operated revolving stage under the boxes of costumes, which I was amazed to hear still worked. It also had a massive permanent cyclorama which, if I could persuade Cliff to light up, defied belief. When lit, the 180 degree concave wall at the rear of the stage seemed to disappear, making the illusion of an enormous gulf between the auditorium and the stage seem completely real. I don't think I ever quite experienced this feeling of space in a theatre in the same way again.

The other side of getting to know the Arts more intimately was going with my parents, at regular intervals, to see plays before their London opening. My first memories of these excursions, was a feeling of nauseous boredom and a longing for the interval, when I would be able to get a glass of Coca-Cola in the cool of the foyer, a treat, because it wasn't approved of at home.

This feeling of being dragged to the theatre went on for quite some time. At first it was limp musicals like *Salad Days* and *No No Nannette,* and then there were dreary productions of plays like *Private Lives* and *Fanny by Gaslight.* But gradually the plays started to change, they started to get wiry; writers like Arnold Wesker, Harold Pinter and Charles Dyer were beginning to make their mark.

Plays were infiltrating the Arts Theatre that connected with my disjointed feelings. I can never forget Ian Holm in *The Homecoming,* Roy Kinnear in *Sparrers Can't Sing,* James Booth in *The Fire Raisers* and other great eye openers; but the highlight, in a kind of contradictory tumble, would come from the university itself....

Standing for the national anthem, before a play started, no matter what, was a daily routine, part of the institution; when the drum role was introduced, everyone stood, without question.

So it was that the house lights dimmed, everyone hushed, as a small figure in a bow tie and tails walked across the stage and down into the orchestra pit to a piano, which had been elevated on a rostrum so the top appeared to be just above the stage. With his back to us, he flicked the tails away from his behind and sat down on a small stool and proceeded to play the national anthem. As if on cue, everyone in the auditorium stood up. There was the usual polite silence, as the audience paid their respect. When it came to the end, the punters sat down accompanied by the slight clearing of throats and shuffling of clothes, the now familiar noises of patrons ready to descend into the world of play. The little figure went back up onto the stage and walked off, leaving a pregnant pause; after a few seconds he came back on again, went straight back to the small stool to sit at the piano and once more proceeded to play the national anthem. This time the audience seemed a little perplexed, if not embarrassed, but decided amongst themselves that he must have made a mistake and dutifully stood up to help him out. At the end of the Anthem we all sat down, the little figure went off for the second time, but almost immediately came back on, went down to his stool and played, would you believe, The National Anthem again: There was a stunned second or so of silence as the penny dropped; then a wave of release filled the auditorium, followed by cheering and clapping. My heart raced with delight. For me this was a revolution, the beginning of a breakdown between what was down there on the stage and what was here in the auditorium.

The man playing the piano was Dudley Moore and the play was *Beyond the Fringe*. I couldn't help but feel elated at what I had seen. It became a huge irony for me, this piece of theatre, because of what had happened with Mr Maxwell at The Manor; but the screw that stuck in my throat was how come Dudley got away with it and I didn't.

The fucking load of cunting shit
The earthly road a stinking pit
The new born babe his lot a cot
Submerged, deprived in full blown rot
The lorry's gone the father shouts
The mother screams get out get out
The years go by a sinking ship
The babe a boy jumps out the pit
He sulks and squirms for his mankind
He hits the streets
Revenge on his mind
"A man I am" he whispers loud
The Family's past becomes a cloud
Blown away by windy days
He tries so hard to mend his ways
Ideas like leaves are brushed aside
Clear skies ahead he's in his prime
A Fallen crest that's left behind
A dot on the horizon in his mothers mind
Her child she sees unreal unkind
He's left her right
He's out of sight
Will he or won't he
I think he might

17

Summoned to the lair
Look into the cauldron
See the stirring of the multi layered one dimensional coloured coat
Touch the surface of the shadow play
Be not afraid
Become as a friend to the foe.
This consumption is coming soon
To a movie theatre near you

In times of being weighed down by fear, the adversary seemed all powerful. But when, in some kind of alchemic contradiction, this uncontrollable terror moved to a broader horizon and on to the big screen, without leaving the shore the enemy allowed us in, even to hold the hand of their child. When my heart was heavy and raging, it was all but impossible to find a way and the dark place of light offered up an essential lifeline.

During my third and what was going to be the last year at The Manor I often used to sneak off at lunchtime, usually with Trevor Hanslow or Alan Willis. We'd go down to the city centre and slink in through a side entrance of The Victoria Cinema. Common to a lot of picture-houses of the day, this municipal building, which was situated directly opposite the Market Square, had well worn marble steps leading up to a gothic foyer of crimson flock wallpaper and brass down lighters. If the door round by the church wasn't open, one of us used to get in for half price two and nine (two shillings and nine pence). Once inside the auditorium, we'd go down to the front and when the usherette had her back turned, open the fire escape door for the other.

At a glance, I could still pass for a 12-year-old so I was usually allocated to buy the tickets, while Trevor and Alan looked old enough to buy a packet of five Woodbines from the off-license. The off-licence was tucked away on the right-hand side of the grand front entrance next to some stairs leading up to a ballroom. The only time I ever went up to The Victoria Ballroom was to see *The Jokers Wild* play. I liked nothing more than to stand proudly at the edge of the stage, look up at Dave Gilmour, who even then commanded the auditoria with his musical riffs, and share a nod of approval with him. I had known him since primary school, when he and his brother would occasionally try to unhinge me with verbal jibing when I was walking to Fencauseway to get the 129 bus home.

There was also a restaurant attached to The Victoria, which remained a fantasy eating place, derived from an advertisement that kicked in before the Pathe news or the first feature; "You can't live without eating, but you can add variety by eating out, so make this your rendezvous again and again etc etc....." it ended with, "our off-license is open for the largest selection of beers wines and spirits in Cambridge". If the cinema was packed out with undergraduates, the last bit of the advert would go like this; "our off-license is open for the largest selection of "QUEERS" wines and spirits in Cambridge. Shouting out 'Queers' had everybody falling over themselves with laughter.

Like many cities in the UK at this time, Cambridge had a breed of these fading picture palaces scattered within the throws of its boundaries. There were architectural differences of course, but when the lights dimmed and the projector thrust its magic upon the screen, they all had that same flickering denominator.

I first became aware of moving pictures through my dad's passion for the art. He talked constantly about this actor or that film which he had seen as a young man. On special occasions he would take me to see movies he thought suitable; Buster Keaton, Harold Lloyd, Marlene Dietrich.... Each time is etched in my memory by the magic of the light in that dark place.

George once took me to one of the few privately owned cinemas left in Cambridge at the time called the Kinamma. The Kinamma was a flea pit of a building where the auditorium stunk of leaky latrines and the roof had a hole which let the rain in. We saw a pioneering picture directed by Jacques Cousteau called *The Silent World*, which mesmerized us with the wonder and deep magnificence of the ocean in glorious Technicolor. This occasion was memorable, not so much for the film, but more for the shock of being in the same row as some boys who started rocking the seats backwards and forwards until the bolts, which held them fast to the floor, started to pop loose. We got out of our seats and went and sat at the back, just before the whole row crashed backwards. I remember feeling bemused at how everyone just carried on watching the film regardless of the ruckus.

The Rex was another privately owned cinema, a sad hangar of a building situated in one of those grey areas, on the outskirts of the city centre, near The Manor. When I was seven years old my mother took me and one of my cousins to The Rex to see my very first film, *The Titfield Thunderbolt*. My cousin became so entranced that periodically he'd rush down to the front and look round the side of the screen to see where the train, featured so prominently in this film, was coming from. Although I was too shy to show such delight, as my cousin had done, the vividness of this colourful picture show whetted my appetite for more, much more!

A year or so down the block, my parents brought me to the Rex to meet up with Gigi and go on a terrifying and intriguing journey North by Northwest. It wasn't until I braved occasional outings on wet afternoons during my third year at The Manor, that I became aware of how the Rex was like the Jekyll and Hyde of cinemas; depending on the clientele and which film was being shown, it had two distinct sides.

George Web was infamous throughout Cambridge at this time as the manager of the Rex. He was a shrewd man who, even with the oncoming advent of television, knew how to make the dwindling popularity of cinema pay. It was common knowledge that he turned the heating up in the summers, to enliven the sale of soft drinks and ice-cream, and down in the winter to sell greater quantities of hot dogs and coffee.

He instigated one of the first showings of *The Wild One* in the sixties when it had been banned outright by other cinemas throughout the UK. When the Rex put on a film called *The Blackboard Jungle* the place erupted. Seats were broken up and the wooden armrests used as clubs by rival gangs who beat the hell out of each other. This didn't stop George Web, on the contrary, he wanted the Rex to become a regular meeting place for teddy boys and leather clad motorbike freaks to hang out, for him it was all good publicity.

Some of these motorcycle gangs were notorious for terrorizing Cambridge; most of them were born and brought up in the sticks, small villages in the Fens, like Fordham, Fen Ditton and Soham. A great deal of the fen area in Cambridgeshire has for a few hundred years seen families brought up in complete isolation and I suggest that some might have seen themselves as being above and beyond the boundaries of the law.

During my last couple of terms at school, I found my way into hanging out with one of these gangs. I knew the leader who was two years older than me, from The Manor. He dominated the whole place and without doubt was one of the toughest boys in the school. Somehow I wheedled my way into his liking me and very occasionally I would go and meet him and his brothers outside the Rex. For a short while before I left school I looked for some kind of acceptance, or maybe it was protection, from these hard men of the shire. God knows what I was doing! I got my first ride on one of their motorbikes, a rocket of a machine that was apparently thought too powerful for the city streets and consequently barred from legal use. But this didn't stop the brothers from masquerading like wild ones and using me as a scapegoat for their feral antics. My initiation into acceptance, by this tribe of leather clad hyenas, was to sit on the back of the captain's Vincent, whilst he, catching me unawares, set off at such a definitive speed that the bike shot out from between my legs, leaving me for a split second in midair, before being smacked down in the middle of the road. Were they taking the piss? I don't know really, but I used them, as much as they used me. They were feared throughout Cambridgeshire and my thinking was that if I went along with their fucking about, they'd look after me when things got rough in other departments, especially downtown on a Saturday night!

The Rex Cinema had an adjoining ballroom, which in its glory days saw the likes of my mother and her first husband waltzing head to toe in plush 30's attire. When I was a boy the ballroom had been greyed out to become a notorious gloomy hall where the so called sleazier bands of rock 'n' roll played. Groups like the Pretty Things, and The Rolling Stones made their Cambridge debut there. I remember an incredulous me staring up at Mick Jagger, who looked like he was about to keel over with a terrible case of jaundice, as the band took us to get our kicks on Route 66.

For me the only a,b,c worth considering in Cambridge, was the ABC Victoria, the ABC Regal and ABC Central. These art deco caverns were built for the sole purpose of showing one film in each separate building – the multiplex was not even a shadow on the horizon at this time.

Occasionally the wide black stage below the massive silver screen, in these stylish barns, was thrown over to live jive and mass hysteria.

Most of the local or visiting rock bands would usually play at the Corn Exchange, the Dorothy, or The Victoria ballroom. Of the Cinemas, The Regal had a front stage large enough for the more commercially successful bands to perform on. It was at The Regal that I went to see Chris Montez sing his hit *Let's Dance*, fantastic, exhilarating! I have a vague memory of the Beatles, who played bottom of the bill, but they didn't seem to make much of an impression; it wasn't until their next gig in Cambridge that I began to take in what I had brushed aside.

Ponji lording it in a punt, with Jan Bredstorf punting, of course!

18

Lying half asleep in Addenbrookes Hospital, waiting for the anaesthetist to arrive for the oncoming descent into tonsil removal, I started dreaming about a girl. I was just about to lose my virginity, when I was brought to my senses by the man in the next bed, spewing forth sexual expletives into the ear of a nurse, who seemed to be hovering a few inches above his head. It was the first time in my life that I had heard full throttle, no holds barred swearing from a grown man. I became suitably entranced. This patient had driven straight across a roundabout and made a head-on collision with a bollard on the other side, because he had been too drunk to realize otherwise. He ended up in hospital with major concussion. Somehow I found out, I suspect from one of the nurses, that it was quite common for private thoughts to pour forth into the public arena when coming round from a general anaesthetic. I became nervous, dreading what might pour forth from my dulcet lips.

In spite of my neighbouring bed mate, whose rambunctious behaviour didn't seem to faze them at all, the nurses were up for anything, specially a laugh. They seemed unashamedly open about their exploits, particularly in the pill popping arena. They made no attempt to cover up the fact that they were moving large amounts of pills from the hospital medicine store, to put somewhere other than in the mouths of patients.

As well as my tonsils, I also needed some fluid draining from behind one of my ear drums, but this didn't seem to concern anyone very much, especially the nurses, who seemed taken up with more pressing matters. This gave me the confidence to take in and enjoy the shenanigans taking place in the ward.

The excitement was tangible; for this was the week which would see the Beatles return to Cambridge, only this time playing top of the bill. And throughout the night before my operation, the nurses took it in turns to disappear out the window, which was, believe it or not, directly opposite my bed, shin down the drain pipe (we were on the second floor) and leg it down to The Regal, where they were keeping a place in the queue for tickets, which incidentally had started to form a couple of days previously.

From my hospital bed the Beatles had started to penetrate my imagination and as soon as I was up and running again, I went down to Millers to buy their second album.

As far as I knew, Millers was the only record store in Cambridge where it was possible to hear and buy into, what was for many, the sounds underlying the beginning of a revolutionary holler from the restricted passages of our time.

Millers had an unusual front window, made up of a large concave trough of glass through which a passerby could see into a bustling subterranean vault downstairs. Here, those in the know listened to the music of the day in small cubicles, before deciding on their all important purchase. These prefabricated booths, weren't as private as they alluded to be. Like continental telephone kiosks they were open at the front to public scrutiny and this made it imperative that my selection fitted in with those who might be hanging around the opening. I rarely had the courage to risk asking for something I wasn't sure of, in case it didn't fit in with the trend. But on this occasion, I had no such fears and went straight down to the sales desk and without hesitation...

Before I could get a word in edgeways, the sales girl told me that *With the Beatles* had sold out.

Disappointed, I slouched my way back up the stairs, wondering how on earth she had known my choice. Were they really that popular? I made my way over to Boots the chemist, which had found a home in a new shopping centre across the road, to see if on the off chance, they might have the coveted vinyl disc. Much to my surprise I managed to secure a copy. Just from the cover, I could see I was holding a piece of art. The photograph on the front of the album had an immediate sense of being chic. It showed their faces in black-and-white, like a stylish picture from Vogue magazine that my mother sometimes read. The acceptable album cover combined with an exciting up-and-coming musical combination of the fab four, meant their sound started to get through to my languid ears.

Soon after I left the hospital and after much badgering from us children, my mum and dad finally succumbed and got the dreaded television. One of the early highlights, of this extraordinary compromise, was watching the Beatles perform live at the Palladium in *The Royal Variety Show.*

When John Lennon spoke out, saying those of you in the cheap seats clap your hands and the rest just rattle your jewellery and then broke into the song *Twist and Shout*, the goose-pimples leapt to attention all over my body. I knew now what the nurses were so excited about, while I was in hospital, those few months previously.

~

By this time I had fallen a very long way short of the scholastic pile. I felt as thick as an overgrown plank in a builder's yard. It was the mere fact of not being able to screw a sentence together, or tie a simple equation to the page without screwing up that constantly pulverised me to the quick.

I felt as if I was being squeezed from both sides of the tracks.

At school, the wrath of physical punishment may have left a lasting sting, but through the sour taste of tears I could see some cruel logic in that. No, the real and lasting source for my chastisement came not from the corporal side, but from the constant humiliation of failing so miserably at basic schoolwork.

My mother and father were no doubt deeply disturbed by my troubles, but the truth was, even with all their education and first class degrees, they were at a loss and didn't know how to help me. They and their neighbours held the mirror up and when I looked at the reflection, I saw a sieve for brains. Despite their compassion, I felt constantly put in the shade by what I saw at the time to be their superior overt intelligence.

Towards the end of my third year at The Manor I sat in on a sober meeting between the headmaster and my parents, where it was agreed that it would be better for the school, and for them, if they found somewhere else for their son to continue his education. Although the petty misdemeanours and my escalating bad behaviour were undoubtedly the real explanation for the school's rebuff, it was the way the teachers put across their incapacity to help with my academic work, which finally got shot of me. One way or another they convinced, my gullible, mother and father to remove me from the building without ever mentioning the word expelled. The slighting remained in the air for many months to come. I felt unreservedly embarrassed for my parents, especially since my mother was now teaching drama at The Manor in the evenings and my dad was on the governing board.

Looking back now, I can see so much pride flying around. How could there be anything wrong with their beloved son, it can only be the fault of that hopeless institution? Then, after hours, days, nay years of head scratching on their part, I think my mother and father finally came to the conclusion that I was a square peg. And the worry of this dilemma got them feeling even more concerned and this just pushed us all further out of joint. I wanted so much to make them feel alright, as I am sure they did me, but we just kept missing the target. My dream always, was to be an equal in my parent's eye, to feel respected and then somehow intellectually accepted. But we were all too nervous, too wary of the emotional disturbance, to ever really untie the knots.

For all my in-school posturing I left The Manor, when I was still barely fourteen, in a wake of anxiety for the pain I had caused my parents and trembling with fear for the next miserable desk to come.

After the summer holidays I moved on to a more appealing place of learning, this time with a mix of girls and boys and run with a more liberal ethos; but in spite of some initial relief, it had come too late.

I spent days sitting in the classrooms of Impington Village Collage, which was situated in a village on the outskirts of Cambridge, unable to move, tied down on a plateau of illiteracy. Like Gulliver I felt as if these ties would never release. The sensation that the head and body were bigger than the surroundings, made any teachings hard to take in without a great deal of physical effort.

Ludicrous as it now seems, a vast amount of my scholastic time was spent sweating with nerves. Even within the tolerant structure of this new school, my faculties were invaded by mistrust and apprehension. No doubt these feelings were accelerated to greater heights by living in a city, which was held up as one of the most sacrosanct centres for learning in the world.

The realities my revered elders tried to convince me with, came loaded with inordinate amounts of fear. Their persuasive and often aggressive pointers, securing as they saw it definitive ways to pin down a future, pushed me away from the heart of my physical reality. In this environment my sense of self bent further out of control. How could I take in the words of man, when life itself was leading me with a million stories on a million undefined paths?

And then there was Russell.

Russell Page was Michelangelo's David with unkempt blonde hair. To me he was an enigma. He was neither boorish nor snobbish, was bright in the academic sense and without knowing it my first hero. Later on we became better acquainted, but for the short time I was at Impington I don't think we ever spoke to each other.

What made him stand out was his continuing melancholic attitude toward the school authorities.

During the longer breaks between lessons I sometimes caught sight of Russell, outside on the steps leading from the main hall, a lone figure of poetic insurgency. He'd sit with a hang dog expression, staring into the middle distance, with a quiet brooding about his person telling the establishment it could never persuade him otherwise.

Russell was in the year above me and although only sixteen, it was rumoured that he knew how various narcotics worked.

At this time the bohemian sub culture was just a whisper in my ear, a sound bite from a distant future and yet somehow I saw within Russell, an echo of this heart beat to come.

There was one memorable occasion which summed up his enterprising talents for making the authorities shudder. In the grounds, within the perimeter of Impington Village College, were several prefabricated classrooms built for teaching science and technology. During his last term, at the end of an apparently normal school day, each pain of glass in these dedicated buildings became Russell's canvas. Protected by the shadows of a summer evening, he quietly and methodically painted every single bit of window space with gloss red paint. His defiance was to me a wonderful expression of daring. His insubordination was not put over with any direct aggression, on the contrary, it was made with an obvious expression only found in ART and it was my first gob-smacked glimmer into the poetic and revolutionary side of BEAT.

"I should never have gone to Cambridge. Cambridge gave me ideas above my station and above my abilities. I never understood Marx. I never could cope with the Richards, Leavis, Williams, Steiner approach to literature."

George Scurfield

19

Having been summoned to the head teacher's office, to meet the well suited, clipped and ready, employment officers, I was asked what it was I wanted to do after I left school. In response to my reply, "A policeman or a clown", a lead heavy silence filled the room. They began to explain with some careful wording how my lack of qualifications meant I was sorely restricted. They said, with a distinctly stilted tone, that the only avenue open for me was to pursue that of an apprenticeship in one of the building trades, but even this suggested a great deal of uncertainty.

Fuck it, I left school with my tail well and truly between my legs and, like a rejected dog, sought comfort in those who posed no threat to what was left of my equilibrium. This meant hanging out with such mates as I could find who like me, were not caught up in a relentless quest for some unforeseen job, with a vague reward, in some unforeseen future.

I wasn't by any means alone. A lot of my friends were told that their futures were a non-starter. Apart from small firms like Marshalls select aircraft industry and The Cambridge Instrument Company there was no manufacturing to speak of, no pride of heritage for the working man in this city. It was simply accepted that they would end up doing menial jobs, usually of a physical nature for small reward. The average labourers wage in Cambridgeshire at this time was among the lowest in the country. And as I was being shoved hammer and sickle into that bag, I counted myself as one of them. I was hurt, infuriated and full of screaming chaos.

We didn't know it then of course, but we had been brainwashed by our teachers and parents, who had in turn been brainwashed by theirs, into a straightjacket of worthlessness. The brochure of our lives told us with colourful clarity that they were over before they started. It was as if we had been herded together into the corral of a dissipated and distracted present. For some this was the end of the line, but for others it was an opportunity to begin the dance. As far as I was concerned the distinction between debauchery, celebration and respect for the now became blurred.

It was generally felt that we had nothing to gain and therefore nothing it would seem to lose, by getting drunk or pilled out on a

Friday and Saturday night. Eventually this dissipation lost its parameters, until such time as the whole week was taken up with trying to put our past and future lives behind us.

By now I found the whole idea of being among lucid people alarming to say the least. I tried to avoid anyone who might show up my total inaptitude for anything remotely academic; this became difficult, if not impossible, around the unquestionable cerebral highflyers who dominated the Adams Road area.

It wasn't until I got a temporary job as a waiter in the hallowed eating halls of Caius College, that I started to see how infantile the undergraduates were. Watching them throw their food around, playing skittles with the glasses and plates, I often felt as if I were donning the robes of a zoo keeper, feeding frenzied wild animals in an enclosure. But even with this newfound insight, I still felt utterly intimidated by the idea that this gothic institution of learning deemed them to be somehow superior. What I didn't realise was how profound and near the knuckle my insights were – and the lessons just kept on coming.

I was at an old boy's rowing dinner, busy spilling soup down the back of one the guests who had been treating me as if I were a slave on a galley. This mishap with the food, at these gowned slob-outs, was the only payback we had at our command and was shown to me by the headwaiters, so I felt perfectly within my rights. A guest turned round unexpectedly from one of the long tables and above the constant din started shouting out my name. I had learnt to carry five or six plates of food stepped up the arm, one on top of the other, in such a way so as not to get food on the bottom of the plates, and managed to keep composure. Barely able to hide his astonishment at seeing me in the guise of a lowly waiter, the voice introduced himself as a cousin and asked me what on earth I was doing there. His surprise along with my awkwardness caught the eye of the other graduates who started to play games, calling me to heel by my first name, trying to trip my certitude. Inevitably their oncoming jibes saw a couple of the plates I was holding go crashing to the floor. My cousin came to the rescue, by picking up the pieces and was very apologetic for any embarrassment he might have caused. Although he was considerate, what I couldn't get my head round was the fact that these louts, for that is how they came across to me, were supposed to be the best of the best, the crème de la crème in the grownup world.

This was a time when the Wimpy Bar was placed within the dying shadow of the waltz and jive era. The echoes of the fifties coffee bar were being left behind, with an intense feeling that nothing could really be seen or heard from the mannequins of those bootlace ties and blue suede shoes. Teddy Boys, were losing their grip as the wild representatives of the working man and their mantle was being passed to the Rocker, while those who wore the Burton suit of a weekend were buying scooters and tarting themselves up as Mods.

I tried to stand proud as a Mod for a few months, but this remained a short lived fantasy. Being a sharp dresser, as Mods certainly were, cost money and the readies, despite my family background, seemed forever in short supply. Through the combination of pocket-money, received with gratitude from my father who gave it out like he was running a very tight ship, and helping out at the shop, I did manage to get the Levi's, a Ben Sherman shirt and a pair of desert boots.

Ronnie Reed and Charlie Weedon, a couple of fishtail parka wearers I knew, offered me a lift, but I bottled out of going down to Brighton, which perhaps on reflection was a good thing. In 1964 the rivalry between the Mods and Rockers culminated in full scale war, making headline news in the broadsheets of the day. I was shown proud pictures of these violent clashes between my friends in the News Chronicle, the Daily Mirror and even The Times.

Even if it wasn't as clearly defined as the skirmishes between the Mods and Rockers, you didn't have to go down to the coast to seek out a war. Cambridge, as it had been for centuries past, was still firmly split between town and gown. The constant conflict underlying these two rivals was well established as a normal, if not disturbing, part of city life. A sinister trait acknowledged by so few, affecting so many and I'd been given the bird's eye view.

When I was growing up there, each undergraduate under the law of the university, had to wear long black gowns. This law was strictly binding, especially if they were outside the college grounds after dark. As I understood it they wore these capes, which were tailored according to rank, so they would stand out from the crowd. This was most important at night because they could be seen by the proctors, who patrolled the streets in the wee small hours accompanied by university constables known to us as bulldogs. These heavyweights had the power to fine, or even suspend undergraduates for breaches of university rules. Intimidating as these college lawmen certainly were, especially when they were in full swing, it wasn't long before I learnt how they had little or no jurisdiction over the locals...

Mick O'Reilly was young wild and Irish and for a couple of years the mere sight of him could terrorise those parts of Cambridge who cared to notice. He usually wore a black suit, white shirt and black tie. From a distance you might say he looked quite smart, but up close, well the cuffs and collar gave it away. If that didn't make the passerby wonder, his greasy rivulets of long black hair, sticking out from under the rim of a bowler hat, certainly did. On a Sunday, if he was feeling confrontational, he would stand in the entrance of the Irish pub opposite the Roman Catholic Church and shout out detrimental expletives about the Irish. Then run like fuck up the road with half the pub, including his relations, running after him. One way or another they'd catch up with him and beat his hide to a bloody pulp.

One night, I was standing with Dougie Brown, keeping him company while he waited for a taxi in the Market Square, when he introduced me to Mick O'Reilly.

I don't really know if Dougie Brown was a little person or not, all I remember is that he was a couple of years older than me and I looked down into his face. Dougie could drink practically anyone I knew under the table. He never shouted or fell about when he drank. The only way you could tell he was intoxicated was by the whites of his teary eyes turning fiery red. At the end of the night if you looked into the windows of his soul it would reveal a basket of drowning kittens disappearing into a whirlpool and there was nothing you could do to rescue them.

Mick O'Reilly came hurtling round the corner full of manic energy and slapped himself between us. At first my heart skipped a few beats, but very quickly I got the sense that he was being friendly. We made our introductions and without any hesitation he took us both toward the Senate House passage to hunt out the proctors. He said they would come after us if we ran off at the appropriate moment! We waited in the shadows and sure enough, some twenty minutes later there they were coming round the corner and it was exactly as Mick had said. The mere fact that we ran off sparked a frantic chase. When we finally allowed them to catch us they demanded to know what College we were from and Mick just said the college of life you cunt, which left them dumbstruck and because we were locals powerless to pull rank.

Over the oncoming months I got to know Mick quite well and he revealed a strange mixture of loving kindness and threatening wantonness.

The last time I saw him was at a late showing of *The Carpetbaggers* at The Regal cinema. In the middle of the film he had gone off to the toilet, ripped out the ball-cock from the cistern, gone back into the auditorium and thrown it at the screen, which left Alan Ladd with a giant bogey hanging out of his nose. This escapade put a stop to the midnight films at The Regal and at most of the other cinemas in Cambridge at that time.

For many undergraduates, the 5th of November started out as a day of celebration in the city centre, but invariably it would end with the festivities turning sour. On one of these autumn days, Ponji pleaded with my parents to be allowed to go into town and watch. They of course refused permission. Quietly defiant to the last, Ponji snuck out of his bedroom window later that evening and got his way. The next day I heard of exploits, which sounded both exciting and terrifying. Petrol was poured into the fountain in the middle of the Market Square and ignited, giving light to a massive police presence trying to quell unrest between the growing numbers of locals and students, who were descending on the city centre, hell-bent on creating havoc. One such incident he told me about was of someone he knew who had run up behind a policeman, lifted his helmet and put a firecracker under it. A gang from his school had been determined to beat the hell out of as many undergraduates as possible on that night and then string them up from the lampposts surrounding the Market Square. I believed it then and still hold it as a reality now.

This tradition was known as grad bashing. I often heard many of my contemporaries speaking out about how they'd got a so-and-so toffee nosed wanker and smashed his skull against the pavements of Kings Parade, or some other suitably hard surface. The anger was entrenched and blatant. You couldn't avoid it if you went to a school overflowing with boys from the thick end of town, as I had. Nothing special to my time; I was told, usually in passing by my elders, that this conflict had been going on for hundreds of years.

It is generally thought that in the 13th Century, following a backlash in Oxford between town and gown, many undergraduates were killed along with many locals. The King granted special protection and privileges to the scholars. A significant number, fearing for their lives, were given a new home in a place called Cambridge. Out of this move grew the university, but so it seems did the rift.

What had really changed? Like the tranquiliser taking over from the straightjacket, our outward manifestations may have become subtler, less easy to pin down, but the one-upmanship of this breeding ground for excellence, continued to stand over the locals like an elephant over a mouse. The ethics from the jewel in the crown of our education, not unlike a dogmatic church, was still feeding fuel into a huge split between the haves and have-nots. It wasn't hard to deduce that this deplorable divide, between the clever people and the thick, came not from the council house tenants, but from the heart of this exclusive city, the university itself.

From the pile I was under it just seemed like the whole shebang was part of the same disease, like opposite sides of the same ugly coin. Because of my academic background and my dumb-head schooling, I was in a unique position of being able to taste and see both of these sides full on. But such was the power of affiliation back then, I didn't have confidence in my insights – I just continued, as if it were my rightful place, to feel snared at the low end of this rigid social spectrum, like a rat trapped in a cast-iron drainpipe. The fact that some of the most outstanding scientists of the 20th century had been firing warning shots across the Oxbridge bows, for the past three decades, hadn't penetrated the entirety of my pensive brain. Yet somehow I still managed to see the writing on the wall. I may not have had the facilities to ride the waves with the literati, but I could certainly see the more obvious connotations of our academic standing, in the world of science and engineering. In the beginning there was thought, and then there was the machine.

Do those ever eager authorities, caught up in the corridors of distinction, have any real idea of what the consequences of their actions might be? When the epicentre of blind, institutionalized, knowledge loses its way and erupts, the fallout can be felt thousands of miles away, the repercussions of which are rarely acknowledged by the perpetrators.

"All our lauded technological progress – our very civilization - is like the axe in the hand of the pathological criminal." Albert Einstein

Who'd have thought that a seemingly harmless theory like E=mc²could have led to our greatest means of mass destruction. It seems we are so certain of the needs of our concrete world that we turn away from those repercussions at the drop of a dollar. Einstein always saw E=mc² as a purely theoretical insight and refuted any responsibility for the H-bomb, especially after the devastation of Hiroshima. The greatest scientist of the twentieth century became a pacifist and campaigner of humanitarian and civil rights in the latter part of his life.

"In some sort of crude sense which no vulgarity, no humour, no overstatement can quite extinguish, the physicists have known sin; and this is a knowledge which they cannot lose."

Robert Oppenheimer, father of the atom bomb, 1948

When I was growing up in Cambridge, there were only two colleges for women, Girton and Newnham, the rest were a breeding ground for a male dominant society, who thought it was their right and privilege to run the world. This was a time when you could still get into Oxbridge through the family name if it was deemed necessary.

Working class graduates, as my father would say, had been trickling into Cambridge, like token pawns, since the late thirties. For some this may seem like a class war, a matter of storming the barricades; but I believe this is a conflict far more insidious and much harder to pin down. Measuring one's achievements against those who have made none; isn't this a national pastime?

Despite what my dad and his communalist colleagues may have felt, a revolution was starting to take place, which saw many of the more adventurous locals seeping in by the back door. The grammar school was gaining some ground, bringing an undeniable sideways shift. A slow change, but it was palpable. Not that anyone from The Manor would ever have been given a place at Cambridge or Oxford, God forbid.

There can be no doubt now that the end of the fifties saw a greater swing on the horizon. Young men and women from opposite ends of the social spectrum were beginning to hang together. The servant and the master could be seen in some quarters sitting at the same table and talking shop. If your ear was truly to the ground, you could hear the buzz being initiated by the intelligentsia and the plebs who were relaxed enough to explore their company of opposites.

On the dance-floor, under the spotlight of stage and screen, through the pioneers of popular music and poetry, by way of social interchange in pubs and coffee bars, through political movements like CND, within the subculture on the streets and even between the intakes of drugs; the early sixties saw that small shift, swelling into a global surge of questioning. With the backdrop of World War Two and the relative fear-bred way of life not that far behind, this was a time, as seen by many, for abundant change.

~

The one constant throughout my time in Cambridge had always been my relationship with water. As the years drew their course, the life force I found with this unending element started to sweeten a competitive need. When I was twelve years old I became a member of the Granta Swimming Club, where, between bouts of nervous diarrhoea, I did as much as I could to keep one stroke ahead of the boys.

My first foray with the Mill Pond in Cambridge was taking part in the 'Swim through Cambridge', an annual event set up by the club for earnest swimmers to show off their aptitude to the gatherings, given window by banks of the Cam. I took part three or four times as I remember and wound up with the last few at Jesus Green, where the swim ended, bemused and frustrated. Before the race I used to notice how much fun other kids were having sliding down the weir from under the mill bridge and really my wish was to be a part of that and be free of the formalities of the swimming club.

By the time I was fourteen, I suppose you could say my wish had come true – for the social element had taken over from the wet. The Mill Pond had now become a meeting place where I would go and catch up with old friends from The Manor.

We hadn't quite cracked the self-conscious nut about being under age at the drinking pens down there, but we could usually coach some kindly elder or unsuspecting undergraduate, into buying us beer from the Anchor pub. Having scored our illicit brews we mingled with the summer crowds above the old mill race, which overlooked the river towards Silver Street Bridge. It was whilst surreptitiously hanging out like this that I first became aware of one Ian Carter or Pip, as he was widely known. '

Pip was always surrounded by ongoing intrigue. From where I stood, he usually seemed to be at the centre of a bunch of like-minded souls who wanted to cut a finer edge. Drawn into his company, I found out soon enough that he was a pill pusher, which made him someone who was sought after, particularly by the Mods!

Pip may have been brought up on the rough side of town, but you couldn't accuse him of being standoffish. We got on immediately. He didn't seem to be entirely comfortable in himself as he appeared to fidget a lot and was constantly looking over his shoulder for the next move. His eyes darted away from one another and all over the place. The only time he seemed to be still was when he got down to doing a deal.

It was shortly after meeting Pip that I started to sell him what pills I could get from the cabinet in my Aunt Alice's kitchen, and through these exchanges we started to become close friends.

I lost count of the times I went down to the Mill Pond to trade medical contrabands, but certainly there was a summer when I was standing with Pip, pint and pills in hand, when suddenly from out of the blue we heard a strange and distant yelling. These yelps and cries, unlike anything I'd heard before, very quickly became louder and more defiant. Everyone became transfixed by expectation, as the sound quickly metamorphosed into the spectacle of a black top hat on the head of a scarecrow, whose arms were outstretched in manic fury, crucified against the skyline. Like a demented cowboy on speed, his legs possessed by wild acceleration, propelled a sit-up-and-beg bicycle with increasing ferocity, towards a packed crowd of summer drinkers at the bottom of the lane. It very quickly became apparent that the rider wasn't going to stop and as if in perfect timing, the throng of gob-smacked onlookers parted, like the Red Sea did for Moses. The cyclist shot through the incredulous crowd, over the top of the mill race and took off in slow motion through the air. The bike and body, as if glued together, landed yards out, in the middle of the river and for a few frantic minutes, just below the surface of the murky water it was possible to see the vague outline of the body still peddling forwards. Very quickly the bike and rider disappeared altogether, leaving a few ripples and the site of a derelict top hat, floating about in the wet stillness as if in mourning for the big splash.

After what seemed like an eternity of silence, a body pulled itself out of the water on the other side of the river and the oncoming crowd went ballistic. Emo had arrived, cut to the quick and broken everyone down to a common denominator of a stunned and delighted audience.

Emo was a good friend of Pips, so it wasn't long before he arrived at our side to say hello. It turned out that he had bought several packets of Morning Glory seeds from Woolworths, downed the lot, gone through hell, thrown up and then, with his head and stomach on fire, seized the first bike he could find and made a beeline for the river.

Imo, pronounced Emo, was a nickname given to him from the play on the initials of his full name, Iain Owen Moore. Emo had Pip's distracted energy, but on first encounter seemed more gregarious, dangerous even.

Like many of my friends from school, they were from the same impoverished area, constantly having to fight their corner in the classroom, at home and on the street. There was little or no verbal communication in their upbringing. Emo basically learnt to talk from listening to the wireless. Pip had been unable to speak, until Emo took him under his wing and gave him the reassurance he needed to find his voice.

It turned out Emo knew my brother through going to the same school. As far as I could make out Ponji was seen by Emo and many of his mates as a total dick-head then, a head-prefect, who was lucky to have survived without being killed. Emo was three years younger than Ponji. Despite the age difference they had a near disastrous faceoff at Chesterton, which almost saw my brother being thrown off a top story balcony, no doubt as a reprisal for some arrogant way he had laid down the law. But this was the beginning of the sixties, times had changed and faces moved on.

Not long after Ponji's further education, where he hadn't excelled as he wanted, my brother started to cultivate a more bohemian image. This overt change meant the likes of Emo and Pip now saw him as someone enticing to be with, someone who wasn't scared of the heights.

Whether it was Ponji who provided the calling card remained to be seen, but the fact that I was his brother, seemed to cement a compelling bond between Emo and myself.

Well there's a place you really get your kicks
It's open every night about twelve to six
Now if you wanna hear some boogie you can get your fill
And shove and sting like an old steam drill
Come on along you can lose your lead
Down the road, down the road, down the road apiece.   Don Raye

20

For his school years Emo donned a quiff, but now his hair was shoulder length and he radiated with a look that was nothing short of handsome. Like Roy Wellford, one of my partners in crime at The Manor, he was brought up on 'Starvation Drive' by the one and only rule that could bring a renegade of the street round to their senses: the fist. He certainly had that same neighbourhood toughness as Wellford, that sense of fearlessness, which so often goes with the territory. Both inside and outside of his clan, Emo had been shafted in more ways than one. Being beaten up was second nature to Emo and, like my friend from The Manor, this appeared to make him uninhibited by the dangers of any physical extremes. Since Emo had no apparent fear of the consequences, he was utterly unpredictable. Legend had it that as soon as he got his road licence he tore up the steps of the Civic restaurant in the city centre on his motorbike, rode it through the entrance, round the tables and out through the swing doors on the other side and never looked back. By all rights he should have been another dead head, banged up on the mortal slagheap of time, but unlike many of his mates, even the hardest ones, there was something which made him wiser to the event. He seemed completely at ease around the feminine side of his nature and this, I now believe, gave him the sensitivity he needed to crawl out from under the pile.

Aside from coming from opposite ends of the social spectrum, we had a lot of things in common. Like me, Emo could hardly tie a word to the page, let alone speak coherently and out of necessity had found other ways to live in a city, which continued to push its scholarly excellence down our dumb throats. All we had left from the start was a capacity to mock these rigorous intellectual walls, which stood guard over the pavements of this distinguished town like a gargantuan weight, lest they smother and pulverise us at the next turn.

To begin with, I believe Emo found me irritating, a little stuck-up even. Perhaps I harboured feelings of superiority, but I certainly was intrigued by his friendship and his bottle. I did my manic best to keep up with his wild wit. Quite often the energy between us would escalate into a kind of competitive frenzy. Soon after we met we found ourselves, in the heart of the city, among a mixture of shoppers and students going about their weekday business. As our heads began to reel with the buzz of the distracted crowds, some spontaneous spirit grabbed us and we started an animated dance in the middle of a zebra crossing. Exploding into life, the gesticulations took over and progressed into abandoned wildness. Hot under the collar and raring to go, we started to strip down to our nakedness. Unbeknownst to us surveillance technology had begun to infiltrate the city and two police cameras were eyeballing us from the crenels of the college roofs. Within minutes the police-car drew up alongside and two burly officers of the law leapt out. They ordered us to get dressed, which we did with deliberate nonchalance.

It's hard to believe now, but our long hair and jeans were subversive to the authorities then. Emo was wearing sandals, which in the early sixties, especially for a young man of his age, was an extremely rare occurrence. For these policemen he certainly must have looked kind of biblical, because one of them grabbed Emo violently by his hair and referring to his Jesus boots barked out "We know you Moses"; and just as I thought Emo was taking the brunt, the venom with lightning quick reflex was spat out in my direction, "but we don't know YOU", which pinned me to the seat of my underpants.

Behind the struggle I was having with my nerves, I saw an ideal opportunity to show Emo that I was someone who could hold their own with the powers that be. Full of mock bravado I proceeded to explain to the officers how I came from Adams Road, and that I was the son of George Scurfield and the nephew of Doctor Alice Roughton. I was relieved and even surprised that this tack of superiority actually worked. After some verbal acrobatics via the walkie-talkie in the siren pit, they let us off with a tight lipped warning.

Emo and I went to calm ourselves over a pint at a pub, filled with ambitious pirates, called The Criterion. He may have remained unpredictable, but it was after this little incident that Emo and I began to feel more relaxed when hanging out together. It wasn't long before I discovered that Emo broke down barriers and crossed the social divide with some considerable ease.

Through my friendship with Emo, I became acquainted with Dave Gale and thereafter with Storm Thorgerson.

As it remained difficult to hold on to any small amount of self-confidence, gravitating towards a friendship with Dave and Storm was possibly going to be an answer, and to some extent it was. I never consciously put them together, or on a pedestal, but that's how it turned out to be; as I saw it then, they were both the intelligent and acceptable side of stoned.

Dave Gale cut a dashing figure, with his jet black hair and dark chiselled looks. On first impression he seemed lithe, quick of step and fiercely cool. Storm was fairer, larger of frame than Dave, he was more extrovert in manner and looser with his appearance. Apart from being graced with looks that were polls apart, they both shared an unequivocal gift of the gab. Unlike most of my friends I had acquired up until then, they harked from the same middle class ranks as I did. Although they were both captivated by Ponji's charms and already knew him quite well, it was their engaging like for Emo and his jocular ways which drew me into their circle.

I first met the witty, ever dapper, D Gale, whose father was a biochemist in Cambridge, at his parent's well-to-do house. He had taken over their home, while they were far away in another country, to have a weekend party, which I hasten to add went on for six months. I tagged along with Emo little knowing what lay ahead of the queue. I had seen a lot of Dave's guests through the windows of the El Patio (the coffee bar round the corner from my dad's shop), but up until now I hadn't been close enough, or more to point bold enough, to take in the reality of who they were.

Over the next few hours I began to realise that it wasn't just the disgruntled few from the thick end of town, who wanted to rip the head from the reed. I found myself among sons and daughters of comparable Cambridge families to my own. Nevertheless, despite the apparent similarity and licentiousness of this familiar crowd, I was still haunted by a blatant inferiority gnawing away at my self-esteem. The fact that most of these heads had passed or surpassed the eleven plus and gone on from there to the various public schools, grammar schools and elite universities of the day, hung over me like a shameful shadow. Crazy though it may seem I even felt their coolness to be superior.

When I left Dave Gale's house, sometime towards the twilight hours of a Sunday morning way back then, I remember wanting above everything else to be accepted and respected by them; but how?

I noticed through a layer of jealously that Emo had no such problem cutting the mustard at this party. It seemed to me that he was the fool on the hill, who basically held the reins to the emotional temperature in the rooms. He was like a safety valve on a boiler. Every time the pressure built up he would go into some articulate trance or wild dance, letting off steam for every repressed feeling within his vicinity and he was loved all the more for it. Uninhibited by gender, his libido seemed to hold no bounds. Emo's character was such that he could smash his way through a plate glass door with enough composure to ask the girl on the other side if she wanted to get laid. He was the anarchist who bamboozled kings. He outwitted wit, steamrollered the rules and made new ones up as he went along.

My thinking was that if I could somehow steal some of Emo's thunder, I would be in with a chance. After all I had won them over at school so why couldn't I do it here.

Some few days after Dave Gale's party I was standing outside Storm's house with a keen friend of Emo's called Pewee, Emo and his quiet girlfriend Fizz. Frances, or Fizz as we came to know her, seemed very different to Emo, her beauty was shy and foreboding. Although her manner was extremely gentle she loved Emo's lawless humour. She stood by his side through thick and thin and put up with all his bull-shit for many years, until one day, much to Emo's devastation, she just upped and left, got married to a Buddhist monk and raised a family.

Storm stuck his head out of an upstairs window and like a well fed king to his courtiers pointed his finger, indicating who could or couldn't come up. To my surprise he chose me. I was ushered in through the front door by an outgoing woman, who I found out later was Storm's freethinking mother Vange, an artistic lady who, by any means, wasn't afraid of a young man's chemistry. Carefully avoiding her eye-line I moved cautiously into her terraced home. She directed me up to her son's bedroom where I became privy to the workings of relatively primitive psychedelic light shows, spent time gazing into small cinema boxes, Zoopraxiscopes or whatever they were called, and stolen away by half finished sketches of fairies and mushrooms on the walls, etched with love and great care by a young artist called Dave Henderson; and oh yes, last but not least, mesmerised by the comings and goings of some of the more enlightened young modernists in Cambridge, who seemed to gravitate toward Storm's magic room in droves.

~

Although I was perhaps now harder on the outside, encrusted like a chrysalis, I was beginning to sense a deep down stirring of the heart, perhaps turning towards a freedom, which up till now had eluded me. This awareness became even clearer when the way I breathed was more fluid and thought no longer a distraction. Thus I was able to begin expanding my horizons; then again however free I tried to be, I still seemed destined to lose my nerve in the face of beauty.

My stringent fear of the opposite sex meant the reality of a relationship with a girl continued to elude me. I couldn't rationalise or take in that this was something that might not be right, because I assumed categorically that I was not worthy of their company. The distance between myself and the ever mysterious, was like looking into an immeasurable desert where the horizon plays tricks on your emotions. The more I reached out the more disillusioned I became. I started to tire of these fantasies that played tricks with my mind and sought comfort elsewhere.

The entrance to the Criterion, or *The Cri* as it was commonly known, was down a narrow passage, which was tucked away unnoticed between the front bar-room of this pub, and a small department store owned by a prominent Cambridge family of the time, called Eden Lilley. The front bar-room, which looked out over a pedestrians-only ally called Market Passage, was mainly taken up with the regular drinkers. These Cambridge locals would use this room for a quiet pint at the end of a working day, or a quick one during a welcome lunch break. It was very much a worker's hangout, rather than anything genteel that might be on offer in the heart of a grand old university town.

Directly at the end of the dark passage, down some shallow steps, through a small poster-covered chamber, where the obligatory cigarette machine stood guard in the shadows, was a much larger room, filled with a scattering of beer-stained tables, benches and well-worn chairs. Here an aftermath of saw dust, between the crevices of grey splintered floorboards, made the scuffed surface seem practically hospitable. This was the meeting place for the hard nutters, motorcycle gangs, the lost and founds, the beats, the poets, disgruntled G.I's, shrouded undergraduates, rock 'n' rollers, and anyone else who found it hard to operate from within the standard journey of leaving school and dying for a living. If a job prospect meant ending up with nothing to gain but a vague feeling that something might be alright in a non distinct future, then this was the place to be.

A long bar took up wall space to the right, which only became noticeable once you were well and truly ensconced inside this paddock for the lean, mean, rough and ready. The overall ambiance that dominated this thriving saloon was the rich musical overtones, made up mostly from the front runners of British blues. Their sounds pounded out from the pulsating belly of a Juke Box tucked squarely against one side of the room..... *There is a house in New Orleans they call the rising sun....*

21

I gravitated towards a friendship with Pete Glass, from hanging out with Emo and Pip, in the hazy mixture of beer, cigarettes and speed permeating the back room of The Criterion. On first meeting Pete's smouldering seemed intimidating, but with time the gentleness underlying his strong image shone through. He was three years my senior, and tough. I had known him from a distance, as an older pupil at my secondary school.

Pete came across as confident about who he was and sure about his place in the world; hard with a soft centre. Being streetwise meant he could knock a punch if that's what the ultimatum required. I couldn't stop myself from being a little in awe, for he seemed uninterested in being a Mod or a Rocker. Nevertheless, his attire had a distinct sense of looking right. He stood in close sync with the rock groups of the time, bands that were on their way to bringing the blues home to roost in the UK.

The whole country seemed to be waking up to this new wave of musical contenders. Groups like the Animals, Yardbirds, The Spencer Davis Group and The Rolling Stones were never out of the charts. Pete stood head to toe in this sound and like Pip he could go that extra yard, because he played the harmonica, or the blues harp, as it was known to those in tow.

I remember sitting with Pete Glass, Emo and Pewee in the shallows of the River Cam, shrinking our newly bought Shrink to fit Levi's. Most people sat in the bath to do that job, but we wanted the world and its oyster see us do it right.

Pete encouraged me to go down to Miller's and buy two LP's by Chuck Berry and Bo Diddley. These two mavericks of the African American folk genre infiltrated the popular culture of the day – their sound may have been geared toward rock 'n' roll, but it was rooted in the Delta. When I got in on the rhythm, I wanted to seek out other true singers who cradled their pain in the blues: Bessie Smith, B.B. King, Howling Wolf and Muddy Waters.

Was I Mod or Rocker, a Beat or a Poet? I wanted to be all this and more, but if the truth be told, underneath this fledgling security I was still just living hand to mouth, in a closed and private place of fear. I sat submerged behind a rakish mask and for the time being seemed to get away with the act. Smoking cigarettes, drinking pints and dabbling with medicines secured from Pip's surreptitious handouts and Auntie Alice's cabinet no doubt helped the charade along.

The main pills that everyone seemed to be taking were called Purple Hearts; these were a mixture of amphetamine and barbiturates. There were others of course such as Black Bombers, French Blues or Dubes, as they were known to me, but basically all came under the same heading, Speed. For the diehards there wasn't, I don't think, any real discriminating between the different tabs being thrown down the gullet. Uppers or downers, leapers or poppers, it didn't matter what they were as long as they pushed back some kind of envelope.

The first pills I ever took in great quantity were the last, because I had a near death experience with them. It was at a party in Cambridge, in some anonymous house heaving with horny teenagers. I found myself lying on a bed with my penis shrivelled up inside my body and my heart racing toward a terrible conclusion. As I lay there the palpitations became so bad that I must have sweated out a gallon of water. Eventually the morning came and I left that frenzied place and the pills far behind. I remember staggering into a daylight that seemed bright and new and saw for the first time in my life, two dogs stuck fast together on a grass verge on the other side of the street.

Pip found it all very amusing. He loved the different shades and colours of the pills that we were buying and selling and looked to me for some kind of backup to his amusement. I obliged by trying to be enthusiastic. It kind of reminded me of swapping cigarette cards in the playground at primary school but with a less innocent twist.

After getting close to being burnt alive in the amphetamine pyre, I withdrew to Adams Road for a few weeks to get to grips with the shock, but the eye of my family made me restless and the urge to go downtown again couldn't be resisted. By now it was clear that I wasn't a pill-head, but I desperately needed something to reassure my lost sense. I had learnt the hard way that getting blocked was not my idea of a good night out and quietly sought a more comfortable way of getting some height without the fallout.

Pete Glass and I fantasised about being like the men, I think they were mostly men, who were drawn to the city during the summer months with nothing more than a blanket roll thrown over their shoulder. In our eyes, these hobos were the real thing not down and outs, but enlightened travellers who really did live outside the system. When I reached the legal school leaving age, I wanted to celebrate in some way and when Pete suggested that we take to the road with a trip to Ibiza, I seized on the idea like a ravenous monk.

We set off on this bohemian trail like two wayward scruffs in search of a dream. I was fifteen years old and full of optimism and hope. Our dress code may have been lax, but we weren't entirely penniless. Pete had saved a bit through his job as an electrician and I had been earning at Scurfield's kitchen shop.

The rough ferry crossing to Calais didn't faze us. I remember throwing up my seasickness on the upper deck, through a running commentary about how travelling with Club Mediterranean was the only way to go, with Pete collapsed on the main deck with laughter.

Our buoyant mood continued right the way through that gastronomic country. Although thumbing a lift in France was totally acceptable then, it wasn't always easy. Sometimes car after car would go by without a bite, and then it became a question of one of us hiding in the grass verge, while the other pretended to be the lone hiker. Whether or not two was a crowd seemed debatable; but it didn't stop one charitable man picking us up and taking us to stay the night in an estranged orphanage, full of lively kids of all walks and sizes, in the middle of tree covered countryside. We were treated as venerated guests and fed accordingly. The morning of our departure came round soon enough, leaving an aftertaste of kindness and a distinct hint of sadness for those young ones who wouldn't make it.

The rest of our time on the road went smoothly, apart from when we thumbed down a huge Citroen van, which stopped too abruptly and was concertinaed by a number of cars piling into the back of it. Disaster, or so we thought; we crept off with the wish of sight unseen and managed to get a ride right into the eastern part of the Pyrenees and Andorra, where there was still a great deal of snow around. We had neither the clothing nor the bedding. I had never been so cold! It was then that I discovered the heat generated by cement from sleeping on cement bags in a shed on a building site.

Then before we knew it we were dropped, as if from the sky, into the middle of the second largest city in Spain. This was a time when long-haired young men were a very rare sight on the continent. Standing out on the ornately tiled streets in Barcelona, we got mobbed by girls and boys alike because of our flowing locks and our well-worn denim jackets and jeans. We played along with their suggestion that we were pop stars. They pulled and prodded with friendly curiosity at our person, questioning our every move, as if we were aliens from another planet.

They all seemed so clean-cut, very precise in their charm and grooming. I think we represented a taste of excitement for what was around their corner. Having snacked out on bread and wine, we wandered the docks, looking for a boat to take us to the stop off island before Ibiza, Mallorca. It all seemed dark and rather foreboding with few people about, except the odd sailor who shouted at us in rapid Spanish when we asked for directions. And then, before we knew it there was the crossing from Barcelona, packed together in a small cabin with a family of Catalonians. We ended up in the lower bunks while the locals, who couldn't settle their sea legs, started throwing up their diced carrots and tomato skins from their allotted beds above us.

Ibiza came and went; drunk on absinth during the day and at night we roughed it, sleeping in a cave partnered by a sack of oranges, which we half hitched from the Market Square in Ibiza town.

Some short time in, our playful friend Penny arrived from England, which saw us getting further into the Spanish allure. She pouted along with the best of them and it was hard not to be drawn into her attractive lure and brooding personality. Penny and I may have had a passionate embrace against the stone wall of a downtown bar, but it was she and Pete who finally took the wedding vows. As their time together became more consuming, I was left traipsing the alleys and rubble of the ancient town on my own, which had a mixed affect on me.

I may have gone to Ibiza with the intention of fulfilling my aspirations as a fully fledged man of the road, but the truth was I didn't have a clue. I sent back a postcard asking my parents to get me off this Hell Island, which much to my dismay was received in a humorous vein. Not that Ibiza was hell; on the contrary it was what was going on inside me that seemed to house those inclinations. But of Ibiza, there were the bullfights, the Absinthe, the dikes from Cape Cod, the nonconformist enclaves, the freshly caught squid, the pans of home-cooked paella and then the sea, the clear crystal blue sea with its riches and endless beauty.

Having hitchhiked back through what must have been somewhere near forty-eight hours of pouring rain, I arrived home in Cambridge, worn out and bleary eyed, determined to keep my head down. Thumbing lifts was not something I was particularly taken to after this mammoth excursion.

On our return to Cambridge, Penny and Pete invited me to be best man at their wedding and I was proud to do so, but as marriage seemed like an extraterrestrial dream to me, I left them to get on with the housekeeping and continued in my own way to search for love.

Some might say that the trip to Ibiza was a blessing in disguise, as it shocked me into realising that I had to do something more responsible with my life, but what the outcome of this significant journey did, was to push that illusive spark still further out of reach. I don't know what I would have done without my parents and their shop.

In spite of the difficulties that went down between us, there were many times when my mum and dad were caught short by their sense of humour. On the rare occasions that they lost the plot, they were like two kids who fell over themselves with laughter. If and when the ironic penny clicked in, my mother simply doubled up at the borderline between salty tears and delirious mirth.

My father's sense of humour, like a lot of us boys, occasionally drifted towards the lavatorial.

George coveted a certain amount of controversy around the shop at two Jesus Lane, but not enough to knock his Cambridge image too out of shape. He favoured his choice of employees to be on the relaxed side. There was one Christmas which had me, Ponji and our Danish friend Jan Bredsdorff helping out; if I have got the year right this was in 1963, which meant the length of our hair became a strong point of contention for a lot of the clientele. Some shoppers were so incensed that they would only be served by George alone. Although this annoyed my father he showed no signs, just took it all in his stride, for there was always a little kickback on the side. He might be serving someone extremely politely one-minute and in the next, go out into the hallway behind the door and release wind; these measures were only ever taken if he felt the customer to be unashamedly snooty or blatantly Conservative.

My father wasn't averse to attractive women holding the fort at Scurfield's. Penny from Ibiza worked there for a time, as did my cousin Margaret Alice who was always done up to the nines, all legs, high heels and eyelashes. Talk about gender, she could bring Jesus Lane to a standstill, especially when she was unpacking a crate of earthenware outside the shop on a sultry summer afternoon; god she was sexy. She and her friend Margaret Fasken lived for some years at number eight and brought a welcome wave of amorous energy to the house. I was a little young to really get the hang of it, but if nothing else, their sumptuous company made me feel less wary of the opposite sex and brought my hungry ears to the attention of Elvis Presley.

No doubt I was still trying to cling to my father's coat tails, for I put in some prolonged and intensive time at the shop when I got back from Spain. Although he seemed positively supportive about this, there was a certain wariness underlying my time there. I don't know why this was, but like most fathers I am sure he wanted what he thought was a better life for his son. While being together offered its rewards, there was always this slight feeling that an explosion could take place if I expressed to strong an opinion of how things should be done around the shop, or if I offered up some political comment that wasn't entirely in line with his. As long as I didn't press the wrong button, watched my mouth and turned in a good performance, everything between us seemed to run smoothly.

George helped me in the moments of spare time between customers, by writing official letters to various theatres throughout the UK, asking if they had a posting for a vagrant like me. To my surprise one of them answered offering me an interview.

I was to meet an artistic director called Donald McKechnie at the Arts Theatre Club near Leicester Square in London. My ever eager parents, who were anxious to see my future as a secure bright star flourish, took me there and practically frog-marched me across Charing Cross Road from the tube station, willing me to get this job. During the interview I told Mr MacKechnie how I had made up my mind that if he didn't give me work, I was going to take off hitchhiking around the world.

Was it my bravado, or a misguided act of kindness, or was he merely taking advantage of my desperation? Either way, he offered me an opening as a student ASM (assistant stage manager) for wages of four pounds a week. George agreed to finance an extra four pounds on top of that, which brought the lifeline total to the grand sum of eight pounds. Donald had got a young worker for a slave wage and my parents were delighted. I was pleased too, but the truth was that the prospect of living so far away from home left me tied up in trepidation; especially as the job was in Barrow in Furness, which as far I was concerned was another galaxy way off the radar.

The caged songbirds fill the air with their sweet music and out on the horizon, the motley crew on board the orange ship sinks without trace, leaving those of us on the shore with the distant sound of another day.
Ibiza 1964

22

I can't really remember if it was months or weeks before I had to leave for that theatrical vocation in the Lancastrian outback, but I do remember thinking how I had better make the most of this short time before it swallowed me up.

It was through Pete Glass that I met a likable guy called Barney Barnes. Barney was the first person I'd crossed paths with who admitted to liking and using heroin, which both intrigued and frightened me in equal measure. He captained a band in which Pete occasionally played the harmonica. Rather than branching out, Barney seemed content to remain on the Cambridgeshire music circuit forever. I went a couple of times to see Pete and *Barney and the Hollering Blues* as they were called, play at a US Air Force Base just outside Cambridge.

Shortly after the trip to Spain, I met up with Barney and Pete at the Criterion for a pint and they introduced me to a sweet couple called Roger Barrett and Libby Gausden. Roger and Libby seemed more like soul mates than lovers. There was something special about being with them when they were together, something which made you feel like you were heading straight down the highway to a field of possibilities.

I became good friends with Libby, when she, Ponji and I went on a memorable trip to Paris together. As well as being extremely pretty, she was delightful company. Warming to a path of humour, she encouraged my comic turns; she was particularly taken by my Frankie Howerd impersonations, which I would throw out to the wind when we were away on our adventures in the French capital.

Roger, who had taken to calling himself Syd, had a shy charismatic persona, which seemed to be contradicted by a natural charm and a mischievous smile. It soon became clear that he loved painting and poetry, and we both shared an interest in theatre. It turned out that he had a Pollock's Toy Theatre which, like me, he'd modified to his own fancy. I'd made a fully functioning Victorian hybrid from an original design very similar to Syds. These made to measure model theatres had lights that dimmed and curtains, hemmed and tucked together by our enthusiastic mothers, which lifted into a made to scale fly-tower. Raising these modified drapes revealed a three-dimensional montage of such magic it could take your breath away. The small beautifully proportioned stage was set with intricate and colourful backdrops and characters. The theatrical sheets of scenery and cast, made of paper, originating in the

1800's *(a penny plain and twopence coloured)*, were pasted on thin cardboard and then cut out. By moving the characters about on wire slides from the wings and working the tableau with voice and subtle lighting, you could bring a dormant picture to life. Despite our age and the apparent cultural shift of the early sixties, Syd and I still found time to go into the imagination of these subtle toys together.

I hadn't really got a handle on Syd's musical flare until I went to see Barney's group playing cover versions of the blues, at the Dorothy Ballroom one night. Much to my surprise Syd was playing lead guitar. His magic was such that for the time he was on stage, he spun a web around the whole room and the local crowd disappeared into that twinkle of music in his eye.

A day or so later, at Syd's suggestion, we met up to go to London in his mum's clapped-out Austin; our aim, to get there by lunchtime. We set off in the morning up a relatively quiet Trumpington Road. Just past the Botanical Gardens we began to gain speed, then, as the car was getting into its stride the bonnet suddenly blasted up and hit the windscreen, leaving us looking into the depths of a black hole. Syd's reaction was to carry on driving. I was about to shit myself, when the force of the wind unhinged the bonnet and it shot over the roof landing somewhere in the road behind us. Grinding to a halt, I rushed back to retrieve the piece of battered carcass and with some makeshift wizardry, we hurriedly tied the injured nose back to the mainframe and shot off like an old-fashioned rocket in a cartoon.

We stopped at a cottage in Haslingfield, a small parish just outside Cambridge, to pick up some amplifying equipment from Rado Klose. I don't think Syd wanted to hang around, but because Rado's family were particularly close friends with my mum and dad, I said yes please when they offered us some tea. Syd's impatience kept poking into the side of my neck, so the tea and cake was cut short. Rado's diligent mum made us some sandwiches for the road. Once we were back in the confines of the old Austin, Syd told me how he knew Rado from school and how they had a mutual interest in music and emphasized what a great guitarist he was. I was thinking, between mouthfuls of bread, how Rado and his three brothers had a natural exuberance and love for life, which always put my overblown machinations into perspective. I explained to Syd that Rado's mum and dad, Helmut and Rita, had known me since being a baby. I always felt comfortable with them, especially with Rado's dad Helmut. When my mum and dad first met Helmut and Rita in 1947, they were living in a bell tent on Madingley Hill, in Cambridge, camped out during one of the coldest winters on record. Helmut joined the International Brigade and fought for human rights in the Spanish civil war. He ended up in a concentration camp in the foothills of the Pyrenees and was cruelly tortured. My dad always said he was the real thing and had great respect for him. Helmut had a rugged, kind character; he was a fastidious carpenter and also worked in the Zoology Laboratory in Cambridge, where, if I was lucky, he would take me to see the terrapins. I engaged Syd's interest further by saying that if ever I was upset when I was little, apart from my mum and dad, Helmut was the only grownup who could bring comfort to my teary, snot-ridden, face. Syd got a kick out that and pushed his foot further down into the floor of the car, bringing us ever closer to his reefer hideaway.

Up till now the only thing I'd inhaled had been cigarettes. Marijuana, had been consumed since before history began; it had been used relatively recently for medicinal and cooking purposes in Europe, but I hadn't come into it. I'd heard that smoking, or if it was preferred eating, the dried leaves of this wild plant could induce a mellow high; completely the reverse of taking amphetamines, which at this point I was certainly never going to do again. Because this simple weed was illegal it was difficult to get hold of, which meant the main purpose of our journey was to go and find some in London. Syd seemed to know the score, for he had contacts at a desperate flat in Tottenham Street, into which he promptly disappeared as soon as we arrived.

I stood patiently on the pavement; waiting for him to come down from god knows what darkness. Just as I began wondering if I should walk away, he seemed to appear from nowhere and presented me with a little paper parcel, of what he told me cheerfully was top quality hashish.

Having stashed our demon prize we collected our thoughts over a pint and then parted company. Syd went back to Cambridge and I went off to seek out Ponji's whereabouts a few blocks down the road.

With the small wedge of Afghani red clutched cautiously in the palm of my sweaty hand, I found my way to Cambridge Circus, where the bonhomie Frenchman from Number Nine, Jean Simone, had fixed up somewhere for my brother to live.

Jean had wangled his way into being an interpreter for the BBC, while Ponji was still working for the market research company run by our cousin Geoffrey; this gave Ponji the time and the financial clout to seek out a place at the London Film School.

When I arrived to stay with my brother in London for the second time in my life, he was settled, as much as he could be settled, in a stealthy centre for the creative, the hip and the stoned.

Squeezed as it was between a perfect Victorian pub and a geriatric hardware store, the entrance to number Two Earlham Street disappeared into the architecture like a rundown opening in a Dickens novel. You could walk past the anonymous door, and you were walking past one those unfurnished maisonettes, plentiful at the time for a token rent, in which anything could be going on.

Once inside, a narrow corridor went directly back from the front door to some stairs that were stripped back to the bare wood. The overcast stairway gave way to a compact landing on the first floor, where Jean Simone, energetic as ever, presided over a small printing press given to churning out pornography and books by Alexander Trocchi, William Burroughs and the like, writers who were banned by conventional bookshops at this time.

Ponji's room, which was adjacent to Anna and John's bedroom on the next landing, was excessively neat in every area, right down to how his toothbrush was placed on the requisite chest of drawers.

Anna and John wore the whole hippie philosophy beautifully. Like a lot of girls from that era, Anna's hair flowed on forever. Open-handed, they were both fair of feature, charismatic, laidback and dressed accordingly. I took a shine to them instantly.

My brother's obsessive neatness was a clear contradiction to the rest of this dwelling place and gave the impression of a man apart. I realise now that Ponji's ability to spawn order in a chaotic environment, stemmed from surviving his time at Number Nine, where he had got into the habit of creating absolute parameters, lest the chaos outside swallowed him up. It was very common in Number Nine, for members of the immediate family to find themselves having to give their bed over to one stranger or another. When my cousin Johnny first got his little bit of money for instance, he immediately went and bought a padlock for his bedroom door. Whenever I spent time with my brother, no matter where he was staying, the door to his room was mostly shut, if not locked. Ponji's habit it seems still needed the disarray to feel at home and to this end, Earlham Street in its small way had become Number Nine and Jean Simone, Auntie Alice.

At the top of the stairs on the third floor at Earlham Street was the bathroom, kitchen, and living room; some short time later this part of the house was knocked into open plan, which then meant taking a bath could be seen by anyone cooking in the kitchen, or for that matter rolling a joint in the living room.

Initially I felt shy of the spirit energy here and sought solace in Ponji's room, where he seemed so focused in what he was doing, so lucid with his intentions. But he and I had changed; I think we must have become more self-conscious about our limitations, either that or the responsibility of being my big brother made him feel uncomfortable. This wasn't to say he didn't want me around, on the contrary he wanted me to stay but on my own terms.

A slight shift in gear was all I needed to find myself in the middle of a house where I became acquainted with friends, who seemed to feel like me about the disorientation in the outside world. But unlike me, they seemed to have the ability to get on with creating a new life from a great range of gifts and colours. It was as if anything could be made, or a job tackled, from a completely fresh and different perspective.

I was so overwhelmed by sliding under the doormat into this new world of cool that I forgot the hash, which I suppose got lost somewhere in the joints that were rolled up from time to time, without much significance, by these inspirational few.

While sitting on the old pine floor in John and Anna's room, partaking in friendly conversation, Jean Simone came and plonked himself down beside me.

There seemed to be no uncertainties in Jean, once he started on a project, no matter how mad, he'd set about it with careless exuberance and wouldn't stop until he got bored; then he'd drop the job immediately and without remorse or hesitation move on to the next. There was no doubt that Jean was generous to a fault, when he had money everyone could eat. He was absolute in his energy, opinions and actions. Without hesitation he told me in his reputable French accent, that I had been an "Absorloot coont" for not allowing him into my tree house when he was living at Number Nine. I felt awkward and fell into my chin, mumbled something about that was then and how it was too complicated to explain. I sat there and breathed in the fusion. He laughed like a cavalier and at some point thrust a joint in my hand. This was the first time that I'd smoked the weed; after some tentative inhalation I felt woozy and digressed backwards into a frisson of paranoia. Not a good start, but as I was to have read to me on numerous occasions later - *perseverance furthers*.

John and Anna helped me to be right at home. We made each other laugh. I felt accepted, but more importantly cool in their company. They really did make me feel as if love was to do with discovery, part of a creative process, without the fixation of a financial price.

We went out to the cinema one afternoon to see a film called *The Train* with Burt Lancaster. Anna's young sister Lisa had come along for the ride. I immediately became infatuated. At first her beauty paralysed my nervous system, but she very quickly put me at ease. Once I got over my initial shyness I got into the swing of things and had her falling about with laughter for the remainder of the day. Her hair was long and dark and she had stardust in her eyes.

London was full of people scurrying along the pavements and I was skating above their heads in the opposite direction, that is, until I got thumped in the stomach on Shaftsbury Avenue by a tattooed oik. After this I became wary, but the temptation to fly was always there and at times irrepressible.

It was never going to be easy, how could it be? One way or another I had been told that I was incapable and would never amount to anything, especially around the structure of the spoken word. So I fell into the 60s like a pea into a pod; well, not quite.

It's like I'm placed in a cylinder made of crystal clear water, where the walls are never ending in thickness; the more I look directly ahead for a way out, the more overpowering the surroundings become, perhaps if I look up.....

The doorbell at Earlham Street rang and Dave Gale who had just arrived back from Ibiza with his girlfriend Maureen came rushing up the stairs. He lay down on the kitchen floor, like Paul Gascoigne did when he scored that goal for England, crying out for the cornflakes he'd been deprived of over the few weeks he'd been away!

My priorities were becoming extremely split between what my parents wanted and what I wanted. I had made the decision to take the job in Barrow, but it felt a long way away from my brother and this pool of new accepting friends in London.

I was to go back and forth to Earlham Street quite a few times over the next decade and witnessed a melting pot of changes, not so much to the building itself, but to the artistic and poetic collaborators that came and went from within its walls. It always remained a strange mixture of obtainable and unobtainable goals. It was a place where lying on the floor all day was acceptable, if that was your bent; but it could also be a house of industrious beavering, a bit like a science laboratory for the artist, where spiritual quest waltzed hand-in-hand with Heath Robinson. It became synonymous for the beginning of psychedelics. The first light shows for the Pink Floyd were put together here, by the ever smiling Peter Wynne Wilson who lived there for a time with his girlfriend Suzy;

like Anna and John, Pete and Suzy were a quintessential couple of the sixties, always ready to make the visitor comfortable with a cup of tea and a joint.

I couldn't avoid the gateway any longer.

I hadn't entered the notion of being an actor yet, but I was already beginning to feel like an out of work one. I was starting to feel like one of those people that they find behind a false wall in the back of a juggernaut lorry between countries. As far as the authorities were concerned I was infiltrating the National space and would always be made to feel I was sponging off the state. In short, I was one of those people who had time on their hands; but with time on my hands....... well perhaps I had a slim chance of breaking through.

By the time I came to make the final move away from Cambridge, Syd was beginning to spend time at Earlham Street. These were halcyon days and he was being as prolific as ever with painting, writing songs and getting his band up and running.

Syd's intoxicating take on my going off to work in the theatre, played a vital part in being able to take that first step towards the train. He took me down to Jimmy's in Frith Street, where we stocked up on free bread and ate Greek stew for a few pence. During the meal he made his intrigue for the illusion created by the actor ever more apparent. Theatre he said is true art. He spelt out that what I was doing was completely the right thing and would ultimately be a great adventure. I wasn't sure if I shared his buoyancy, or his belief, but by encouraging me to feel better about the path I had chosen, he spurred me on to find a new kind of home up there in the North of England.

Starry-eyed an' laughing as i recall when we were caught
Trapped by no track of hours for they hanged suspended
As we listened one last time an' we watched with one last look
Spellbound an' swallowed 'til the tolling ended
Tolling for the aching ones whose wounds cannot be nursed
For the countless confused, accused, misused, strung-out ones an' worse
An' for every hung-up person in the whole wide universe
An' we gazed upon the chimes of freedom flashing.

Bob Dylan

23

1964 saw the first Habitat store open in Chelsea; Nelson Mandela is sentenced to life imprisonment in South Africa; thousands upon thousands of troops were sent into Vietnam to knock out the Red Peril; plans for The World Trade Centre are announced and a record breaking seventy three million viewers tuned in to watch the Beatles on the Ed Sullivan show. Television is still broadcast in black and white and BBC 2 is to make its first screenings, giving the viewers a record breaking three channels. The Labour Party wins the election by a narrow victory, ending 13 years of Conservative rule and Harold Wilson becomes Prime Minister.

My frazzled brain was spinning off in all its sixteen year old directions, every which way but here! The further out into the world I went, the fiercer the cold. Like rivulets of water running their course on a frantic journey toward winter, my mind began to freeze up inside until eventually it became difficult to see any logic at all. My intuition was telling me I should break the ice, try to dissolve it, melt it any way I can, but I just couldn't get a handle on how.

Barrow-in-Furness might just as well have been on the other side of the moon; to get there in those days you had to travel to Crewe and spend the night on a desolate station bench before venturing further north the next day.

Time on the train gave me a lot of space to reflect, which I hadn't had in ages, if ever. I started to become more aware of just how lost I really was. Somehow my state of affairs just didn't add up. Staring out into the middle distance I started looking for that elusive logic.

The old fashioned railway carriages, the ones with a corridor and compartments where watercolour paintings of quaint holiday locations were framed in unison above the plush seats, heaved their way up to Cumbria and came to a grinding halt. For a moment, it seemed like I was the only passenger in the whole world. I caught myself and managed to push the journey into some kind of proportional perspective.

Cambridge had left me with a bitter and sweet pill to swallow. I may have felt engulfed by a void of invisible fears, but that prestigious university town where I was brought up, had gotten smaller, and in retrospect was beginning to seem like a trap, where the intellect weaves a web to catch the fly. Where my family fitted into all this remained a quandary; after all weren't they seated at the head of the table with the other demigods of Cambridge?

When I ended up with my own company, I was constantly thrown back into a state of mind which left me with a "why should I bother and what's the point" syndrome. So much energy, so much grief, all for some illusory concept, just words, signifying, much ado about nothing.

There weren't any hideaways anymore unless you count sleeping and drug taking as a way of hiding, which my commonsense was still together enough to tell me was a physiological short term solution to a long-term problem.

Eventually we began to weave our way along the coast at a Sunday pace. The weight of my thoughts filled me with eternity and pushed me into a heavy sleep.

Inevitably the train arrived at its destination but I didn't. The daze of the trip, along with an acute sense of tiredness, had me traipsing the wet grey cobbled streets of Barrow in bewilderment. The back to back housing grew severe in prospect. As I began to wonder what the fuck I was doing there the theatre loomed into sight. Built as it was in red brick, it seemed to stand alone on land that wasn't too far away from being like a bomb sight.

The only door open from the outside of the theatre led down to an old scene dock, where Bob Dylan's *Chimes of Freedom* was filling the silence. The troubadour's voice was coming from a battered radio hanging among sawdust covered cobwebs, above a tidy tool bench, which was placed squarely against a heavily painted wall, chipped and worn from years of use. On first glance the rest of this space, which was full of ghosts from past productions, seemed chaotic, but gradually my practical eye brought it into some focus. The old canvas flats from previous shows were stacked according to size against one wall, while an enormous rostrum heaving with pillars and props another. Almost as an afterthought, a mortise machine, a lathe and some well-used hand tools sat, ready for work, near the wide double doors that gave the only opening to the daylight outside.

Because it was a Sunday most of Barrow had taken the day off, but when an elderly man walked through the false door, etched with precision by the scenic painter, in the centre of this muddled space, and said "How do", I knew the theatre hadn't.

Without a by your leave, he told me to put my stuff down in the corner and come and help him lift a huge wooden frame, called a flat, which he had just finished canvassing.

Later I got digs for four pounds a week, which left me the rest of my money to spend on food, cigarettes and beer, and that was it really, my introduction to the theatre and the stage carpenter Mr Jack Pearson.

~

I had to make a monumental effort to disguise what was going on inside my skull. I did this for the most part in mendacious ways. When I found myself in social situations challenging to my abilities, I started to lie my way through them like a rabid explorer hacking his way through a wild jungle.

What happened on the first day is a blur, all I can remember is that I took myself in hand and navigated the occasion with the social niceties at my disposal. I felt like an orphan at a wedding as I sat in the circle for the introductions of welcome, given with shy aplomb by Donald MacKechnie. After the read through we had tea and the actors as I remember were not hugely forthcoming. I would have to work hard to win their respect. I felt relieved that I'd made the first hurdle.

Once the rehearsals proper were under way, I was allotted my slot for the next fortnight. The first play *Meet Me by Moonlight* gave me and the other first-timer Jinni Steel, an easy ride; we were merely sent out to scrounge around the town for props, which meant we got to know each other quite quickly.

Apart from some damp fumbling among the wild grasses on Granchester Meadows in Cambridge, and some self-conscious French kissing tricked along by a glass or two of the strongest cider known to man on the dance floor of The Dorothy Ballroom, I was basically still a virgin. So Jinni's blonde hair and full lips kept this hungry horse wild for his oats. She was friendly enough, but there was always an underlying feeling of mistrust between us. When the night finally came tumbling in, the bed on the set remained empty - she was prim and proper and I was lost and found.

The play had no sooner opened and the company was rehearsing the next, which in this case was a farce, *One For The Pot*. Jinni and I were thrown in at the deep end on this one. Along with the other ASM's of the day, we had walk-on parts. This was nerve wracking fun, but as the stage struck me dumb I don't think I quite lived up to the occasion, so I was glad when I was back in the workshop for the next production.

Jack Pearson was a retired shipbuilder, a stocky, grey-haired Lancastrian, with dry probability in his wit, who took me under his wing. This was really when I began to take the first step toward some kind of genuine professional confidence. He taught me with great patience everything about building sets, getting things going fast and finished the quick way; for this was fortnightly rep, which meant plays were put on during a season every two weeks.

Having initially felt closed out by the main actors, the armour gradually fell away and we became more relaxed in each other's company.

James Hayes and I started out as walking companions. Softly spoken, with a strong sense of purpose, he told me of his earthy upbringing in Limerick. I got to love his keen Irish sense as we tramped the city hunting out props and cheap places to eat. One day he started to tell me how he didn't want to stay locked in as an assistant stage manager, because he had his heart set on acting. There was something conclusive in the way he put across his love for the art that made me immediately think of my mother and I started to feel extremely homesick.

I just didn't have the sense of clarity that James seemed to have and I became jealous. I wanted the classical strength he had for theatre, the clarity with words, of being able to put them on the plate of the character and hand them to the audience with no shame. But I had to settle for the lot I'd been given. James had sown the seeds though and from here I really started to covet the airs and graces of a professional actor.

Looking back I was sixteen years, going on four. God help us, a four-year old in a giant's body, who'd made up his mind to gain his family's respect by becoming a star of the stage.

The legitimate ASM's had all been to drama school and working in stage management was their permit into acting. The very thought of going back to a school, even if it was a drama one, sent cataclysms of horrors through me, so that was out of the question. The only choice as I saw it was to infiltrate the work-front taking in as much as I could about this intangible art.

One of the main jobs for an assistant stage manager was to sit in on rehearsals and take notes for the director, making sure that all the props needed for the next production were listed and collected.

Having to follow the play for prompting, with so little time at hand, was excruciating and made me read and reread the text before rehearsals started, learning the words phonetically, as best I could like a parrot. Then, praying that I wouldn't get caught out on the day and that the nervous sweating would go unnoticed, come across as a spontaneous sight reader.

Once the play is up and running the ASM who is prompting (or to give it the theatrical vernacular 'on the book'), has to make sure that all the props at the beginning of the show are in place and ready. When I was 'on the book' for a production of *Private Lives,* I made the mistake of not checking the prop list thoroughly enough and left out the cigarette lighter, an absolute essential for the player to do their tuxedo piece. If a minor catastrophe like this happened it was customary, after the curtain had come down, to go to the leading lady and then the leading man and apologise, which I dutifully did. To my utter embarrassment they made me go down on one knee and bow my head and ask for forgiveness. After much reprimanding on their part, I was allowed to walk out of the dressing room backwards as if leaving royalty! This made me acutely aware of how deeply unpleasant some actor's power games could be and I hated it.

It sounds like I'm talking big company, but it wasn't. At any one time during the first season there were no more than six main actors. Donald had to box clever with the budget and brought stage staff into the company, those who could act, to fill out the gaps.

The turnaround from one show to the next would often leave the stage crew with prolonged periods without sleep, and by the time the first night of *Dinner with the Family* came along, most of us had been awake for 24 hours. I was working with the designer, who, as the pressure mounted for the opening, ended up like all of stage management doing every kind of job. We were getting ready to let the French windows in from the fly tower. Such was my tiredness that his spindly character and manic disposition tickled the heart of my funny bone. That we were both in the fly gallery was tempting fate, particularly on an intense first night like this. Because this main flat was so heavy it was suspended by two separate ropes; the designer had landed up in charge of one rope and yours truly was in command of the other. The green light came on and fraught with our sense of responsibility we released the breaks. The oncoming exhaustion got the better of me. The sight of my colleague struggling

156

with his load gave me uncontrollable giggles and the rope holding this monstrous weight began to slip from my hands. In an out of body moment, I could see the far sides of the gothic windows jerking towards a lopsided catastrophe and started to hear what I thought were gasps from the auditorium. My friend the designer became furious, which made the hysterical weakness much worse. Just when I thought of letting go altogether, a hot and fuming Donald MacKechnie, who had rushed round from the auditorium in the nick of time, appeared out of no-where, jammed the break and rescued me and the blithely unaware actors down on the stage from a horrendous calamity.

At some point the company put on the compulsory Shakespeare play, in this case the Scottish one and Roger Forbes was brought in for role of the main man. As far as I was concerned Roger cracked the ice. He was an actor's actor, decked out with a cravat and double breasted blazer, a charming compulsive gambler, who liked nothing better than chatting up the clients and spending his wages at the bookies.

As his days were spent in the theatre, he had no time to get into town. Very early on in rehearsals Roger surreptitiously took me to one side and put five shillings in my hand, then he asked me to place it on a particular horse running in the three-thirty.

Inside the betting office the whole business of filling in the form got the better of me, the name of the horse escaped my rattled brain and I lost my nerve.

When I came back empty-handed, Roger was a little flummoxed and said he would personally take me to the bookies and show me how it all worked. These occasional outings for a flutter got across to me that the theatre wasn't the be all and end all of our existence. With Roger there was more to life than treading the boards and it was very important he felt, to have a laugh.

In the year and a half at Barrow, with much determination, partnered by a great deal of guesswork, I worked my way up from the humble beginnings of a student ASM to a fully fledged stage manager. Saddled in there, were occasional forays into acting. In the end I was being paid properly. I even managed to save some money, and the work realised an equity card.

I made two professional mistakes that stand out now, one not so bad and the other one nearly catastrophic. Whereas in Cambridge I pretty much felt that I was making mistakes all the time. What Donald

MacKechnie did by giving me a break, was what my schooling had never done – lift me out of a constant fear of failing.

I had become the acceptable and slightly unpredictable stage manager of the day.

Theatre as far as I could see, had to be run on the principle that what the people wanted the people got. As with many other theatres throughout the British Isles then, an enormous amount of compromise had to be made. These were desperate times for an institution which depended on an audience that was beginning to get what they wanted, by way of entertainment, from the box in their living room. Ornate repertory theatres like Her Majesty's in Barrow were on the brink of closure, or opening their doors to daily rounds of bingo. This meant trying to find ways of pleasing the audience, by putting on plays that had that common denominator. Occasionally something would happen whereby the speed and time of a distinctly limited rehearsal period, whipped up a spontaneously rapturous show that would have the audience completely captivated.

A wonderfully surreal adaptation of *David Copperfield* and a light hearted Christmas production of *Pinocchio*, among a few others, lifted me as an audience beyond the stars. These were moments when the conjurer brought together the ingredients to leave a lasting impression.

No doubt Barrow had been a learning curve, but even with the unequivocal moments of enchantment, my feelings of insecurity were paramount in undermining a lot of my time there. It seemed to me that fear ruled the roost. I dare say this wasn't helped by the artistic director flaring up like a minor tyrant at regular intervals if the play wasn't working to his order. He would often reach an explosive boiling point, during the technical or dress rehearsal, and let off steam by lambasting stage management, or some of the lesser actors; a charade within a charade, highlighting the fortnightly turnaround.

This apprenticeship may have given me an opportunity to prove to myself and the world that I had more than a few bells and whistles at my disposal. However, the manic resolve, which I needed to keep up a reasonable front, blinded me to the result. Because of this I never really appreciated what I could do, or really took on board the company I was working with. I felt most at home in the bar after the show, regaling the actors and mixing with the locals, where I became the reigning champion for drinking a yard of ale. Little did I realise how much of this creative work-time at this theatre had actually gone in; a lucky trait that seemed to accompany me on my continuing journey into the ether. On the back of my reputation at Her Majesty's Theatre in Barrow, I was offered a job as stage manager at the Library Theatre in Manchester, and turned it down. Despite these winnings, the thought of continuing with full on responsibility behind the scenery wasn't where I wanted to go. I suppose I had the excuse of my age, after all I had only just passed the threshold of my eighteenth year – anyway, I'd made up my mind about wanting to act hadn't I? Or was it that I yearned for something unobtainable here, something which wasn't second-hand, in a new and undisclosed world.

She looked so steadfastly at me: with a kind of doubt, or pity, or suspense in her affection: that I summoned the stronger determination to show her a perfectly cheerful face.
Charles Dickens (David Copperfield)

24

When I left for Barrow George and Cecilia were still living in Cambridge. Having been dominated for too long by the head-wise environment, Auntie Alice and the house next door, they decided enough was enough. By the time of my return from Barrow, a year and half later, they had sold number eight and moved lock and stock to an exquisite hideaway in a place called North Creake in Norfolk. The decision to move was made without my knowing much about their plans, so it was hard not feel squeezed out of the equation. I spent some few weeks at their cottage, which seemed small when compared with number eight; or had I just grown too big for the boots – either way, it wasn't long before I felt compelled to move on.

I landed up in Paris, with the intention of staying with my oldest sister Elizabeth. My thinking was that I would get closer to her and perhaps find a niche for myself in France. Believing that my sister had well and truly established herself as a dancer, I arrived full of sanguine hope.

She was working nights in a musical at Theatre du Chatelet and it was great to see her down on the stage performing in harmony with the rest of her shipmates. I always loved to see Elizabeth dance and as far as my limited experience could see, with great flare. I was full of pride and excitement when I went round after the show, to meet her and friends, who welcomed me into their colourful circle as if I was one of them.

After she had changed we went to eat in some great restaurant, where all would embrace her with hugs and kisses before laying on a tantalising spread.

Visiting restaurants was a frequent and vital part of Elizabeth's clockwork; a gastronomic escapade to make her life more acceptable. As she saw it, eating out was the celebratory reward for being alive.

She smoked Gaulloises akin to a trooper and spoke French like a native Parisian from the rough side and fitted right in. Wherever she went in this wondrously kept metropolis, she seemed to have an intimate connection.

Sometimes the talking after these meals would go on well into the early hours and we'd finish off by walking through the scrubbed cobbled streets to the markets, which in those days were in Les Halles. The workers that knew her there called her Babette and gave her anything she wanted from the fresh produce, which was brought in during the night in readiness for the city on the following day, for free.

We would end the hours of darkness by having onion soup in a small distinctively French bar in the market, where it was cooked for the beret brigade and tasted as delicious as anything you can imagine. Having knocked back their breakfast Cognacs the stall holders would go back to work, leaving us to retire to our beds and sleep it off until the afternoon.

Once I got used to the lay of the land, I found my way back to Les Halles on my own, where I would seek out company among the array of prostitutes, who hung on my every gesture, in the doorways of this theatrical place. Each house of disrepute seemed brimming with different ages, different weights different styles. As far as output was concerned, there was just about any kind of taste accounted for and all done and sold, with the know-how of a skilful sales person. I was too scared to ever make the move and I think after a while they realised I just wanted companionship. They seemed obliging and even went as far as having a laugh and the occasional cup of coffee with me, as they helped with my abortive attempts to push my French into a more colloquial regime.

In France, at this time, a place for a beer and chat with friends was the complete opposite of the same kind of establishment in the UK -there was usually good food if you wanted it; no uptight laws deciding if you were young or old enough; no debauchery or "Time Gentlemen Please". Everyone and their uncle, from les enfant, to le bourgeoisie, from music, to Babyfoot (table football), from pinball, to cancan dancers, from gigolos to farmers; anyone could hang out in the bars of Paris, if they chose to do so and with absolute impunity.

Elizabeth was sharing a flat with a folk trio called *Les Enfant Terrible*, who could rock most groups of this kind I'd heard, in my limited incarnation, out of the water. It was through one of the singers that I was introduced to a way of life in the Paris bars.

The baby of the group Jean, a handsome dark figure with the Gitan nonchalantly held at the corner of his mouth, taught me to hang out in French fashion. I became a champion pinball player, learnt to play Babyfoot and began to see that I could entertain and communicate with the locals, in spite of being a verbal disaster.

As I became more accustomed to this new way of life in Paris, I began to see that those closest to my sister had to pay a price of some emotional kind. If it wasn't one of the dancers, it was a flatmate who had done something untoward which led to the falling out. Good mates found themselves involved in such a way that it was hard for them not to feel they had fallen into a trap.

With the ongoing domestic complications between my sister and her friends flaring up with increasing regularity, the atmosphere, especially after a boozy night, was steadily degenerating. Elizabeth would usually end up at the centre of some domestic wrangling concerning the cleaning, or a non-payment of one bill or another.

With some sadness, brought about by these heated exchanges, Elizabeth convinced me that we needed a more upmarket lifestyle. After some in-depth talks she decided it would be a well deserved wheeze if we looked for another apartment. My savings from Barrow were all but used up, which meant this change in our living arrangements pivoted on my asking George if he could help me out, until I got settled into some kind of work here.

With a bit of assistance from my dad, we ended up living in something far beyond our means, furnished with seriously ornate Regency furniture, round the corner from the Arc de Triomphe in the Rue de Tilset.

Things marked out well for a while. Elizabeth went out of her way to demonstrate to me that a life in France would work out as it should. I didn't see the picture quite as rosily. With her knees beginning to give in, dancing was becoming more and more of a hurdle, which meant less work. She never gave up scheming and dreaming. If it wasn't going to be dancing there was always something else in the pipeline; playing guitar, singing, or even acting.

When we got down to the nitty-gritty, usually late at night after a meal, the bitter cards she'd been dealt by the family would inevitably emerge. The encroaching dawn began to leave these endless discussions with a feeling of despair in the air, which was beginning to seem insurmountable. Along with her increasing difficulties and my missing earnings, the lack of money tightened the strain between us. I was beginning to think that the questions that were clamouring to get through my door were not really being asked or answered here. I continued in the back of my mind in vain expectation.

Elizabeth managed to arrange some interviews for me with a couple of people she knew in the film industry. My sister believed in my abilities enough to set up a meeting with a French stunt coordinator in a bar. I felt this was more for his fancying Elizabeth, rather than any stagecraft I might come up with. I was a good enough actor to put it across at the opening like a Frenchman; "Oui je parle français, absolument". Unbelievably, he introduced me to the director of a film he was working on, who much to my surprise agreed to give me a job; that's as far as it went though. My French, or rather lack of it, let me down at the seventh hour. With me nodding and saying yes at inappropriate junctures, I found myself unable to take in the bulk of instruction, and the scene I was in fell apart. The reality being that I was hardly in command of my native tongue let alone that of another country.

Due to my appalling language deficiencies the director, spitting brimstone and fury, asked me not to come back. I was generously paid a fee, but the outcome left me thinking yet again about what I wanted, or more importantly needed, in terms of a social interface. It now seemed certain that getting some sort of job in France was a pipe dream.

During this interim period, I slunk back into the now familiar heap and ended up hanging around bars on my own, and going to watch films for long periods of the day at small distinct picture houses, scattered about the city, called the Cinematheque.

The Cinematheque in Paris at the time was great value, in that you could spend as long as you liked, a whole day if necessary, watching films of a selected genre for one franc. One day it would be all Hitchcock films the next Buster Keaton and so on – the French just went that extra mile with cinema.

In everyday life Elizabeth was a soldier through and through. She'd go to the bottom of the pit swim around, climb out and start again. However, as an artist she found this very difficult to do. There is no doubt that her aptitude was such that she could have done virtually anything and been very successful, but lack of self-belief and her need for approval were so strong they constantly gunned her down.

The reality of making a genuine creative statement means having the guts to stand up and be counted, to be prepared to fail, to stand up in public fall and stand again. As I came to know only to well, the roller coaster of acceptance and non-acceptance was Elizabeth's stumbling block. She just didn't have the wherewithal to see that key opinions made by others were part and parcel of the artistic way. Very little in terms of artistic endeavour seemed to work out for her and they certainly never seemed quite right in the eyes of the family. We were so often uncomfortable with her artistic expression, her chutzpah, her honesty. This had a huge impact on how she felt about herself as a performer. I know now exactly what she must've been going through, especially in regards to feeling confident about what she could or couldn't do in front of an audience, but back then I hadn't got a clue.

The places where she lived turned into treasure troves, which mirrored her abundant personality. Without spending much money she could bring a derelict house round to an Aladdin's cave of cosiness. She knew how to make a party when there was nothing to celebrate; she always loved the ritual of mealtimes particularly in a good restaurant. Then there was that certain something inside her that wanted more and it was this something that always seemed to bring her down into a dysfunctional mire of despair. I started to feel as if I were in the same ditch and in the cold light of day, I probably was, but I couldn't do anything about that at the time. I wanted with all my heart to help her, but I just didn't know how. It was hard not to feel that by staying with Elizabeth, I would find myself sliding into a pit of impossibilities and I began thinking that the only way out, was for me to leave.

The excuse I needed came rapping at the door in the guise of Dave Gilmour, Willie Wilson and Rick Wills, the trio who made up the bulk of Dave's group The Jokers Wild. They were back in Paris, after a small tour down in Spain, looking for gigs and seeking out my company.

Elizabeth and her singer/dancer friend Mattie introduced Dave to a few people who might help him, in exchange, his group agreed to work a couple of sessions with Mattie. Her rendition of *Sugar in the Morning* sung through a sad hung-over demise wasn't quite what they were expecting. In spite of their different styles, they came up with some passable recordings. What the Joker's Wild did was make the blues rock, which meant they were playing where Elizabeth and her continental friends didn't really want to go.

Although café society in Paris was brimming with music and art at this time, it tended to lean toward a folksy, more romantic idiom. This didn't mean the poetry wasn't strong and gutsy; Juliette Greco, Jacques Brel, Georges Brassens and even the late Edith Piaf, were still the muse for many writers and artists on the left bank; they held the key. Jazz was very acceptable, but Rock 'n' Roll, in the developing sense, was perhaps considered to be a little crass, cheap even.

Despite numerous attempts to find places to play, the gigs weren't exactly forthcoming for Dave's group, which meant we had time on our hands to hang out together and have a laugh.

My asking complete strangers in the Paris streets if they'd seen Gill, an imaginary character I dreamed up for the occasion, had passersby going out of their way to help. "M'excuser vous ont vue Gill?" excuse me saw you Gill? "Qui?" "Gill, he's a big man who plays the saxophone and eats cat's tails for breakfast". "Un grand homme a tenu l'extérieur la porte de magasin, là-bas". "Qui?" My surreal attempts to converse with adorably proud Frenchmen, who didn't like to lose face by not helping out, saw some dandies literally taking me by the hand to show me where they had last seen him. As I got deeper into the thicket of this primitive form of street theatre, Rick and Willie would follow a few safe paces behind and inevitably ended up with tears of laughter cleaning their cheeks.

It was clear that I needed a break from Elizabeth to think things through, to see if I really could continue the domestic way of life we were pertaining to. She didn't like this idea at all and became really annoyed when I moved away for a few nights to some sleazy hotel room, which Dave had rented to accommodate the band. Here was one small space for four bodies, where the moth eaten carpets and rickety armchairs were used as makeshift beds.

Dave spoke fluent French and played Baby-Foot like a demon. He certainly looked the part. With his rock star features and long hair, the select night clubs just simply opened their doors to us.

The Birdcage was one such place where we would sit in luxurious leather comfort, soak up the exclusive atmosphere and enjoy the comings and goings of some of the popular artists of the day. Each member had their own bottle of whisky labelled with their name, which was taken down, when they were in town, from neat dark shelves under the stairs and drunk at appropriately lit tables.

Occasionally I would end up going to the Birdcage on my own, but the only way to get in if you didn't have the clout was as a guest. So early on I used to wait outside until some kind-hearted night diver came along.

It didn't take long before I became a regular who could flip the coin into the jar with the rest. I was beginning to see that by going out on a limb, I could get attention and bring whoever was in this club to see humour in the tale. On form I felt as if I was the main attraction and my fifteen minutes as The Birdcage mascot came easy. Adlibbing with imaginary boss-men who would tan my hide for misbehaving, had me pirouetting across the furniture like a flash and asking the punters, those who were willing that is, to save me from the devil's claws. This kind of improvised act, or rather spontaneous emotional explosions stemming from the surrounding inhibitions, had me gaining some sort of solid ground as a performer. It also meant the misfit inside the confines of my body could take a backseat for the day. It wasn't my job to entertain so I didn't feel obliged to indulge the clientele too much, or the staff for that matter. I could be as risqué as I liked. Inadvertently I had stumbled on the key that makes the audience lap it up all the more.

The girl standing at the bar seemed to be focusing her attention toward my table, which made me feel a trifle uncomfortable, for she was beautiful in a Jean Shrimpton kind of way. When I looked away, I could still feel her eyes focused on where I was sitting. Eventually she came over and asked me if she knew me. I held on to my seat, my beer and managed to remain cool, then said "I don't think so". I was to say the least flushed to the core by her interest. She sat down opposite and offered to buy me a drink. It was as if an angel from heaven had fallen into my lap. It turned out that she was with a friend who was sitting at a table near the bar. I couldn't really work out whether they were together because, as soon she sat down with me, he walked out without her. A few minutes passed and she asked me if I should like to come back with her to the hotel. Inside my heart was racing a million to one, outwardly I took it all in my stride and decided in my foggy vanity that what was right for her was good for me and accepted her invitation.

I had reached a state of obsession, in terms of making my persona into a mask. No matter how extreme the social intimacy, it was vital that I didn't let this facade slip lest the truth be seen.

After we arrived at the hotel, she took me up to a luxurious suite and then she left, leaving me a little bewildered with her friend from the bar, one Ramses Shaffy. I found out later that Ramses was a folk hero in Holland, who had lifted the Dutch image to a more flamboyant place with his hit songs, but at 18 years old I didn't know him from Adam.

Ramses was charismatic and gentle in manner, which made me feel relaxed in his company. We drank whisky and talked into the evening.

Some few hours later he casually asked if I wanted to take a bath. I may have felt a little perplexed at this suggestion, paranoid even, but the drink had taken the wind out of any anxiety and the thought of a good soak sounded good, so I said why not.

As the bath was filling he set up a little table next to the tub with a briar pipe and a small box of hashish. He brought me a robe and started to take on an almost servant like role. I got into the bath and was somewhat taken aback when, after a few minutes, he decided to get in with me. Despite some vague nervous disposition hitting in, I felt compelled to go along for the ride and sat opposite him, a little tipsy no doubt, with a bemused expression about my face.

He lit the pipe, which was lock-stock full of pure hundred percent Afghan red and handed it over to me. My sense of wanting to lose myself and not be seen as a spoiler took over. I consumed two huge puffs and, as what often happens after inhaling a bucket full of hash smoke, gravity began to take control of the senses, then my body and the water became inseparable.

After some stoned time I think he could sense that I had become as one with the bathwater. I was aware of this man at the tap-end of the tub trying to warn me, but I couldn't respond and when he pulled the plug there was an overwhelming sensation of being sucked down the plughole, a liquid mass.

With a distinct feeling of being left behind in some distant drain, I managed to pull myself out of the vacuous tub in a dignified manner. Dripping wet, I fell further into a stoned and captivated spell. I allowed Ramses to dry me down with a towel, in such a respectful way, I felt as if I were a prince with his butler. With a discreet bow, familiar to those who have staff, he ushered me out of the bathroom towards the bedroom. Finally, as I stood before the empty bed, the penny dropped, and I went ballistic. I started crying out for mercy, weeping, sobbing, and pleading for anything, for the fire brigade, for the police. Falling to the floor and desperately fawning at his feet, I begged him to forgive me; "I'm sorry. Please, I am in the wrong place, I've made a terrible mistake". He must have felt dreadful, because as far as he was concerned I was doing fine until this emotional vomit suddenly burst into the room. A few seconds of silence elapsed, by which time I felt ill. I stood up, made one last attempt at a bid for rescue, "hall for an amalance", reeled around a few times, with the room and Ramses in tow, and then collapsed.

Having passed out on the bed, I didn't wake until late the following day. Nothing was mentioned of the previous night, though it still howled insistently, like a distant cat, crying out from the back alleys of my mind. Ramses showed a lot of concern for my wellbeing and that afternoon took me to the finest oyster bar in Paris, where I was introduced to the French king of rock'n'roll Johnny Halliday. During those few short minutes of introduction Halliday, for the hell of it, broke ground rules by taking up a pile of plates and started hurling them with precise energy, one after the other, down the central corridor between the tables. Having made his point, he left with the feeling that he could tear the place apart and still be treated as a god.

Back on dry land, I went to support Dave, Rick and Willie who were playing one of the few gigs they had put together in that sumptuous city.

I couldn't pluck a harp to save my life, but I loved what music did and when it came to the sound I wanted them to rip the place apart. As the band started to really get down into the music so did I. The temperature rose and I felt compelled to fire up the dance floor. Those aloof Parisians moved in, jiving, jumping, writhing; and then the band really took flight.

When in-between sets I heard the Who's *My Generation* for the first time, blasting out from the in-house sound system, the depth and breadth of their music got into my gut and tore my feet even further from the ground.

After the gig the boys took me to a club, where cages, full of half naked ladies gyrating to the music, hung precariously from the ceiling. The whole place was seething with slight, gorgeous girls, dancing and making time together. They seemed very friendly and wanted to smooch at the drop of a hat. One gorgeous starlet took me by the hand. We started to glide together and before I knew it she fell into my face. Just before I got too carried away Dave called me over to a table, where Herman, of Herman's Hermits was eating a breakfast plate of egg sausages and chips, and informed me, with a wry smile, that practically every girl in this club was a hermaphrodite.

After a few more nights of camping out between chairs in the tiny hotel room with Dave, Willie and Rick, I decided it was time to go back to Elizabeth and tell her about my next move.

I desperately wanted female company, but if ever this vulnerable occasion really presented itself I fell apart at the seams. I put up a laissez-faire appearance, but felt utterly unworthy of their intimacy. I saw this vulnerability as a weakness and semiconsciously began to put the girls in my life in an untouchable space. If I caught the eyes of platonic beauty, it was as if I were trespassing upon hallowed ground. By the time I added everything up, any real involvement with the opposite sex made me feel as if I had committed some kind of terrible crime.

Despite the free thinking ethos thrown around in our family, there were no coming of age talks; the little I'd learnt about sex was from snippets of smutty talk in the playground. At the dawn of my puberty I started having rampant wet dreams, which usually concluded in the naked presence of my mother. One day, over this furtive period, my mother stopped me on the stairs at number eight and said sharply "Matthew if you must masturbate please use a handkerchief". As an afterthought she threw in with a little less abruptness, "as it makes added work for the laundry basket". The dichotomy, of this distinctly erotic climax, nearly destroyed me with heinous guilt.

Having a girlfriend during those formative years in Cambridge, became a complicated task. If it wasn't frowned on, it was so open to ridicule. Even at this time in Paris, I still felt the natural curve of female friendship to be utterly out of bounds. After so many years in the wilderness I was dying for the caress of a lover.

There was no doubt that the underlying nature running between Elizabeth and me, was bordering on being incestuous. I never talked about this, occasionally she would joke about it however and wasn't that far away from making serious suggestions. For a moment there it seemed a tempting proposition. I wasn't her full brother, maybe we could even ignore the blood tie and as I hadn't come close to being comfortable with the bosom of a woman, I was dying to leap in.

We held the mirror up to each other and although she was a good nine years older than me there were many similarities, especially in the way our paths were mapped out. Looking into Elizabeth's eyes was like looking deep into a well, where the surface of water is far down in a dark place. As I become accustomed to the space, the image gazes back a clearer reflection and I sit with disbelief and extreme discomfort at what I see.

I could no longer cope with my sister's incessant need for fetching, carrying, nursemaid, and general helper. The only way out as I saw it then was to walk away, leaving her with an enormous amount of anguish and anger. In hindsight I see that she wanted a man in her life, more like a father. Inevitably this role I did my level best to fulfil was impossible. The reality of being her younger brother got lost somewhere in the maze.

Her sense of rejection screamed out at me when I came to say my goodbyes. Feeling that she would never forgive me, I left abruptly and hitchhiked back to England.

I knew exactly where I had to go and what I wanted to do.

25

Turn off your mind, relax and float downstream,
It is not dying, it is not dying
Lay down all thoughts, surrendered to the void,
It is shining, it is shining.
Yet you may see you the meaning of within
It is being, it is being
Love is all and love is everyone
It is knowing, it is knowing
And ignorance and hate mourn the dead
It is believing, it is believing
But listen to the colour of your dreams
It is not leaving, it is not leaving
So play the game existence to the end
Of the beginning, of the beginning   (Lennon & McCartney)

It could be said that this was God's grace, but at the time the name of God hadn't knowingly entered the universe I was in. Nevertheless the true sense of well-being I was to rediscover, over the next crucial years, often seemed to swathe me with a holistic sense, a sense perhaps of soulful worth.

It was 1966. The Beatles are more popular than Jesus Christ. The war in Vietnam rages on. Against death threats and extreme violence Martin Luther King leads a civil rights march in Chicago, where they are met by screaming white throngs hurling bottles and rocks. Bob Dylan is booed at the Free Trade Hall in Manchester for playing with an electric band. The kiss of death, coming from the insatiable heart of the industrial world, engulfed the village of Aberfan in Wales – a gigantic landslide of coal waste swept down from the hillside, devouring buildings and killing 116 school children and 28 adults before it came to rest.

The first thing I did when I got back from France was to go straight to Earlham Street in London, only to find out that Ponji had moved elsewhere and Syd had taken up residence on the top floor.
    The printing press, which Jean Simone used for churning out illegal literature on the lower floor, had been confiscated by the law. Some of the rooms were etched with charring from a fire, in which Ponji and friends were lucky to have escaped with their lives. Jean Simone had

moved to a farm in Wales with a girl who had enough money for him to play with tractors and horses until something more enticing came along. Seamus O'Connell, a gentle giant of a man, with a head of hair matching that of King Charles II, had taken over Jean's room. Seamus chain smoked rollups and drank pints. His high IQ had him working with hulking reel to reel machines called computers during office hours. Despite appearances he didn't do drugs, which meant sitting alongside his friendship offered some warm respite, when it was needed, from the druggy carousel.

Emo and Pip had made it up to London and were tagging along with Syd, basking in the light of his rising star. They may have come from opposite ends of the social spectrum to Syd and indeed my good self, but this divide didn't stop them from giving as good as they got. Syd loved their fearless humour and cool dress sense, but most importantly, at this ambiguous time, he needed their kindred support.

Pip was looking more like a pirate than ever with his wild hair, handlebar moustache and roving eye; he had moved onto the harder stuff, which in the short few years to come, would lead to his undoing and untimely demise. For the time being Emo and Pip were firing on all possible cylinders and their streetwise sensibilities, held them in good stead, a way of survival, which had allowed them their only way out from the constraints and margins of a loser's life in our home town.

Pip and Emo held a mirror up to my own sense of loss, which made being with them both comforting and awkward in equal measure. They weren't sure if they could last the weeks in London at this time and asked me what I was going to do. I had what I thought was a way of surviving the short run by staying with Ponji, but I couldn't say this because I was fearful of them tagging along. I wriggled out of it by saying I'd probably go back to Cambridge, which was in fact the last thing in the world I ever wanted to do.

Syd was friendly and still retained his sparkle, but was a little more reticent than when I last saw him. His band Pink Floyd had moved on from covering the blues, gaining notoriety for playing experimental music performed in beams of light, which were projected through bottles of water. Coloured oils were dropped into the water. The light, shining through the bottles, splintered in all directions, creating paisley like patterns all over the players and much of the audience. Hidden among this lightshow, Syd's shy nature really got into the music. Being at these gigs was like being under the sea dancing with fractured sunlight, the effect was mesmerising. These pioneering sessions broke new ground at a club called UFO in London's Tottenham Court Road, where the audiences were growing by the week. Syd's song *Arnold Lane* was about to be released, destined for the top twenty and the band was lean and hungry for more. But it seemed to me that his intimacy was tugging elsewhere. He very much felt like someone who wanted to be in the centre of the laboratory, rather than selling his wares in a hard and fast market place.

As I sat next to him in the open plan room upstairs in Number Two Earlham Street, all those years ago, he came across as a young boy on the edge of a fairy tale, in a place apart from the ambitions of the managers and the rest of the group. Their incessant need to orientate the music, towards a more secure aspect, seemed to be pulling Syd's artistic aspirations away from their roots. There was some kind of incongruous misfortune afoot; for it seemed that without those very specific roots, he would never have been able to create the music and songs, which were to put the band well and truly in the driving seat.

Once the sixties were up and rolling, a kind of unsaid acceptance seemed to wash through the ether; whether one liked it or not, art could be anything from a blank canvas to a masterpiece. Artistic freedom seemed to be the main driving force, which begged the question as to what artistic freedom really was.

History may tell us that this was a time of a renaissance for the arts. Initially this may have been the case, but I think for many, despite the ethos underlying the time, art in the broadest sense was not unlike it is today, a front for an underlying need to score the hat trick of money, fame and fortune. The music scene was no exception.

Syd wanted to make and explore sounds and if it was successful that was a bonus, but I don't think that was the draw. His latent insecurities appeared to lie at the heart of a struggle, which seemed familiar to many artists in the sixties. His innocent temperament appeared to be ill-equipped for the wiliness of chart success. From the side lines I saw an apparent indifference to the framework of the rock 'n' roll industry, give rise to a great deal of animosity between him and his growing musical train.

Despite the flux of the music business, the main thing I remember, upon revisiting Earlham Street after I got back from France, was Syd's insistence on sitting me down on the floor, in a haze of excited hash smoke, and listening to a new record by the Beatles called *Revolver*. The pioneering sound with its evocative lyrics was an absolute inspiration. With their popular fan base spawning out across the globe, it gave the distinct feeling that a massive sociological change was in the air. I thought

I had evolved, but on hearing this album I was floored; I hadn't even started.

Being artistically free was for me a partial issue. At the back of my mind was an instinctive need to fill the emptiness, not with art, but with the confirmation of an essential sense of life, as the Beatles advocated in their latest embodiment, *Tomorrow Never Knows*. And with this in mind I left Cambridge Circus and Syd to seek out Ponji's company in another part of town.

~

I emerged from the bustle of South Kensington tube station, into a glorious sunny day in that late summer at the epicentre of the sixties, with outright optimism toying with a dream of love. If there was any shit-faced doubt, I made damn sure it was well and truly tucked away in the bottom drawer.

It wasn't hard to find the apartment block because it looked out from the corner of Old Brompton Road and Harrington Road in Georgian grandeur, with the name Egerton Court clearly written above the entrance for all to see.

I crossed the road from Dino's Italian restaurant, just as my brother had instructed me to do, and made my way up the sweeping incline of the stairway to the first floor and rang the bell. The wooden door with a wire-glass panel on the upper part was backed by some ageing white fibre board, making a tentative step towards the security and privacy of what might be going down on the other side. While waiting, I marvelled over an intricate wrought iron gate paying homage to the old fashioned lift on this landing. I dared to push the button and there was a wash of clanking sounds as the lift, which I was to find out soon enough had recently been used by Polanski for his film *Rosemary's Baby*, pulled itself up from the ground floor. The stairs it seemed went upwards to further floors and I was about to take a closer look, when the door to the flat opened. A hypnotically beautiful girl, in a paisley patterned and extremely short summer dress, stood in the doorway. Her fair hair flowed down to the waist of her perfectly proportioned frame; she seemed delicate and kind in manner.

Once I'd established who I was, she asked me softly if I would like to wait for my brother in his room, which was directly opposite a scruffy galley kitchen, toward the end of a narrow corridor. She introduced herself as Jenny and with the same gentle manner as she had ushered me in, offered me a cup of tea, which I gladly accepted.

When Ponji finally arrived, the sun had slunk away for the day and the assortment of rooms in the flat filled with the bustle of friendship and intrigue.

Ponji was as pleased to see me as I was him. He made it clear from the start that I could stay as long as I liked and what was his was mine to share. We talked a little about Elizabeth, but mainly about the great films he had been seeing for the course he was now on. Ponji put across his time at The London Film School with enthusiasm, but I sensed some growing dissatisfaction with how things were turning out there.

I tried to bolster the positive aspects and shared some of the undoubted depth and thrill of the cinema we had gained together over the past decade. I told him of the stack of classic films I had clocked up at the Cinematheque in Paris. I reminded him of how he had wangled his way into going to the The Film Society when we lived in Cambridge and got me to tag along. The Film Society was run by Dave Gale then and he steered us into that university club without question and with absolute respect, plunging us into the minds of Bergman, Cocteau, Truffaut, Renoir and others. We became entranced and immersed in an underworld of dreams, painted so vividly by way of those masters of the silver screen.

There was no doubt that Ponji had got the film bug, but something didn't seem to hang quite right for him.

He put an LP on the record player, lit a cigarette, lay back on the bed and allowed the gentle jazz rhythms of Miles Davis's *Sketches of Spain* to fill the soft smoky air.

It wasn't until we turned in for the night that my brother disclosed the reason for his late arrival that evening. He was seeing a therapist. A somewhat controversial move on his part as his analysis involved taking LSD. I was a little taken aback; not about the acid as I remember, for up to that point I had little idea what the letters LSD stood for, but mainly at his admitting to needing therapy. After all, you had to be mad to see a psychiatrist, didn't you? I said I would abide by his wish with regards the family and keep this strictly between ourselves. I remained cautious, but inquisitive. Ponji was my big brother and I still looked up to him.

As my brother's weekly encounters with the shrink became part of his stride, any initial misgivings I might have struggled with soon took a back seat, particularly as I began to familiarise myself with his new home.

What was clear from the outset was that each room in this flat was tailored to the personality of those that dwelled inside them and each one of his friends had a sense of purpose. It seemed clear from the start that they knew where their hearts lay and in what direction their paths were going.

Nigel Lesmoir-Gordon and his partner Jenny were the prince and princess of sixties royalty and their room, the largest in the flat, never in all the time I was there felt flustered. Dave Gale, who wanted to be there, but constantly believed that he shouldn't, had the smallest room; his bed was a split-level affair above his door, maximizing the space underneath for his clothes and fervent pen pushing. Next to Dave Gale's room was Aubrey Powell's and this was very much a space dedicated to being grounded; sleeping in partner with his guitar on the floor, where the steady reminder of the blues beat out from a record deck in close proximity to his pillow. Moving right along came Ponji's room, which was in a sense at the centre of the flat; it wasn't as large as Nigel and Jenny's but it did have adequate space for a double bed, a wardrobe and the infamous armchair, which seemed to have followed my brother's lead from his bedroom in Cambridge like an old friend.

I had already spent a little time with Storm in Cambridge and wanted more of his genial company. So, I gravitated towards his room, which was sandwiched between Ponji's and the communal bathroom, like toast to butter and very quickly found myself engrossed in conversations of an existential twist. The closeness of the carrot coloured walls made the room where Storm slept seem like a womblike vault.

My survival process at Egerton Court was to turn up the anarchy volume, which I could now do at the drop of a hat. This basically meant trying to push my new friends into any place of uncontrolled laughter, often at the expense of making myself look extremely silly. Finding I was rewarded with encouragement, I made no apologies for giving out what I thought was the key to my freedom. It may have seemed to those on the outside like I was sinking into some kind of wasted washed-out space. But as I saw it then I was undergoing a transformation into a deep-seated all encompassing present.

Despite my continuing need to play the fool, smoking marijuana with Storm was done in an experimental vein, in the knowledge that we were partaking in something profound. There were many times when the cosmic joke teased the boundaries beyond the mythological line and found us doubled up on the floor in sublime laughter. That stoned mirth may have often got the better of us, but inhaling a joint was primarily about relaxing the cerebral part of the brain so that it became fluid, without any fear or threat of what might be round the corner. Like a stage whisper heard from the wings, the word was loud enough. Our existence didn't need redemption from the outside. The grass was not greener somewhere else, because it was right here at the tips of our nimble fingers.

By becoming more relaxed in Storm's company, I found I was begging to let go of any self-conscious need to stop the flow. Thus I became hooked, not on dope, but on what my friendship with Storm revealed. He wore the suit of a mentor and gave me confidence in my own interpretations. He was four years older than I was and had already come away from the University of Leicester with a BA Honours in English and Philosophy.

The first thing he did was to begin to pull into focus the books that had taken him a step further into the mystery of the universe. One such book was *Childhood's End* by Arthur C. Clark; for some nights I would lie on the floor room while Storm read out loud, digesting and dissecting the work as we went along. Then there was Aldous Huxley's, *The Doors of Perception and Heaven and Hell*, which he knew back to front and sideways. Eventually he brought my attention to Albert Hoffmann, the man who in 1938 by a chance encounter in his laboratory in Switzerland brought LSD into the world.

As I took the first step towards my childhood's end, I began to gain enough poise in my cerebral faculties, to realise that they actually worked and quite well. At this fruitful time in my life, Storm presented me with a new found security, which was an important step in establishing how I was to live out the rest of my life. When the end of a day drew in, an essential interest in our existence became the pivotal spin at the centre of our lives. It was Storm who had the greatest impact; his intellectual agility got through to mine and was releasing me from the chains which had been holding me fast for so long.

It may be hard to believe but this was the first time in my life that a dialogue of such standing had taken place – conversation nearing mature fruition. I was so used to someone of Storm's intellectual calibre blanking me out, or playing the superior game, and was delighted when he didn't. This acceptance had been a long time coming. Finding I was immersed in a place full of discovery, my reality started to take a head-changing step into new hemispheres.

Life, as all encompassing, became more of a certainty with these exciting new friends from Cambridge, who were undoubtedly brought together through the need for artistic and spiritual kinship.

I'd finally managed to squeeze into Emo's shoes as the definitive jester at the heart of the court. As I saw it then, this was my passport to courage and survival.

~

Out of the six players who lived at Egerton Court Nigel and Jenny were the most difficult to get to know. Seeing them and their room as elite couldn't have helped. Like Jenny, Nigel was always beautifully turned out. With his long hair, paisley jacket, velvet trousers and clean cut looks he really was the part.

As far as establishment and authority were concerned no wool was pulled over Nigel's eyes. On one occasion when the drug squad came barging into their room, Nigel, cool as cucumber, followed the police around, moving the stash from under their eyes as they were going about the search, turning the investigation into a daring game of hide and seek.

As an undoubted aristocrat of the sixties Nigel Lesmoir-Gordon summed up what I thought at the time to be a real understanding of fearlessness. When the plot fizzled Nigel held his own with the best of them. This was brought home to me one day, when I was looning around madly with him and Jenny in the corridor outside their room, (trying to vie for attention no doubt). In the middle of the carry-on he pulled his penis out, and placed it in my hand Groucho Marx style. I may have appeared unflustered, but the truth is I was shocked by his indifference and well and truly put in my place. After this I gave him the space and respect he deserved, the graces I hadn't been calm enough to employ previously. Through this trifling encounter I became a little more aware of how reading social interaction was often a lot more complex than skin deep and I began to see Nigel and Jenny for who they really were.

Nigel was a metaphysical poet who had no truck with convention. Like my father he had been to Oundle public school and like my father he knew right from the start that he was an outsider. But unlike my dad he wasn't going to eat his shorts over it. He was one of the first so called Cambridge beats to stand up in public and recite his own poetry. Nigel never compromised his dress sense. Whilst I was buying second hand sailor's loons for twenty two shillings from the Chelsea Market, he was wearing the elite clothes of the sixties like a true Edwardian dandy, bought from exclusive boutiques like Quorum and Granny Takes a Trip, on the King's Road.

Jenny came across as extremely good natured, perhaps with a suggestion of being a little fey; but dig deeper and you'd find real salt of the earth. During one of our many colourful encounters, I had nicknamed her Gladys which she took on board with the greatest of humour. She really was a person grown out of flower power, beautiful with a butterfly touch.

Synonymous with the time, their bedroom was kitted out with soft white Afghan rugs, which were spread across the bed and floor in a neat but relaxed fashion. Complementing the classical fireplace, was an antique dining table, which seemed to move around depending on the day that lay ahead, but for the most part it took up central position in the room. Occasionally I would find I was sitting in a stoned place at this table and get caught up in Nigel and Jenny's quest for the Holy Grail. The seeds from the Avalonion bag were planted somewhere in the depths of my subconscious here. During the day the curtains were often drawn across the large bay windows, spreading a filtered oriental light across the room. It wasn't unusual to see the likes of Mick Jagger, Alan Ginsberg, Marianne Faithful and other such poetic mortals of the time come and go from the mystic portal of their bedchamber.

Through one of his many friends Nigel had a connection with Albert Hoffman's laboratory in Switzerland, which was good for us because it meant he was able to get his hands on some of the purest LSD produced at that time. This was no watered down affair. You can't compare the large doses (typically between 200 and 1000 milligrams) of LSD taken at that time, to those of today (between 20 to 100 micrograms). This is no idle boast, just an idea of the seriousness of what was being undertaken then.

It was no accident that I would end up taking my first acid trip at Egerton Court, because it felt absolutely safe to do so and I chose Storm to take me to the gate. He relayed clearly that where and how the drug was administered, should be done with careful consideration. Although we saw ourselves as guinea pigs, testing human nature to the limit, experimenting with LSD was certainly not going to be an overly altruistic affair, for there was too much excitement in the air for that.

By the time I came to leave these shores for unknown seas, I was well primed and hoped somehow, perhaps naïvely, that it would bring out the best in me.

That such a tiny amount of liquid on a sugar cube could have such a huge impact, still fills me with unease and amazement.

For the first half an hour or so, on that fateful late afternoon, it felt like nothing was happening. Then little by little I became aware of the senses taking in how extraordinarily beautiful it was just to be able to taste, to see and to hear; to be pushed gently into finding the reality of something lost from the virtue of a child. Clearly this wasn't about going somewhere; this was a gradual dawning of awareness, where the surroundings become natural to be with, in the richest possible sense.

My initial fear of taking the drug began to vanish and in its place was the heightened simplicity of being in the unexplainable undeniable magical now. The contours of the worn carpet on which I sat became a sea of living cloth; the clothes that I was wearing started to take on a definitive feel. The inhalation and exhalation of the breath made wonderfully comfortable the festooned body. The pores of the skin, the nervous system, nay the whole being is a cacophony of absolutes, fitting with ease into the magnitude of their surroundings like it had never been otherwise. This was a timeless place of beauty and wonder.

At some point I stood up, acknowledging the fluidity of movement to be an indisputable motion that came to fruition outside the intellect. It seemed as if the physical transition was being blessed by something full and legitimate from somewhere else, in direct correlation with a deep understanding inseparable from the inner self.

Storm offered me a segment of orange to eat, which I accepted as if it were a carefully chosen gift and it hit my taste buds like an exploding symphony.

The ears had become bathed in surrounding sounds. The sounds weren't harsh or sharp, nor were they soft or muffled; they were what they were in all their glory. Even the traffic noise, or the distant thrust from the jets of an aeroplane going towards Heathrow, seemed magnified into an enthralling, if not audacious man-made logical depth.

I wandered out into the hall, where normally the floor would have seemed too tacky to lie on, but in this instance I had no hesitation. I found myself beginning to explore the physical possibilities; I placed my legs up against the wall with my back at one with the floor and started to stretch into the vastness. I began to see that the place I was in was no longer a limited dimension. It may have seemed arrogant to entertain the idea, but when I reached toward the horizon a bit more, I could take another step and walk up the wall and across the ceiling; this may seem ridiculous but the realm of possibility was there.

Did time pass, or were we merely still, with an endless universe passing through and around us?

As the dawn broke silently over the city, we went down the gradual incline of the stairs and out into the radiant air. We glided across the road with ease to the tube station and became mesmerised by the coming and going of the oncoming rush-hour. The swarms of people hurrying to work, like fish in search of water, just seemed ridiculously mind-boggling. Near the surface of their lives was the astonishing revelation of an exemplary existence. To put so much energy into something so far away from the nature of their true selves seemed absolutely crazy. Storm and I were undoubtedly the minority, but I believe it was they who were lost.

It is not my intention to advocate that the taking of such substances might enable us to see, hear, or taste in such a way as to realise a God-life. I cannot deny however, that this journey brought with it an assimilation of parts of my childhood that were left behind in Cambridge and Shepreth. What was brought into focus during that auspicious trip was the realization that I had plunged into the molecular structure of air, like I had into water as a child, and found myself flowing in the wonderment of a powerful reality. I had returned to an innocent linking with a fathomless earth.

Christmas comes to many children as a time of great excitement and if you can pause for a moment and go back into how that excitement feels then you may have some understanding of what was being celebrated in terms of our lives. For some the innocence beneath the surface burst forth in a cosmic universal dance and quite honestly, when the skipping on the lawn started and the daisy chains of reason were strewn around the neck of beauty, it did seem as if the spirit had its hand in love. For others the dance became buried in short lived jubilation at the bottom of the garden in a place of horror. When the horrors came you were lucky if you escaped, some didn't and they went under never to return. Those of us with our heads in the sand, in our naiveté, or is it in our arrogance, assumed that this was just down to the drug.

It is true that LSD opened doors to darker places; somewhere down the road, Punk emerged from the heart of the love child like a repressed kangaroo into a boxing ring. As far as I could see Syd Barrett went punk before Johnny Rotten had even brushed his teeth. But because punk wasn't acceptable then, his oncoming wildness seemed out to lunch, especially to a fence sitter like me.

As I was to find out soon enough, there was no doubt that taking acid was a risk. If fear was the basis of your personality then there was a high chance that a heightened sense of fear might leap out and grab you. By the same token, if you had an open heart, there is no doubt it could push you towards a heightened sense of love.

After several weeks of dossing on Ponji's floor I was seeing less and less of him. Ponji and I loved, and clearly cared, for each other, but our differences were starting to seem insoluble. This was becoming apparent in our behavioural patterns, especially under the lanterns at Egerton Court. When the night drew in for instance, I was up for smoking spliffs in Storm's room and being dazzled by the likes of the Doors, Jimmy Hendrix and other such rock luminaries – whereas Ponji was usually lying alone on his bed, listening to the gentler rhythms of Miles Davis or Mozart, carefully preparing his head for the day that lay ahead at the London Film School.

I think in the end I avoided slipping into Ponji's room when he was awake, because he was concerned about how his younger brother was swaying in the psychedelic maze. I couldn't allow myself to be distracted by the difficulties Ponji was having on my behalf, lest it upset the enriching time I was having with his flatmates. After all, wasn't getting stoned about enabling our ears to hear the music well and our hearts to see our loved ones true? It wasn't about yearning for the future, or the past, was it?

Is it a bird? Is it a plane? No its Matthew after France and before the fall.

South Kensington 1966/67 taken by Ponji

181

26

It seems there was a hunger in my upbringing that had me wanting a deeper understanding of freedom. Whatever the intention, I had taken from my parents an unequivocal need to explore social boundaries at their limits. When the extremity of conservative law came down too heavily it was considered acceptable to fight back, especially with regards right wing injustice, this was after all a united democracy.

I had inherited a fundamental desire for a fairer society. I wasn't able to see that to a large part, this was a social concept an idea of freedom, which had its roots sown into a Dickensian past. This meant a conformist misconception lay dormant in me and like an agitated seed this would eventually grow, turning the world I was in upside down.

For the time being then, I saw being free as an external issue; and this licence, signed in full by my socio-political parents, meant kicking any doubt off the playing field and putting a question mark over traditional barriers. I was convinced that the only way forward was to draw attention to my surroundings in any way I could and release the sheep from the shepherd. A ridiculous premise, because if I had looked closely at my life I would have seen how full of contradictions it was. But to hell with that, by standing on the table and creating drama in the centre of friendly gatherings, such as lunchtime in the canteen at the Royal College of Art, I'd show the world how imprisoned we are by etiquette.

I used Storm and Dave Gale, when they were studying film at the Royal College of Art, to gatecrash my way through the free thinking doors of that noble establishment. By way of chasing rabbits, I soon found myself amid the company of pioneers, going headfirst and heart-first into new realms of their artistic lives.

The dean of the Royal College of Art at this time, Christopher Cornford, whose son had been to the same primary school as me, was a friend of my parents, not close, but he was someone they respected and likewise he them. I think because of this connection he chose to turn a blind eye and may even have encouraged my improvisations within those inventive walls.

And so it was that for a good two years I became a rather anarchic, if you like eccentric, young guest of this esteemed institution, and for the most part was welcomed with open arms.

Punctuated with a little manic resolve, I set about trying to befriend the students, who to begin with were rather bemused at my dealing a deck of cards to those I didn't know and making an existential quip in passing with those that I did. When they found out I didn't really have a qualified place there, one or two apprentices took an aggressive stand toward my anarchic ploys. Then gradually they got to see how I was not so much a threat, more a puff of smoke, there one minute and gone the next. When those corridors of art finally began to accept this wilful presence, the friendship became a mutual affair. They accepted me as someone who wore his heart on his sleeve, someone who wanted to dance, cry and sing with the best in the field.

Through a deepening friendship with this creative centre I became intrinsically involved in filmmaking, playmaking, pottery, photography, painting and graphics. Many of those I was involved with went on to become masters of their respective paths. Along with Dave Gale and Storm others were Tony Scot, Patrick Uden, Elizabeth Fritsch, Alfreda Benge, Franco Rosso and Stephan Goldblatt. I'd hoped that by slipping in through the side door, the entrepreneurs among them might use me as an actor when they went out into the working world.

Up until now my only real connection with Dave Gale was held together by light hearted tension. We'd loon around for brief interludes, usually on passing amid the scurrying of cockroaches in the kitchen at Egerton Court. He was an all-time great mimic; among others he did a hilariously clipped impersonation of a spivy teddy boy and had the Bee Gee's down pat.

Our brief encounters were to become more of a lasting fixture when he directed *A Spurt of Blood* by Antonin Artaud at the RCA and was brave enough to give me the part of the knight. If this wasn't prize enough, he also managed to persuade a handful of unique, gorgeous, talented girls to be in the play.

My dreams of companionship really did come true here. I got much more than I ever bargained for. In the female corner there was Hester Strong, Frances Vaughan, Lindsay Corner, Jane Walker, Margareta Bourdin and Jenny Spires. I had a particular infatuation for Jenny. I'd known her as a fellow Mod from Cambridge. Just being in her company gave me goose-bumps and trembling knees.

Richard Longcraine, who was later to become a well established film director in his own right, worked the special effects like an enthusiastic professor of technical wizardry. For this short lived play, which was to be staged in the round, Longcraine and his colleagues carved an enormous hand, between four and five feet wide, out of polystyrene, which was supposed to be that of God's. The idea was that on a given cue this monolithic fist, with its protruding forefinger, was to be released from on high then swing down and across the stage. They set this up with an elaborate wiring system, which was attached to the giant wrist by a fuse wire, which in turn was attached by way of electrical circuitry to a hook and a remote switch somewhere high up in the ceiling.

I got to wear a full suit of armour, the genuine article made entirely of heavy steel. I could hardly move my arms let alone walk into the arena. For my entrance through the audience, Dave insisted that I have the visor down, which meant my vision was seriously impaired. Clanking aside, I managed to make it to the edge of a central platform, the side of the stage, and then sat down – this was the cue for Longcraine to switch the switch connected to the fuse wire, thus releasing the hand of the almighty.

I heard the faint swoosh as the great hand glided past the back of my head. I spoke a couple of lines and by the reactions from the audience I thought I was doing exceptionally well. Through the tiny slit in the visor I managed to catch the vague outline of someone rushing across the stage with a fire extinguisher. I thought this person to be a surreal extra, put in without my knowing at the last minute. When I suddenly heard Dave Gale at my side, trying to manoeuvre me off the stage, I knew something was up and had to grudgingly accept that the sound of the audience oohing and ahhring wasn't to do with my commanding performance. The hand of God had caught fire. If it hadn't been for the quick footed, there was a serious possibility that we could have turned the main hall into a heap of cinders.

I can't remember if we got to the end of the play or not, but the evening cemented a strong bond between the cast, the crew and the audience. It certainly brought Dave Gale and me a lot closer. While I may not have pulled it off as a great knight, in the clear light of day, it was sharing quality time in rehearsals with the girls that brought a new kind of confidence to my domain. They made it very clear that they liked me. This was of course a mutual affair; I fell in love with each and every one of them. Oh and I almost forgot, somewhere in there I lost my virginity. Oh boy! Enough said.

Sometime later, way-out in this college slipstream, I allowed myself to be stamped with the unflattering nickname of 'Beaky', because of my Romanesque nose. Privately I thought I'd seen the end of that kind of thing when I left school. If my guard was down, this nickname still had the power to send me crawling off, sight unseen, to the ugly bug ball. It seemed my self-esteem was still fallible after all. Under no circumstances could I let my friends know that I might be unhinged by something as trifling as a label, as it wouldn't be seen to fit in with those freethinking ways, so I played it up. Ladies and gentleman welcome to The Chicken Show – here's 'Beaky'

Water as they say flowed under the bridge and any misgivings that I might have had, by being branded with this new name, were to be taken much more lightly when my path was to cross that of Pete Townsend's.

The ever amiable, bespectacled Richard Stanley was a contemporary of Storm and Dave Gale's and like them attached to the film course at the RCA. He approached me out of the blue one day, with the suggestion that I might be the central character in his graduation film. As with other last year student films the main actors would be paid a token daily fee of ten shillings. This certainly wasn't why I chose to do it, but it sure did help as I was basically living hand to mouth at this time. If there was a story to this celluloid journey, it was about a day in the life of an adolescent outsider trying to relate to his surrounding world; suited me down to the ground.

Richard Stanley had been at the same art college as Pete Townsend and was a good friend, as too was the cameraman on Richard's film, the kind unimposing harmonica-playing Chris Morphet.

I had seen The Who play, a few years previously, in a small venue in Cambridge. As a relatively unknown band they took us pill boppers for the rock and roll ride of our lives. Since then they'd hit the stratosphere as a world class act; in other words they were now mega. Pete Townsend was to me nothing less than an almighty god. When I found out that he was to play my brother in the film and compose the music I nearly fell through the pavement. I tried to take it all in my stride, but when the reality of working beside him came along I fell feet first into a self-conscious pit and lost my nerve. Here I was, one minute showing the world how to be free by pirouetting across the floor stark naked, if that was my desire, then tripping up with red faced silence when a real star played the tune.

On the first day of shooting I couldn't get out of bed. It wasn't until Richard and Storm quite literally pulled me out that I took to the floor. Through a daze of sandman eyes I placed one foot in front of the other. I tied my senses to the surroundings and pulled my body through the dense vortex, like Spiderman climbing the side of a tall building. What was extraordinary here was the power of persuasion. How the thought of something in the future can turn us inside out and so readily away from the present. I was so afraid of the outcome of filming that it pulverized me to the quick before it had even begun.

Pete's feet were well and truly on the ground and he did nothing but encourage my ease. Nevertheless on that first morning, however hard I tried, I still felt like I was wading through treacle.

When the board clapped, the heart jumped and I managed to convert the overloaded performing I had to contend with, into something which seemed to get nods of approval. This wasn't hard to do, as the scene mostly consisted of Pete driving around Hyde Park Corner, in his grand open-top American car, with me beside him interacting like mad with the surroundings.

Having got a few takes under the belt I began to relax a little. Just as I was getting into my stride, the day was cut short. Pete had to go early, because that evening The Who had a concert, at the Saville Theatre in Shaftsbury Avenue, with the new kid in town called Jimi Hendrix. In passing Pete asked me if I would like to come along. He had it seems enjoyed my company and the filming. Jimi Hendrix play? How could I let any coy stargazing get in the way of this stride? Like many other heads throughout Briton, the echoes of Hendrix's debut album, *Are You Experienced*, was still permeating my nervous system and of course I said a resounding yes!

On the night, The Who topped the bill but it was Hendrix's virtuosity which stole the show. He was just extraordinary. Beautiful, angry, dangerous, classical; what more? With a sound that had never been heard before, he and his guitar blew the world we were in through the roof. However, Hendrix setting fire to his guitar with a tea spoon of lighter fuel couldn't touch The Who for their rampant theatricality. Their set seemed to continue the myth of an extramarital affair with the trappings of the world, especially those of the music industry.

Compared with the arenas most groups of their stature play in today, this Regency theatre, full of upholstered seating and ornate deco, made the night seem like a close encounter with a new friend. Anyone with an open mind could see the writing on the wall. What had started off as a spontaneous mistake of guitar breaking in some far off gig in the past, was now a full on way of smashing their way through the mask of a technical world going mad.

Gigs and road-shows aside, what really put me at my ease over those few days of filming with Pete, was his sharing shy explanations with me, of how he came to terms with his noble mask in the playground. My being called Beaky seemed to fade into insignificance. He had been teased and bullied for his looks a damn sight more than me during his school days. He had taken the hurt and made it into a virtue through playing the guitar. I understood the quality and the quantity of his pain. I was on home ground here. I wasn't a musician, but I could mimic my way out of a paper bag.

What Richard Stanley tried to get me to do in his film, was to directly mirror my surroundings by dancing with the elements and taking a high dive into the underground. It was the kind of show he'd seen me do so often in the halls of the Royal College of Art. Looking at it now, I see an innocent boy making head and tails on the roller coaster of a topsy-turvy cityscape.

The director wanted me to sing a ditty with rock undertones at the end of the film, which, along with the film score, Pete was to produce and arrange. I told them categorically that I was tone deaf, but Pete soon talked me out of that one. We worked the song at his tiny studio, which at that time was on the top floor of his pretty Regency house around the corner from Buckingham Palace in Victoria. Over the next few hours I came up with something, which remarkably was a little more than acceptable.

Richard Stanley decided to call his film *Beaky*. Courtesy of my prominent nose, I started to realise that I wasn't going to be the next Robert Mitchum. I had however, gained further confirmation that a need for feeling cool and handsome was something which had to come about from how one sits on the inside. What permeates through to the outside world is what binds us together.

To introduce me to the other members of the band and give me a more intricate idea of how they operated on the road, Pete picked me up in his Lincoln convertible late one afternoon. The hood was open to the elements. Exhilarated we took off up the motorway towards central England, to the city of Birmingham. We arrived at the *Mothers*

Club sometime in the early evening where he told the manager to give me anything I wanted from the bar. Pete then took me round backstage to meet the rest of the band where I was greeted in choral unison with Beaky! I was shown a milk crate of champagne in the corner of the dressing room and told to open a bottle. As I was bending down, the back of my trousers were grabbed from behind then ripped from my legs. I stood up with the front half of my sailor's loons dangling from my thighs, to find Keith Moon holding the other half in his hand and looking firmly into my eyes to see which way I was going to twist. I managed to conceal any apprehension and sneered my way, with a kind of mirrored psychosis, through a few pirouettes of intensity. Pete came to the rescue with a spare pair of trousers and I spent the rest of the evening getting paralytic in case I had to dance another tune with Mr Moon.

I played along with the night as I thought fit, by getting drunker until it was time to go back to London, by which time I could hardly stand.

Halfway down the motorway we had to stop in the darkness and I fell out into a chasm, which seemed as large as the Grand Canyon, then threw up all over the grass verge. Pete came round to where I was puking and asked me how I was doing. I distinctly remember, looking back toward the glittering lights of the Midlands, telling him that the world was all shit, nothing but a crock of shit. He helped me back into the car and we set off again, this time he made sure *The Piper at the Gates at Dawn* was crying out from the car stereo. Hearing the Floyd seemed to hit a wrong note and in a haze I tried to tell him that it wasn't working. After some struggle I fell back in the seat and gave into the music and the fairy tale in Syd's voice did begin to calm me down. As the car settled into the journey I began to take in Pete's fascination, which bordered on a kind of obsession, for Syd and his band.

We stopped off at a motorway café, where the stalwarts who knew The Who from years of touring, gave us a warm welcome and a hearty breakfast.

Back in London Pete dropped me off in South Kensington and on parting suggested that Storm, who had been working on the technical side of Richards's film, and I come round to his house for a meal mid week. As if in a dream I gladly accepted and we set a time.

Even Storm, who wasn't renowned for his silence, kept a somewhat subdued place at the table. Pete talked his way through the meal, which had been cooked and served with a great deal of domestic care by his unassuming wife, who looked a bit like the actress Geena Davis when she smiled. He started telling us about one of his latest projects, the story of a nowhere man, who, caught up in a world of cyberspace, loses his way in the real world. I can marvel now at how close to the bone of the future he seemed to be, but there and then I had no idea what he was talking about. Pete gave the impression that he thought the world in which we were all heading was to be something of a Hi-Tech nightmare. At this time the Internet was just a speck in the eye of the United States Department of Defence, it hadn't even entered the minds of the domestic market and yet Pete seemed to have an uncanny handle on where the path of this technology, that is so common to us today, could take us.

I don't know how he knew, or where these nightmare insights came from, but they did and his Orwellian mind wanted to turn the audience inside out with his revelations.

Inevitably we got round to talking about Pink Floyd. I couldn't help thinking we were perhaps there because of this. He did seem to have a loaded interest. It was common knowledge that he would often go and hang out at the side of the stage at UFO, the club where the Floyd played in the early days, to watch the band submerse themselves in psychedelic light shows and their space-age sound.

As he talked on, the night drew its curtains across the sky and eventually it was time for us to leave. When he saw us to the door he asked us if we would like to come with our friends from Egerton Court to see The Who play on the campus at Essex University. There was no question that we wouldn't. On closing the door he quipped in with, "See if you can get Syd to come". I had a suspicion he wanted to show how his musical dexterity could match the Floyd's. We didn't like to lose face by telling him that we were losing touch with Syd and his marbles, so we said "sure".

We never told Syd that we were going to see The Who play; he just turned up with his car at South Kensington and Egerton Court. Without a word passing between us I ended up going with him. This wasn't as easy as it might sound, because Syd was beginning to do away with boundaries and rules by then, especially those of the road. The run down to Essex went by like a distorted flash. I don't think we stopped at one red traffic light, which left me scorched to the back of the car seat. Apart from the occasional grunt and smile, Syd didn't say a word.

The Who played a superlative set and as an appreciation for their guests, a blistering rendition of *Arnold Lane* (Pink Floyd's first top ten hit) to see out the night. All I could think of during the entire show was of being wrapped around a lamppost if Syd drove me back to London, and of how I could wriggle out of this predicament without offending him.

The lesson of not worrying about what's to come before you get to it still hadn't sunk in. By the time the show hit the final note Syd had simply disappeared and through some slip of time I ended up going back with Pete, who groaned the while away by complaining about the lead singer being out of tune. Once he'd got the dialectics of the night off his chest, he then wanted to know what I thought of the gig. I felt relaxed enough to tell him that I couldn't really take it in, because of my concerns about Syd and the lift back.

After the filming our paths were to cross less frequently, but if ever I turned up at Pete's front door, even on the hop, he was always welcoming. There was an overt intelligence at work when Pete was around. Years later he was instrumental in helping Lena (my wife) and I find a rehab centre for my step-son Sean in the UK. The only person I could think of who had been there, back and three times round the block was Pete and he went out of his way to lend a hand. On and off I remained in touch with him; but as the years came to pass, I had the feeling that he thought I had lost something gained from those spunk driven days. Perhaps he was right and I was holding on to some obscure rationale and walking as the crow flies. But if he had really taken the time out to see who I was, maybe he'd have seen a friend who needed to change, rather than someone who couldn't spin the tune his way.

I was born with a plastic spoon in my mouth
The north side of my town faced east, and the east was facing south
And now you dare to look me in the eye
Those crocodile tears are what you cry
It's a genuine problem, you won't try
To work it out at all you just pass it by, pass it by

Substitute your lies for fact
I can see right through your plastic mac
I look all white, but my dad was black
My fine looking suit is really made out of sack   Pete Townsend

190

27

With my parents now living in Norfolk, I thought I'd left Cambridge well and truly behind. I was still imbued with relations at Number Nine and many of my friends at Egerton Court had family connections in our old home town, so with some reluctance I occasionally ended up going back.

That summer, I had taken a second carefully prepared acid trip with Storm in Granchester Meadows, where the magic of the natural environment enveloped our senses like a delicious feast. I realised then how you can't actually equate nature, or indeed a place with a label. There we were in the middle of a miraculous spread, with space to evolve. Cambridge or Timbuktu, the beauty of our surroundings could have been anywhere. So I decided, albeit a little tentatively, to make the break that year and spend Christmas in Cambridge with my friends – for that city, which I felt had dealt me a poor hand, now seemed an easier proposition. Making this move wasn't, of course, as easy as it sounds, for I was plagued with guilt about not going home.

Usually I would have gone, as did Ponji, Elizabeth and my sisters, to continue the unbroken custom of a yuletide gathering with my parents. As their house was now much smaller than when we lived in Cambridge, any family gatherings were a lot more hemmed in. It had been particularly hard the previous year, because Elizabeth found it extremely difficult restraining the hurt she had for my walking out on her in Paris.

Atheism and Christian rhymes aside, Christmas was a big deal at our home, a fanciful Victoriana feel good time, with real candles on the tree and lots of tangerines in the stockings.

Following in the German tradition on my mother's side of the family, meant the bulk of giving and receiving at this auspicious time mainly took place on Christmas Eve. For an outsider, particularly those with

Christian leanings, the way we went about Yuletide festivities must have been a mite confusing.

My mum and dad put it about quite openly, that they didn't believe in the Christian god. If they had any divine leanings at all they were of an atheist kind, if there can be such a thing. Their spiritual beliefs, or lack of, didn't stop them from putting up an extremely decorative Christmas tree, playing games and singing the odd carol when the sleigh bells came around.

Christmas was certainly a strange time of year, which either seemed to leave me wanting something I didn't get, or getting something I didn't want. For my years of childhood I usually equated this with what Santa Claus did or didn't end up bringing me. Like the time I got a toy six shooter with a reel of caps that slotted into the body of the gun, when the truth was I wanted a different and very particular sharp shooter, which I'd seen gleaming in the toy department of one of those small family run stores in Cambridge. The gun I dreamed of was a more authentic model, as in the westerns, with realistic bullets. These bullets pulled apart and could be filled with one or two individual caps, then placed in the chamber of the gun six at a time and fired off accordingly, leaving the participant to grapple with the very tense reality of reloading behind some make-believe shelter in some make-believe world.

When it became clearer that Father Christmas was really just a kindly extension of my own father, it began to dawn on me that it wouldn't be possible to get what I so often desired, particularly as he so often seemed strapped for cash. Then as the years passed I began to see that this wanting actually had its roots in an emotional need, a need which I have, for most of my life, refused to accept was really there. Like waiting on the gift that never quite materialises, I hung on in some kind of vain hope.

As with a lot of families the idea of giving and receiving at this time of the year had a virtue in itself, but once the novelty had worn off, which it inevitably did, the gorgon reared its ugly head and the festivities usually turned to stone. These annual gatherings would start off well enough with much eating, drinking and joviality, but then the customs became hard going. The games usually turned sour, especially when Elizabeth or I started losing. If it wasn't that which kicked the goalposts off the pitch, then the inevitable wrangling between Ponji, Elizabeth and our mother, with me and my younger sisters fighting our corner somewhere in the middle, certainly did. There never seemed to be a clear reason for the lid blowing off the box, as it was constantly a minor domestic quibble that triggered the explosions. From the woeful tears in the kitchen it wasn't hard to deduce that the turkey was just too big for the oven.

For the winter of my first breakaway, which through a process of elimination I deduce to have been the one between 1967 and 1968, I just simply wanted to see if I could make it through the festive season on my own, or at least, away from my immediate family. And when Storm suggested we go to Cambridge and spend Christmas with his girl friend Libby at her parent's house, I rallied to the challenge.

So with the guilt of not going home never quite subsiding, I hooked up with my friends. The fog of roach inhalations may have blurred the window and may even have blinkered me from the cold hard truth of day to day living, but it didn't mean I wasn't aware of the clutter.

Libby's sister, her mother and Libby herself provided the boys in their life with a meal of such quantity and quality the gluttony nearly killed us. We drank, slept and when we could, smoked copious joints, to see the nights away behind curtains, garden furniture, or anywhere else we could find for our reefer madness in their salubrious home.

When it was decided that we had pushed the boundaries a little too far out of whack for Libby's father, which wasn't difficult to do as he was constantly in danger of bursting at the seams, we moved into Storm's mother's house. This meant lounging around where the usual unusual gatherings took place, in Storm's old room.

Various friends from London dropped by – one came bearing New Year's greetings from Seamus O'Connell, who'd invited anyone who wanted to come, out to his father's infamous house in the country. I liked Seamus and from the few times we had hung out together at Earlham Street got to know him quite well. Seamus was like a big North American Indian. His shoulder length dark curly hair and horn rimmed glasses, made him look as he was – someone with a very high IQ. I had never met his mother, but when Syd had taken me up to London to score dope for the first time, I was told that the dishevelled house he had gone into belonged to her. She was, apparently, someone who practised what she preached, which in her case, for the good of humanity and free will, was the occult. She pretty much turned a blind eye to everything anybody wanted to do as long it didn't include murder. So her house was a refuge for just about every kind of free loader, druggie, mystic, poet and blues maker in the land. If Seamus's mother was like that what was his father like? I decided to go along for the ride and as far as I remember, so did a few others from the Cambridge underground.

For some of those nights in Cambridge, I slept at Number Nine, where I was greeted with a lot of withheld frowns about how my life in the stoned lane was turning out.

Elizabeth was on one of her excursions from France, staying with friends in another part of town. She merely came to Number Nine to visit. I don't think she ever felt comfortable around the idea of staying there; the memories from when she was a little girl still turned her stomach. The emotional baggage continued to be complex between us. She hung around hoping we would nosedive into a fall. A habit we caught from our mother, where we can be beastly to each other, all fall to pieces, say sorry, wipe up the tears and continue from where we left off without resolving a thing; it aint gonna happen. Instead, I told her about the outing to Seamus's father's house and she wanted to come.

It had been agreed, for those who wanted to go on the outing, that we should all meet at Number Nine; the idea being – follow the leader so no one gets lost on route.

Early in the afternoon Emo turned up, then Dave Gale. There were others too but I can't remember the names. Last to arrive was Alan Stiles who pulled up outside the house in his gleaming boys-own Morgan, a sports car that was forever breaking down, but always looked as if it had been polished for the occasion.

Hanging around in the Oak Room, waiting for the oncoming bodies to congregate, it wasn't long before Elizabeth, who had dyed her hair bright turquoise to earn some extra money for some promotional event in Paris, grabbed Emo by the arms. She looked into his eyes and told him straight up that he was an angel and that deep down he was a non sexual being. Emo lapped that up, but it left the rest of us who knew him, choking on our incredulity. Leaving Elizabeth at the centre of much attention, I went to the bathroom to alleviate my bladder. By the time I came back she and Emo were in dispute about the properties of methane gas. As if to get her point across, Elizabeth broke off mid-flow and said to Emo "Watch this"; she sat down on one of the ornate sofas in the Oak Room, cocked her legs in the air and lit a huge fart; a rocket like flame shot out from between her legs. Emo had met his female foil. I could see the colour drain from his face. Crestfallen I crept out of sight to bury my embarrassment.

What Elizabeth did in the privacy of our own home was one thing, but here, in front of my revered friends, was too much. I was thinking about leaving when Dave Gale came up to me in passing and said how amazing my sister was. His interjection was all I needed for me to change my mind. With my tension eased considerably, I decided to stay and adapt to the grain. In truth Elizabeth had called our bluff.

Alan Stiles stood out from the crowd, not only did he look like Clint Eastwood, but like an Eastwood character he didn't tip his hat to anyone. He worked the punts when I knew him, those that were kept in the river under the windows of the Anchor pub, with another soft centred hard guy, who lived like Alan on neither side of the law. They worked it like a closed shop. Alan, who actually had a heart of gold, often found himself in the midst of a stand-down. If trouble bumped into him, as it inevitably did, he was always deeply considerate, but if someone pushed the limit and swung a punch, he was usually fast enough to simply deck them. Elizabeth loved Alan as did I, and my dad. The feelings between him and my family must have been mutual, because he was always turning up at our house in Cambridge. Alan was born and brought up on the same street of malnourishment as Emo. Emo used to sit on Alan's knee when he was a toddler; this must have meant he was a lot older than any of us. But no judgment came with his age; as far as we were concerned Alan knew what we were about and let us get on with it. He had been around the world enough times as a merchant seaman to know the ropes. He chained smoked woodbines, rolled big spliffs and loved a pint. He lived with a fantastic looking girl who had a black bouffant hairdo and mesmerising eyes accentuated by lots of dark eye shadow, giving her beauty an air of a dancing firefly. Their arguments were infamous in Cambridge. If Alan got on the wrong side of her, she would lay into him with a passion and ferocity, matching anything Anna Magnani might have come up with. In their company the possibility of fatality was a very real prospect. If I hadn't seen her hurling any object she could lay her hands on, directly at him and in quick succession, I wouldn't have believed it myself

With Alan and Seamus leading the way, we made our way out on the road like a small friendly wagon train in search of new frontiers. The hedgerows and highways passed by at an easy pace and it wasn't long before we hit the depths of the Hertfordshire countryside.

Arriving was like waking up from a full on dream and emerging from the car, like being dropped from the sky into the middle of a lush evergreen jungle. There were no fences no walls, just foliage dripping with life in all directions. The path falling over itself to please, tumbled through a saturated glade and led us almost indiscriminately to a spacious opening, dominated by an extraordinary looking house. This delicate looking building, commanded a lot of space. It was two floors high and comprised of single skin walls that seemed to go up a mile, built entirely of small handmade bricks. Straight out of a fairy tale, it was like something beautiful a child might have built out of paper and cards.

From the inside, the outside walls seemed precariously thin. There were hundreds of small gaps between the bricks, spraying pinpricks of light all over the wide open interior, giving the impression of an inverted star. Relatively it wasn't an old house. Seamus's mother and father had built it themselves in the early forties, around the time Seamus was born, brick by brick, shovel by shovel. A labour of love before they went their separate ways.

Quite simply this skeletal home, which looked as if it could be blown over by the next big bad wolf that came along, had an ephemeral quality, as if it had been painted with subtle brushstrokes into the overgrown landscape. The Chase, as the place was called, was brought about by artists unhindered by the laws prohibiting such a piece of work today.

There was no sign of Seamus's dad, but the drive was well worth the effort for what lay ahead.

While the others refreshed their taste buds with a cup of tea and rested their limbs up on the gallery, a floor and matching balustrade that split the interior of this auspicious space in two, Dave Gale and I decided to see where Emo had got to.

Unbeknownst to us Emo had followed his nose into the nearest neighbour's garden and found himself head to toe with the most celebrated sculptor of the time.

Traipsing through the lush flora, with wild grasses still annoyingly wet from the heavy dew licking at our trouser legs, we began to see a few familiar bronze figures peeping out from the undergrowth. The more we looked the more we started to see. As well as contemporary statues, all sorts of objects came into focus, from carefully placed boulders through to driftwood, pebbles and assortments of shells; there was even a skeleton all weathered into the environment, as if it were an organic counterpart.

We bumped into Emo who was on his way back looking a little bemused. He said he'd had a kind of transcendental experience with an amazing guy who had the same surname as him. It was he said like the man was expecting him. I think Dave must have known and chose not to say anything, but I am sorry to say I had no idea.

Emo pointed us to an enormous shed situated in the garden of this next door house. We stepped with a bold stride into the wide entrance and there at the other end of this industrious space, among a rich array of sculpture, was Henry Moore, refining a full shaped model for a bronze to come made out of plaster.

It took a few minutes before he looked up, which gave us time to take in the enormity of it all. There were scaled down replicas of many of his most famous pieces that seemed randomly placed everywhere. There were many variations of a family group which looked almost abandoned, as they were, among the piles of clay, plaster and tools. As well as two large work-tables, there were sketches of work to come and that which had gone, sprawled across a table and pinned to a large section of wall. Radiant female figures stood proudly amidst the assortment of other work vying for our attention, all bearing that monumental theme.

Henry Moore must have had an affinity with Seamus's father because without any defining of boundaries the two gardens bled easily into each other. By the same token I think he was used to guests just appearing out of nowhere, because he didn't bat an eyelid when we walked into his private space. Without, I hope, appearing to be too fawning, we expressed our admiration for his art. He tackled the continuum of his privacy and our curiosity by saying he would get his daughter to show us around.

And she did; over the next hour or so Dave Gale and I were treated to a tour of the grounds, with such love and kindness it took our breath away. I learnt more in that short time about combining the elements than I would have ever done with a lifetime in the classroom.

Meeting a person, who had such an affinity with nature's gifts and at such a time, was so special. Here was organic matter, solid or otherwise, moulded, shaped, chipped, carved and cast to a beautiful earthborn shape, recognizable and intangible in equal measure.

We may not have met Shamus' dad or settled for very long in his parent's magical hideaway, but like a child who finds his way back home from being lost in a daydream, the day left us with a kind of natural contentment that doesn't come along very often.

On the way back to Cambridge there was an unusual quiet in the car; with me and Emo as passengers this was a feat in itself.

As some of Seamus's guests had decided to stay the night, Alan Stiles had ended up driving back on his own.

After a little time, we got to a place on the road where the incline went on forever. With Alan trailing behind we eventually made it to the top of the hill and as with many long climbs there was a sharp decline. The road down was very long and fiercely steep. We were picking up speed, faster by the second, when Alan's Morgan came alongside with him throwing his arms around inside the hooded cockpit. Alan's facial contortions very quickly had us in hysterics and the faster we got the more grotesque they became. We must have been going about eighty miles an hour when he started waving the handbrake madly at us. We suddenly realised he'd lost control not only of his senses but more importantly of the car. By now he was ranting, mouthing something about us getting in front. His predicament became clear. We were to go bumper to bumper with his car to slow him down. Our driver dithered and then bottled out, leaving Alan hurtling forward with the bottom of the hill coming up fast to greet him. Luckily his deftness at the wheel was such that he shot up a side road and eventually slowed to a halt. We towed him the rest of the way home.

That time in Cambridge was the last I saw of Alan. He ended up as a roadie for Pink Floyd when they became one of the world's most successful rock bands. He went to America with them and put down roots there. *Alan's Psychedelic Breakfast*, a track on the Floyd album *Atom Heart Mother* pays tribute to him.

Elizabeth now had a better understanding of who these friends of Ponji's and mine were and what I was doing with them. Nevertheless, it was still hard for her not to hold a grudge for my walking out of her Parisian life. We said goodbye with jovial hugs and jealousy undertow. She went back to France and Emo and I took off to London with Storm in his big black Buick.

The journey back to the swinging capital brought with it the reminder of our financial restraints, with Storm accusing Emo of not paying back a fiver he had lent him a few days previously.

We stopped off to see someone we knew in a huge detached house just outside Royston. This decidedly eccentric friend loved soul music and lived alone in the attic. His parents, who were supposed to preside over the rest of the house, never seemed to be there, or if they were they kept a very low profile. He had inherited £10,000 from a family estate, an awful lot of money then, and despite his better judgment, decided to spend the bulk of it on good quality dope. When we arrived he had in his possession an oriental smoking devise, which I was told was a hubble-bubble, loaded to the gills with the finest hashish money can buy. If that wasn't to your liking he had a smaller smoking device, the simple chillum, packed with regular high grade grass. And for those of us who preferred there was always a plain joint doing the rounds. We smoked, talked, laughed, kindled our friendship and got raging high.

Resuming our journey, Emo and I fell into the back of the car mellow yellow, but soon the journey got on the worst side of the driver. Storm continued to berate Emo about the fiver he had lent him. I got a little fed up with the rumble and suggested to Emo that if he promised to pay me back, I'd give Storm the money. Then we fell asleep sprawled out on the back seat. We dropped Emo off at a flat he was sharing with Dave Gilmour and continued on to Egerton Court. I can't say I wasn't worried about getting my money back.

Dave Gilmour and Emo had a job working for Ozzie Clark and Alice Pollock, two hugely successful designers, who ran a boutique in Chelsea, for their one off clothes, called Quorum. Dave was driving the van and Emo worked in the shop driving everybody either mad, or charming the pants off them. When I turned up Emo was in full female regalia entertaining the punters. He didn't have my money of course, but he said he would get it if I came with him and Dave, to drop some clothes off for a fashion show at the Chelsea Town Hall.

It seems that Dave surpassed the criteria of what was constituted as handsome. The modelling agencies were always trying to persuade him to pose and parade for them. Even when we arrived at the Hall they were trying to sign him up. Overcome by shyness he darted back into the safety of the van, with Emo and me following close behind, teasing him to take up this glamorous job. We carried on cajoling him all the way back to the Kings Road, but Dave was adamant. Not many days later he landed himself a life changing job playing the guitar.

Emo finally got round to paying me back the fiver outside Quorum, where we bumped into a friend who was in charge of a small studio used for the sole purpose of dubbing pornographic films. The friend told us we could earn £25 a session doing the voiceover if we so desired. Emo thought better of it, I took the bait.

If you could go at it with a distinct lack of shame, this was money for old rope, a simple job with few words and a lot of grunts and groans. I met another budding actor, whilst working on this conveyer for sex in the fast lane, a kindly soft spoken guy who reminded me of Syd. He had the same wry smile in his eye as Syd and like me seemed terribly uneasy about the whole ordeal. Any embarrassment we endured soon turned sweet for him, because a few weeks later he landed the part of Benvolio in a film of Shakespeare's *Romeo and Juliet*. In contrast to what was going down for us this was a massive break. We parted company and although

I was green with envy, I managed to find enough humility about my person to wish him well. Like the young actors I'd met in Barrow, his bid for stardom left me yearning for the same kind of attention, which I just assumed he got because he'd waded through three years at one of the principle drama schools. It seems I still had a long way to go if I was to have any chance of catching up.

If they believe this then they'll believe anything.
(Photo taken from an advert for vermouth)

28

Ponji seemed to be finding his way alright. When he left the London Film School, he found he was in demand as a film editor. This intricate job suited his meticulous eye. There is no doubt that if he'd continued working the frame he could have become very good at it, but unbeknownst to me there was something inside him that had other objectives.

Ponji was settling into a job with a Soho film company, when he started to dedicate himself to a path of inner development under the guidance of a spiritual teacher. As he began to explore what he and many others saw as the science of the soul, his time at Egerton Court reached its finale with an enlightening trip to India, where he was initiated by his beloved master.

On his return from this dazzling subcontinent, so full of the life force was he that even the more heathen among us couldn't help but see the effect. Something triggered the light, because despite what the sceptic might think, he literally seemed to be shining with abundance. Some friends said to me, having been with Ponji directly after he arrived back from India, that they would have taken the next plane out to the Punjab if they'd had the money; some did.

With dedication at the forefront of his life, he gave up his job as a film editor in London to devote himself entirely to this newly found spiritual path.

Sat on the sidelines I refused categorically to accept the shift. Even though I could see the very significant change in my brother, I was dumbstruck when he decided to move back to Cambridge. Maybe it was the feeling of loss, but my take on what he was leaving behind left me totally confounded. It just seemed perplexing that he needed something over and above the wonderment of our life as was. Why couldn't he work and live in London and still lead a spiritual existence? Why did he have to let go of absolutely everything? These were questions that would continue to plague me for decades to come.

I believed that despite knowing me since birth, Ponji still couldn't find it in his heart to trust me. It seems he had never really disclosed his innermost feelings. Later on, when the demons began to diminish the shine, my brother tried harder to convince me of his spiritual beliefs, but as he failed to tell me why he had taken them on in the first place I continually felt like I'd missed a cue.

Ponji's desire for a more humble life meant he wouldn't need his room in the flat anymore. As far as my time at Egerton Court was concerned, these changes, which had come out of left field, put me in an awkward position, as I would no longer have the luxury of living rent free on his floor.

Because I still fell miserably short on the money front, a friend of Storm's from Cambridge, Dave Henderson, was chosen to take Ponji's room. Dave H was a real artist, a gaunt handsome figure who was to spend a lot of time, often days and days alone, as one the world's unsung heroes, with his canvas and paintbrush. Like my cousin Francis, Dave H gave the impression of someone with a translucent body. He once answered the door to the flat when some fellow hippy had rung the bell, looking straight through Dave H, the hipster said "Oh hello man, is there no one here?" then turned away and left without so much as a bye word.

Like Ponji, Nigel and Jenny followed the spiritual quest, with the same journey to India. When they returned they decided to buy a house in Battersea, which in those days was the cheap side of the river. Their room at Egerton Court became vacant and immediately after they left, Syd moved in.

Syd wanted to be initiated onto the Sant Mat path just as Ponji, Nigel, Jenny and many other of his Cambridge friends had been, but he was rebuffed and told to come back later. This I was told can happen for many positive reasons. But being cast aside at this time and by such a redeemed person, seemed to add to an increasing disassociation that was starting to separate him from the ones he loved. He very quickly grew dark around the eyes and stopped speaking to most of us.

The first I'd heard of Syd's departure from the Floyd was when Emo and I met up with Dave Gilmour in Kew Gardens one afternoon.

While we were lying on the grass imbibing the air, Dave pulled out a crumbled bunch of fivers and slapped a couple of notes into my surprised hand. This was a lot of money then, especially to a non earner like me. I was about to ask what it was for, when he interrupted my train of thought by saying something about money in the grand scheme of things. Then he casually said how it was alright, as he was now receiving a healthy and what looked likely to be regular wage, having taken Syd's place as lead guitarist for Pink Floyd.

As far as the Floyd was concerned, Syd was now out of commission. But it was already clear that the first two Albums were selling enough to bring in an income that would enable his other-worldliness to experiment as a solo artist. Which he did like a man possessed, all over Egerton Court, using pans, pots, clocks, the bath, the bathwater, anything he could get his hands on to make his increasingly off-kilter sound.

A lot of the time, like Syd, I felt disenfranchised, like an autocue that gets misunderstood. Fortunately, unlike Syd who had started to mistrust most of his friends, I could still see how the sanctuary of others kept me afloat, gave me courage.

The moments, where I was convinced that I'd touched heaven on earth right here and right now, compelled me to hang on in there. However, when Ponji's time in London drew to a close these thin spiritual threads became more and more obscure. The odds of my being a full on real hippie in a material world were not looking good and I started to fall.

On the surface the game always had to be seen to be played and on the occasions when my discomfort got the better of me, those around told me with absolute conviction to be cool; "Don't worry about the flies in the sugar man, it's all cosmic". Privately this hip intervention left me fuming. Turning off the incessant chatter of the mind and floating down the stream, as the Beatles told us so eloquently to do in their song *Tomorrow Never Knows*, was becoming an increasingly difficult ordeal.

I felt alien to the likes of the so called spiritual teachers like Maharaji Mahesh Yogi and Maharaji Charan Singh. I was, I realise now, sour to the taste of such sweetness. I was too uptight. As far as I could see, the Beatles, my brother and many of his friends had fallen into the treacle jar and I couldn't get a handle on it at all.

Like guiltless new born children we gazed forever onwards, towards Noah's great rainbow. A philosophy of its time, which for many seemed innocent, but I had reached an impasse. I could only really be a part of it by sitting behind a mask of virtue, lodged in a self-conscious and quietly agitated place. There I would lie, in a room full of beautiful people, hidden in a remote part of the back brain. This part of the anatomy, like a voyeur obsessed, was forever soaking up everything out there, often peering into the confines of someone else's mesmerising and intensely private space. The sixties may have flaunted a parade of free love, but sometimes it was just downright embarrassing.

Without Ponji around I felt like I'd lost a foothold; but Storm, Dave Gale and Po shared my scepticism for this wave of saccharine mysticism hitting our shores, so it wasn't like I was really alone.

I wanted to stay on at Egerton Court, as I thought it might provide a way forward, after all I had got to know my new mates pretty well by now. They seemed so enterprising, particularly Storm, who I now saw as a close, if not powerful, ally. It was Storm who suggested that I spend the nights on his floor.

From becoming Storm's guest, I got to know many of his friends well and none more so than Nick Sedgwick. Nick could laugh until he cried. He was a delightful audience and like Dave Henderson he really wanted to brave the path of the warrior. They were true philosophers who saw art and poetry as the main way towards getting this ride. Nick's energy was constantly bursting with excitement and euphoric delight. He was someone who wanted to know the deeper score. Always on the line, his straight forwardness allowed me, if not demanded that I be myself, which I found difficult to do without reverting to the usual acting out.

My hairline was starting to recede, but in all honesty I thought of this as a natural progression. Ever since I came into the world my dad was bald and his baldness added a certain flavour to his charisma. I surely never saw it otherwise and I think my buoyant acceptance of hair-loss, helped Nick to see the humour in his receding hairline.

Storm, Dave H, Nick, Po and I sat around and pooled our ideas. We wanted to make a life which didn't compromise our integrity. The idea of a collective consortium came up, in which each person would be used for their particular artistic bent; anything from decorating to filming, therapy to theatre. The others may have seen it differently, but from where I sat, this is where the beginnings of the design company Hipgnosis were sown.

Richard Stanley's film *Beaky* went on to win a couple of awards at the various film festivals out there in the grown up world. Not to be outdone, Storm had the idea of making a film with Emo and me as wild protagonists. He had already made a 16mm black and white short with Emo and Pip, which for anyone lucky enough to have seen it, was wildly funny. Storm had the necessary qualifications and there was no doubt that Emo and I had a flare for acting; it may have lacked some refinement, but even in the most poignant moments we couldn't hold back from the cue.

After some discourse it was suggested that it would be a good idea to begin this celluloid undertaking out in the country. Realising this could be a way of contributing to my time at Egerton Court, I suggested my Aunt Fanny's, which was situated in the heart of the Essex countryside. This was a place that would impress my friends, at the same time I would boldly use the generosity of my aunt and uncle to put us up and feed us, thus buying me some quality time with my friends in London.

Ponji on the right and friends in India

29

I was nine years old when my dad took me to the railway station in Cambridge and left me with the station master, who in turn put me in a secluded carriage next to the guards van on the Essex bound train.

This journey to Sudbury was the first time that I'd experienced travelling any real distance alone.

Left to my own devises by the guard, I started struggling with a leather strap that held the window in the door to the outside closed. After a lot of effort I managed to unhook the strap from a small brass button, on the inside of the carriage and the window went crashing down into the wooden carcass of the door. I didn't have the strength to pull it back up and spent the whole journey with the bellowing sound and smoke from the steam engine pouring in through the window. I couldn't resist sticking my head outside, to see if I could catch sight of the engine as the train hit the bends, but withdrew quickly, retrieving a face full of black soot.

Having arrived safe and sound in Sudbury, my mother's sister Fanny and her husband George, along with my cousins Pauli and Corinna, came to pick me up. After the friendly hellos, which I shyly acknowledged, they took me to their home in the village of Gestingthorp. My dad and I had decided that I should try out the vacation here for a day or two to begin with, in case I got homesick. Like Ponji and Elizabeth before me this excursion was to become a regular event during many of the school holidays.

Gestingthorp Hall was a big rambling mansion set in the middle of a grand country estate and came attached with a small working farm. The gathering of crops from the manageable fields, allowed my cousins and me to ride on the combine harvester and play jump and hide in the bales of straw.

My understanding is that the Cooke's bought Gestingthorp Hall from the Oats family. Captain Titus Oats was one of the explorers who accompanied Captain Scott when he went to the South Pole, the one who said "I am just going outside and may be some time".

After that doomed expedition the remaining Oats Family made the largest room, upstairs at Gestingthorp Hall, into a small museum commemorating the explorer. When Auntie Fanny and Uncle George took over The Hall they decided to use this room as a studio for Fanny to paint in and hold art classes. Fanny was passionate about painting, especially with oils. She would try to encourage anyone with a similar inclination to turn a brush to the canvas. Even I crept up the darkly lit gothic stairs to attend a couple of painting sessions and of course, I had a boyhood fascination for the few remnants of Antarctic artefacts left behind from when the Oats lived there.

Run by the Cookes, The Hall retained a sense of fading aristocracy. There were staff on hand, but they only seemed to come in the mornings to work a spot of cleaning and help out during breakfast, which was served from warmed silver platters in an imposing oak panelled dining room. The only other gastronomic interludes, served in this grand room, were usually to honour an occasion worthy of the space, like a wedding, or the hunt. Apart from breakfast, regular meals were taken by the old AGA in the large friendly kitchen, well worn from years of use. Like Cecilia, Alice and the other sisters, Fanny did most of the domestic organising, the washing up and the cooking.

Electricity had only been put into The Hall in the mid Fifties. Despite this modern convenience there was little or no central heating, so the house was freezing in the winter. It seemed especially cold, because Fanny had that same stuff and nonsense attitude to roughing it that Alice had at Number Nine. I somehow found it disconcerting to see Fanny and George huddled in front of a two bar electric fire in one of the smaller rooms, with the ravages of Jack Frost knocking away at the door to the hallway inside the house; perplexing, because I'm sure they weren't exactly poor.

Gestinthorp turned with the seasons; the winters may have been harsh, but the summers could be exhilarating. There were special outings, like being taken for an eccentric camping expedition down to Cornwell in the Cooke's convertible Rolls Royce, where I got a flavour for riding the waves on a small board and tasting Cornish ice-cream for the first time. Then there was the excitement of standing next to Pauli's older brother John out on the field beyond the ha-ha, while he launched one of his beautifully crafted model aeroplanes into the blue unknown. The ha-ha was basically a ditch, one side of which was a vertical retaining wall and the other sloping grass, to stop livestock getting across to the front of the Hall. We used it as part of a daring game of leap-and-tag and it made a perfect mote to keep the dragons away in one of my elaborate fantasies. If playing castles didn't tickle your fancy, there was mucking about in the boat on the lake far away at the bottom of the front garden, and swimming naked in the freezing swimming pool secluded among the cypress trees; or if you were good at it, which I wasn't, playing a game of tennis on the hard court; there could be all this and more in the summers in Gestingthorp.

I spent most of my time during the holidays with Pauli and Rinnie, who treated me pretty much as a brother. Rinnie taught me to kiss, which to begin with was fraught with anxiety, but left me feeling warmly rewarded. Among other things they introduced me to their taste in popular music with the likes of Lonnie Donegan, Burl Ives and Spike Jones. These great singers and twisters from the fifties were played out from 78's, turning on a posh horn gramophone player in the grand Georgian drawing room. They spoke of the fun they had with Ponji, how he would start telling them great stories which he was never be able to finish, how he would start climbing anything difficult and tall, before he had even settled in. They liked Elizabeth but Ponji was their idol, they doted on him; his arrival brought with it excitement, a sense of great daring and ongoing adventure.

When I was a boy, I found Grandmother Hopkinson to be a ferocious beast of a woman. She spent the last years of her life going from one daughter to another and if ever it was her time to come to Adams Road my mother's moods would darken. On arrival Granny gave the family a shoe box full of chocolates to appease us, then having settled in, took her position at the head of the dining table and with fierce determination got on with her crocheting.

She resented young boys, which after seven tries, perhaps stemmed from not providing one for her husband Bertram. When she thought it was her business to do so, she would reprimand me and if she thought I'd gone too far hit me with her clenched fist and the protruding knuckle of her middle finger. I hated her for this and always wished she would die. She lived well into her nineties, which I suppose was fortunate in a way, because it gave me time to find some last minute compassion for her and her formidable ways.

By the time the Egerton Court lot came to shoot the film in Gestingthorp, Granny was well into her eighties and living full time in a large ground floor annex adjoining the side of the Hall, which had its own entrance and all the amenities needed to be fully independent. By this time her right eye had been replaced with a glass one and along with her fearsome character this made her very intimidating indeed. She often attended evening meals in the kitchen and there was something extraordinary about seeing her in the company of Emo, Dave Henderson, Storm Thorgoson, Nick Sedgwick and all. She held her own very nicely thank you. There was one memorable evening when she came to the table fighting from all sides, picked up her fork and demanding to know what it was, speared a burnt sausage as if she meant to kill it. Her action was delivered with such force that her glass eye shot out of its socket into her soup. Ignoring the guests, as they looked on in stark disbelief, she sifted around among the noodles and juices for the marble like eye, wiped it off with her napkin and put it in her cardigan pocket, then carried on eating as if nothing untoward had happened.

Auntie Fanny went to Slade Art College in the1920's and she was a highly gifted painter, but like the rest of her sisters she didn't seem to have quite enough belief in herself to really follow through with her talent. An all too familiar trait that seemed to come back and haunt my family, near and far, time and time again.

Fanny may have had a heart that lay with the bohemian, but this didn't stop her from taking on the trappings of an archaic life style in a mansion and marrying an old fashioned gentleman, who was a partner in the family run law firm in London.

As a traditionalist, George Cooke carried the convention of the Hall ever onwards, a true Edwardian centre in the village. There was hunting, croquet, cricket, the Hall versus the locals and many of the other recreational goings-on, grown out of bygone English ways.

The five Cooke boys attended Winchester, Marlborough, or Eton Public School and like their father and his father before they were expected to go to Oxford or Cambridge then into a life in the City at the office.

As far as I know George commuted to London every working day for most of the many years they lived in Gestingthorp. He'd leave the house extremely early in the morning and get back late in the evening. I imagined that Fanny felt for a great deal of time that she was widowed to The Hall, so by the time the sixties came along, I think she was dying for some artistic irreverence to shake things up around the place.

While I am sure Uncle George found the idea of a bunch of weekend hippies invading his private space somewhat alarming, Fanny welcomed us eagerly.

The film that we went so readily into the Essex countryside to shoot was to be called *The Mad Bugger.* There wasn't a story as such but there was a theme, with the main idea being that Emo and I should offset each other in the most anarchic way possible. My character was a floor mat, someone who was seen to be like a refuse disposal bag into which any old garbage could be put. Without my knowing it this role I played so willingly, showed up my underlying relationship with Storm.

Both Emo and I went out of our way to get attention from the people around who we saw as potential guardians and Storm was no exception. It may seem naive now, but we had been locked into this survival habit for so long it just seemed like a natural part of the course. Storm's role was to control us, like an arrogant trainer with two performing monkeys. In the film, as in life, he'd promote the games. He went out of his way to keep us at the end of a leash, and the nearer the edge we got the longer the lead.

Sometime into the shoot we began filming in a chicken run and as is my want, I suggested that I should have a fit on the muddy floor and Storm seemed delighted by this idea. On action I went into full throttle and ended the take with a Neanderthal step, by eating a mixture of mud and chicken droppings. Once we had got that one out of the way the idea came up that Emo might defecate on my face. Who suggested this, or whether or not this actually happened is irrelevant. The very fact that we entertained the idea isn't.

I hadn't realised just how far I was prepared to go to be liked by someone who I thought held the key to my future; all under the watchful eye of my relations. The words 'far out' were beginning to reach an ultimatum, if not a deafening conclusion.

To many members of my family, I must have seemed completely and hopelessly lost. No doubt this was the case, but I had taken this route because no other seemed forthcoming. I had become super adept at getting stoned aloofness to help me blend into the grownup world. Smoking dope had become second nature. I may have been swept a long way off from the shore, but I was still determined to stay afloat.

Little did I realise how I would have to drift a lot further out, until the tide would eventually begin to turn.

Like bees we were drawn back to London, as if it were a gigantic soup plate of honey. The sweet, enticing spells made the temptation to dive in so intense that drowning seemed inevitable. Integrity is almost impossible to maintain unless one stays firmly on the rim and who was really strong enough to do that? Well one of us was. Dave Henderson went back to Gestinthorp Hall a few months later and lived there for well over a year to continue his search for the grail through painting.

Back at Egerton Court the aftertaste of *The Mad Bugger* hung in the air like the smell of some uncooked fish. The two reels of 16mm negatives, sat undeveloped in film cans inside the fridge for months, until they moved with Storm to his flat in Belsize Park, where as far I know they still sit, tucked out of the way like some terrible self-conscious truth.

Gestingthorp Hall

30

It wasn't hard to remember that Storm's girlfriend, the ever buoyant Libby January, was the daughter of a successful estate agent in Cambridge, because the for-sale signs yelled out her surname outside many houses in the shire. She and Storm would quite often go down to her parent's house for the weekend, which meant four square meals and a rest from the dance in London. Sometimes they would invite me and anyone else, who happened to be around, to go with them. I think Libby's parents were a bit flummoxed by us, especially her father, who was by any standards quite a corpulent conservative man. If ever we ended the evening by watching television with Mr. January in their living room, he always made sure we stood for the Queen; in those days the BBC finished broadcasting well before the midnight hour, with the National Anthem.

I helped Storm with Pink Floyd's *Ummagumma* album cover, when the doorway and garden at Libby's parents house, was used as a framework for one of his surreal ways of looking into perspective. I remember it, not so much for the occasion, but as my last ever excursion with Storm and Libby together, for it was shortly after this that we all parted company.

While she and Storm appeared to be very close, it seems Libby had worked out, well before any of us, that Storm's insecurities were such, that he saw achieving closeness as an intellectual pursuit.

Most of the time Libby and Storm seemed very happy with my company, but if ever Libby decided to stay the night in London, it was a question of two's company and three's a crowd. I'd then make a tentative move toward Po's room and lean on him for hospitality, which wasn't always easy.

On the surface Aubrey Powell or Po, as he was known to us, was not someone I'd normally choose to hang out with, because he wasn't comfortable around too much angst. Spending time with him meant choosing one's words carefully. His business sensibilities came first and made him a hard nut to crack. I'd worked out quite quickly that Po was dogmatic about day to day living, particularly about keeping the shekels coming in, and as I was continually broke, this often made me feel as if I'd outstayed my welcome.

Money may have held a key position in Po's life, but it wasn't necessarily the financial loop that found a way to his heart. He loved music especially the blues, and could, when he got down to it, play the guitar like a man possessed. Po was an out and out raver who, if he chose to do so, took me on a sweeping ride of musical possibilities.

In one of our more poignant moments, he disclosed to me that when he was outside, he could become dwarfed to the size of a miniature doll, with the streets and buildings taking on gigantic, towering proportions. Then something would trigger the brain to change his perception and in a blink of an eye he became a giant, looking down at the roof tops. He used to like the odd spliff, but he wasn't by any means delusional, so these Alice in Wonderland insights he had were extraordinary.

When we'd gotten to know each other a little better, Po began to give more of his time and I found on rare occasions, his company to be wildly exhilarating. If I was with Po for instance and Emo dropped by, I could find myself floored by the riotous banter going down between them. Lazy Sunday afternoon, we had no mind to worry. It was a good thing that these seriously jocular times were infrequent – otherwise the incontrollable effort from laughing so much could have seriously ruptured my spleen.

Despite the camaraderie and the rock 'n blues interludes, Emo and I continued to be a financial liability. The bottom line meant that Po found trust in two dossers like us difficult to realise. Sadly we seemed shy of ever really taking a step through the looking glass together, but we got damn close.

Aside from some token handouts for appearing in student films at the RCA, earning regular money continued to elude me in London. Along with letters, telling me firmly to get one of those jobs that resting actors get, my father stretched to putting a little cash in to see me through. I didn't feel much like an actor, but I thought, perhaps in vain, that if I could hold on a little longer, the wave of creative excitement breaking at the doorsteps of the RCA might lead me to a more fruitful stronghold. In light of these dreams, George's insistent letters made me painfully aware of how I wasn't really holding my own. So when Jenny approached me out of the blue with the suggestion that I might take a job with Sue Miles who ran the restaurant at The Arts Lab in Drury Lane, I seized the opportunity like a hungry monkey grabbing for a banana.

Apart from bringing in some badly needed cash, I got to know the Lab quite intimately. It seemed like the perfect place for me to work, because it gave me an ordered routine in an environment advocating social freedom. I could flirt with a happening or two and get into talking with one of the many performers or artists and leave without shame if I felt too exposed, as working in the restaurant gave me the perfect get-out clause.

Converted from a huge abandoned warehouse, the Arts Lab was kicked into life by the ever amorous Jim Haynes, and it was for a time the most controversial centre for theatre, film and art in the UK, if not the world. Jim Haynes had an office tucked away up a couple of narrow steps at the back of the building, with wall to wall mattress covering the floor. There was no furniture, just a mass of books and papers spread-eagled around the sides of the room, and his typewriter taking centre stage. Don't get me wrong, I only peeked into his office when I felt the weather permitted, which was usually in the middle of the afternoon. Once when I thought it was all clear in the lobby I stole a moment to peep in and to my dismay I saw Germaine Greer, Jim and a couple of others in there and they weren't drinking tea.

On the same floor as Jim's office there was a very adaptive studio theatre, a gallery and the main entrance. On the right hand side just inside the entrance was a large semicircular reception desk with piles of flyers, posters and other such give a-ways that adorned its parameters, but there was rarely anyone behind it.

The restaurant on the upper floor was a lean spacious affair, with some scrubbed tables and benches taking up most of the space. A juke box was the only other piece of furniture and it stood alone under the window pounding out the rhythms of the day.

Serving behind the hatch and clearing tables meant I met a lot of the artists who came to play their part in the building. Of the many dignitaries that rang my bell I suppose it was John Lennon, who seemed the most intriguing because he was so shy and polite, quite the opposite to what I expected him to be. He and Yoko Ono came to The Arts Lab a few times. She seemed to lead the way, whilst John remained a cautious step behind. They did one of their performance happenings in the lobby once and John became a little more animated, when he broke an egg into Yoko's small bag of white flour. This work of art was then shrouded in mystery and displayed as a piece of sculpture near the main entrance with a little rope fence around it and a sign saying John and Yoko.

I found the theatre in The Arts Lab to be a somewhat alien affair. In all the time I worked there, I don't think I ever saw a show; this wasn't to say I didn't peek in on a technical run and get a glimmer of what was round the corner. It could have been Van Morrison's band Them, or perhaps it was The Peoples Show, or the writer James Baldwin, or maybe even the black activist Michael X inciting the next radical move.

The Arts Lab was the happening place in London. At its height you could just turn up at any time, day or night, get a bowl of soup, meet a friend and be privy to some up to the minute event put on by many of the extraordinary performers, artists and musicians, who seemed to be attracted to the place in droves. I had a fleeting glimpse once, of someone on all fours, spread-eagled on the floor like an insect, under a sparse structure made up of scaffolding poles. The creature was Steven Berkoff, who would reappear sometime later as a main player in my life. (I don't think Steven performed *Metamorphosis* at the Arts Lab, so he must have been trying it out; either that or I was observing him rehearsing *In the Penal Colony*)

Working upstairs wasn't all honey and roses, it could also mean I was subject to some verbal abuse, especially from disgruntled hippies who thought their lot in life should be put up front and heard.

I saw the tide turn the heart of love toward a darker side here. It was becoming clear that a number of radicals were beginning to believe that a more demonstrative need for change was necessary to get their act across. Martin Luther King was giving way to the The Black Panthers, Dud and Pete to Derrick and Clive, the Beatles were on the brink of splitting up and in my free-wheeling work corner, Punk wasn't that far away from throwing a hammer at the works. "Thanks for this bowel of chilli con carne man". "What about payment!" "Money doesn't exist in my universe man, deal with it".

The Arts Lab was a goldfish bowl and although I was swimming about on the inside, I never really felt comfortable in the water. For some, who were more susceptible to change, it became a place they might walk into wearing a tie and suit, then wander out without a watch and in a kaftan full of beads.

Not for want of trying, I couldn't really get the hang of it at all. Strangely I felt shy there, especially among the main players. Surprising really, I wanted to fit in and fantasised incessantly of firing on all four cylinders there, but it just didn't happen. I had my moments though, but they were usually small waves, upstairs in the restaurant.

I remember vividly how the basement was done up like Jim's office, where the same mattress flooring turned it into a very intimate space for showing films; a great place for crashing out that inevitably became an addict's haven. The time and the space were running away from themselves.

I don't think The Arts Lab closed down as such; it just ran out of favour and fell to the demise of the junkies and disintegrated.

Maybe he was like this with everyone, but Jim Haynes seemed to have this way of looking through me like I didn't exist. Years later I bumped into him in the bar at the Traverse Theatre in Edinburgh, I introduced myself as someone he knew from working at the Lab in the 60s; he was nice enough, but he was quizzical. I don't think he really had any idea who I was and why should he have done, after all, I could have been anyone.

A movement is accomplished in six stages
And the seventh brings return.
The seven is the number of the young light
It forms when darkness is increased by one.
Change returns success
Going and coming without error.
Action brings good fortune.
Sunset.
The time is with the month of winter solstice
When the change is due to come.
Thunder in the other course of heaven.
Things cannot be destroyed once and for all.
Change returns success
Going and coming without error.
Action brings good fortune.
Sunset, sunrise.
A movement is accomplished in six stages
And the seventh brings return.
The seven is the number of the young light
It forms when darkness is increased by one.
Change returns success
Going and coming without error.
Action brings good fortune.
Sunset, sunrise.

Chapter 24, Syd Barret 1967

31

The tail end of the sixties reached a pinnacle of injustice for many heads, with the drug squad raiding Keith Richards's home in Sussex – among others he and Mick Jagger were arrested and made an example of by being imprisoned. It was a well publicised and celebrated bust, which saw the demonstrations and outrage reach out across the lands. Thousands of people particularly among the young were smoking marijuana at this time, and it was decided by some of the hippy intelligentsia that a change in the law was necessary. This shift was kicked into fruition by a young man of the day called Steve Abrams who ran a drug research company called Soma (Society of Mental Awareness). At Soma's instigation a full page advertisement was put in The Times, calling for a stark reform to the law regarding cannabis. It was signed by sixty-five prominent figures from that time; including Francis Crick, David Dimbleby, Brian Epstein, Graham Greene, Francis Huxley, George Harrison, Dr Ronald D Laing, John Lennon, Paul McCartney, Ringo Starr and others. The outcome of this public declaration was the *Wootton Report*, which was influential in how the law is today, regarding the penalty for the possession of soft and hard drugs.

One of the signatories in the advertisement had been Dr Ian Dunbar who I believe was the Medical Director of Soma. He was one of two doctors that we knew of who was able to prescribe a tincture of cannabis to those who needed it on medical grounds.

Around this time Storm and I had wangled a meeting with Dr Dunbar at his surgery in Notting Hill Gate. We managed to convince him that we needed the aforementioned tincture, using some limp excuse about getting paranoid from smoking dope outside the confines of the law. He was our Dr Roberts and just signed the paper.

Storm and I would collect our fortuitous prize from a chemist in Shaftsbury Avenue, take it back to Egerton Court and make up our medicine. This consisted of pouring the said tincture over some tobacco in a small tobacco tin, and then placing the mixture in a preheated oven, which evaporated the alcohol, thus leaving the tin full of a dense, but workable concoction. This was to be the beginning of the end...

Dave Gale and I came hurtling back from The Arts Lab one evening, with the lash of speed tearing a tear from our eye. We had managed to cross Grosvenor Place from Hyde Park Corner and started to make a getaway for the last stretch home, when we were pulled in by a police man.

To the officer, who waved us down, we must have looked like two wild men of Borneo, with our long hair ripped in all directions by the wind. He started by asking us the formalities; is this your scooter, do you have a licence etc? The law regarding head protection was on the cusp of change and he asked Dave if we'd thought about wearing helmets. I was feeling a little cantankerous and quipped in with "Of course he has". The authorities were still unfamiliar with what was going down among the bohemian enclave, especially those who looked like us. The officer looked us up and down, then said after a short pause, "I suppose you're the sort who smoke that marugoweeni". I retorted again, as cool I could muster, "as a matter of fact yes", which immediately propelled him into a kind of military drill.

We were hauled off the scooter and told to stand with our arms down by our sides. Instead of being impressed Dave Gale couldn't believe what I had just done. As he was telling me from under his breath, what an idiot I was, I brought out a tin of the aforementioned substance to show the policeman, who then thought he'd struck gold. "What's this?"

"Legal marijuana, I get it from a doctor on prescription".

"Oh yes and I'm the King of Spain, keep your hands where I can see em" he said, as we were escorted like prisoners of war across to a little police station, which unbeknownst to us was tucked away under the big arch in the centre of Hyde Park Corner.

We must have sat in that tiny waiting room for two or three hours before the sergeant behind the desk, finally tracked down Dr Dunbar, who in the end legitimised the contents of the tin. The policeman, who had been somewhat aggressive in how he had handled us, now came back a humble servant, ingratiating to the extreme; it was sir this and sir that, as he showed us to the door.

During the wait Dave Gale had kind of given into the inevitable and no doubt thought I was a total lunatic for behaving as I did. Back at

Egerton Court however, our escapade came across as a rebellious wheeze. We were offered some hash cake to celebrate our home coming, which, because of his wired experiences with psychedelics, Dave took umbrage to and went to his room. I quietly dismissed this as being nonsensical paranoia on his part. But a few days later my world was going to place me squarely on his side of the tracks...

Storm and I shared a passion for going to the movies. We would often go with a flask of tea and a lunch box filled with sandwiches, especially useful if it was a film like South Pacific and involved an interval. *2001 A Space Odyssey,* fitted this criteria perfectly.

Although only recently opened at one of the big-time panoramic cinemas in Soho, Storm and I had queued up to see Stanley Kubrick's ground-breaking film a few times over the last weeks. Now we felt we were ready enough to see it again, only this time under the influence of Lysergic Acid Diethylamide.

Sitting in the cinema, waiting for the film and the trip to kick in, I started to drift, when somewhere from a distance I began hearing my parents calling out my name. Although far away at first, it was clear that they seemed to be telling me something a little severe and distinct. I got more and more drawn into the sounds of their voices until they were actually coming not from the auditorium, but from deep inside the confines of my skull. As the LSD got into full swing, their presence, having been minimal, became overwhelmingly accusing and loud. "Matthew", they kept saying, "WHAT DO YOU THINK YOU'RE DOING?"

Pummelled into a maze of doubt and guilt, the workings of my brain began to rip themselves apart. The power of my parent's voice was so strong that it took me to the very edge of my being. Totally wide awake, while completely absorbed in a literal nightmare, I was no longer capable. Whilst I was aware of my surroundings, I had lost all association. Sucked into a subliminal state of mind, banged up and twisted away inside, toying with another world. This appalling paralysis went on for hours and in all my years on the planet it was to be the most horrific experience I've ever encountered.

Storm led me back to South Kensington and Egerton Court, like a medium attached to a terrified ghost. He stayed by my side for the remaining hours, as the horrors continued to bite into my senses, until nature's balm finally enveloped me in sleep. I was fortunate in being able to regain a grip on my equilibrium, but the scar remained, a steadfast reminder of how easily sanity spins into madness.

The outcome of this horrendous trip meant my pride was shot to pieces. I was no longer able to ride the high ground and everything was far from cool. It was as if I had been turned inside out and the screaming contradictions were there for all to see.

Hard though it was to accept, I now had a much better understanding of what Dave Gale meant when he said he suffered at the hands of personal demons. He had been spooked to the core by the devil's hydra and made it clear to us that he wasn't at all comfortable around tripping, or smoking dope. If ever he found himself digesting these mind shifting substances, either on purpose, or by accident, he said it left him with a fuck sight more than a paranoid after taste.

He too could go into cataclysms of paranoia when threatened by an oncoming visit from his parents.

For Storm and I these parental allusions and drug induced nightmares were something to be smirked at; how ridiculous to be afraid of your parents. "Just relax man take it in your stride, it's just a cosmic interlude before the real thing. Be cool", but he couldn't and now I had been slapped, well and truly into the reality of how he felt.

At present cannabis can be prescribed by doctors in the form of extract of cannabis and alcoholic tincture of cannabis. Until very recently the demand for these preparations has been virtually negligible. In recent months however, there has been a striking increase in the amounts prescribed. Our enquiries, supported by what we were told by our witnesses, indicate that there are a number of doctors who are beginning to experiment with the use of cannabis in the treatment of disturbed adolescents, heroin and amphetamine dependence and even alcoholism.

Clause 99 of 'The Wooton Report' 1968

32

A saucer full of secrets it might have been, but it became clear as time drew its course that my role in Storm's life was increasingly going to be about being on the receiving end of his ardent commands. I helped him, in whatever way I could, to develop early record covers for Pink Floyd, Ainsley Dunbar Retaliation and a few other bands of the day. He managed to scrape together enough work through contacts and friends to keep things evolving. Although he'd allow me to have a say in how a piece of art might be, he invariably seemed to have the last call. Despite our undoubted friendship, his persistent compulsion to be boss, especially around our artistic endeavours, was beginning to wear very thin. Somewhat anxiously, I started looking for a way out.

I began to drag my feet across Storm's bough, especially for the short time we spent together in the darkroom, where his incessant commandeering role came in too close and the chemicals made me nauseous. No doubt if I'd been more lucid, I would have been able to say no at the necessary moment and stand up for myself, but I didn't have the wherewithal to grow away from this dependency. My need for reassurance meant the balls to stand as an equal in Storm's company still eluded me, particularly in the work environment. I fitted with ease into the hands of the puppet master and he was more than ready to pull the strings.

By spending time with Nick Sedgwick I began to gain a vague understanding of how it wasn't just Storm who created the scenario we were both in. By sharing these frustrations with Nick, who had become a real friend, I came to understand how I had fallen head long into Storm's game, how I had virtually made a conscious choice to be his yes man.

Finally, it was beginning to sink in. If I wanted to survive in the adult world I needed to be myself, rather than constantly trying to please by being someone else. Easier said than done – little realising it would be a lifetime's work, I was determined to make this a lesson I could learn.

There was now a rapid amount of change in the air. Ponji had for all intents and purposes walked out of my life. Dave Gale and Storm's time at The Royal College of Art was drawing to a close. Syd was beginning to walk on the balls of his feet, lose touch with the ones he loved and was starting to live in a darker place. All these changes were making me feel unsteady and I was starting to see the return of fear as a prominent pillar in my life.

I had discussed with Nick how we might get a place together, but I still didn't have the guts to take that small step. Then, with what seems now like a perfect piece of fortuitous timing, Dave Gale came up to me late one afternoon in the corridor of Egerton Court and with enough gravitas put it bluntly; "If you don't get out from under Storm's wing, he will smother you to death". This was the push I needed to tell Storm what to do with his directives.

For some short time we all moved away from Storm and he was shattered. Severely traumatised, he took up therapy. His retrospection didn't last long; he soon relapsed back into his old head boy routine. Over the next few years I occasionally met up with Storm, but the reality was, he only really wanted me around if he could force-fit me into his schemes. This isn't to say he didn't teach me, directly or indirectly, an awful lot at a crucial time in my life. My few years with Storm opened new doors and he undoubtedly planted the seeds for my investigating a more interplanetary self.

Nick and I moved into a two roomed flat near Notting Hill Gate to share our thoughts and lick our wounds.

What my friendship and dialogue with Nick had done was to bring me much closer to Dave Gale's way of perceiving things. By becoming more confident in his and Dave's company, I started to share some of my more private feelings. As the trust between us began to grow, we revealed a great deal of interest in how we become fragile and how easily our worlds can collapse. And although I couldn't quite get to grips with it, or perhaps more to the point, didn't want to believe it; I started to further question my own values and how, despite the freethinking spirit of my family, we weren't actually standing as securely as we thought we might be.

Since 1966 Dave Gale had been going to weekly therapy sessions with a controversial therapist of the time David Cooper.

Along with Ronald Laing, David Cooper was perhaps best known as someone who saw psychiatry as institutionalised, complacent and even dangerous. Cooper coined the term *Anti-Psychiatry* and was instrumental in bringing likeminded persons, like Dave Gale and I together to form the *Anti-University* – a way of joining, exploring, learning, without the domination of institution.

I went with Dave Gale to an extraordinary forward thinking event in the summer of 1967 which was put on at the Round House over a period of two weeks called *The Dialectics of Liberation*. During those few days I witnessed a diverse selection from many cultural fronts talk about what liberation really meant in their lives. Dr R. D. Laing, Alan Ginsburg, Stokely Carmichael, Herbert Marcuse and Dr David Cooper were among those that took part. They put across, with commanding clarity, the necessity for a diverse psychological shift to take place in our society, if we are really to create a place of true freedom.

I was learning how the idea of freedom is bandied around in social and family circles, like so many footballs on a football pitch, when the reality is that for those who saw these ideas differently, the doors to the playing field were closed and locked tight against their access. I began to get my first real understanding of how liberation wasn't restricted to how things swing on the outside, and that if we were going to change then it was going to have to be a change that came from within ourselves.

And the ships were set adrift.

Dave Gale went on to form the theatre company Lumiere and Son with Hilary Westlake. Dave Henderson spent a great deal of time, sometimes days alone, painting his masterpieces. Nick Sedgwick went to live in Mexico and became a prolific poet and writer. Storm and Po mapped out a way ahead for record sleeves and rock videos, establishing Hipgnosis as a ground breaking design company. Nigel and Jenny came back from India to start a family and the film company Gordon Films. Syd moved out of Egerton Court into a flat around the corner in Earls Court and shone for a while as a crazy diamond, before falling headlong into the abyss. And last but not least, shortly after my declared independence from Storm, I stumbled into a heaven sent world of genuine love.

~

Vivien Kurz was a sensitive eye-catching pre-Raphaelite New Yorker, an underground actress, who was well known in certain circles, particularly for a film that came out of the Warhol Factory called the *Match Girl* – a New York fairy story loosely based on *The Little Match Girl* by Hans Christian Anderson and directed by the avant-garde film maker Andrew Meyer in 1966. Vivien and I first met while I was working on Richard Stanley's film *Beaky* and immediately had an attraction for each other, but she was going out with one of the crew members, who I was told had fits of psychotic jealousy about her, which was understandable given how attractive she was, so I avoided any major flirtations. A month or so later I was invited to a party and met up with her again. That night as they say, the world fell into place.

Vivian seemed like a natural occurrence, something familiar that made me feel real and connected with myself again. She wasn't a night owl as such, but neither was she a great daytime person. The outside world just didn't seem to exist when I was with Vivian.

In-between bouts of sweet warmth, and soulful love-making, she'd roll up small spliffs – we'd get stoned, listen to our favourite music, get the munchies, sleep, laugh, argue and philosophise. Whichever way the wind blew, I wanted to be with her.

She shared a flat with her friend and confidante the actress Francesca Annis, around the corner from Egerton Court and it was here that I was to spend a lot of time with her. I was the most possessive lover in Christendom.

Despite her need for an eiderdown way of life in the city, I managed to entice Vivian out of London for a few days to meet my parents in Norfolk. George was particularly forthcoming and seemed to like her a lot; whilst my mother was a little reserved, however even she wasn't totally averse to Vivian's charms. I was relieved and delighted at their acceptance. I thought I was on to a winner. Undoubtedly my parent's approval was, it seems, still important to me.

Following many months in her gentle company I became acutely aware that Vivien seemed distracted when we were together, perhaps stemming from the fact that my lack of artistic clarity made me a dumbwaiter – meaning however together I came across to her on the outside, I was floundering like mad on the inside. Vivien was all too aware of my inner torment and whatever strengths I could bring to our sumptuous table started to pall. We tried in vain to make things work, but in the end she became wary of a future together. She took to the road, with a short trip to Morocco, to think things through on her own and this culminated in her going back to America.

Her departure was heart breaking enough, but then she sent me a letter, which was to be earth shattering. She wrote that despite our love she was no good for me, and that it would be better for both of us if we were to end any thought of getting back together. She finished the letter by declaring her warmth and asked if it would be possible to remain friends, despite the unhappy ending.

33

After my break-up with Vivian I set out to protect myself against the women I got involved with. I don't think this defensive stance was anything overtly conscious, or new, it's just that it became cunning and more prevalent. I certainly didn't realise that I was going to have to acknowledge the chronic distrust for the female form and put it to right, if ever there was going to be real maturity in my life.

As those tremulous cords were eating away at the better part of my heart, I tried to keep my head down and wished my spirits high. It didn't take long before the ancient engrained habits caught up with me. Convinced by the turmoil, I slid back into the old subdued pile of low self esteem.

With some stoic determination and after god knows how long, I returned to the realms of the living. I was again feeling really squeezed by my parents, who kept writing letters of concern about my nonexistent finances, suggesting firmly that I should settle down immediately and take on a job. Easier said than done – I knew by now that the only way to deal with this disquiet was to become an actor, but my lack of self-belief was undermining me on every front. I just felt hopelessly incapable. Even with Barrow, those few years previously, and the recent skirmishes of acting at the RCA, I still didn't have the confidence to use what I'd learnt and step onto a more conspicuous rung of the star-studded ladder.

After weeks of living hand to mouth, bumming around and not caring too much, my conscience finally caught up with me. I managed to find some work; this mostly consisted of decorating my cousin's market research offices in Soho, which thank god were a bit like the Forth Bridge.

The merry-go-round turned slowly for the better. I got back into going to the weekly *Anti-University* meetings. These gatherings of freethinkers took place in living rooms, cafes, pubs, rented halls and anywhere else that wasn't tied to an organisation. This was a way of giving, taking and learning without any notion of an institution dominating the dialogue. I started to mix with some extremely intelligent, interesting people, friends who brought a renewed challenge to the foundation of my life.

The early meetings for the *Anti-University* took place at Nicholas Albery's house. Nicholas was a lovely guy, an enthusiastic self-deprecating hippie, who survived Oxford University and the sixties and went on to become an innovator of workable alternatives. He spoke out about the ecosystem, how it just wasn't sustainable, before Greenpeace was founded. He never owned a car and was one of the cofounders of Neals Yard in Covent Garden, when it really was an oasis for alternative whole-food and holistic medicine. He wasn't afraid of standing up in front of the status quo to express his difference or indeed concern. It was typical of him to invite the beginnings of a radical movement into his family's opulent home in Kensington.

The *Anti-University* meant talk of revolution, not anarchic revolution, but a revolution of the heart and mind.

A ruffle-feathered, beard-mumbling, David Cooper rocking backwards and forwards in cross-legged position in the Albery's Regency living room, was indeed something to be reckoned with. David Cooper was an existential and indeed controversial psychiatrist, a nonconformist who, along with R.D. Laing, questioned the orthodox treatment of madness. This was heavy threatening stuff back then, not that that concerned them too much. For them there were no absolutes, or fixed parameters, no tangible boundaries. They strove for dialogue in all relationships particularly in traditional ones like doctor-patient, mother-daughter. However challenging to the orthodox system or to them-selves, there was a possibility of change. With Laing and Cooper you could never pin anything down to a right or a wrong way, in fact they had many differences, but one thing became clear, there had to be a more collective responsibility for madness in the family/society, if we were to survive.

I immersed myself in Cooper's works and those of R.D. Laing and became convinced that my state of mind hadn't just come out of the blue. The realization that I wasn't isolated gave me the strength and conviction to accept a greater depth and vulnerability in my life. A picture was emerging of someone who was admitting to wading through the mire and wanted out. I was beginning to learn how I could only be my true self within the safety of isolation. When I was with my friends and family for the best part I'd play an elaborate game of pretence. The more convoluted this fake presentation of myself became the harder it was to stop. At times this compulsion had become so extreme that my life at its centre seemed completely pointless.

~

I met Ann Friend from going to the *Anti-University* meetings. She was straightforward, courteous and took a deep interest in anyone who cared to find out about who she was.

She had worked out that the only way to survive was to make sure she got enough money from her old man, who by her say was rich enough, and come to England from the US, get set up and do therapy.

Ann was like the high priestess of reality and non reality. I am not sure if she meant it that way but that's how she came across to me, especially when she was on home ground, surrounded by cats, consulting the tarot, in her lofty tower situated on the top floor of a rickety house in Powis Square. Here she resided slap bang in what was then the thriving head culture of Notting Hill Gate.

Without malice or agro Ann had a way of questioning my outlook, which on occasion made me feel as if the floorboards were slipping away from under my reality.

There was no way I was able to fully understand where she was coming from, or what she wanted then; but I felt intrigued and at the same time extremely threatened by her emotional insights regarding my family.

Why was I threatened? Privately I allowed myself to sense the intensity of the entanglement, but for anyone on the outside my family was hallowed ground. Someone who came into that circle and started to challenge these fundamentals, like Ann did, posed a threat.

It was a foregone acceptance that when I was with my parents, they were the grownups and for the most part I was still the child, whose livelihood they were still very concerned for. I had no idea just how locked in the past the need for us to remain entrenched in this relationship of infantile dependency really was.

The couple of times I took Ann to visit them was unbelievably scary. I think I was too frozen up inside to really equate what was going on, but looking back there was no doubt she had her finger on the pulse of who we were.

By now my parents were settled into a comfortable way of life in Norfolk. They had less money, but my dad's dream of continuing his work as a poet and running a small bookshop had come true. The last thing they wanted was to have their bedspread disturbed by an upstart like me, so when I went to North Creake to see them with my new-found insights, I came up against a subtle wall of disinterest. Understandably they were very dubious about anything that might dampen the spirit of their idyllic life. I had no intention of destroying or taking away from anything they were doing, on the contrary, I felt very proud of them. But it was beginning to dawn on me that perhaps some of their children were paying a price for the life they had chosen.

The image my parents presented to the world of liberated truth was beautifully crafted. They spoke of Poetry, Freedom, Socialism, Love and Loyalty with such flare and certainty. Although I felt well out of their league I wasn't entirely uncomfortable with it, but I was starting to notice how this altruistic outpouring came from a place which somehow seemed carefully guarded.

Much to my dismay, when Ann was in my parent's company she wasn't in the least bit intimidated by their intellectual finesse, and the possibility that they might not agree with her viewpoint. She went out of her way to question their beliefs, their conclusions and insights.

They seemed dubious about allowing any of their flock responsibility above and beyond anything they might be in control of, and I think Ann knew this. Ann had worked out so much about how dysfunction in a family can come about, from her own. When she started to say to my parents that I may well be seeing a lot more of the social complexities than they might imagine, you could feel the hairs rise on the back of their collective neck.

A few days after Ann's visit, my mother told me how it was imperative that I shouldn't be taken in by the tidal pull of a woman's needs; she said "I ought to be very wary of my desires for the opposite sex blocking my path to the stage and acting".

Although I'd slept with Ann a few times it was never going to be the central issue in our relationship, as I was too scared of her power; but this didn't stop me from wanting some of her emotional knowledge.

The great love in her life was an extremely sensitive man she'd met, who had a drink problem. It was because of this relationship that I went with Ann a few times to Al Anon meetings and open AA meetings in London. Through Alcoholics Anonymous I started to get a real understanding of how the person with the drink problem so often becomes the family scapegoat. I began to learn how the family as a whole makes up the merry-go-round of an addict's life and if one person, whether they are the drinker or not, tries to get off the ride, all hell can break loose. We need the boozer as much as they need us, if it is otherwise we no longer have a role to play. In turn I saw how the family so often needs someone to be seen as neurotic, or if you like mad, so the rest of us can appear to be seen as together, or more to the point sane.

I was looking for alternative ways of understanding my own strengths and weakness and thought naively that my family might go into this with me.

There was now no doubt that as a unit we were starting to become fragmented, but we were just too stuck in our habitual ways to really deal with the skeletons in those dark corners. How much proof did we need? Elizabeth, who was still living in France, was surely disintegrating into the life of an alcoholic, Ponji for all intents and purposes was about to throw the towel in, Lucy was still full of angry tantrums, Sarah suffered with bouts of low self worth and I was in a place which wasn't too far away from all of these. At times, usually after some terrible argument, we became full of remorse, but ultimately we were too proud to do anything about it.

As far as I could see at the time, the only way forward was to admit to the mess and by admitting to it; perhaps we had a chance of moving on from the constant need to wallow in it. However, I had underestimated our pride and our absolute resolve not to rock the boat. The way we dealt with this rather large family blemish was to go into a kind of united denial, which blanked out the part that didn't seem to be working as it should. As long as we appeared to be happy we could do what we liked; walk around naked, get plastered to the wall, drop acid, smash windows, anything but ask the question why.

On a one to one basis my father reluctantly went as far as admitting to having read books by Carl Jung and Sigmund Freud in his undergraduate days. He made it clear that he was a great admirer of Mahatma Gandhi, Martin Luther King, John Hume and other such advocates of non-violent ways of obtaining social rights. It was obvious that my father believed in a spirit, which connected the everyday world, but he couldn't at this time in his life move away from the safety net. And as far as my mother was concerned, well she just felt threatened and immediately closed down further discussion by saying, usually in a puddle of unadulterated sobbing, that if there was a problem particularly with regards Elizabeth and Ponji, it was all her fault.

I understand how my visits may have been coloured by previous encounters, where the whiff of hash smoke put exception to the rules, but now I was pleading with a clearer head and an anxious heart. In the end however, I was to wound up and over wrought to find a way to communicate, without one of us becoming grossly uncomfortable and very defensive.

After one of these stays my mother, in a moment of quiet desperate support, slipped me a cheque, something that George wasn't to know about. Despite her generosity, the profundity of being constantly brushed aside was still hard for me to swallow.

Usually when I left my parents home over this period I felt utterly defeated and deflated. I guess looking into these complex parts of our personalities was just too painful, and seemed to put us all in an unworkable situation.

Despite the celebrated bid for freedom my parents had an enormous hold over me. I little realised how hopelessly dependent I was. Foiled in a gigantic emotional web of wanting, I hadn't got enough inner resolve to deal with this on my own and would inevitably end up losing my rag. Angry at their indifference and at what I felt at the time to be their lack of respect, I would so often take off with a kind of fuck you attitude churning around inside my gut.

When the time of introspection and reflection subsided a feeling of overwhelming remorse came over me and the only way forward, as I saw it then, was to appease the situation and them by setting myself up as an actor. There was it seems no way out of this crucial step. Despite the fact that my twenty-first year was just round the corner, the maturity of age seemed destined to elude me. The same old doubt and the same old fears returned to lodge themselves in the pit of my stomach and yet again I began to feel it could never be otherwise. There was however, some far off voice that just couldn't let go. Thankfully a fundamental part of my heart remained vigilant. Blessed with the simple fact of being alive, I had underestimated nature's determination to work the spirit and the soul.

34

My cousin Brian Harding, from my father's side, stayed at number eight when he was gearing up for A-levels at the Technical College in Cambridge. It has to be said that I felt a little out of my depth with Brian. He was it seems succeeding very well in his studies. We never really connected until we were in a play together directed by my mother. This production was a diffident attempt on my mother's part to show the teachers at my secondary school that she meant business. Rather than face the authorities directly, she decided to show them up, by teaching drama there in the evenings as part of a further education package. The long and the short of this saw Brian and me falling over ourselves with terrible nervous giggles in a neat top-hat adaptation of *Lady Audley's Secret*. The outcome had the opposite effect to what I think my mother had hoped for, with the teachers feeling sorry for her and wondering how on earth she could have given birth to such a loser. But it cemented a tenacious bond between me and Brian.

Like me, Brain had an unpredictable personality that bubbled over with energy. He would appear to be going along minding his own business when all of a sudden he'd make some left of field connection, to something someone had said, which really hit the funny bone. Then somewhere round the corner, without an audience, he'd sink, engulfed by the black dog.

Despite our mixed attempt at playing the stage, he went on to sing my praises as an actor to his friend Julian Hough. Brian had befriended Julian through a mutual interest in acting while they were at the Cambridge Tech together. From here they decided to pursue a career in the theatre and started on this noble path by applying to various drama collages in London. Julian eventually got into Drama Centre and Brian into

Guildhall. It didn't take long before Julian started coming to our house and thus began an endearing friendship.

Like me Julian came from the academic side of the fence.

On the rare occasions that I went to Julian's house in Grantchester his father was always in a darkened library with his head up the backside of a book. Julian's father, Graham Hough, was a brilliant English Professor, but he seemed to me to be another Cambridge intellectual who hadn't got a clue how to relate to their children. They may have had their moments, but he just seemed so catatonically engrossed, so wrapped up in his head that he could hardly say hello to Julian, let alone find a way to show his love. I don't remember seeing his mother there, but I did meet her years later when she was living in London. By that time Julian had fallen into his self destructive ways and was hitting her for the odd fiver to keep his drinking up to the mark.

Julian had a sister who was not that far away from the flames, but it was Julian who eventually walked into the fire. His life flashed before us like a shooting star, a troubled soul with many sides. It wasn't until I saw him in The National Theatre of Brent's *The Messiah* that I really became aware of his originality as a performer, which combined with his unique humour and spiritual optimism, put him and this show into a league of its own. In his dark moments of struggle, which came to dominate the latter years of his life, I saw in Julian the two distinctly definitive sides of a Cambridge boy in stark conflict, the yobo and the academic – raging, writhing, punching and plunging together – until they would bring him down fighting tired to the floor.

By the time I got round to applying for a place at Drama Centre, Julian was at the end of his second year and knew from experience what kind of pupil the college liked. He helped me put together the pieces from *Hamlet* and *Tartuffe* that I had chosen as the key to my entrance.

I got the audition down pat and I would probably have got in on that alone, but I had to be sure. After the main show case with the teachers, I had a one on one interview with the principal Christopher Fettes, in which I saw the need to burst into tears and plead my case. This line of emotional blackmail proved to be over the top, but effective. Fettes was forthright and advised me that they would give me a place, with the proviso that I see the college psychiatrist beforehand. Although bemused by this conclusion, (what me mad, I don't think so) I agreed unconditionally.

I gave the therapist, whose office was in a natty part of Primrose Hill, my sanest impersonation of a sane person yet and he charmed me all the way. I thought the session had been a push over, until he leant across his desk and suggested that I attend group therapy twice a week for a month just to be sure.

Sitting as one of the so called patients in the circle of chairs at the Paddington Day Clinic had a familiar air about it, but the formalities of rank that were held in place by the men and women in white coats, was not something I'd encountered before.

When the sessions started the doctors remained within their clearly defined roles. As soon as we finished, whether it be at the end of the day or a tea break, so did they. I found this most disconcerting. Because of my previous experiences in groups like that of the *Anti-University*, I expected the dialogue to be on a more equal basis. I thought, naively perhaps, that there were no boundaries, apart from the ones we draw up inside our hearts and minds.

I was in with a real mixture, this was not some middle class play pen time, this was a fucking dip-shit cock sucking mother of a whore see how you like it time. When it came to spitting out their truth, some of the rawer patients exposed extreme pain and the indifferent way it was dealt with, was a stark reminder of what it's like to be on the receiving end of a doctor's cold professionalism.

As the doorway of why I was there faded away into the distance, I got deeper into the swing of things and I made it my goal to challenge what I saw as a ridiculous hypothesis.

What does being mad mean and if we are mad as some clearly are, does it have a beginning and an ending? These were the questions I put quietly and politely to the doctors in the kitchen one afternoon and the answer was adamant; "This is neither the place nor the time, can you please wait until we're back in the circle". I was flabbergasted, madness as they saw it, had a cut off point. It was a given that I could control my urges until someone with authority decides the time. In reply I said, "Looking at a state of mind in this way is a ridiculous hypothesis", because as I saw it, "the flaw, if there is a flaw in madness, is its unpredictability and if it wants to be mended, it will probably be mended on the back foot, and not necessarily at some predisposed time of their choosing". They tried to catch me out by looking at me as if I was mad, but I couldn't care less about that. I looked them straight back in the eye and waited for their move, but they didn't know what to say.

What was clear to the doctors was that I had enough confidence to put them on the spot and they gave me the stamp of approval I needed to be in the sanity club. I seemed to have this way of being able to steer through the woods without crashing into the trees. Of course I didn't allow them near to anything vulnerable in my life, because I just couldn't find it in myself to really trust them.

~

I remember Vivian telling me how the convention of Drama School was one approach into acting, but not necessarily the right way for me, and to some extent this turned out to be true.

My time at the Drama Centre was full of diverse contradictions. This was the year the Beatles came out with their swan song album the immaculate *Abbey Road*, but I was hearing it from a distance, always in someone else's room, or some Hampstead squat, with my inner ear far from relaxed, making out that all was calm and in the groove.

Given the state I was in, I suppose it was extraordinary that they gave me a place at all. I had got into Drama Centre on a wing and a prayer and was as high as a kite on this achievement alone. The first year started well enough, in the autumn of 1969, on a wave of euphoria and excitement.

Christopher Fettis and Yat Malgram presided over Drama Centre as if they were the guardians of a royal dynasty. They were both extraordinarily charismatic and very little got past them. There was nothing they didn't seem to know about acting, theatre and life.

Once when I was having a conversation with Christopher about the need for change in British Theatre, he said with an intensity that pinned me to the wall, "If there was to be a revolution then it has to come from within the structure as is. If you feel the need to change theatre Matthew, then join up and turn it around from the inside". I couldn't really fail to get the gist of what he meant, and somewhere in the back of my mind his words kind of stuck. At the same time I couldn't help thinking how it was only six years previously that the radical thinking teachers and students at the Central School of Drama walked out as a collective body and started up the Drama Centre. An unsung revolution and a dangerous prospect, for they had left with nothing but their frustration at a syllabus they thought to be unsatisfactory and with only their talents to depend on.

Christopher was a master teacher, a director who had a thorough understanding of a character's psychological makeup. His manner may at times have seemed intimidating, but he was supremely good at steering the student away from the self-conscious and putting them slap bang in the middle of what, where, when and how.

Yat was less forthright than Christopher. His softly spoken Swedish accent may have given him a certain vulnerability, but he was no less intimidating; his focus was such that a twist of his tongue could turn hot blood cold. He had by all accounts been an exceptional dancer and there were times when one got a glimmer of this, especially when he gave a demonstration of something he was putting across in his movement class. During the war Yat joined the Ballet Jooss and through this encounter he got to work with Rudolph Laban, the visionary dancer, choreographer, and movement theorist. In close collaboration with Laban, Yat evolved a unique way of helping the actor find and embody the character. Every internal action has an external reaction. Directly or indirectly, from subtle to gross, every physical movement has a driving force that comes from inside the physiological vortex.

Across the board; the way acting was taught at the Drama Centre had tremendous clarity. Strictly based on the theories laid down by Constantin Stanislavsky in Russia, and later by Lee Strasberg and Uta Hagen in the States, it came across as carefully crafted law.

Each character in a play wants something. How they get what they want makes up the drama. If a character has no driving force then there is no play.

The action of the characters drives the forward momentum of the Play, and finding out how to play this action, physically, emotionally and mentally, took up most of our time there.

Sometimes when I was overwhelmed by waves of extreme contentment, seeking out a character in a play seemed a futile proposition. Other times I was unreservedly immersed in the teachings. Squeezed between these two constants was my all too personal baggage, which I found nigh on impossible to leave at the college gates.

If it was required to go into the depths of a complex character, we were taught to use a tool, which had derived from the teachings of Stanislavsky, called 'emotional memory'.

'Emotional memory' drew on a personal realization of some event in one's own past, which might help to bring you closer to the feelings of a character in a play. So for instance if the character had a scene which might require a moment of intense tears or laughter, you were encouraged to draw on your own personal experience of these emotions. It is often said of an actor, "Oh they were so good they were the character" I was told that if the actor used it to their advantage working with 'emotional memory' could go a long way towards helping them achieve this goal.

I have heard it said many times that the mature actor learns to leave their dirty washing back in the sink where it belongs. At the time this was difficult for me to realise, as it was my want to bring too much self enforced emotions to the piece being performed.

Hold the mirror up to nature – theatre is life and life is theatre. Perhaps it would have suited me better to say, where does my life end and the play begin and to have settled for a happy medium; a bit of my own life thrown in here and there, a little flavouring to give added realism to the art; but I had no idea how the ins and outs of my demons worked back then and it was they who took control.

The first year culminated with a presentation, in front of all the teachers, of a Maxim Gorky play that Christopher directed called *Enemies*, in which I played a large part. I got very positive feedback and this was enormously pleasing. If my sense of worth hadn't been cowering so efficiently behind the mask, I would have benefitted enormously. The heartfelt communication on the stage, with luminaries to be, such as Geraldine James and Don Warrington felt right and stayed with me.

The intensity of my double thinking may have gone unnoticed. However, I had fallen well and truly into the trap of what a lot of insecure actors do when they try to see themselves from another's view point. I was acting at being an actor and in the end this complex charade was to have me running for the dark.

I was back in the ring again, with my life seriously on the line and if I flunked this time I really was dead on the green. I owed it to my parents, to the tax payer who, despite my lack of academic qualifications, had given me a generous grant. I owed it to my contemporaries in group eight, but above all I owed it to the teachers of the Drama Centre, who put it across very clearly that they believed enough in me, not to fuck up.

Over the year I absorbed an awful lot, but with my abilities back under the microscope I just didn't have the where withal to stay the course. Because my brain was too fired up, I couldn't hear the music and at the penultimate moment lost my nerve. No amount of self deception, or reassurance from my contemporaries, could stop me from falling into the familiar nightmare of being back at school again and fuck up I did.

It was working with Yat in the all too familiar classroom on his movement psychology, which finally pulled the trigger. We were required to write a lot of pedantic things down on the trot and I got into a terrible internal panic, trying desperately to put the words neatly to the page. My pride was such that the disgrace, in not being able pull off this relatively simple task, had to be hidden at all costs.

It's hard to imagine now, but this was a time, when the word dyslexia hadn't established itself, a time when anyone one who couldn't read or write was either working class, or a laughing stock.

This was before credit cards, when the only way to withdraw cash from a bank was with a cheque book and some form of identification. There were many occasions when I'd make out that I'd left my wallet somewhere and tell them I'd be back to write out the cheque once I'd retrieved it. Then it was out on the street looking round for a library or bookshop, frantically seeking out the help of a dictionary. Then return to the sales person or bank clerk with the cheque written out before hand. It may seem ridiculous, but I was that far away from being able to ask for help and I went on to hide the shame, at the cost of my place in this remarkable college. I felt like the runt in a pack that prides itself on its literary heritage. If only I'd been calm enough to think it through, I'd have seen and heard the many friends, who were rooting for me under the umbrella of this extraordinary church.

Christopher tried to persuade me not to leave, but I was adamant. I felt completely confident and totally calm about my decision. I even went as far as quoting a psalm from the bible to him; "The Lord is my shepherd I shall not want …I will dwell in the house of the Lord forever".

I made it clear to any of my friends who tried to stop me that I was leaving because it was my chosen path to do so. I wanted everyone to know that I wasn't some weekend hippy or fly by night pretender. I was a true believer, the real thing, whose love for the universe was far greater than anything that might be pulled together in some antiquated hall in Chalk Farm. Somewhere deep down, paradoxically perhaps, I really did believe this.

Yea, though I walk through the valley of the
shadow of death; I will fear no evil: for thou
art with me; thy rod and thy staff they
comfort me.
Thou preparest a table before me in the
presence of mine enemies: thou anointest
my head with oil; my cup runneth over.
Surely goodness and mercy shall follow me all
the days of my life; and I will dwell in the
house of the Lord forever

35

My mother's reaction, when I told my parents in the kitchen at North Creake that I had decided not to go back to the Drama Centre for the following year, was so over the top that I nearly fell of the stool. She exploded with grief. "Matthew" she spluttered out between outrage, tears and disbelief, "How could you, what have you done!" I was so shocked by her outburst that I quickly disintegrated into an infantile heap.

Overloaded with remorse I left for London feeling as if I had raped my mother and killed my father.

On the way back I stopped off to see my cousin Francis at Number Nine. We spent time together cutting the weed and shooting the breeze. He wasn't at all surprised to hear that I'd caved in before I got the chance to go through that gateway into acting. He knew those self-deprecating demons well, from battling his own and wanted to help. We discussed how I might find a way of living in Cambridge without compromising what was left of my integrity. But it was impossible, especially around Number Nine, where being in Aunt Alice's company was adding to an emotional backlog of dangerous proportions. I had seen her betrayal around trust, which she had recently demonstrated when dealing with Ponji's truth and I wasn't about to let her anywhere near mine.

I saw very little of Ponji directly after he got back from India, but the times I did meet up with him I couldn't avoid the teachings of his spiritual path. I continued to dismiss his piety and the more I resisted, the more determined he became. I genuinely felt too screwed to the floor to ever start with a God life. I was and still am genuinely uncomfortable around any kind of dogma. What I really wanted to talk about was my own plight, but if ever I showed any sign of weakness, he always turned it back round to the teachings and how it was all to do with the power of mind. This was something I wasn't ready to hear. I found it hard to get away from thinking that the extreme intensity he had around these spiritual laws, stemmed directly from the major players in his life, who were never really there for him.

My feeling was that his spiritual master had to some extent fulfilled the role of surrogate father. Some light was also shed on his mistrust around the opposite sex, when he explained on numerous occasions how he wouldn't get involved in a relationship with a woman, as he believed categorically that they were the goddesses of Maya, the figureheads of illusion.

About a year after he had moved back to Cambridge, Ponji must have been severely plagued by his struggle for those enlightened heights, because he sought out the one person he thought he could confide in, Auntie Alice. At the beginning of my year at drama school, he went to her for help. In doing this he must have been very vulnerable indeed. I am convinced that Ponji was finding it progressively harder to rationalise the darkness in his life, especially in the light of his spiritual path.

The prayer wheel was spinning out of control, which for those who choose a spiritual path is not an entirely uncommon phenomenon. In the right circumstances a novice monk, whose struggles with God are raging, can be advised to cease their meditations for a while and the fervour will calm of its own accord. Rather than searching out this resolution, which would have been a long way outside her domain and therefore nonexistent, Alice, in a professional capacity, had him committed to the local loony bin, where he was given Electroconvulsive Therapy.

As far as I could see ECT just accelerated his feelings of low self-esteem toward their devastating conclusion. I cannot believe to this day that I or anyone else in the family didn't try to stop, or even question that appalling decision.

When I went with Francis to visit Ponji in Fullborn Mental Hospital on the outskirts of Cambridge and saw him on the ward along with a lot of desperate cases, I nearly broke down. I was confused and furious. Confused because she was our Auntie Alice and furious because I just couldn't agree in any way what so ever with her professional conduct.

In fact I was so angry that from then on I found it hard not to throttle her when I was in her company. When I broached Alice about Ponj's lockdown, I told her through a mist of gritted teeth and clenched fists how I wanted to kill her. She just looked at me in a calm and detached way and said, "That would be very unwise".

I was struck dumb. She had floored me with her lack of remorse. Why wasn't she concerned about my wanting to do her harm, or even the slightest bit interested in finding out why Ponji was stuck in such a painful place? She was a psychiatrist for fucks sake. Even if they didn't see eye to eye, surely any decent human being, would want to know why part of their family had broken such a big personal link in the chain.

She may simply have been averse to going into the quagmire, but whatever lay behind it, this encounter strengthened my belief that professional doesn't necessarily mean right, and made me even more determined to ring my bell a long way from her shores.

I said goodbye to my cousin Francis and went back to where I'd lived when I was at Drama Centre, mainly to sort out my stuff and stay for a few days while I worked out what I was going to do. It was a relief to spend time with Joan Goody, the owner of the house, who ironically happened to be my mother's best friend. She may have been bemused by my abrupt decision to break off my acting course mid-flow, but in her usual way was unflustered and non-judgemental about what I had done.

Joan met my mother during the war through their connection with the Ballet Jooss. When the company was in Cambridge Joan would come to Number Nine to visit her brother Peter Wright, who was a dancer with the company. Immediately after the war Joan married Jack Goody, one of my father's closest friends from his university days. Ponji and my cousin Francis had nick named him, Jack the Black Goody, partly out of his anthropological dealings with the African continent, but mainly I think because of his dark moods. For the most part I remember him as a volatile man, particularly when he was around Joan, so to me the name made sense. Whilst he was setting himself up as a prominent intellectual in Cambridge, he was humiliating Joan at every turn of the way. By the time we moved to Cambridge their marriage was on the rocks.

I sometimes fantasize about what it might have been like had she and my father swapped partners. It seemed to me that Jack and my mother would have been better suited, my mother had balls and perhaps had the tenacity to stand up to Jack's ferocious passion; whereas Joan was a quieter soul more akin to my father, a kind of kindred spirit. In the end Joan managed to get out from under Jack's metaphorical boot and started to set up her own life. She eventually moved to London and became one of those unusual teachers who could turn unworkable and antisocial pupils around. She worked in some of the roughest schools in London and later on became a champion for multicultural teaching in the classroom. Perhaps if I'd been a little less shy about my problems at drama school she might have been the perfect person to turn me around. But life as it was for me then wasn't like that and now it was time to move on.

I drifted around in London doing the best I could, making money by taking whatever odd jobs came my way. I found a flat in the Fulham Road for a time, which I shared with two friends, but left when the angst and financial responsibility got too much. I took accommodation in bedsit-land, where it was just a question of rent and the responsibilities were down to a bare minimum. When it became too hard to handle even that much, I spent a few nights on the benches in Hyde Park, where the fear of some arsehole attacking me from behind kept me half awake during those dark hours. With one eye on the outside and the other in a dream, I'd doze reticently, until the morning breathed a sigh of relief across the spacious lawns and dew covered flowerbeds. I hated feeling dirty, so measures to keep clean were at a premium. I went to this hotel in the Earls Court Road a few times to have a wash. As long as I strode confidently across the lobby like a regular guest, it was easy to get past the front desk and up the central stairway to the first floor. Then it was a matter of finding a room with the door ajar, sneaking in and getting a surreptitious soak in the tub. Security was a lot less stringent than it is now.

More than anything else, it was the continual shame that kept beating a path to my door that had the greatest impact on my well being. I felt like the usual nonlinear freak walking into a one dimensional overcrowded market place, only to find there was no way out. Trapped by embarrassment, hemmed in by inadequacy, I reversed into the backend of a roach.

Eventually I got some painting and decorating work with someone I met at Earlham Street, John Whiteley. John was a fantastic tonic and being around him at this time gave me the self-assurance I sorely lacked. There was no judgment with John; sleeping rough and being down and out were just acceptable parts of life's tapestry. It didn't mean it wasn't hard, but because it was acceptable to laugh in the face of adversity there was no shame pulling at my shoestrings. The only other person who I felt this grounded with was Emo.

It's funny how things work out, because around this time I bumped into Emo in the street in Notting Hill Gate. I hadn't seen him for well over a year.

After the manic jovialities had worn off, he told me how he was spending a lot of time with Dave Gilmour who was starting to climb rapidly to the heights of fame and fortune with Pink Floyd. He gave me a phone number and we left it at that.

When it came to falling, the one person who sat in the seat and could go down to the bottom without turning a hair was Emo. A few days later I called the number he'd given me and Dave answered. He and Emo asked me out to the country, where they were living. With some reservation I accepted their invitation. I wanted to be in Emo's company, but I wasn't sure if I felt comfortable enough to share my worries with Dave in the picture. I didn't want to be the one to put a dampener on our time together. Dave always seemed so content, happy even. He had mapped out a path and stuck to it – making music was his lifeline and his life.

He and Emo picked me up from the train station and apart from their cheerful manner, the first thing I noticed was the car. Dave was driving a brand new top of the range BMW, which was given to him in part payment for some music Pink Floyd had composed for an advertisement selling these well made German automobiles. It seems his passion for playing the guitar really was beginning to bring in the big money. Driving through the dark to our destination, he couldn't have been nicer and Emo's buoyant mood was delightful, but still I remained cautious.

Dave's house was like an enormous cottage, a perfect sprawling English rose. There was plenty of land attached, trees, fields, lawns and gardens overflowing with flowers – the whole setup seemed enticing. While Dave strummed and tuned a favourite guitar, which no matter what he was doing was never far from his hands, we spread ourselves comfortably across cushions on the floor and over tea and biscuits touched on the past.

There was no way I could bring myself to talk about running away from drama college. I told them how I had recently been back to Cambridge and Number Nine, to meet up with my cousin Francis. I was dying to share my anguish for Ponji, but held back from telling them how impossible things had become for him after he moved back there. Skirting the issue I asked them if they'd seen our old Cambridge mate Pip.

Dave and Emo filled me in on how Pip had been caught with dope in hand at the airport in Greece. When Dave was on holiday there Pip came over to visit and was thrown in jail for his endeavour. Not good. Trapped like a rat with hard drugs then, especially in that part of the Mediterranean, could mean months, even years locked up. Pip was such a heroin aficionado that it had all but killed him. The needle had dug so far; searching relentlessly for a vein meant he lost the life of his left arm. The good news was that being in prison in Greece meant he was forced to go cold turkey, so when he was released, many months later, he was clean. Dave and Emo seemed pleased with Pip's recovery. I couldn't help thinking that it wouldn't take many weeks back home, before the grey skies of England would have him searching for a seam again.

While I was concerned for Pip, I just couldn't let go of my own battles, which continued raging against the sides of my skull like a tempestuous storm.

I think they could sense I was stifling and drifting.

Inevitably they asked me how Ponji was doing and expressed their fondness for him. I told them he was as energised as ever about Sant-Mat, his spiritual path, and that they had more chance of seeing him than I did, as he was now spending a lot of his time with Storm in London. I desperately wanted to tell them how Ponji had been zapped by the medical profession in Cambridge and how we as a family had basically stood by and let it happen, but I couldn't.

Was it that the embarrassment of Ponji tumbling from grace into an insane asylum was just too much? Or was it that I wanted to spare them the pain? Either way I couldn't bring myself to mention this dark and terrible truth.

Dave continued to strum some fortuitous licks on the guitar. Emo went to make another pot of tea in the kitchen. In his absence, expressing concern for Emo's welfare, Dave asked me what I thought Emo should do. I was perplexed as I thought our friend was surviving from day to day with more vigour than most of us. I said I wasn't sure what he meant, at the same time I was thinking how I was really in the same shoes as Emo. Keeping up appearances, I said that Emo may not have money, but wasn't he worth his weight in gold, as a friend didn't he give back as much he got. Ever since the beginning Emo just had this way about him. Admittedly he could be really difficult to get to grips with, frustrating and unpredictable, especially if he thought he was being misunderstood, but ultimately for those of us at the opposite end of his social spectrum, he was groundbreaking, intriguing and extremely funny.

When Dave, whose family background like mine was prodigiously academic, was in his last year of schooling in Cambridge, Emo was working in the coal yard. They started becoming friends from chance meetings on the top of the double-decker bus which took them home every Saturday. From the start, there was a kind of unsaid kinship between them that crossed the social boundaries and expressed an undoubted spirit of the time – you could just see the play of innocence between us when Emo was around.

I may not have had the nerve to express what sat in my heart like a stone, but just being in Emo and Dave's company at this time lifted my spirits and gave me courage for what lay ahead.

Matthew, in the early 70's

36

I got back to London and bumped into Robin Cooper. Like Ann Friend, Robin was someone I'd befriended at the *Anti-University* meetings. He said he was in the middle of getting a Philadelphia Association house up and running in Portland Road and asked me if I'd like to come and help. He also said it was going to be one of a few places that the PA was hoping to set up for people to go nuts in, without the usual interference from the head police. He knew I was good with my hands and asked if I could do some of the work there for a small but regular wage. I had nothing to lose and went along with it. He never for one minute made me feel like he was helping me, but help me he did.

I was coming to the end of my twenty-second year and just about managing to put some sort of style across – it was 1971.

A few years previously in 1965, Dr R. D. Laing, the internationally renowned psychiatrist and some of his colleagues created a charity, which became known as the Philadelphia Association. In doing so they took over a large renowned property in the East End of London called Kingsley Hall; a building with a history well suited to their work – as among other things it had been a shelter and soup kitchen during the general strike of the 1920s – it was where Mahatma Gandhi chose to stay when he was in England fighting for India's independence in the early thirties. Against all odds, Laing and his allies set about creating a place where people, ill-equipped emotionally, might live in a secure environment and get to grips with their inner states without being completely shutdown. It was a place that set about challenging the established rigid assumptions of normal and abnormal behaviour. As it was then this was a voice in the wilderness, a therapeutic asylum where the use of tranquilisers, straitjackets and ECT were hailed as being a barbaric thing of the past. Out of this community was born the model for other such shelters in and around London, the first of which was in Portland Road.

Whilst reading psychology at Edinburgh University Robin Cooper became disillusioned and frustrated with his studies, but all this changed when he came across Dr R. D. Laing's book *The Divided Self*. He was greatly encouraged and wrote to the author who agreed to meet him. Robin then decided to take the therapeutic path and after graduating, he started analysis in London with a colleague and close friend of Laing's, Dr Hugh Crawford. It was Crawford who brought to life the Portland Road community and Robin was one of the first people to move into the house, which is where I came into the picture.

Robin was a richly intense person, his enthusiasm for the ideas that Laing advocated as a way forward was unrelenting. There were no games with Robin; he was passionate, straight forward and unpretentious. He was in the middle of his own struggle when I met him, which put us on the same ground, apart from one small difference, he was taking a therapeutic route, where as I was on the brink of admitting to internal conflicts, but wasn't really prepared do anything about them. This didn't matter to Robin though. He just gave me the space to be who I was when I was and if I could get into the goings on at Portland Road that was great too.

The PA community began its satellite life away from Kingsley Hall in one of those large Victorian houses, familiar to many parts of London, that were beginning to find a new lease of life then, as those who could afford to do so, got rid of the aspidistra and gave them a full on bricks and mortar face lift. The Portland Road house had been stripped back to its basic old pine amenities, so that any incoming resident could make it their own.

My job began by working on the basement which common to a lot of those terraced houses had a big problem with damp. I started by tanking the walls in the basement and went on from there, plastering and finishing. I hadn't really done anything as elaborate as this before, especially for anyone else, but it was one of those rare building jobs where everything went along according to how it was planned.

For the first couple of weeks, Robin was the only person living there. Between whatever else he was doing, we'd get together in the kitchen, break bread, drink tea, and dig a little deeper into who we were and what we felt we wanted in the world. He made me feel that these breaks were as much a part of the job as working on the house.

Before long a young woman was brought to the house; a real contender, a heavy weight, who was, as far as I remember, the second tenant after Robin. As Hugh Crawford stipulated, like everyone, she was a work in progress and as there was a slight concern that she might harm herself if she was left on her own. This meant it was imperative that there was someone responsible in her company all the time. I found myself roped into the scenario, which wasn't a big deal, as it had come about as natural progression.

She wasn't by any means a weak person and at first I found being in her company daunting. But it became pretty obvious after a short while that she had her own ways of sorting herself and as far as I could see it worked. One of the things she did, to bring her head back under control, was to run a freezing cold bath and then sit in it until she felt grounded.

The next person to be brought in was a youthful slight angelic Frenchman, who had a problem with staying and leaving. After he settled in, as much as he could settle in, he would appear in the kitchen doorway, or at the bottom of the stairs and even sometimes at the bottom of the ladder I was on, ready with his endless goodbyes. Suitcase in hand, he'd tell anyone who happened to be around that he was leaving. It was like he was testing us. "I'm leaving now, I am going", he'd say. When he saw that no one was bothered either way, he'd walk out of the front door and down the street, carry on walking until he realised no one had stopped him, then he'd come back to the house and do the whole thing all over again. One of the other things he did was to pick flowers from a front garden of one of the neighbouring houses then ring the front door bell and when they answered, give the owner the flowers; at first they were grateful, but eventually the street got fed up and after a lot of complaints we had to stop him. This reaffirmed something inside him, and made us all more aware of how difficult it would be to deal with his insecurities in this kind of a neighbourhood.

At Robin's suggestion, I sat in on some of the early Portland Road meetings and once again the internal presence of my parents took over. It seems like a joke now and I was hardly aware of it at the time, but their will and mine were locked in a kind of pathetic struggle, trying to define what was needed, what was best for me. The power of their hold over me was so strong that I really felt I had no choice, other than negating what was around me here. If I had been a little more confident, I'd have taken a proper place in the circle at Portland Road and made my doubts and insecurities known. After all, this was a place which advocated the use of plain language for a plain and simple resolve. Yes it had its difficulties but what community doesn't. Here people were allowed through the door when it was felt they had something human to address, or as Robin put it, to go through, or to weather. This didn't mean a house of anarchy, it meant a place of healing that was readily accepting of human dilemmas; dilemmas which when taken to the extreme can often lead to a place of seemingly insurmountable loneliness and pain. Apart from the electricity bill or the rates, I don't remember any paperwork. I just remember a fundamental depth of interest in each person, from each individual, regardless of who they were or what they did.

Most of the meetings were conducted cross-legged on the floor in the front room at Portland Road. When Laing was present he hovered just outside the circle observing and saying very little. At such times, so powerful was the paranoid legacy in my life that I told myself he was being aloof, that he wasn't joining in because it felt beneath him to do so. In spite of the amount of clear knowledge I'd gained about who Laing was, I was determined to make him into the bogey man. With Crawford it was slightly different, at least he had a beard like my dad and sat on the floor with us, definitely more of an equal; but even through this rational acceptance, I still made him into someone I wouldn't leave a kid with, let alone myself. Oh I said my bit, but it was always about externals, about the house, about the practicalities needed to bring it towards some kind of completion. Like my mum and Auntie Alice I was all for fixing the world on the outside, but never in a million years would I reveal the plank in my own eye.

Looking back I was in the perfect environment to tackle the rifts in my life. A large part of me wanted to settle in, but by wanting to do what was right for mummy and daddy, I felt compelled to make Laing and Crawford the enemy and to step away.

A family is responsible as a whole as well as individually and like I had learnt from AA, if we can all admit to this then no one member needs to be the scapegoat. I understood this in theory, but I still couldn't for the life of me step off the hallowed family merry-go-round.

Even though I thwarted Laing and Crawford's image, I still managed to retain a semblance of justification for their insights, which meant their teachings kind of stuck. Once again it was one of those fortunate strokes of fortuity where, despite my bouts of panic, I had retained a lot more than I realised at the time.

As life with Robin and working at Portland Road started to bite, I began falling into the trap of seeing myself as a victim. Torn between the teachings of Laing and what my parents advocated left me jarred with angst. I started carrying guilt around like a rucksack full of sand. I found myself seeing so many different sides. One thing I wanted badly was to make George and Cecilia see that I could amount to something, while at the same time retain some kind of emotional integrity for my own insights, but the reality of a balanced outcome was slipping further and further away.

It's funny how things work out, because in an indirect way what Portland Road did was push me to the bottom of the barrel, to a place where the only way to survive is to turn around and face the demons.

It was very difficult to do so, but somehow I'd made it clear to Robin that I couldn't really get comfortable with Laing and Crawford. I trusted him enough and was able to tell him that their presence made me uneasy. Again Robin accepted my dilemmas as a perfectly acceptable part of the journey.

Out of the blue one day Robin started telling me how he needed space and time away from Portland Road. He had come to the point where he could give up his room if it better suited a person more in need than himself. He felt that the distance might now be more appropriate to his oncoming role as a therapist. I don't think he would have liked being garlanded with that label, maybe confidante is a better word, or as Alice Miller says in her inspiring book, *The Body Never Lies,* enlightened witness.

Suffice it to say, Robin had been given the opportunity to move into a flat on the top floor of a high-rise block in Fulham called Lannoy Point, and asked me if I would like to take on a room there. I had little idea at just how depressed I really was, but as always I never let this get in the way of a forward shift in my life, and since I wanted a way out of bed-sit land, I gratefully took hold of the opportunity.

Some weeks into the move, I retreated deep into the absolute fear of my family's disapproval. I made my way to Lanoy Point, shut the door, and left Portland Road behind me. Robin had gone to Wales for a week or so to do some rock-climbing and to continue renovating a derelict smallholding he'd acquired, which he was hoping would become another human place for human things.

With the heavy weight of contradiction swirling away inside, I just went deeper into the mire of depression until I could no longer move. Left on my own, I hit the bedroom floor like a dead weight and turned out the light. If I was to make it now I would have to rise up from the dead.

37

During the early part of the summer of love, which for those of us who weren't there, meant those warm months in the middle of 1968, a council tenant struck a match in her kitchen on the 18th floor of Ronan Point in east London and triggered off a massive catastrophe. The explosion, from that innocent domestic gesture, caused one side of the tower block to collapse like a deck of falling cards.

I hadn't really taken in this appalling tragedy, in which four people died, until I moved into the flat in Fulham with Robin those few years later.

Soon after Robin and I had settled in, some council workers turned up at Lannoy Point, which had the same design flaws as its big brother Ronan, and started nailing random planks of wood across the mass of pre-cast concrete panels that formed the main structure of the building.

Although I was aware of its short comings, the physical insecurity of this flea bitten hi-rise apartment block I was living in, mattered not one little drop. For all it was worth, I was through, finished, and washed up on the shore of defeat. How had I allowed myself to be beaten into this terrible impasse? Was it because the lid on my anger had become so heavy that I was forced into submission? I certainly felt I had no articulate means and I couldn't trust myself to go anywhere because of my seething rage. I was furious with Cambridge and my schooling, angry with peace and love, I was livid at my parent's liberal acceptance of the tightening knots in my life, and when all was said and quiet, I was sick and tired of the continuing need for my self-deluding lies and never ending conceit.

The load had become unbearable and under such strain my body could do nothing else but collapse. It was like one of those clichés from a hard-boiled detective novel, where the hero is thumped from behind and disappears into a black hole.

Out for the count, hours turned into days and days into nights, until such time as some incidental banging and shouting in my head gradually brought me round to the sounds of the real world.

The last thing I wanted was to entertain any idea of a visitor, but so determined was the knocking that I felt compelled to make it stop.

Feeling as if I'd been hit for six by a juggernaut lorry, I dragged my feet into the lack lustre hall; then pulled the last remaining drop of optimism out of what had surely disintegrated into a sceptic tank of agitated self-hatred and opened the door. To my surprise I was greeted by the quietly commanding, ever empathetic Mick Rock.

Mick looked like Bob Dylan did when he grew his hair, went electric and started wearing shades. I first met Mick when he was reading French and German up at Cambridge. He was one of those rare undergraduates in the city who dared to cross the line. Some of us lesser mortals often ended up in his rooms at Gonville and Caius with the view of taking a hit of some kind. Mick was always optimistic about what was around the corner. No matter how plastered things got, he saw the outcome as being for the best.

Other than please his mother, he was never sure what do with the degree in languages he got from that exalted University town where I was brought up.

I had some catatonic laughs with Mick. Like Nick Sedgwick he was a great audience, especially when we were out on the edge of the stoned abyss together.

Mick ended up at The London Film School in Covent Garden, as Ponji had done. Eventually he made his way into the world as one of those supreme heads who never really lets the side down, and found a successful niche for himself as a photographer and friend to some of the main players in the rock'n'roll fraternity.

The lift was out of order. And because Mick had made it up fourteen floors to the top of this piss infested building, to ask me if I would come to a yoga class with him and his mesmerizing missis Sheila, I felt compelled to listen.

Mick's wife Sheila was adorably enigmatic. The roots of her family had emigrated from Japan to the US, so Sheila was born and brought up in New York, but retained that Zen like interest in the spheres. She came to the UK in the late sixties and like Mick caught a ride on a highway to the stars.

I fell in love with Sheila as soon as I set eyes on her. She had a younger sister called Bambi who I once took to Aunt Fanny's in Gestingthorp. When we had settled in for the evening meal, Bambi asked Fanny if the hall was haunted and Fanny in the inimitable Hopkinson way said "Oh yes of course". Bambi being a classic New York babe and entirely used to city life, got so spooked that she demanded to be taken back to London as soon as the sun came up. I think I was trying to get to Sheila through Bambi, at best a bad idea. Because of this, my relationship with Bambi went into a kind of murky misunderstanding. She moved into a maisonette that had become my home on the traffic spun Wandsworth Bridge Road in Fulham for a while. Bambi and I toyed with the idea of being lovers, but I think somehow she never really trusted my motives, quite right too. Our time together was to remain as friends, purely platonic. Unlike her older sister she never really felt comfortable in the UK and a few months later went back to live in the States. I wasn't to see her again. Then I heard how she had got into heroin and some short time after this she died tragically of infections from sharing the needle.

Mick and Sheila eventually went their separate ways. Mick went to live and work in New York, while Sheila stayed on in the UK and with much integrity discovered a sublime gift for revealing the subtle tones found in the light and shade of photography.

I was reluctant about attending any kind of spiritual seminars, because the syrupy quest found in these devout corners, be it eastern or western, left me feeling like a grossed out monkey. But as Mick had made such an effort on my behalf, I couldn't find it in my heart to say no to him and the yoga mat. So I hauled my body along to a Buddhist centre in Airlie Gardens for that initial yoga class, like a pygmy pulling on an elephant.

My first yoga teacher, Penny Nield Smith, wasn't short of having a theatrical personality. Done up with her brightly painted fingers and toes, she biked from class to class in South London, like a lady of the lamp, ready to throw out any nonsense that came her way.

It was very clear from the start that what she was teaching could in no way be considered wishy-washy.

To begin with I found the simple fact of doing something physically taxing, extremely hard. I was so out of shape that any exertive movement brought on so much nausea. Nevertheless I surprised myself and continued with these weekly classes and even started doing what yoga I could at home. As I progressed a little, I began to see some improvement and with this apparent development, the clouds that had been hanging over me started to shift.

Initially I think it must have appealed to the background of engineering in my psyche, because I found myself responding in a favourable light to the logic of this universal science.

Eventually I would become intrigued by the workings of yoga at a deeper level and find myself drawn toward the unlikely pursuit of a more spiritual note; but for the time being it was enough just to marvel at the daily transformation of the body from something sluggish and dead, into something dynamic, vibrant and alive.

Penny was generous with her knowledge of yoga and within a year or so of intensive time in her company, she made it clear to me, that if I wanted to take my practice to the feet of the master, I would have go on from here to a different teacher.

With Penny's blessing I managed to get classes with a woman called Silva Mehta. Silva had a foreboding character of Slavic proportions and on first meeting seemed very austere. She reminded me of one of those prima ballerina teachers who ends up with a cane in an attic somewhere, teaching young up-and-coming dancers, beating out the steps at every turn.

Despite my obvious hippy leanings, Silva took me under her wing. She was very precise in how she put across her interpretation of this ancient art. Through going to her classes, which were by no means easy, I began to see that I had a certain amount of physical control over the malaise.

Once the more obvious benefits of yoga started to evolve I became somewhat obsessive about my practice. I rose like the proverbial phoenix and began to go at it fire and tongs, day in and day out month after month. As I was to find out later, in some aspects yoga had become like an addiction.

Intuitively, I never really believed that a life, lived as a journey through to the future, was ever going to be satisfactory. And as I was told ad infinitum, that the raison d'être for my being alive was to "Look to the future", it became very difficult not to buy into the habit of having a profound mistrust for the present. Being fully engaged with the here and became to be seen as a stumbling block, and as resolving this was considered nothing less than a waste of time by my elders and family, I couldn't help feeling as if the train had left the station without me. There was no doubt that those never ending distractions were driving me toward a head-on collision with god knows what. But like some quirk of fate, yoga came along at the right time to steer me away from this predicament.

As I became familiar with some of the more obvious dimensions found through the practise of yoga, it became clear that the body has to be fearless and confident if we are to learn anything truly profound. Here was a newfound stability that allowed my nervous system to settle. I began to realise that much of the mistrust I had for a distracted journey away from the present, was bang on line. What the usual suspects seemed to advocate wasn't the infallible truth after all.

I had no idea, as I continued unrelentingly in the pursuit of some deeper understanding of this forgiving art, that I was heading towards classes with Penny and Silva's teacher, who at the time was a relatively unknown Indian yogi by the name of Bellur Krishnamachar Sundararaja Iyengar.

BKS Iyengar came to England in the 50s from India as a private tutor to Yehudi Menuhin, whose life and music had been transformed by the way Iyengar taught him yoga.

In those days Iyengar saw himself as a servant and no doubt was treated as such. But despite such prejudice from the echelons of high society for race and yoga, word got out through friends and acquaintances of the renowned violinist, that Iyengar was a supreme master. Gradually, at Iyengar's instigation, his lessons reached further afield and into a more public arena.

By the time I started doing yoga Mr Iyengar had been coming for yearly visits to the west for well over a decade. He would stay and teach in the UK for several weeks. I now consider myself as being very lucky to have crossed his path then, because this was still a time when his classes were small enough to take on a more personal and intimate nature.

At the tail end of 1971, at Silva Mehta's instruction, I landed up in the basement gymnasium in Paddington Street and well and truly on my feet.

There was no outward manifestation of eastern mysticism or religious ritual. There were no candles or incense burning; in fact the only sign of anything remotely deferential about the occasion was the distinct pecking order of a few women, who seemed to be scurrying around like a lot of demented hens, trying to instil seriousness and order into the arrival of their revered master.

What could easily have been mistaken for just another physical education class for adults was to become the beginning of a monumental journey into the possibility of change.

To say Mr Iyengar was charismatic is an understatement of the highest proportion. From the very first meeting it was impossible not to notice the way he resided in the body, which he often made clear with animated pride, was the true temple of god.

After the short introductions, he began by saying that he was just a teacher, someone who was there purely to pass on as much understanding of this deceivingly simple craft as he could. He talked a little of his meagre background and how yoga had saved him in his youth from the ravages of tuberculosis, malaria and other life threatening illnesses, which he had suffered throughout his childhood. He demonstrated with remarkable ease some of the asanas/postures; then with an imperceptible join, he started the class with a flame of passion that could bring even the most sceptical to acknowledge the fire.

For the first time in my life I was in the presence of a teacher who got across the wonder, beauty and magic of the world by firing up the reality of my own being. Suddenly I was with a man who was asking me, at every step of the way, if I wanted to live or die.

"When I began yoga, there was, I am sorry to say, no wise, kind teacher to lead me. In fact my own Guru refused to answer any of my innocent inquiries on yoga. He did not instruct me as I do my students, offering them step-by-step guidance in an asana. He would simply demand a posture and leave it to me or his other students to figure out how it could be realized".

BKS IYENGAR

38

Mr Iyengar was the consummate actor, at every turn he had the audience eating out of his hand. From the very beginning I wanted to be like him, everything he said and did seemed to make perfect sense. When he spoke of movement it was never contrived, when he stretched it was into the vastness. He'd say "What's two hours yoga, if it allows you to sit with God". The inhalation and exhalation of the breath had never taken on such significance. He had learnt so much from his own rigorous practice about the depth and profundity of the human mind and spirit. He emanated irrefutably how the subtlety of the nervous system came together with the heart, soul and spirit, to unite in the real meaning of yoga.

In his early years, it is said that illnesses combined with malnutrition, were to lay the young Iyenger directly into the arms of fatality. But providence had a master plan in the guise and path of his eldest sister, who married Tirumalai Krishnamacharya, a man who, by the time Iyengar was in his early teens, had immersed himself well into the workings and philosophies of yoga.

Some time forward Iyengar managed to retrieve a few major pointers from his brother-in-law, who from all accounts was a brutal yoga teacher and an unforgiving task master. When all was said and done, he brushed Iyengar aside as being too sick and weak for such a strenuous path. But Iyengar was made of stronger metal. Grateful for any morsels of information that his brother-in-law passed his way, he began rigorous painstaking work on his own body and started piecing together what was to become the backbone of his teaching.

He spent hours and years in his practice like a prospector in the hills panning for gold. Later he came down into the valley to give out what he had found and for the willing pupil it was like receiving a precious and life enhancing gift.

Before Iyengar came to the west yoga was either altruistic idealism, contortionism, or a safe afternoon hobby, something for dabbling one's toes in, but never to be realised in the fundamental sense. For many westerners Iyengar made real the possibility of a physiological and psychological change at an intrinsic level.

His marriage to Srimati Ramamani, who was to bear him six children, brought yoga out of the shadows and into the twenty first century. With his wife's unrelenting support he showed that to be master of yoga didn't necessarily mean an esoteric life alone in a remote cave somewhere.

Using himself as a guinea pig, Iyengar worked out the clearest and easiest way to put across what he had learnt for himself and then generously passed on this knowledge with a full and compassionate heart.

The way of the artist had as much a part to play as the scientist, or the engineer and the skills of their trade were brought to the fore in his classes. Along with any other titbits he might have gathered from his journey across the lands, he worked on the dilemmas and needs of his pupils in his own practice and gave back only when he had a definitive solution.

He could persuade the unlikeliest of pupils into action. Even for the very sick, there really was no such word as can't. In his class, it was always a question of how. If an asana/posture came with strain or difficulty, he would, in a flick of the eye, find a way to release the body and make it fly and then when it was necessary, like a skilful falconer bring the bird back to roost.

The down beats were as important as the up beats, the inner life was as essential as the outer; harmony between the two worlds was vital, if the path of yoga was to be realised. He said our obsession with wanting to be ahead of the game, meant we were losing touch with the body and in turn a vital balance in our life was being lost. Lest we find ourselves adrift in space unable to get back to earth, it was imperative to have our feet well and truly on the ground.

The down beats in my life were no longer to be scorned, now I could embrace both sides of my wayward life and begin to work with it.

At first Mr Iyengar got hold of the little boy in me who didn't like to lose and enticed me deeper into the realms of yoga with small competitive rewards. In turn, I began to see the small boy beneath his exterior and he allowed that door to be open; the happy boy who was proud to wear his new gold watch or the ever so slightly rockabilly tweed jacket. He was a mate, as well as an untouchable teacher.

If you withdrew into a constricted space he'd have a way of cajoling you out. In equal measure, if you were getting too big for your boots he'd find a way of slamming you back in. There appeared to be no boundaries within his personality and this could make going to his classes a terrifying, but exciting prospect. You could never be sure which way he was going to blow. He might castigate someone who was bendy for showing off and pour praise over someone else who was tight, for being intelligently connected with their body.

Intelligence, he said, was to be alert and aware – back-brain back body, front brain front body. How do the feet connect with the floor, what is happening to the skin on the back of the leg as we stretch into the "Waspness" is it releasing or contracting? Are we restricting the breath, so on and so forth?

I once asked Mr Iyengar how he judged me as a pupil and he said that my inner life was written all over my face. He had an uncanny knack of reading the skin like a book, knowing who you were and where your weaknesses lay, before you even set foot on the mat.

Right at the beginning he came along side me and said with some vehemence, "Mattchews, there isn't just dope dope, there is yoga dope too". From then on in I realised that this was going to be one hell of a challenge, but somehow through this encounter, I also realised I was absolutely in the right place and that this was the real thing.

Here was someone who seemed to know how spiralling thoughts can take one out of the body and consequently disconnect it from the all-encompassing here and now. Knowledge, he said is no substitute for practise. Being in the present was about finding harmony with the body and emanating with the very pulse of life from the feet down to the head up. I was in my element. Through practising yoga I started to gain a deeper and more strident connection with the earth and through that very simple fact, found a legitimate way of saving myself from the emotional disturbances, which had for years plagued my confidence from the inside.

Once after a very intense class, which I felt proud to have got through without too much effort, he said "Mattchews I will always out ego you". Out ego me? Was he throwing down the gauntlet or just simply acknowledging that he was aware of the arrogant side of my distinctive personality? I suspect it was the latter, but he said it in such a way as to leave me wondering.

A little later on I was sitting with eager anticipation in the front of a pranayama class. As the class settled into the quiet rhythms of the breath, he suddenly said "Mattchews if you do not stop making this noise I will have to send you out of the room!" No doubt he was referring to the zigzag thoughts, pouring out in all directions from my distracted head, but as far as I was aware I hadn't made a sound. I spent the remaining part of the lesson reeling with angst at what he said. I couldn't for the life of me understand what he was talking about – in front of forty or so people he had humiliated me and I felt really shaken. It wasn't until years later that I was to get the full gist of what he meant. One of the greatest challenges for me in yoga and indeed in acting has been about quietening the brain, realising the agitation, letting go of it and getting on with the play.

Meditation was truly alive and well in Iyengar's company, the spirit of a master class was always there, but he didn't suffer fools. If you were asleep or preoccupied he made sure the culprit was brought back into line with a thwack. This was never, in my opinion, cruel or malicious, it was vital to the safety of the practitioner that they be ready and alert to the dangers on this highway.

Taking on the responsibility for one's own inner life was a primary factor in his teaching. It wasn't, as I believe some came to think, simply about gaining a certificate and making yoga into a career. Teaching he said was of course very important, he emphasised that we are all teachers in our different ways and can teach people to different degrees. But he also made it absolutely clear that ultimately teachers must be prepared to learn from their pupils and then there is a continual rapport.

When Mr Iyengar taught, there was always something different in each class, something new in each moment and the material of yoga never ran out. Exchanging was taking place all the time; we were constantly opening to a new world, which left no space to get bored. I saw how you could apply this even to other studies, be it mathematics, acting or anything at all. If the teacher is prepared to learn from the pupil, then the pupil becomes eager to give, then there is real love, and real communication. Iyengar never just used his authority, as the 'guru'. He never taught by saying, 'you are wrong and I am right.' Though he did often point out, using sharp discriminative wisdom, that if you work the body like this you live, but like that you die. He was adamant that in the end you should find your own way as he did; if necessary, use whatever you can to help align the body correctly. Stay alert and respectful to one's own inner physical and spiritual intelligence, seek out the teacher within the body as he had done, that was the ultimate message I got from Iyengar.

It would be very tempting to end this story here, in a kind of glorification of the yogic way, but like they say in the scriptures, this was only the beginning. Over the next thirty years or so right up to the present day, I would keep delving deeper into the reality of keeping my feet firmly and truly on the ground through the practise of yoga. There can be absolutely no doubt that it gave me an extremely focused space to fall back on, especially when the intellect and the voices of defeat came in too loud.

Unquestionably, from an external view point there were many benefits in what yoga did for me. It certainly took me a long way into attaining some success as an actor, but it wasn't until the autumn of my life, when I was really prepared to take responsibility for the emotional pain, that an extraordinary sense of worth began to emerge in my practice. In the beginning, a hidden nemesis in me used yoga as a way of gaining power in the world, which eventually backfired. If this book is to mean anything I had to address this fact.

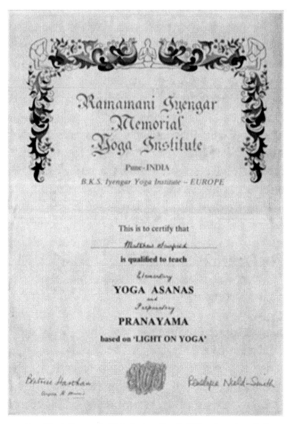

A certificate is no substitute for practise, but it's a proud reminder.

39

At well over seventy years old, decked out in a bikini and wellington boots, Auntie Alice was on her hands and knees in a vegetable patch at the bottom of the garden at Number Nine. For a few split seconds I became rooted to the spot and nearly lost my nerve. This powerhouse of a woman, who had dominated much of my family's life, now looked sort of vulnerable, if not a little pathetic, crouched as she was on all fours amongst the cabbages. If it wasn't for the dark thoughts of how far she could go, when entrusted with the truth of one of her kin, I could easily have lost my nerve. But this was no time to dawdle; I had made up my mind and was quite clear about what I had to do.

Without any sign of being startled at my sudden appearance, she came right in with "Hello Mitty how nice to see you". I had done with the niceties and gone beyond caring. With no hint of fumbling, I spilled the beans; "Auntie Alice, can you please lend me £2000?" There was a pause as she took in what I had said. "What's it for?" she asked with quiet directness. Trying not to sound too childish I laid it down as bluntly as I could; "I have been offered an unfurnished maisonette in Fulham and the people who have the lease want the money for fixtures and fittings or what they call key money". I started to explain what this apartment would mean to me, commented on its size and how it would be very useful, not just for my own domestic security, but for my siblings who might need a room in London any time soon.

Somehow I wasn't surprised when she said yes, but I was taken aback when she said she didn't like to loan money as it always seemed to make relationships complicated in the long run. I thought to myself how you couldn't get much more complicated than what was going down between us at that moment. She then stipulated that she would give me the money as long as I didn't tell anyone in the family, particularly George and Cecilia. With some ingratiating ineptness rumbling around in the back of my subconscious, I accepted with as much gratitude as I could muster. We went up to the house and her apartment, where she wrote out the cheque.

I couldn't believe what had happened. She had given me, what was in 1972, a princely sum almost as an afterthought. Once the formalities were done with, we had a glass of well-fermented apple juice in the kitchen and as she was going about her domestic duties, she asked me what it was I was doing now. When I said teaching yoga, she just asked "What about the RSC, have you thought of applying to the Royal Shakespeare Company?" When I couldn't answer she added, "Well I hope you know what you're doing". Yoga was brushed aside as if it didn't equate, which I put down as understandable, since anything outside her sphere had little or no relevance.

When I left Number Nine the following morning to head back to London, I was over the moon at having won such a prize, and from a woman who I thought saw me as nothing less than a mischievous low-lifer. However, below the level of joy lurked a vague unease, perhaps connected to the rule that lending or borrowing money ties you in deeper.

~

I met Amarilla at one of Silva Mehta's yoga teacher training classes. She was very pretty and self effacing, and had a way of charming the pants off me. I liked her as soon as we said hello. She and her partner had been the previous tenants at 87 Wandsworth Bridge Road and I was thrilled to hand over the money and take possession of my own front door.

Amarilla's family were free thinkers, who went as far as sending her to a school founded by the radical educationalist A.S. Neill, called Summerhill. I knew about Summerhill, because my old friend Storm had been to school there. At the time Neill's philosophy on how children should be taught was very controversial. Children he said should be allowed to live their own lives and not be dictated to by anxious parents, or hedged in by the ridged assumptions of the teacher. I thought this sounded wonderful, but Amarilla had mixed feelings about Summerhill. It was she said, more like Lord of the Flies than Lord of the Rings. She felt it had left her badly equipped for a life in the outside world, like me, she seemed to feel at times like she had been a sacrifice on the altar of her parent's beliefs.

Whether her schooling had anything to do with it or not, she was certainly uncertain as to the merits of living a life in the fast lane. Rather than just rushing blindly for the ladder of success, she seemed predisposed to a broader way of looking at life.

I danced like a demented frog in my new home, hopping from room to room with pride and joy. I was now the exclusive tenant of a maisonette comprising six rooms, two of which were huge, and I didn't have to answer to anyone.

Amarilla and her partner had left me with a blank canvas of stripped pine floors and white walls, so for my taste it didn't take much refurbishing. The two front rooms that looked over the traffic heavy Wandsworth Bridge Road were the largest; the one on the top floor was to become a yoga studio and the bottom one a living room and a crash pad for guests. Next to the yoga studio was a smaller room which would become my bedroom, underneath this room was a workshop. The other two smaller rooms would be bedrooms for next of kin or friends, who might stay for awhile and help out with the rent. Even in 1972, £33 a month rental was cheap for such a large flat. It was protected by the rent act, which meant the rent could only go up at three yearly intervals and only then by a certain percentage, which added to the security.

Thanks to Alice's generosity I was able to take a huge leap. The knock-on effect of living somewhere where I could practise yoga, with enough space to throw a big party was shaking my tail feather like never before. The more I practised the more confident I became and the more confident I became, the more my life seemed to turn around for the better.

The fickle power of those inner doubts may have lingered in the wings, ever waiting for a time to creep in and take over the helm, but for now the skies were clear and a path of optimism seemed mapped out.

Through teaching yoga and continuing with any house maintenance that came my way, money was finally beginning to line my pockets on a regular basis.

I really began to believe that anything was possible, it just needed clear energy and I was privy to more than enough of that. The more yoga I did the more energy it seemed to produce. It was like I had tapped into a main reserve and was now reaping the rewards. Yoga had given me a nervous system, which now seemed resilient enough to face the outside world. Life would still prove to be a rollercoaster, except the trials that came before me now were no longer seen as insurmountable difficulties; they became stories which had the possibility of taking shape with a creative twist.

~

Amarilla rekindled a flame of interest in me for the teachings of Jiddu Krishnamurti. Although he would have torn down such titles as being superfluous, J Krishnamurti was known as a philosopher, enlightened teacher, or even by some as the chosen one.

I went with Amarilla to hear the talks given by Krishnamurti at Brockwood Park School in the south of England. I had seen him a couple of times in the late sixties, but was now a lot more appreciative of who he was.

Krishnamurti was a slight unassuming man whose physique belied the way he put himself across. Whenever I take up one of his books or listen to one of his talks, I find it is always good for me to be reminded of his beginnings. As a boy he was seen playing on a beach in the Bay of Bengal and brought to England in the early nineteen hundreds by Annie Besant and the Theosophical Society, to be educated and set up as the new messiah. If he had been a charlatan, as several of the guru's infiltrating the west turned out to be, he could have easily taken advantage of the many adoring persons and patrons who started to surround his life, but instead, much to a lot of people's dismay, he declined the part of great teacher. The step down from this role gave him much of the substance for his future talks.

In 1929 he wrote 'Because you have placed beliefs before life, creeds before life, dogmas before life, religions before life, there is stagnation. Can you bind the waters of the sea or gather the winds in your fist?' He said, 'according to my point of view, beliefs, religions, dogmas, and creeds, have nothing to do with life, and hence have nothing to do with truth.'

When I'd seen Krishnamurti in the past, I was divided inside by what he was saying. I am in no doubt now, that this division came about because the fortitude of those parental figments still held a rein on how I related to freedom. I don't think I was really aware at this time but one of the greatest rewards yoga was presenting me with, was a sense of perspective on my own state of mind, which was rapidly gaining a lot more space for new and unknown horizons. I could now begin to hear and see the talks given by Krishnamurti without trying to overload my ears with judgemental thoughts of right and wrong, good or bad and all the other dualistic ends and means, separating me from the clarity of wellbeing.

Whenever I had tried to live my life from a basis of an accepted intellectual understanding, by knowledge alone, I had become intimidated to such an extent that I became paralysed. Unable to break free of that conditioning, I was always lead back to the same place, failure. Now I that the science of yoga had taken up the backbone of my life, I increasingly began to see the overall limitation of thought. I had the facility to empty the vessel and take in the world.

Knowledge is an important tool, but there is no doubt to me now that it has become a top heavy one. If we use concepts and ideas at the expense of our heart, aren't we seriously in danger of wiping ourselves from the planet. Places like Cambridge and Oxford, where arrogance in knowledge breeds like a disease, have a lot to answer for. How can we go on telling the world that we know what's best for it. We only have to read between the lines, look closely into the families whose lives are predominantly held together by academic glue, such as the one that I came from, to see the dead weight of dysfunction. Isn't it time to clean up our own backyard and stop with this assumption that *we know best*, as it just seems to add alienation, misunderstanding and sorrow.

My time in Cambridge led me to believe that my life was shot to pieces, before it started. Like Iyengar, Krishnamurti was to turn the tables even further round, to put things into perspective and to make my Cambridge years seem like a ridiculous distant hypothesis. Krishnamurti said of education that it is a complete failure because it has overemphasised technique. He said 'In placing such importance on techniques we destroy ourselves. The exclusive cultivation of technique has produced scientists, mathematicians, bridge builders, space conquerors; but do they understand the total process of life? Can any specialist experience life as a whole; only when he ceases to be a specialist?'

Hearing Krishnamurti speak increased the ever-growing profundity and joy I had for living in the eternal present, making it an even stronger reality. Now all I had to do was live this truth under the spotlight! But did I have the courage to live in the world without a system of beliefs, or more to the point traverse the stage, without the props?

40

The beginning of the seventies saw the demise of the actor manager. Laurence Oliver had been superseded by Peter Hall and the theatre for the most part was presided over by a stranglehold of definitive experts. The director was king and actors and writers were now pawns in their game. There were some who screamed outrage from the wings. Joan Littlewood was outspoken on this front and despite her massive input, enriching our lives with shows like *Oh What a Lovely War, A Taste of Honey, The Hostage, Fings Ain't What They Used To Be* and giving actors who were otherwise dead in the water a chance to blossom, she was branded on a daily basis as a nutter and a rank outsider. The actor was open to ridicule and derision in rehearsal by the man out front. They were mostly men, white males, whose so called academic supremacy gave them control. Innocent passion for the play became an object of cynical derision and was best kept hidden away, out of the rehearsal rooms, in the backrooms and closets of these civic institutions called theatres. These establishments of play were becoming the legacies of architects, politicians and local dignitaries who felt the need to leave their plaque on the wall and a building behind when they died. Most of them wouldn't trust an actor with a barge poll, let alone have tea with one. It became imperative that these buildings of pride were presided over by specialists of the day from Cambridge and Oxford, experts who knew that the play came not from the heart and soul, but from concepts, iambics and sterile technique. There were exceptions to these rules, but they were usually found in the provinces or somewhere out on the fringe.

But hey let's not trip before the fall, it was one of those days when London was dancing, where even the grouchiest neighbour seemed blessed with an innocent heart.

With the rush of a great yoga practice permeating my nervous system I left the front door behind me and hit the streets.

On that sunny optimistic afternoon in 1973, two years after I had left Drama Centre, I had arranged to go back there for an interview with the hope of re-establishing myself as a student again. I did indeed have a meeting with the teachers, expecting them to ostracise me for leaving so abruptly – so the first thing I did was apologise. To my surprise they were unanimous in their praise and told me categorically that I was ready enough to go and work in one of the leading theatre companies. Present at the meeting was my friend Andy Norton, an ex-student who now directed and taught there. Andy made it clear after the meeting that this wasn't a ruse to be rid of me, but absolutely genuine.

Stunned by their confidence I made my way back home via the Kings Road, where I bumped into Francis Fuchs. Francis was a vegetarian from birth, a mild mannered left wing activist who got straight down to the nitty-gritty. I'd known him from my days of playing around at the Royal College of Art. During that period he'd given me a well paid leading role in a film he was instrumental in making for television called *Images*. This black and white short, utilised my talents and those of the actress Imogen Hassel, in a series of spoof commercials, to illustrate how the goggle box was predisposed to corporate gain, so he knew I had some notion of how to play the stage. Over coffee he told me of this plan he had for taking a satirical swipe at the established process of reporting news, using theatre as the medium. The idea being that as bulletins came in from around the world, the writers and actors would come together during the day and make up tongue in cheek skits of these newsworthy events, then put them together as a spontaneous satirical gig in the evening. Having explained what it was all about he asked me if I would be interested in getting involved. I said I would do it and as an afterthought threw in, "On the condition I can do a little something at the end of each show as a kind of highlight". Much to my astonishment he agreed to this request. A few days later I met up with the other actors and writers involved. The show called *Here is the News* found a keen audience and gave me the chance to polish my buttons in public. Other members of the cast included John Gorman from *The Scaffold* and the late great Norman Beaton.

I was introduced to Norman by Francis Fuchs on a street corner in Sloane Square – he unashamedly had a huge spliff on the go, while talking about going to the parameters of the play and then seeing how far we could go. Norman left Guyana for London in 1960 and managed to find a post as the first black teacher to be employed by the Liverpool education authorities. It wasn't long before the hypocrisy in schooling got him disillusioned and he quit – finding his way as a radical writer and actor, he became instrumental in developing Afro-Caribbean theatre in Britain. Norman had a natural ease with the audience and eventually made the headlines when he exploded into everyone's living rooms in the late 80s with the sitcom *Desmond's*. Great to work with, he cheered me on to play my part with as much guts and thunder as I could muster. With Norman there was no time for nerves, the diabolical cultural divides in our society were too in your face for that.

This newly formed company had to be open for change on a daily basis, not just on the topical front, but in the cast as well. This satirical show established a short life for itself in a new but as yet unused building in the Kings Road called The Gallery Theatre, which soon after became part of the Chelsea Cinema complex. A few months later, after a short break, we were asked if we would like to perform in the recently opened New End Theatre in Hampstead. The New End was so tiny it always felt packed to the seams. The intimacy certainly put me on the spot. My little act, of a mimed birth growing into an adulthood of wild blues and release, had become a bit of a tour de force. One evening the designer Iona McLeish was in. She was very complementary and said she would put my name forward as a candidate for a play she was working on in Wales.

Next thing I knew I was camped out in Cardiff and playing to an audience of excited school kids throughout The Welsh Valleys, in a play based on the myth of Sir Gawain and The Green Knight. The director Elspeth Walker encouraged me and the rest of the crew ever onwards, making sure there was a laugh at every turn in the road. If the gigs meant we had to stay away for the night she made sure the hotels were rambling and eccentric. Tim Albery and I got on very well; he was a dynamic stage manager and drove the van through the hills of Wales like a maniac, with the radio blasting out rock 'n' roll from the dash board. Because I knew Tim's brother Nicholas and his irreverent alternative ways from the days of the *Anti-University* I felt I had a familiar friend in Tim. Their father was the theatre owner and impresario Sir Donald Albery, so theatre you might say, was in Tim's blood. We remained good friends until I was in a surreal play he directed in London at the Institute of Contemporary Art in the early 80s; where I think my unpredictability and terrible weakness for giggling on stage, put him off from ever working with me again.

Sir Gawain and the Green Knight ended its rip roaring success of a tour as a Christmas play in the Sherman Theatre in Cardiff, where it never quite caught the same depth of imagination as it had in the valleys.

For what it's worth I see this as the real beginning of my time as a professional actor and somehow felt confident that from now on things could only improve.

Yoga was at the forefront of my daily routine and I wasn't about to bite off the hand that fed me, but practising was difficult, especially in digs with a bedroom full of wardrobes and an impatient proprietor. One afternoon the landlady came barging into my room and caught me standing on my head. After the shock had worn off, she exclaimed in her broad native tongue that I had the devil in me and would continue to do so if I kept on behaving like that. I could see that she might have been thrown by seeing me in my underwear, but to be in the middle of some strange bodily contortion as well was just too much. For her peace of mind, as well as mine, it was imperative to find somewhere more suitable accommodation.

By now I had become friends with some of the staff of The Welsh National Opera and Drama Company and was given the opportunity to move into a room in a house which belonged to the publicity officer, Loesje Sanders.

By the time Christmas came around I felt able to go to my parent's home in Norfolk with some great reviews. They leapt to their feet with pride. There was no doubt that acting presented a doorway to their hearts. They seemed nonplussed about yoga though and gently dismissed my yogic ways as if it were an article of clothing that didn't look or fit quite right. And although I half expected this response, I still couldn't help feeling rebuffed by their subtle dismissal. Little did I comprehend the fact that this and other such rebuffs were driving me into honing a deeper internal intelligence; it was like I was being tested to see if this new foundation in my life was really solid.

Back in Wales, Loesje and I spent an increasing amount of time together. It turned out that she came from a Cambridge family. She had a great love for opera and opened my ears and eyes to this intriguing and epic side of theatre. She gave me that extra boost I needed to focus on acting with a little more clarity and self belief, convincing me further that it could be a way of life.

At the beginning of 1975 the main company was going to stage a production of *Macbeth* and Loesje encouraged me to put my name forward.

Ian Watt Smith, who carried the label, director of productions, agreed to see me. After I'd finished reading from the play he told me I'd made a complete hash of it. He had no hesitation in telling me that the beats were all over the place, he said read it again, this time punch out the iambic pentameter. I couldn't follow what he was talking about, but he tapped out the rhythm on the floor with his foot and I went along with him, doing my impersonation of a speaking clock. As I was to learn later he was just one of many directors and actors who thought that technique was the main gateway to great theatre.

He gave me a part in the play, but it was in a ridiculous production of *Macbeth* where the design took over from the content. The stage was dominated by one big rostrum, which sloped at a ludicrously steep angle, from one side of the stage to the other. The colourful array of talented actors, slipping and sliding precariously on the set, managed to rescue a sinking ship and bring the play to some kind of passable entertainment. Ronald Lewis played the main man with thigh length boots, in the top of which he kept his fags and various pills, which his body needed to remain up to scratch during the run. Collett O'Neill played Lady M. Nigel Terry, who played Malcolm became a good mate, as did David Bailie and Jenny Lee who played Lord and Lady Macduff. The design may have taken over from the content, but the way in which the actors muddled in made the play work, if it worked at all. The production left me a bit nonplussed, but I still felt seduced enough by the spotlight to want more.

Acting seemed like a possible medium to be involved in without bringing harm to myself and others, but because the cynical aspect of show business was so overwhelming, it very easily evaded the subtleties of the heart and I was still very much in two minds about it.

I got back to London and did what a lot of actors do when they're out of work, I demoralised myself by going along to the labour exchange to squeeze money out of the state and I hated it. Why is it, that unemployed people are treated with such contempt? Does the financial burden really place such a weight on the rest of us? Most people want to feel worthwhile. If given the right incentives and pointed in the right direction everything in a person's life must surely be possible, but here there was a continuing sense of dejection and restriction.

Fortunately I could still hold onto some semblance of sensibility. This wasn't about getting a job. The strength here lay at the feet of how I reacted to a world turning its back on me. If the head is chock-a-block with the bitterness and sting of constant rejection, the heart can become hard with resentment, by which time it's very difficult to get up and running. What I was able to do, if only by a hairs breadth, was to empower that side of myself, which like many of us opens up like a dark void when faced with unemployment. The knock on effect of feeling worthwhile, automatically creates a want to do action. No doubt I was lucky, my life was never just about taking the one path, for bad or for worse, my parents had given me too much of a curiosity into what makes us tick for it to ever really feel like that. My upbringing had given me enough initiative to want to work it out for myself. There's always the possibility that living outside the system, of travelling against the grain, will capture the nervous system, but I had an instinctual insight. As the clouds in my life have lifted, I have realised how fortunate I was to have had parents who wanted me to explore the greater possibilities of life. They gave me the initial courage to head out on the highway of independence. Even though this journey was to prove much more daunting than any of us ever realised, it came to imbibe me with enough fortitude to lift my head out from the sludge of the labour exchange.

However, despite these more overt family strengths, what I hadn't grasped was that if I wanted to change still further I would have to let go of the detrimental parts of my past, which for all my yogic ideals still had the power to shake my confidence like a dog with a ragged toy. Among the positive aspects in my family, an overwhelming negative legacy lays engrained like a weathered stain on a clean white sheet. If you can't grasp a PhD on your way out the door, don't bother showing up for the game. Until I could dig out the roots of this misery streak, in a truly fundamental sense, I would always be dependent on some sort of nanny, state or otherwise.

It was good to be back in London, with enough room to get into some intensive yoga again. I just accepted that by exploring further this fine art, I was gaining a greater affiliation for life in the external as well as the internal world.

Ponji was still a frequent visitor to the flat, forever playing the spiritual card, but he could never settle. My sisters Lucy and Sophie rented rooms for an indefinite period. Lucy was starting to take a closer look at the dark side of our family ghosts. She sought the guidance of a councillor at a time when it was thought by our family to be distinctly ambiguous. She wouldn't give in, as I had done, to her pride. Although I didn't have enough courage to show it at the time, Lucy's therapeutic wrangling became the emotional barometer I needed if I felt I was really losing the rails. Her inner resolve helped me to see that my ongoing demonic battles were not hallucinogenic leftovers from the sixties crash pad. Lucy didn't do drugs; she was always straight down the line. Our dialogue may at times have blown up into over-the-top arguments, but she was always a steadfast reminder that healing begins when we finally admit to wanting help, something I was still unable to do.

In short, there were to be many guests and lodgers who shared the flat with me in London over those oncoming years, which I found both difficult and exhilarating – difficult because my erratic nature could be exposed and exhilarating because I loved connecting with the many diverse and unpredictable characters who turned up.

Emo and Pip came to stay for a while. I couldn't always handle Emo's impulsive character or Pip's addiction to heroin and made that absolutely clear by giving them the cold shoulder. Although I remained close to them both, I seldom saw Pip after that. I wasn't surprised when I found out that the needle had finally swallowed him up. I was shocked when I heard that he allegedly got himself killed by a psycho, after he came on too strong to the man's girlfriend. Emo always maintained that Pip had been the perpetrator of his own death.

Whatever entanglements, good and bad, the many friends and relations who came and went through the flimsy front door into my private space always remained a challenge to my love and sensibilities.

A few weeks after I got back from Wales, I revived a popular yoga class in a hall just off the North End Road. One of my pupils was Francesca Annis, who I had got to know very well when I was going out with her flat mate Vivian in the sixties. She now owned a house not far from my place in Fulham and we would sometimes hang out together. Occasionally she would phone Vivian in New York to say hello and tease a little by asking me if I wanted to talk to her, which made me blush like a twelve year old. Francesca was a real tonic, she was confident, without any sign of arrogance, not only in life, but as an actress as well. She was already very successful and I could have easily been jealous of her, but because she was so open and generous in her personality it just never crossed my mind to be so. She saw yoga as an important part of her life and was an extremely receptive pupil. We started talking about playing Shakespeare one day and I told her how the job in Wales had left me feeling unsure how to handle the verse. She suggested I write to a director she knew called Peter Gill.

The idea of writing job letters didn't appeal, so I decided to paint a picture with watercolours and write a poem.

Shortly after this Peter Gill's assistant Michael Joyce called me and an appointment was arranged. Right from our first meeting Peter's enthusiasm and energy had me dancing around the room. Unlike my previous encounter with Shakespeare, he left me with a feeling that I had talent, and as long as I immersed myself in the world of the play the buttons would take care of themselves. The production of *As You like It* was to be a delightful eye-opener, with an inspiring cast.

For the few weeks Peter and Michael continued casting, I wangled my way into spending a lot of time with them. Despite this closeness they kept me in the dark as to what I was going to play, which left my mind open to the fantasies of leading roles. I can't say I wasn't disappointed when they finally decided on my playing William and other parts. However, Peter had a way of making all the actors feel like they were main players, so it wasn't hard to bring enthusiasm and fun to the job. He was imbued with a kind of love for the actors that seemed to make them fall at his feet with willingness.

Loesje's house was in an area of the Welsh capital called Splott, so I was familiar with the place where Peter was born and brought up when I met him. He told me endless stories about his upbringing which was working-class and tough. Splott is situated next to the Docklands in Cardiff's Tiger Bay, which was, when Peter was growing up, a multinational area in the midst of terrible depression and decline. Even when I stayed there the neighbouring kids ruled the local streets like colonies of feral cats.

Peter's childhood may have been hard, but his family gave him the space for absorbing the written word with compassion and intelligence. He was self-taught and had been an actor himself, so he knew exactly how it felt to stand in the middle of a great vastness without a clue. He put actors' sensitivities before anything else, but he wasn't by any means weak. One of the things he did with poetic rigour was to make sure that they hit the right note and not for the rhythm, but for the sense; find the sense in the line he said and the rhythm will take care of itself. A lesson often missed by the experts.

When lifted from the page, *As You like It* exudes a kind of revolution from the dark tones of restriction, into the freedom of love and that's exactly what happened in the company. As we went into the weeks of rehearsal we played ate and drank the play until the cup overflowed.

Such was the trust, the actors, who needed help, weren't shy about expressing their insecurities with the verse. Much of the rehearsal was spent creating a comfortable and confident base from where to speak.

There was never any separation with Peter, he was one of us, but he was also a captain who knew when to pull in the ropes. He had a distinctive way of keeping the company happy and contented, even the sardonic Leslie Saroney who was brought in to play Sir Oliver Martext cut a smile during the tea breaks. I knew David Baillie and Anthony Douse from the *Macbeth* company in Wales, which made me feel even more like I was part of a growing family.

The camaraderie continued to flow into the opening night at the Nottingham Playhouse, then moved on to Edinburgh where the play was the international hit of the festival. Jane Lapotaire was the first actor I'd met who said she never read reviews. She said if you can't take the bad ones then you shouldn't really believe or take in the good ones. After this I tried to read them with a certain amount of indifference, if at all.

Clive Barnes wrote of this production in the New York Times '*...it was the best play I saw during the festival...Mr Gill... has a feeling for the way young people act, and his staging of 'As You Like It' seemed to be an Arcadian testimony to youth... The pattern, the mood, and the particular bucolic elegance are his own. This is an 'As You Like It' lost and dreaming in a Shakespearean summer, Jane Lapotaire is enchanting as Rosalind - perhaps the best since Vanessa Redgrave - gauche, confident and beautiful, and John Price makes the most personable Orlando. The charm of the production was quite simply in its insistence on the text and its feeling for the mood and tempo of the play*'.

Paul Dawkins played the forbidding Duke Frederick and reminded me of Charles Laughton, offering up the sense of the lines with every ounce of his body. He was a natural actor, who just came on to the stage and spoke words with such relish it seemed as if he had owned them forever. During the middle of the run in Nottingham Paul became ill and needed to be replaced. I was sharing a flat which belonged to one of Loesje friends, with Peter and Michael when they got the phone call and they asked me to be ready. My adrenalin started soaring through the roof; however I was extremely nervous about biting off more than I could chew. I think Peter picked up on this, add to that the unpredictable side of my nature and it was just too much of a risk. So when it was arranged that Anthony Douse should step into Paul's shoes I was both relieved and let down by the decision.

Alun Armstrong kept the spirit yearning for more with his Geordie stories and songs during and after rehearsals, like a definitive *Touchstone*. He was a master of timing and made sure that Sue Porrett, who was playing Audrey, and I had the lines in our scene down to an absolute art. He taught me to be more than ready with the words. During the first few weeks when I left the stage as William I got a round of applause; I had no idea why or how this was happening. When one of the other actors asked me how I did it I became self-conscious and the clapping stopped. Alun was unrelenting with his energy and commitment to the scene, with him there was no time to wonder or to analyse why, you just got on with it and in doing so the applause returned.

George and Cecilia came to the first night in Nottingham and I felt completely and utterly as if I'd hit the right note for them. They seemed pleased as punch to see their boy making good in such an accomplished production and I basked in their approval.

The artistic director of the Nottingham Playhouse at this time was Richard Eyre, who had recently moved from the Edinburgh Lyceum. He had persuaded Peter to come up from London and direct *As You like It*, which was a major achievement in itself, as Peter became distinctly ill at ease when away from home base. Richard was delighted by the play's successful run and made it known whilst we were in Edinburgh that he wanted to work with many of the actors.

Art is rational and a source of any social action
We have problems because we have intelligence to define and passions committed to hope
And whoever of the week is willing to fight now has already won

The everlasting city and men will not be built
In new-hewn marble from quarries of gods
But from the rubble of human struggle
Go to the wall and build in the ruins

Edward Bond Liverpool 1975

41

I arrived back in London with rivulets of success cascading through my veins and wanted more. I had dreams of playing leading roles and imagined a greater respect from my contemporaries as I strutted around on a star-struck stage.

I got wind of an audition with the Liverpool Everyman. This time I really did bite the bullet. Because I had left Edinburgh with such optimism, I somehow knew I'd got this job as soon as I entered the room.

At this time The Everyman was at the height of its fame for being a provincial theatre that did cutting-edge stuff; it presented a platform for a new wave of writers such as Alan Bleasdale, Willy Russell and the Liverpool poets. A lot of the actors went on to become world-class acts: Jonathan Pryce, Barbara Dickson, David Morrissey and Pete Postlethwaite, to name some. As the new artistic director, John Roche brought in his own chosen flock; there were a few who stayed over from the old company, most notably, Julie Walters and Bill Nighy.

The opening play, Edward Bond's *Lear*, was to have four weeks rehearsal and run for the same amount of time.

On the first morning, the company sat around in a circle and after John had given his optimistic welcoming speech, he told us who was playing what part. Like a silver ball falling into place on the roulette wheel, I froze in my seat when he announced that I was to play the title role of Lear.

I was staggered, why hadn't I been told beforehand. George Costigan one of the other cast members knew that he was going make his directorial debut with Roy Minton's play *Death in Leicester*, Hugh Armstrong who was brought in to play McMurphy in *One Flew over the Cuckoo's Nest* knew what he was going to play. But muggins here hadn't got a clue!

Maybe I got what I wished for and was being ungrateful, but I realised there was no way I was mature enough as an actor to play this part, especially within the given time. After the first meeting I took John aside and told him in as many words that he had picked the wrong guy. He said you're the only person who can play this role in the company and I hired you to do just that. A big part of me just wanted to disappear, but I didn't. I was always susceptible to flattery and took the rope to make my own noose.

The next four weeks were to be a mixture of nightmare, adrenalin, excitement and long sleepless nights. My catastrophic insecurity with words made learning lines the priority. All that remained over the next few weeks was to ram them into my head, learn them like a parrot and hope the sense would follow suit. I kept up the pretence of being in control, but internally I was completely and hopelessly out of my depth. Being actors most of the cast were sensitive to my needs and gave me every encouragement, but the whispering in the wings got louder and I felt a huge sense of separation setting in as the dawn of the opening got closer.

My digs in Liverpool were part of a depressing squat and my room was on the ground floor. I was fidgeting and sweating in my bed of nerves one night, when a drunken bag lady climbed in through the bedroom window and collapsed on the floor. This freaked me beyond belief and I lost control of my senses. I shot out of bed completely naked, screaming at her to get out. I was so over the top that it brought her round to immediate sobriety. She was subsequently so scared that she leapt back out of the window faster than she fell in, leaving a heavy cloud of alcohol and rank odour behind her.

As far as I was concerned the opening of *Lear* was a catastrophe and the following day the director told me he was seriously thinking of firing me; but he didn't.

Later when the days became mine, yoga was given the space it needed to help and things began to get a little better. It took me the best part of three weeks to get a handle on the part and the play. Then one night, toward the end of the run my parents came to see the show, along with the playwright himself Edward Bond, a few local dignitaries, including Willy Russell and Roger McGough. It was a packed house and I rose to the occasion as if my life depended on it. Everything came together and an extraordinary journey took place.

After this my whole perception of who I was working with changed. The other actors revealed themselves as distinctive individuals whose sensitivities were as complex as mine.

David Fielder was nobody's fool and emerged as an ally who had been with me all along; he was prepared to go to the end of the earth, well not quite there, but at least to the end of the play and back. Bill Nighy, who liked to rock the night with the soul, became a friend and told me how he didn't think the play was playable until then. An actor who was going out with Julie Walters at the time came up, and introducing himself as Pete Posthelwaite, reiterated what Bill had said, that I had made what he thought to be an impossible part fly.

Pete and I have never worked together, but our paths were to cross at frequent intervals and we eventually became good friends. Several decades down the line we ended up being distant neighbours in the hidden county, this was never planned. As he would say, it was just another indication of divine providence.

Perhaps all the grief had been worthwhile after all, as the respect from such esteemed company was prize enough to stem that old negative draw.

I may have toyed with the horrors before walking in Lear's shoes, but after this special night was through, there was always admiration and respect for those actors who go the extra mile for their part in the play.

What I discovered by being in the hot seat on that fateful evening was a man who rules the stone empire of his mind, a king who loses his power, breaks down and breaks through. To all intents and purposes he goes mad, but this abhorrent disarray brings him to a wiser and saner place, where he sees, not with his eyes but with his heart, the play.

ELISABETH AND EDWARD BOND

Orchard Way, Great Wilbraham, Cambridge   28 November 75

Dear Matthew

Lear at Liverpool ment a great deal to me. More than it
did at the Court - although you had much less money and
time. I dont know why it ment more to me. I could have
picked holes in parts of it (especially the writing). My
feeling had to do with the honesty of your acting and John's
work on the play. The play could be done as melodrama - but
it isnt melodrama, its very simple and ordinary truth.
Your acting had the same quality - you didnt do anything to
impress or move the audience, but everything you did was
a reaching out to understand the situations and to support
them. Its usually done the other way round, and the situations
are taken as an opportunity for the actor to exploit himself
- which is why most acting is a con. Your performance
was very valuable to me as a writer, I learned somethings
about the theatre. It was also smashing to watch you rehearse.

Im not going to write to John, I know him too well now and
it would seem too formally to send him a letter. But I would
like you to show him this letter - so that you both know
you are thanked.

         With love,

         Edward

42

Hypocrite; *One who puts on a mask and feigns himself to be what he is not.*

Although Liverpool had been head changing, it left me with an overall sadness I hadn't expected and for the umpteenth time I seriously began wondering if I had the tenacity to really pursue the path of rogues, vagabonds and players. But the decision, if there ever was a decision, was never going to be mine to make...

I had underestimated my lack of ability for being honest with the opposite sex. When the seductive opportunity arose for me to sleep with a girl, I used my new-found strengths and leapt in. The next thing I know, she's pregnant.

Once again my lack of maturity let me down. I didn't have the guts, or more to the point didn't even know how to ask about contraception, which seems so embarrassing and ridiculous to admit to now.

I told her categorically that I wasn't capable, financially or otherwise. I said I was too screwed up, that I couldn't take responsibility for myself let alone that of a baby.

It wasn't supposed to be like this; how could I have allowed this to happen!? We were both emotionally adolescent, unable to ask each other what was appropriate or needed when we were together in the love nest. I was blind to my desires and because I was the stronger, it seemed like the decision was mine to be made. I persuaded her to have an abortion. We created a life together and destroyed it, all in a matter of months.

This left me feeling that I hadn't moved on, or really matured as I thought and once more I collapsed in on myself. I was back at the bottom of the juvenile heap again, only this time I had yoga, or so I hoped. Yoga was my only constant and thankfully merciful; but I couldn't avoid the fact that the seeds of truth had been sown and now I had to reap the consequences. Weeks passed as I kept on with my practice; in fact I was fervent to the point of punishment. I managed to keep things moving along financially by decorating, and doing odd house repair jobs for various friends who were moving steadily up the ladder of affluence. But as far as teaching yoga was concerned, the door shut down on that one inside. I felt as if my days of being a moral contender were over. I looked to the road as means of distraction.

By now I was the proud owner of a motorbike, a Triumph Tiger 100, which I had bought for the princely sum of £83. I made the decision to escape by riding it down to Italy, so the bike would have to be in top notch condition. The Tiger 100 was built like a giant Meccano set, so it wouldn't be that hard to revamp. The bike was old, but it wasn't by any means past its prime. With a bit of careful handling, and some mechanical manoeuvring, it could easily be brought up to scratch, n the place that I thought fitted its character; the garage at Number Nine in Cambridge.

I took the bike to bits and from the engine up did a complete rebuild, replacing worn parts with new. My thinking was that if I got to know the bike from the inside out, I would have a better understanding of how to fix it if something went wrong.

Whilst I was in Cambridge I caught up with my cousin Francis again, who had just come back from staying in Ghana with the lawyer Joe, the cool black guy who played the piano in the Oak Room when I was a little boy. We spent a few hours during the evenings sitting beside a campfire in the garden, and whilst doing so, I noticed how the bottom of Francis's spine was badly collapsed. When I brought this to his attention he didn't seem that bothered, but he had, he said been concerned about his eyesight. He showed me eye strengthening exercises which he had got from a book by Aldous Huxley; this involved placing the palm of the hand over one eye whilst circling the other from the sky to the earth and he said it really helped. I expressed that I was glad, but I continued to be seriously worried about how badly out of shape his lower back looked. He said he wanted to live in London for a while and try his hand at various artistic ventures there. I offered a room in my flat and was happy when he accepted. Apart from giving us some time together, it would be useful for covering the rent while I was away.

Within a few days I got the Triumph back to a place worthy of the road, but before I set off across the European Continent, I went to see my parents in Norfolk, who had now moved to a house attached to the bookshop in the market town of Fakenham.

George and Cecilia were quite accepting about my motorbike, in fact they didn't seem at all concerned, which I felt good about.

The bookshop had become a focal point for many writers and poets, who needed some literary respite, in this quiet enclave on their way to the coast. My father took to the role of bookseller like a quill to ink. As with the shop in Cambridge he had a love and an eye for it, except now he'd be picking up rare additions at car boot sales and selling them on for a song rather than flogging a dead pan. Peering through the shelves of new and second-hand books, with a gentle greeting for the customer, he really had become like a friendly unconventional character you might stumble on in a Victorian novel.

One of the great joys of visiting Fakenham at this time was getting to know my youngest sister Sophie. At number eight Sophie lived for most of her time in an imaginary world with imaginary friends. She was now at the latter end of her schooling and her imaginary friends had been taken over by real ones. She said she had a hard time at school, but she gave the impression of handling it a lot better than I ever did.

Sophie had suffered, like my other sisters, from being at the butt-end of my teasing. Being the youngest, meant her age and innocence made the games I played very real and in some instances cruel. My acting out the role of Bill Sikes had her quaking in fear. I'm thankful to say my unkindness seemed to have no lasting effect on her. Now boys and girls alike sought out Sophie's company and they would hang out at our parent's house, seeking out her social wisdom. From where I sat this role appeared to be well suited to her gregarious positive nature.

The thought of crossing the valleys and hills of Europe brought to mind a knight in search of the Holy Grail. I knew there was an oasis out there and I was determined to make that my goal.

With the roads leading to the English Channel disappearing behind me, I hit the fast lane into Paris and just when I thought I'd got a grip on the highway the Tiger broke down.

I pushed the heavy bike, with a weary stride to my step, up the road then gave in to tiredness. By this time the sun had slunk away with the evening and I set up my tent, with a lot of fumbling around, in what seemed to be a total black out. I had a night of strange dreams where rockets and snakes were whizzing backwards and forwards through my bed. When I woke in the morning and stuck my head out between the flaps of the tent, I saw how I was camped on the grass verge, not more than an arm's length from speeding cars and death defying juggernauts on a motorway.

The roadside assistance came and picked me and the Triumph up and took us to a garage in a small village on the outskirts of the French capital. To save money I asked, with the little French at my disposal, if it would be possible for me to fix the motorbike myself. Rather than being thrown by this request they seemed knocked out by the idea. They were incredibly enthusiastic about the workings of the combustion engine and not only went out of their way to help, but gave me the backyard and full use of their many tools.

I immediately set about stripping the bike down and found the culprit pretty quickly. When I had taken the engine apart in Cambridge I had neglected to put back one of the push rods correctly and this intricate part of the engine was now bent out of shape. This was a disaster as I thought it would be impossible to get a replacement. I needn't have worried though; in his inimitable way one of the mechanics managed to track down the Triumph auto dealer in Paris. He then drove me into the city and to the shop. After examining the damaged push rod, the man behind the counter said that he couldn't replace it as it wasn't a stock item, but when I expressed upset and concern he said he should be able to turn one out on a lathe situated right there in the back room. Having expressed my thanks, he added how it wouldn't be ready until the following day. The extended timeframe didn't faze my mate the mechanic at all. In fact we went back to his village where I was treated as one of their own. I put the tent up in a small paddock to the side of the garage and finished the evening with a generous helping of French hospitality.

A day or so later, with the bike back in order, I said goodbye to my new-found friends, as they jumped in and out from behind car bonnets bidding me bon voyage and bon chance and set off once again. This time I decided to keep to the smaller roads, as I found the French motorways somewhat unnerving, the Tiger 100 was fast, but not that fast.

Before I left Paris I went to see my sister Elizabeth, who had found herself a tiny one room apartment in the Vietnamese quarter. She was playing guitar and singing in a couple of night clubs to bring in some cash. Despite smoking and drinking like never before, she seemed well, but it felt strained between us. I couldn't help feeling that, after all these years, she still harboured a serious grudge for my hasty departure from her life in France.

We went out in the evening of course, to celebrate. I started on about yoga and she showed some interest. The next morning she watched as I went through a restricted practice. I think because of her training as a dancer she saw it purely as an external form of expression.

I told her to come to London sometime soon, but our lives were so different now, or so I thought, I wasn't sure if it could ever work out between us. A sense of overwhelming sorrow lingered in the air as we said our goodbyes. I drove away from her doorstep with all the unanswered questions of our combined lives buzzing around inside my head. As I was wondering if the pain in our family would ever be resolved I started to drift, but the immediacy of the glistening cobbled streets soon brought my attention back to the job at hand. I weaved in and out of Paris traffic making a beeline for the tree lined country roads, which seem to go on forever in certain parts of France, and give you all the time in the world. I didn't want to stop anywhere except to refuel and to get directions.

When I asked a well-weathered woman, who was dressed all in black and hoeing a field of vegetables, if she could tell me how to get on the main road for the city of Valence, she was delightfully effusive. I managed to catch the odd word, but I think she could see I wasn't really taking much in. The next minute saw me standing by her side in a rustic kitchen with her drawing a map and asking me if I was hungry. I was starving and gratefully sat around a table with her welcoming family, feeling a little awkward when the plates of meat started appearing and totally perplexing my hosts when I declined them. When they finally understood my plight they showered me with salads, cheeses and bread, which I wolfed down with their perfectly rough homemade wine.

Eventually I got down to the southern part of this aromatic country and started moving closer to Italy, making my way across the freezing Alps. Back on the main roads the journey outside started to become an internal one, as the fight with the cold took over. Astride the motorbike, without proper gear to keep me warm, was like tearing down an unending tunnel of ice. Unable to stop for fear of isolation and hypothermia, I started to increase the speed, with the chiselled subways of hard rock and dramatic countryside disappearing into a pinprick of heat somewhere at the tip of my mind to keep me going. Finally I crossed the border between the small mountain villages of Larche and Argentera, and just when I was beginning to think my fingers and toes were going to fall off, the weather started to change for the better as the warmth of the Italian sunshine began to embrace my journey.

The Italians loved motorbikes then, especially British ones, so whenever I stopped, even at traffic lights, it brought in a few admirers. The motorways in Italy are beautiful feats of engineering and seemed to be less busy than the equivalent in France or England. Back on the road, with the soft wind racing against my face and the ancient hills chasing away cares from my eye line, my spirits soared to record heights.

The journey unmasked a new affair of unending beauty, where the Renaissance falls into a logical place and reveals its true nature. Through towns and villages of recovery, across winding roads of sun swept Tuscan beauty, this was a natural masterpiece painted with subtle shades of blended colours that opened my eyes to a heaven on earth.

Going south, I took the old Roman road out of Florence and finally made it to the quiet parched village of Le Corti, invigorated and ready for the call that lay ahead. I had reached my oasis.

I met Dona Holleman while she was assisting Iyengar in London. She lived and breathed yoga and was open for seriously keen pupils to practise with her. There was a kind of adventurous quality about what she was putting across.

Dona came out of her house and I could see by the smile on her face and the twinkle in her eye that she was genuinely pleased to see me.

It had taken me a while, but I had finally won Dona's friendship. I carried on with her uncertain company and she ended up being very good to me, fun and a great sport. I'd been coming to Italy over the past three years for several weeks at a time, between acting jobs, and had made a network of friends through Dona's yoga classes. I was even starting some small carpentry projects and other maintenance work to pay my way while I was there.

It went without saying that I would go to any of Iyengar's classes when he was in the UK, but finding the teacher in every pore of the body, when he wasn't there, was like being at the foot of an overwhelming mountain, wondering if the climb is possible on your own. How could anyone traverse such a steep and treacherous terrain without help; logically Iyengar was the living proof that it was possible. I tried to find teachers in the UK who had some mastery over this misleadingly simple holistic science, and through one link and another started hanging out with Dona Holleman. Dona had spent a good part of two years and more in Iyengar's company during the sixties, practising, helping him teach and being generally put through her paces.

As with many organised businesses the politics of yoga in the UK at the time seemed like a distraction taking away from the essence of what yoga was all was about, and I think Dona felt she'd had enough. So leaving the gossip and tittle-tattle behind her, she moved to Italy, a country she loved, with a view to setting up classes there. She had a loyal following of a few devotees from England who would go over to her classes whenever they could, and I placed myself as one of them.

During these frequent visits to Italy, Dona was kind enough to put me up. If I remember rightly she was a little unsure at first as to who or what I was, but she persevered with her teaching, until there was distilled clarity in the body of light.

As long as they showed commitment and dedication in their practice, she wasn't shy about sharing what she had learnt with others. From Dona I really got some understanding of the restrain and isolation necessary for a monk's life. There was no get out clause, you either got on with it or you left. The days and weeks were mapped out by a clock denoting which asanas/postures came where. First thing in the morning was sitting for the subtleties of pranayama/breathing, which was followed by a short break, then, depending on the day, we practised back bends or forward bends, or balancing postures, or variations of all three usually for around two hours. At four o'clock in the afternoon it was always half an hour's headstand followed by half an hour's shoulder stand. In between practising Dona would teach classes in her studio which she had set up in Florence. This kind of routine was typical for the weeks I stayed and it really taught me to look into yoga with an internal eye. Yoga became as regular and normal to me as brushing my teeth, wearing clothes, or taking a bath, which meant it became abnormal if ever I missed a session.

There were a few other guests at Dona's on the afternoon I arrived with my motorbike, and having had our introductions, it was straight into a head and shoulder-stand practice. We then set about preparing some food, and as we settled into the evening, I started telling stories of my journey through France. The humour soon took over and by the time we went to our beds we were full of laughter and the anticipation of another day.

In yoga, when it is practised unconditionally, with a total respect for the human form, there is no escape from the ravages of the mind. In life the mind eventually catches up with the body. As I went through the next few weeks I became more familiar with this karmic law

I had learnt this simple rule in drama collage, but I hadn't realised the worth. When a character walks away from the drama of their past, they usually have their head down in some kind of repose. If they are walking towards the future the head is usually up, looking forward, animated with anticipation for their wants and needs. This very straightforward illustration informs us how the past and the future dictate how we stand or move in the present. When someone bears the weight of their past and future burdens for too long, it will inevitably hamper the stance of the body now. I realised I was not infallible to this law, but there were times when I was arrogant enough to convince myself that I was. Initially the challenge for me in yoga was to live truly and completely in the present, but increasingly I thought this wasn't going to be possible, because I saw what I'd left behind as being irreversibly corrupt.

If I can fix the wrongs or heal the wounds of the past, then I can open the gates of the temple with a clear conscience. If I continue to sow seeds of misfortune in the present, I will forever be bound to the past or the future and therefore unable to truly master the art of yoga.

Whilst staying in Italy this time, the circus inside my head caught up with me yet again and was to propel me with even more vigour into the world of dramatis personae...

One Sunday Dona took me up to a traditional Tuscan villa on the other side of Florence, which looked out over hills of olive groves and elegantly proportioned fields, where goats chew on the shirt tails of shade in the gently buzzing afternoon. This beautiful house was home to Vanda Scaravelli. Vanda was an awe inspiring lady, who was born into a distinguished Florentine family and was one of the first dedicated Iyengar pupils in the west. She was one of those rare members of artistic aristocracy, who felt just as comfortable sitting on the floor with a bunch of hippies, as standing in a room filled to the brim with royalty. Her house was often teaming with renowned creative people from all over the world. One of her closest friends was J Krishnamurti and it was through Krishnamurti that Dona and Vanda became close friends. In those early years in Italy they spent a lot of time together playing the piano and helping each other out with yoga.

After some time in their company, I became aware of a nagging desire to tell them about my immaturity with the opposite sex, and how it had led to stealing a life; if you like confess to my crimes. But I was finding that every time I opened my mouth a tale of avoidance came out. Vanda and Dona were extremely patient with me, however at times I think this tolerance began wearing a bit thin. Before it slipped away into confusion and disinterest, I'd come up with an elaborate way to catch their attention, and then bottle out of saying what I really wanted. As if from a disgruntled audience, I was greeted with cries of "Why are you telling us this?" or "Get to the point!" I leapt out of the real issue by saying, "I think I have this need to act". "Then act", they would say; "But I don't want to lose this vital thread of yoga"; "You will never lose yoga", they would say, "It is in you and forever will be".

Indeed, I was locked into a need to practise and continued to reap many of the benefits. I may not have touched on my underlying truth with Dona and Vanda back then. Although I was to some extent now wearing the mantle of yoga, much like a costume in a play, it was as they said yoga was in me forever.

Italy and Dona had given me a light heart and I wanted so much to give something back. I felt unworthy of teaching, but decided to stand up to the music, and with the companion of yoga close by my side, walk back through the stage door.

With Dona's support I put on a one-man show about birth and death which contained mime and words. *Una Serata Con Matthew* was a little rough around the edges but proved successful to the small international audience, herded together by Dona and friends in the Palazzo Strozzi, around the corner from the grand Cathedral of Florence.

The adrenalin from putting on this show lifted my yoga practice to a more focused space, and I was beginning to see how being an actor could benefit yoga, in the same way that yoga teaching does. They inform each other. Then I started wondering if I could mix and match without any compromise back in the UK. This would mean setting the conditions before I started a job. But all this was fantasy because I hadn't been offered any acting work and it looked increasingly likely that I wasn't going to be either.

As Italy became a way of life, I began to let go of these theatrical daydreams. Then late one afternoon, as the sun was leaving a wake of soft hues and the certainty of another day across the Italian landscape, Richard Eyre called me out of the blue, with an invitation to tread the boards at the Playhouse in Nottingham.

43

A few hours after arriving in Nottingham, I found myself sitting on the floor of Richard Eyre's living room, in a core of awkwardness, speaking reticently, if not proudly, of my recent travels across the European continent.

Having made me a cup of tea, he asked me what I'd been doing in Tuscany, which he said was a part of the world he liked very much. I said something about exploring the outer echelons of yoga, which didn't seem to make much of an impression, but when I told him how I'd put my hand to house maintenance over there to help pay my way, he seemed intrigued and suggested, with a wry smile, that the room we were in needed decorating. He was joking of course and was a bit taken aback when I offered up my services with the brush.

I'm not sure who was taking advantage of whom, if at all; either way Richard found it hard to say no, which meant my first job in Nottingham was giving a small portion of his home a paint job.

In some ways Richards's sensitivities reminded me of my father. Although a generation apart, their backgrounds were similar in standing and in manner. They both went to public school, ended up reading English at Cambridge and leaning comfortably to the left, but above and beyond this, they resided in a self-conscious inner vortex, where shy intensity oversees the rumblings of an unfair world.

Even though we were to spend a good deal of time together over the next few years, both professionally and personally, Richard and I fell short of ever really delving into a shared past.

I'm not sure if he was aware that we had performed together in a previous life. As I have mentioned in an earlier chapter, I remember his street attire as being dapper in Cambridge. The way he used to hang out during the rehearsal of *The White Devil*, the play we were both in then, brought to mind a cool dude with a keen appetite for living. I certainly can recall a production of *Espresso Bongo*, which was put on during the following academic year with Richard playing the Cliff Richard part, for it heralded some controversy around the city by vying for the darker side of jazz. This role would have suited Richard's style as someone who flirted with the bohemian part of Cambridge life. I'd seen him on more than a few occasions saunter into the El Patio, (the coffee bar around the corner from my dad's shop in Sydney Street), wearing shades and the coveted leather jacket, to hang out with the so called Cambridge beats. Later on, when I found a way into the centre of that eclectic mix, I heard many stories from mutual friends about his satirical impersonations and wanted to witness them, but alas that wasn't to be.

Some thirteen years later in his living room, we let the past hang in the air with nothing mentioned and nothing lost; this was a relief for me, as it meant I didn't have to reveal the true extent of my academic worth.

By the time I came to leave Richard's neat home, I had to accept the fact that I was just too shy of setting any parameters around where or how I could do yoga. Given my past experience of digs in the provinces this had to be a priority for me and I started to tie myself up in a rather large knot over this tiny conundrum. As always I needn't have wasted my time fretting for the theatre provided a perfect home for the yoga mat.

The Playhouse in Nottingham was one of those architecturally designed theatres that left a lot to be desired, especially with regards an actor's needs. Most of the dressing rooms were designed and built as if they were prison cells without windows. During the day the front of house was a bit like an empty airport lounge with locked down shops and void of people, but on first viewing I realized there was going to be more than enough space for practising yoga.

Richard worked the scenes of Brecht's *Trumpets and Drums* with the relevant actors to be called for rehearsals when needed. Although this meant an abundance of time for yoga, it wasn't until the latter end of the rehearsal period that I would catch up with the overall style of the play and discover the full ensemble.

Two of the actors, John Price and Caroline Hutchinson, I knew from *As You Like It* and meeting up with them again, saw a family of friends continuing to grow. Caroline was adamant that I should teach her some asanas /postures whilst we were in Nottingham. The theatre staff saw this as a bit of an oddity, for yoga as it was known then was still confined to the women's institute, or at best a Himalayan pastime. Despite any doubts they might have held, word started to catch on and a few other members of the cast joined in, most notably Zoe Wanamaker, David Beams and Judy Liebert.

I discovered that teaching actors yoga can be extremely exhilarating. I think one of the reasons for this, is the willingness they have to go somewhere different in themselves, to let go of a known reality and go into another, usually without hesitation.

In a society that craves a certainty carved in concrete, the actor's insecurity is patronised and treated as bit of a joke, it is certainly hyped out of all proportion by the media. However, if the actor has enough courage to fill his or herself completely with the character and disappear into the landscape of the film or play, society can respond in a meaningful way, often setting them up as heroes. When Robert De Niro submerged himself unconditionally in the part of Jake LaMotta he was given an Oscar, when Meryl Streep walked headlong into the holocaust as a Polish immigrant for *Sophie's Choice*, she emerged with every award under the sun, when Daniel Day Lewis gave himself over to the wheelchair in *My Left Foot*, they sniggered in the wings, at the lengths he was willing to go to for his craft, then gave him the Best Actor award, and the list goes on.

Actors who are worth their salt realize that becoming friends with emptiness and insecurity are an essential part of the job. This was a serious ordeal, but nevertheless an essential one for me to aspire to. If I wanted any success in this precarious business, there had to be a balance between the emotions and knowledge.

It was beginning to become clear that if the void of the self is full of surplus baggage when taking on a role, it leaves little space for the complexities and demands of the play. When I can let go of those nagging peripheries I am more able to take a true step into the unknown. The same could be said for my yoga practice – the more I am immersed in the character of the body, the more I become integrated with the play of my surroundings. I knew from my inklings of experience that going into the body of yoga, like going into the character of a play, shouldn't mean separation – in fact quite the reverse; if I practised with intelligence and awareness, I became more in touch with my surroundings not less.

I was starting to see that this apprenticeship with yoga and acting were joined at the waist. If I could dance with the incessant jangling of nerves, I was convinced I had a good chance of making the grade in both arts. Embracing and using the uncertainty, was becoming a familiar and integral key to my finding a way into the narrative of the play. Likewise, it seemed the play of anxieties was needed to take an initial step into yoga, and in return yoga could allow a deeper release from those very uncertainties. I just had to be willing to evolve behind the mask.

As yoga and the demands of the theatre continued to be an inspiring partnership, a familiar pattern began to emerge, which was to take me years to fully respect and understand. If I pushed too hard in yoga it very easily became empty, devoid of intelligence, just a way of getting from A to B. It was the same in acting, when I pushed too hard, the character became out of sync, at worst uncomfortable and inappropriate to the overall narrative of the play.

If the pain of pushing too hard is ignored, as it often is in gymnastics, football, or other such sports, the participant frequently gets hurt, or comes a cropper at a later date, bad hips, bad back, arthritis etc; but in yoga, as in acting, the pain and fear have to be realized and respected both physically and emotionally. I was starting to see that if these two vital parts of the journey are worked with, they can become a crucial guide as to how and how not to work an asana, or how to play or not to play the story.

~

The first play Richard had me involved in, George Bernard Shaw's *Trumpets and Drums*, wasn't the greatest success, but that didn't matter to me. Apart from an attempt at a love song, sung with acute embarrassment and for the most part out of tune to a bemused Celia Foxe, I was happy to be treading the boards with virgin intention and in the company of some great friends. I felt grateful to be given the adrenalin rush, which brought my yoga practice still further into shape.

Once the play was up and running most of the company went back to London on the Saturday night for that day and a half off. Usually I wouldn't have bothered, but as one of the other actors, Thomas Henty, lived near my flat in Fulham and volunteered a welcome lift, I decided to go.

It was strange being in London at this time as I felt like a visitor and not someone who was part of the fixtures and fittings. My cousin Francis was now living at the flat, trying to make a life for himself in the big city. Although he was making great use of the small workshop at the centre of the flat, putting his skills with graphics and painting to canvas, he could be woefully discouraged by the slightest flaw. He was his own worst critic and would more often than not become despondent about any of the fine artwork he produced; finding the blot always larger than the landscape.

Ponji habitually showed up at our home on Wandsworth Bridge Road. He still played a big part in Storm's life and helped him out whenever he felt strong enough to do so. With Hipgnosis, Storm and Po's design company, in such demand my brother was put to good use, especially when they were in the midst of a Pink Floyd extravaganza. When the rock'n'roll took Storm away from home he would often ask Ponji to keep his young son company. Through this relationship Ponji found a welcome respite in Storm's flat in Belsize Park. When he wasn't staying at Storm's north London apartment, my brother would cross the city to our cousin Geoffrey's in Turnham Green, or perhaps it was to Sally's in Fulham.

Much to Ponji's surprise, our friend Emo had taken to the Sant Mat path, also placing himself at the feet of their cherished master. These small steps toward the spiritual threshold saw Emo get his own place together on the material plain and my brother often crashed there, a divine sanctuary on his way to Damascus. Wherever he ended up Ponji was always welcomed. When he didn't have the fortitude or inner reserves, to stay with any of his loyal friends, he would consistently turn up at Wandsworth Bridge Road.

Ponji could usually rally to the call, but when he couldn't, as he put it, live up to the fickle nature of the mind, he got despondent and then everything could be hard work. He would sit on the stairs in my flat declaiming how he was just a tramp and that his body nothing but an illusion. His spiritual convictions had reached a distinct mixture of rational and irrational proportions, and when they peaked at that certain volume, it was very difficult for me not rail against him.

He was still convinced that I was missing the point by not having the degree of commitment he had found, taking to the path of a living saint. For my part I saw the teacher as coming in many guises (as in zen in the art of flower arranging, archery or even motorcycle maintenance) and not necessarily just in the human form. I found it easier to release myself in acting and in yoga if I was purged of beliefs, not caught up in them.

We continued to go round in circles, arguing the ins and outs of such spiritual maintenance. As if to make a point, Ponji sometimes spoke about killing himself to break, as he put it, the shackles of his soul. Then he would stress that I wasn't to take this personally. He'd add almost as an afterthought that he'd reached finality on the worldly plain and that taking his own life seemed a logical step. Although I came to hear this argument many times over, it continued to be extremely challenging and ultimately left me very frustrated, wondering why our relationship had reached such an impasse. I found it difficult not to feel upset by the obvious lack of belief in each other and continued to castigate him for making such foolish quips. To anything I might have held up as an objection, he'd try and stop me with what had become a familiar argument; "The body is a transient vehicle holding back the journey of the soul"; to which I would reply, "The body is the journey of the soul".

I may not have found grace in my brother's eyes, but because of an increasing familiarity with the yogic path, I was starting to get a glimmer of what I thought he meant when he talked of the body as being an illusion. The energy in my yoga practice was starting to permeate my body like water going through a fountain, and in this sense it did seem like the body was a transient vehicle, which in turn was beginning to present a freer and more willing mask for the play.

The intricacy of what energy is, in its finite form, is as much a part of the body as water is to the riverbank; they are inseparable. It is possible to take water from the river but not the river from the water, in the same way that is possible to take energy from the body but not the body from energy. Perhaps when death comes to take us, then the body could be seen as a passing thread, but overall I still saw this argument as hypothetical and not conducive to the reality I was living in, at least that's what I told Ponji. He left me with a question that has kept washing up on my shore ever since; if life and death are one and the same, then wondering or worrying about death doesn't make any sense, since it is a place we're already in. Isn't it?

~

I went round to the house in Chiswick, in the pouring rain for the lift back to Nottingham as per Thomas's instructions and knocked on the front door. A woman who I presumed was his mother answered, she was wearing a white hat that looked like a turban and seemed a little intoxicated. She ushered me into their dining-room, where to my utter amazement I was introduced to Tommy Cooper, who was looking for all the world like Desperate Dan with his cow pie. This massive statue of a man was sitting in a throne-like chair amidst a catalogue of antiques, at the head of a large gothic table, which was crowned with an oversized plate of mashed potatoes and sausages.

From the moment I entered the room to the moment I left, it was non-stop banter. Within seconds of my introduction it had stopped raining and the gardener immediately went outside to water the flowers. "Hah… Hah…Look at that" said Cooper, "the pogonias are getting their just deserts". Whilst commenting on the gardener's apparent naivety and between mouthfuls of bangers and mash, this comic legend was rummaging about in a big paper bag of jokes from his brother's joke shop; out of which he pulled a little figurine of a monk, whose oversized penis shot out from between its habit, when he tapped the miniaturised head with a nearby wand. "Hah… jus like that". Mrs Henty, Tommy's wife, came back in with the tea, lent cautiously towards her husband's ear, then with an inebriated pitch to her voice said, "I was the dirty comic and you were the clean one, that's why you made it and I didn't". Referring to her hat he said "you can take the bandage off now love, the operation was successful". They continued with this cut and thrust dialogue until it was time for us to go.

When we left the house to embark on our journey back to Nottingham, it was like their boy was leaving forever. They both stood in the doorway of the porch waving handkerchiefs as large as flags and in-between unadulterated sobbing and gulping for air, it was; "Goodbye son, we love you, come back soon".

Halfway up the M1 I started to regain my equilibrium. Thomas Henty was Tommy Cooper's son, no wonder he knew so many jokes. He loved it that we loved his dad and loved it even more when David Beams did his Tommy Cooper impersonation upstage to him during the playing of *Trumpets and Drums*.

It was no secret that Tommy Cooper lived for a live show, it was his life. When he was playing in Sheffield, Thomas took David Beams and I and a few others from the cast to see him perform. They had wired it so we could hear him over the front of house speakers, telling stage management how he wasn't being paid enough and that he wasn't coming on unless that was put to right. He filled the auditorium with uncontrollable adlibbing from beginning to end.

The stage was full of apparently meaningless tricks and props, some of them he'd use and some he didn't. There was even a garden gate that stood on its own, which if it took his fancy he would walk through out of pure whimsy. When he executed a piece of magic, it always seemed in isolation to anything else. The gags were tossed out front, with sweat, mania and nonplussed amazement, to an audience who, when they managed to get their heads out from under the canopy of laughter, kept pleading for more.

We went backstage afterwards to find Mr Cooper within the confines of the green room, still in full swing and surrounded by hard luck comedians all vying for a place in his company, no doubt hoping some of the hysterical charisma would rub off on them.

He continued entrancing all with his natural clown and we left him in the midst of a delighted carry on. Apparently he would continue playing the floor like this, until the morning encroached, when his backstage audience would be superseded by the theatre cleaners. Eventually he would go back to his digs and like Elvis Presley sleep it off until the evening, then rise to start all over again. He was an extraordinarily vulnerable giant who was besotted by and proud of his son. It was a great thrill to have seen him in front of a live audience, his true element, and of course to have been in his company.

~

Trumpets and Drums may not have lit many fires with the Nottingham public, but Ben Jonson's *Bartholomew Fair* was a different kettle of fish. Richard's ingredients worked with such triumphant allure, that they queued around the block to get tickets for this one. At his best Richard had this knack of putting together a cast which could make fireworks for him out of a play, and this production was one such number. The setting for *Bartholomew Fair* was aimed at breaking down the boundaries between the audience and the show. Deirdre Clancy's design had the front of house done up like a Victorian carnival. A veil of kiosks, roundabouts and other such fairground paraphernalia, transformed the theatre inside and out, captivating the imaginations of the punters before they had any intention of sitting down to watch a play. The actors, playing the parts of the fairground riff raff, intermingled with the audience as they came into the theatre, which gave the evening an archaic if not anarchic feel. To bring this about with gusto, Ken Campbell was brought in with some of his co-workers from *The Roadshow*.

I hadn't seen or heard of Ken before my stint in Nottingham, but his reputation was wildfire. He was a maverick who put together a theatre company in the 60s which was ripe for the time; *The Ken Campbell Roadshow* was apparently a mad ride of improvisation and fresh plays, which spawned such actors as Bob Hoskins, Dave Hill, Jane Wood and Sylvester McCoy.

One of Richards's greatest feats at Nottingham was to persuade the Playhouse board, who from all accounts were dead set against associating the theatre with Ken's work, to embrace Ken's challenging, vaudevillian ways.

During my time at the Playhouse, apart from working in the company as a performer, Ken wrote and directed a play about a local boxer called *Bendigo* and a musical called *Walking like Geoffrey*, both of which turned out to be riotously brilliant and hugely entertaining.

On first meeting, Ken seemed to be utterly intimidating. He came across to me as a chaotic part of my life that I was trying to get away from. Ken somehow managed to ride the hippy byway down the straight lane of conventional theatre and it seems with little compromise. He had an animated way of speaking, firing the words out with squashed nasal inclination and wide eyed enthusiasm.

Typically, having regaled with animated eloquence any theatre hobnobs who might pass his way, he wasn't ashamed to say how he'd be dossing down on a floor of straw with whatever animals or persons that might like his company for the night. He really did seem like a vivacious theatrical character plucked from another place and time, where Will Kemp walks hand in hand with Stephen Hawking and ET.

There were many stories of his directorial ways, from extraordinary to uncontrollably intense. As I got to know a few actors who had worked with Ken when he sat at the wheel as director, I came to see a mixed reception; for some, the wild card meant he could be extremely taxing to work with.

Ken took a kind of cosmic approach to theatre. For him it was more interesting to gain access to the play by way of left field and if this meant compromising the actor's integrity then so be it. I remember being told by one despondent actor how he had complained to Ken that he was being upstaged by some unyielding business during their scene, and Ken simply said, "Well if the other thespian is more interesting than you are, then that's who we want to watch!"

As a performer Ken was very keen on finding the physical stance of the character before he made an entrance. I remember standing in the wings with him during a production of *The Alchemist* when he asked me how his bodily deportment had been on the previous night. I said his arms were held aloft in such and such a way, with his head cocked to the side like a demented giraffe and he said; "Ah yes", then he took up the same posture and walked his body, like some giant dynamic puppet, straight onto the stage and into the scene without a join in sight.

He favoured the place where science-fiction meets science fact, in a time zone where there are few boundaries. He started a Theatre Company called The Science-Fiction Theatre of Liverpool, which he wanted to make into a permanent fixture on Mersey Side. I was with him in Nottingham when he was turned down by the Arts Council vis-à-vis the grant for this company. He saw this rejection as a slight and it threw him into a kind of short lived stupor, which had us drinking the night out together and commiserating over the straitjacket ways which hold the British institution of Theatre in place.

Ken showed me how getting caught up in too many thoughts about the play during the play, can become a distraction taking the actor away from a chance for real magic to blossom. This held in the practice of yoga as well – going into the openness of the universe, through the gateway of an asana, is only really made possible by letting go of the habitual patterns of thought.

Richard Eyre may have given me ample opportunity to play parts that would extend my range, but I don't think I was really able to hear or receive his belief in me at this time. This didn't stop me trying to coax him into giving me a larger slice of the actor's cake.

Somewhere between the grease and the face-paint he called my bluff and offered me a demanding role in a kids show, written by Graeme Garden, playing an eccentric explorer in search of Olympic utopia. I made a damn good swipe at the part, but I still didn't have the calmness of mind to consistently ride the wave. There was one occasion however, when I was speaking out to the mass of young faces in the stalls and the play stopped in its tracks. My eye-line hit that of a young boy and for those few eternal seconds I saw in his eye a perfect reflection of myself. After this I started to become a lot more relaxed and saw the audience to be more like a friendly giant rather than a judgmental enemy.

I remember lying a little forlorn on the couch in the Playhouse green room one day and Ken said, "You look like an alien entered your body in the night", then he asked me what the matter was and when I told him I felt disillusioned about my acting and didn't think I was cut out to complete the course; he said "Wait until it gives you up".

With his advice in hand my prudence sought a clearer furrow in the field; this and the possibility of plaudits, kept me on course for that wondrous place within those boundaries which hold the intrepid mask of illusion together.

On the first day of rehearsals for *Bartholomew Fair*, Ken was late for the read-through and the rehearsal room seemed to go into a lull of anticipation. Just when everyone had given up thoughts of his arrival, he came hurtling through the double doors on a skateboard, bursting at the seams with energy, and the rest of the day as they say was swept off its feet.

For the role of Wasp, in this brilliantly bawdy play, I shaved my head to within a millimetre of the skull and from the outside I guess I looked kind of brutal. I certainly didn't feel tough, or hard, but I must have made an impression, because one night the actress Anna Nigh came to see the show and through this encounter Anna saw fit to recommend me to Steven Berkoff.

Ponji, in the late 70's

44

Unlike Ken Campbell, Steven Berkoff was a reluctant pioneer of the stage. I say reluctant, because when he was starting out in the theatre, he felt out of place in the conventional market place. Constricted by the method of the day, he traversed his own way through the mantle of naturalistic limitations, which seemed to headline the main style of theatre in the sixties and seventies. Steven landed as a diffident outsider and for his own survival he very quickly had to push aside any hesitancy and become fully committed to challenging this status quo. TV and Film were in full swing, dictating the style. Naturalism had become like a religion. The larger than life actor-managers like Henry Irving had passed their twilight days with Olivier handing over the baton to the so called subtle, natural approach needed for the relatively new medium of video and celluloid. Actors were being trained and called upon to portray the world we live in as a one dimensional landscape, where the language of men speaks out through the waste pipe of the kitchen sink. As Steven saw it, portraying the truth and weight of so called gritty realism on stage was strangling the stylised mask, making it an irrelevancy to the trappings of modern theatre.

In short, Steven had been ousted, booted out from the accepted bastions of theatre, and unlike many of his contemporaries, such as Terence Stamp, Albert Finney and Tom Courtenay he was left out in the cold. Through an essential need to stand his ground he kicked back, developing a style of acting and theatre, which was to radically influence how we look at the art today. He emerged like a Minotaur from the underworld of the East End, where the taste of pain and blood was as normal as an act of love, to seek out retribution amidst the demi-gods up west.

The impression I had of the East End of London when I was growing up was a distinct mixture of thirties cloth caps, pearly kings and queens, jack the ripper knees ups and squalid pea soupers. A romantic view, no doubt planted in my subconscious by my father's socialistic ideals and the B movies from bygone days, where actors presented the cockney vernacular from the background of a polished RADA training, in the days before John Fernald and latterly Hugh Cruttwell were the principles; 'Cor blimy mahte, lord luv a duck watch your step'. If it hadn't been for my schooling where my head was chewed up and spat out of the working man's lot, I would no doubt have been none the wiser. Steven's work was to light the blue touch paper and reawaken the sleeping dragon, an explosive boiling point of hurt and pain in me, a hurting, which had been unsafely and stoically tucked away. Working with Steven meant the voice of discontent was pummelled, beaten and mashed, then channelled through the creative doorway of the stage into the freeways of the expressionist mask.

Steven's vitriolic attack on his own background rips through his play *East*. The poetry constantly tells us how the characters want to be anywhere but in their own backyard. Here was theatre which wasn't ashamed to magnify the reality of who we are, to reveal the truth behind the sentimental working-class rags, which had been scattered at the feet of magnanimous polite theatregoers for so long. This was no *Look Back in Anger*, or flippant liberal idealism, this was a punch of social unrest, cutting a knife through the conventional British theatrical institutions of the day. By the time punk had begun its assent into the minds of the *Guardian* readers Steven had already written, produced, directed and acted in his play *East*.

I may not have come from the same background as Steven, but my experience of the Oxbridge divide had left me with enough fury in my gut to want to blow the door off its hinges. I saw in Steven the same frustration and anger as in myself, Emo and other friends from my Cambridge days. No wonder *East* provided such a vehicle for my buried senses.

Anger may be the liberals' dirty word, but in working with Steven I began to realise that anger and energy are one and the same. When a high-voltage body of energy is misdirected it becomes destructive, but when it is wired creatively it gives us an enormous amount of essential power.

Learning to play in Steven's shadow was a remarkable lesson to me about the structure of performance and how it can take the actor to unimagined heights. This was a place where the warrior stands proud with the beast. No need for self-conscious embarrassment, spew forth and link the verbiage with gut wrenching visceral communication at its most honest.

Most directors saw themselves as anything but autocratic, but when the chips were down they didn't really give much away. They were part of what I saw as the university brigade; a group of wily head twisters, who found their way by hook, or by chance, into controlling the arts as defined by the RSC, RNT, BBC and other such strongholds of the actor's domain. The fat controller was well established in his ivory tower and the overall ambiance, which permeated from his insatiable centre, held an airlock to the breath of change in the arts. Actors were two a penny and treated by many as not much better than scum. Stories of horrendous behaviour by these megalomaniacs were legendary. From Lands End to John o'Groats, the dictatorial way cried out like the bay of hungry hyenas in a desert. And as Michael Cain made clear, the only way out of this strangle hold was to earn enough 'fuck off money', which he and many of his contemporaries did by taking their short lived careers in the theatre, and placing them at the heart of the American movie business.

Although providence may not have set up Steven Berkoff's camp on the other side of the pond, it wasn't long before he got his act together on the home front. His enthusiasm to challenge the main guard may at times have seen him wearing the very crown he wanted to avenge; but it would be far too simplistic to make him into the scapegoat, as many of his critics chose to do.

Steven had infiltrated the British stage with his play *East* against all odds, at a time when it was considered outrageous blasphemy for him to do so. He held the mirror up to an institution tacked together by a straitjacket of Oxbridge respectability. *East* was pretty much something those varsity boys tried to sweep under the carpet of irrelevancy and sometimes the critics were damning to the point of disgust, but Steven's strengths defied even these onslaughts.

Until working with Steven I think I just assumed that a life in the theatre belonged to a side of me that would always be restricted. I believed that if I wanted to be an actor it was always going to be in a place removed from my primeval reality, which meant it was never really going to relate to anything I'd encountered in my youth. I just accepted that working in the theatre was a bit like how it must be to work in a bank. I assumed the theatre was exactly the same, except the deal in question wasn't money, but literature, and the currency was the English language.

When I first met Steven and his lieutenant Barry Phillips in 1976 at an audition in a small hall just of Baker Street, they quickly put me at my ease. I went full on and gave them a tirade of a monologue from *East*, with more than enough energy to fill a circus tent. And they came back with more than enough certainty in my abilities to play the part.

The rehearsals for *East* were like nothing I'd ever experienced before. The physical framework of the play came together like a carefully choreographed ballet. If I got near to expressing any doubts, Steven dismissed my fears categorically.

Any reservations I might have had were immediately laid to rest when we got in front of an audience, where I saw the real power of the piece blow the lid off the theatre.

There is a beautifully written speech of resolution at the end of *East* given by Sylv and when I heard Anna Nygh's rendition on the first night, I wept. It was as if it were written for a large part of me, which I had all but buried in a dead and bitter heart. There's nothing romantic about the characters in *East*, nevertheless it oozes with poetic justice and I think that's why so many actors thought it was the play of its time.

45

Being in Berkoff's *East* brought with it a flavour of the West End, my first TV and film roles, an agent and even an accountant, so it could be said that I was now established as a fully fledged professional actor.

In 1978 we finished touring *East* in Australia on a definitive high. Ending the run of this play in Tasmania was a bit like hanging out your dirty washing in the heartland of an old colonial reserve; nevertheless, despite the home county formality, they lapped it up and we left them in a theatre packed to the rafters, begging for more.

John Pryor, who'd been responsible for the music in *East* across the Antipodes, shared a sense of humour and a passion for the Beatles. In short we got on well and decided to make a stopover together in Indonesia on our way back to the UK.

We spent some time travelling rough shod on steam trains in the company of goats, baskets of chickens and many friendly people. We hiked along makeshift roads through dense Sumatran jungle, and travelled jam-packed inside buses built for midgets, where the head banging proximity of the roof made the confines of these tiny coaches excruciatingly uncomfortable. It wasn't until I clambered out of a jolting bus through the window that I sussed the luxury of riding out on top of the roof. Lodged in with the luggage wide open to the elements, the lush all encompassing scenery became the backdrop for a thrilling and now decidedly comfortable journey.

It was hardly surprising when John and I decided, after several weeks in tight proximity, to go our separate ways – including the months of being on stage we had been together in rehearsal rooms, in trains, in planes, in restaurants, in clubs, in bars, on tour for what seemed at times like an eternity.

Shortly after we arrived in Java John made up his mind to go up north to Malaya and then back to the UK.

Despite missing his affable company, I was glad to have time on my own for a while, as it enabled me to take in more of this culturally diverse country without having to make combined decisions as to where to go, or what to do next.

I basically went where the wind took me and ended up with some extremely heart-warming families. I couldn't believe how friendly and inquisitive everyone was. You got the odd malcontent who wanted to learn English and leave his homeland, but overall they were the happiest people I'd ever mixed with. Every village, especially in the more remote and less westernised areas, welcomed me as an esteemed guest. At that time, aside from some fervent bureaucratic corruption, Indonesia was an easy going place. There may have been political unrest simmering away in the background, but many religions seemed to coexist in harmony under the same sky. Hindu temples, Buddhist shrines, Islamic mosques, through to many Christian churches sat together amongst the paddy fields and jungle habitat.

Part of the Muslim culture dictates that the stranger is God and is treated accordingly, which meant that they would put their home and family at your disposal when you arrived at a village. I wasn't really aware of how strongly they held to this belief, until one inconceivable night, when the aftermath of their generosity had me lying alone on the headman's large bed with terrible stomach cramps. Knowing that if I released any kind of pressure from between my legs all would be humiliated and lost, I sat up and managed to bring myself to the side of the bed. Once standing, I made my way with clenched buttocks and small sideways steps to the door of the large central room, where we had eaten the meal some few hours earlier. I had to cross this room to get to the one and only lavatory. On opening the door, my heart sank. I was confronted by a sea of sleeping bodies. Every villager and his cousin seemed to be spread out across the floor on nothing but straw mats, making the reality of getting across to the bathroom, without a terrible accident on my part, an inconceivable logistic. I closed the door as quietly as I could. Fraught with anxiety I clambered out of a small window above the bed, with as much agility as I could muster, trying desperately to keep everything in the lower regions under tight control. Outside in the dark, it was as much as I could do to remove my underpants, whilst the rest of my person just exploded with splattered relief. Banana leaves aren't an entirely satisfactory substitute for paper as they are a little on the rough side, nevertheless I cleaned myself off as best I could with this and whatever other foliage was around.

I awoke in the morning to a barking dog and the sound of some fervent brushing outside. Peering sheepishly out over the window sill, I saw a subdued mongrel standing next to a man sweeping the street with a look on his face that said it all; what kind of wild animal could have made such a terrible mess as this!

All you had to do was to take the bus from one community to another and some intrigued person would come and take care of your needs. The further away from the tourist route the more interested and friendly the locals became.

A fishing village in Java took me in hand for a few weeks. On the first evening some kids congregated in the middle of the village green to watch the snowy black and white pictures emanating from a television set on top of a ten foot wooden pole. But their interest soon dwindled from the electronic mishmash radiating from the box above their heads, to the much more intriguing spectacle taking place nearby.

The dancing, flickering oil lamps, casting shadows from intricately made one-dimensional puppets onto a large screen atop a bamboo platform in the middle of a field, enticed us toward the doorway of an ethereal world. As the evening settled in under a glorious canopy of stars, the audience, from great grandparents through to infants suckling on their mother's breast, became more and more entranced by what they had come to see. I was struck by the way the puppeteer and musicians are never hidden; we are free to wander, to be taken in by the illusion at the front, or watch how it is created from behind. Being able to see through the facade like this doesn't in anyway detract from the play; if anything, because the players are so engrossed in what they are doing, the play becomes more compelling. There is no way I can say I understood the language, but along with the enthusiastic audience that had come from miles around to watch these vaporous shadows cast their spell, I became captivated. The sounds of the chanting, the drums, bells and xylophones along with the dexterity of the puppeteers took us on an epic journey. From birth to death, through love and war; the mythic story became utterly mesmerising. A heavenly atmosphere wrapped us all in a veil of wonder and magic, which saw us well past the midnight and through to a new dawn.

Some time into my stay the men from the village spent the whole day fishing. Later, when the night came tumbling in from the sea, I was embarrassed to find out that the feast of sea food being cooked on the shore in those twilight hours was in my honour. I swallowed my vegetarian pride and dived into a warm night of great company and sumptuous simple fare, grilled to perfection on the dying embers, not a stone throw from the water's easy edge.

Once I started to see how simple it could be to take advantage of the undoubted Indonesian hospitality, my conscience increasingly got the better of me. No matter how hard I tried to blend in, it was impossible not to stand out. Compared with all these agile bodies, I was a bulky tourist with my rucksack in tow and big western frame. It felt gross just to carry a camera, especially one costing more than most grown men would have earned in a year. A part of me longed to be able to let go of my few possessions and really live and work with these people, but the reality was I had neither the strength nor the humility.

Whilst staying in the more touristy areas I was told by other foreigners how it wasn't uncommon to have someone climb into your bedroom at night and take everything from under your pillow. It was difficult not to buy into these scare stories, especially when one ended up in the company of western travellers.

In these parts it wasn't all honey and hibiscus; on one occasion, in a busy enclave of Bali, I ate a mushroom omelette, which turned out to be doped. Nice, but a little later I passed out on a beach and if it hadn't been for some New Zealanders coming to my rescue, I'd have lost all my valuables.

Eventually I landed up in Surabaya, which, like a lot of cosmopolitan Indonesia, seemed to tie a mixture of past and present comfortably together. The Buginese schooners, used for carrying an assortment of cargo throughout this sprawling archipelago and docked as they were, in fine array by the wharf, looked as normal as they must have done hundreds of years ago. The bustling walled harbour with its mysterious aromas was full of pimps and prostitutes, sailors and tinkers, tailors butchers, candlestick-makers, painters, tapestry-makers, carpenters, metal-smiths; traders from all walks of life. There were kids vying for your attention wherever you turned your head and vendors selling a rich variety of food at every step of the way. There were numerous beggars some with no arms or legs, skilfully lighting cigarettes, manipulating anything from a matchbox to the money bowl with their mouth. Women, carrying everything from a few grains of rice to building bricks on their heads, walking with upright poise whilst breastfeeding the baby, seemed to get to where they were going without the surrounding hustle hampering their flow.

Some of the men here seemed aggressive though and even carried knives about their person, which for the first time began to make me feel really uncomfortable.

When I left England to explore this diverse continent I made it known to anyone close that I would be away for some months and not to be concerned if they didn't hear from me. Whilst standing amidst the intense bustle of Kali Mas harbour I started thinking how it didn't feel as safe or as friendly as I might have liked, and went headlong into a paranoid vision. I could be killed here and no one back home would be any the wiser. This primeval fear prompted me to get out of the Indonesian tract as quickly as possible.

Trying to remain calm, I raced back to Jakarta and caught the first flight out to England. Flying from one cultural extreme to another in a matter of hours made the acquisition of a plane ticket seem like a magic wand. Compared with the demented dust ridden hustle of the Indonesian capital, London was like a quiet sedate village.

On my return to England, I met up with some old friends from Italy at one of the only vegetarian restaurants in the centre of London at this time called Cranks.

I had befriended Mike and Pixie through Dona's yoga classes in Italy; we had much in common and ended up practising a lot of yoga together. They both loved to read and despite being a slow reader, way off from their league, it was hard not be excited and inspired in their company. Mike's taste in books reminded me of my dad's; he turned me on to American crime writers particularly Raymond Chandler and Mickey Spillane. Pixie shone with a freedom I had only seen in those who have worked out a life beyond that of material gain. Mike Hollingworth was Australian born and Pixie (Celia Lillas) Finnish. Both of them had made Italy their home from home and spoke the native tongue as Italians do; in fact Pixie was fluent in several languages, and as such an interpreter in great demand. Italy was yet to join the European Union and was a country extremely muddled bureaucratically. Somewhere in the mix Pixie suddenly found herself without the correct paper work needed to continue living in a place she loved; so they had come to England to decide on what to do next. Sitting in the restaurant with them at this time was Pixie's sister Lena. We made our introductions and had lunch.

Lena was accompanying her two sons Sean and Spencer, to a school in England and escaping a wrecked marriage in the Bahamas. I found it hard on first meeting not to be blinded by her attractiveness, but our rapport went on to become so much more than just skin deep.

One of the things that Lena and I had in common from the very beginning was this wariness of pain in a relationship. For me this was as much about causing hurt as it was about receiving it, so we got involved, but held back from giving too much away. I invited her to camp down at Wandsworth Bridge Road and this temporary measure turned into a permanent stay.

For those first few years, the holidays saw Lena going back to Nassau with the boys, so my time with Sean, age fourteen and Spencer, age thirteen, was usually for short bursts. On the occasions we were together they became a huge challenge to my sensibilities. Young though they were, there is no way I can say I was emotionally equipped to take on such prolific individuals and there were times when I wondered what I'd got myself into. Their ceaseless need for lucidity eventually brought home the lack of maturity in my life. Later, after they had walked across many of my irrational land mines, with a heart of forgiveness they helped me to see the light of day with a lot more stability than I might have done otherwise.

Lena and I spent a good many years in London; she got to know a lot of my friends in theatre and yoga. I introduced her to many of my old mates from Cambridge, who took to her immediately. She loved Ponji and was equally taken with Elizabeth, who would periodically come hurtling in off the Channel ferry in a clapped out old Renault laden down with antiques, which would have been bought for next to nothing in France, hopefully to be sold for a pretty penny in England.

Unlike his older sister, Ponji gave up going to our parent's house a year or so after he got back from India, because he found it all too difficult. Elizabeth still held on to the dream of a united family, a dream which usually saw her tumble well before the end of her stay. She would spend the night with Lena and I in London, on her way through from Normandy to Norfolk and then again on her return to France. Always looking for creative ways to make ends meet, she was now living as best she could with what was left of her unique talents; whether it was singing for her supper, wangling her way with a film crew to interview Tina Turner, or mending an intricate antique vase for a stallholder, her versatility just about saw her through. There was still a certain reluctant rivalry hovering over our relationship, but things certainly seemed to get a bit better between Elizabeth and myself with Lena around.

Lena couldn't get over Elizabeth's waking up routine, which involved brewing up a twelve cup espresso pot, drinking all of it while puffing quietly away on her Gitanes. It wasn't until the hit, from this lethal concoction, had gone round her system a couple of times that she would feel ready to face the day.

It was hard not to slip into the semiconscious frame of mind of feeling superior in Elizabeth's company. By now I didn't smoke and only drank the occasional glass of wine. I was a fully fledged vegetarian; she on the other hand, devoured meat, still smoked like a chimney and drank copious amounts of wine.

I tried to explain to Elizabeth that becoming vegetarian wasn't an altruistic move on my part. You don't have to look far to see the fascism in vegetarianism, wasn't Hitler one? "My need to become a veg-head" I would say "was merely a practical rumination that evolved out of practising yoga. It's easier, if not essential, to get into most asanas/postures on an empty stomach and vegetables digest quickly." She remained unconvinced.

Both Lena and I enjoyed a domestic life together in London and had gone as far as we could with fixing up a flat that didn't belong to us. We thought it would be both challenging and fun to take on a more demanding project and in 1983 we decided to buy a place of our own. House prices had started to accelerate at an unforeseen rate, so buying somewhere we could call home in London was out of the question, besides which we had been toying with the idea of living further out in the country. After weeks and weeks of scouring the British Isles from Scotland down to the West Country, the perfect property fell into our lap by way of a simple phone call from an old friend of mine from the sixties, John Whiteley. Our search ended when we bought a derelict corn mill up an overgrown lane in Shropshire. At this very same time we found out the exciting news that Lena was pregnant.

We had to twist the financial truth at every turn to get this project off the ground. Although I was earning what was for me good money, like a lot of actors it came to my pockets at irregular intervals and on paper the maths didn't really add up. The conventional channel of high street banks and building societies shut the door with polite firmness in our faces. In the end we went to a broker in London and on the back of Lena coming into a little family money and our erratic earnings, we managed to convince a mortgage society to lend us enough money to begin the building work. On top of the loan, every spare penny, from any television and film work that came my way, was spent on bringing this ancient pile of oak and stone back from the grave.

An architect friend of John's drew up some plans and helped us to put together a list of appropriate builders for me to interview. Most of them were somewhat bemused at my asking if I could work alongside the team as a labourer. Out of the applicants we whittled it down to one. Gordon Redge came highly recommended and on first meeting seemed totally unfazed by my request to stand alongside the cement mixer. He was it turned out, well up for the challenge.

Gordon was a strong energetic, big framed man. It would have been hard on first meeting not to notice his healthy face, full of Shropshire weather. He had that intuitive fearlessness that only seems to come along when you can let go of thinking too precisely on the event. Like me he was dismissed at school as being a waste of space, yet when the chips were down, he knew exactly what was needed to make the wheels go round.

The lower part of the front facing gable wall of the mill room, at our home to be, was around four foot thick and built of heavy irregular stone. It had a small broken window, the only opening, knocked into the wall as an afterthought. The rest of the wall, from around eight foot up to the apex of the roof, bulged precariously away from the main structure as if in defiance of gravity and was made up of a magnitude of frost beaten bricks. Inside there were two stories of huge oak beams, which had hardened like steel with the test of time. There were no floor boards; this meant that when one was standing where the mill once worked the corn on the ground floor, you could look all the way up, between the beams to the roof, two stories above. In some parts of the roof, which had been covered with corrugated asbestos sheeting, there were cracked and gaping holes to the outside. The years of incoming rain had left much of the inside looking leaky, sad and saturated.

Adjacent to the mill room was a small cottage that was originally built as a cruck-framed house in the latter part of the twelfth century, but was now beaten into submission, with remnants of those ancient days, buried behind a tacky façade of fifties make-dos, dust and cobwebs.

The experts with PhDs after their names came to inspect the structure of the bad gable wall and discussed for several hours the pros and cons of how it could be fixed; papers were drawn up, but no conclusions were reached.

On the first day Gordon came to work there were no formalities, no papers read, or long winded explanations, he just went straight to the action. By the end of the morning he had, with some help from the author, got the inside beams supported from floor to roof with Acro props. By the end of the afternoon we were well into covering the outside with scaffolding and by the end of the first week, we had taken down the whole of the gable wall, making us ready to start from scratch with the foundations.

Gordon's know-how was paramount for this job, there was very little time for floundering. Here thought was used as a tool, as a steering wheel to get to the right place on the hoof, in tune with the physical action; reminiscent of the yogic way. This didn't mean that you couldn't discuss with him what you wanted beforehand, on the contrary, as long as you didn't preach or talk down, he was up for learning something new and different at every step of the way. Admittedly Gordon had years of experience – he had learnt an awful lot from his father, a man steeped in the tradition of the building trade – but I think he knew intuitively from the start how to work a construction site. He made fitting stone and laying bricks seem like a fine art.

Over the months of working together Gordon and I became good mates. He taught me an awful lot about building and working the shovel. Above all he showed me how to persevere when the going gets repetitive, boring and tough, about how to turn that last corner when everything is dead set against you doing so.

Although he was a man who could pretty much put his hand to anything practical, his self-esteem had been hammered by the education system. It wasn't it seemed going to be much different for his son, who was going to the local secondary school, he too was on course to being wrapped up and spat out into the world with that same shameful label 'failure' written all over him.

When I was renovating the mill with Gordon during the week, Lena was still working down in London at a whole food restaurant until she became too pregnant to do so. I ate drank slept and relaxed at John and June Whitley's down the road in an adjoining village. June was the sweetest kindest person you could want to meet; this wasn't to say she didn't have an edge, her favourite poet was Bob Dylan, she loved having a laugh and wasn't shy of a sassy night out; but most of all she was a person born out of a Pre-Raphaelite age and in this sense suited John's romantic nature down to the ground. I had known John since I was sixteen, from when he lived with my brother at Earlham Street in London.

John served his apprenticeship as a painter and decorator, at a time when learning a trade was considered an art as well as a job of work. Besides working with lime and paint pigments, he came away with such skills as plaster moulding, marbling, laying gold leaf and stencilling. He was one of the last men to be conscripted into the army after the war. He was put into the Grenadier Guards and for a time stood outside the gates of Buckingham Palace, with one of those big black furry hats, standing upright for Queen and country. Eventually the reality of being in the army ground him down and he went on strike. The sergeant major stood at his bedside counting down from ten, screaming for him to stand to attention. 'What is it Whiteley, trouble at home, girl friend trouble?' John had had enough and refused to have any more part of it. He was court-marshalled, put in prison for six months and dismissed from the army for refusing to get out of bed.

Like Gordon, John was an artistic soul who had been ousted from the bastions of education way back when he was fifteen years old, with reject stamped all over his box. First and foremost John was a philosopher then a painter, craftsman and great comic, oh and when he put his mind to it he made a mean salad. But they hadn't picked up on any of this; they had misread John just like they have misread so many others.

By the late summer months of 1985 the mill part of the property was completed and Lena I moved in. Our allotted budget meant the attached cottage had to become a separate renovation job, to finish in our own time. If it hadn't been for John and June's hospitality the run up to this change in our lives would have been very difficult to achieve. As it was they made our introduction to the hidden county, (hidden because no one south of Watford seemed to know where Shropshire was on the map then), a seamless joy.

Lying in bed at night Lena was busily reading holistic birthing books while I constantly had my head up a builder's DIY manual. This theme continued during the day, with me engrossed in brickwork and scaffolding and Lena gently bathing her big belly in the summer sunlight on the nearby bank. Toward the end of our stay at John and June's, Lena gave birth to our son Mick, which lifted us both into a new world, transformed by his sweet and gentle presence. It wasn't long after this that we moved into the only room that was habitable on the top floor of the mill – amazing for the three of us to be in our new home, albeit with only one light bulb, no furniture and unplastered walls. We loved it, there was still a huge amount of work to be done, but we had a wonderful base from which to start. Life seemed full of every possibility.

Lena's two older sons, Sean and Spencer, had shown her how time with a child is precious and fleeting. Experience revealed how our worlds change, radically, from one day to the next. She cherished fully the child in her arms. Not to say I didn't find my time with Mick beautiful, he certainly was a new light in my life, but I didn't quite have the presence of mind, as Lena had, to fully realise how swiftly this special time with him would pass.

Sylv:

We will not end our days
in grey born blight – and stomp
Our hours away in fag end waste.
And kiss the minutes till they budge
While we toil in some stinking
factory – but what's the future lads
for us – where were the stars when we
were born that ordained our birth
and death should be stamped out like
jelly babies in a jar to be sucked out
and chewed, then spat out at the end to
croak away before a flickering light
– and fill-in forms at dole queues and
stand behind the sacks of skin that are called
men and women, translated into numbers
crushed in endless files – we will not end
our days like this – waiting, while ma and pa
make little noughts and crosses upon
coupons called hope or death – we will not
end our days like this.   *Steven Berkoff (East)*

Above: Elizabeth tuning in the late 60's

Elizabeth leaping into life on her houseboat

Sometime in the 70's

Emo and Dave in their Ozzy Clark jackets 1968; between them flowed a spirit of our time

George and Cecilia in the kitchen The Old Mill 1986

George and Cecilia, France, late 80's

Matthew and Mick Rock, during our
Mephistopheles act, early 70's
Photo by Shelia Rock

From top to bottom: Bamby, Dave Henderson, Matthew,
friend and Sheila Rock, late 70's. Shot by Mick Rock

Emo on the right and me still rolling after all these years, sometime in the 1982
Photo by Mick Rock

East, Australia 1978.
Left to right:
Roy Macarthur
Barry Phillips
Matthew Scurfield
Sara Mason
Steven Berkoff

Having just
thrashed Steven
at pinball down
under during the
run of East in
Sydney 1978

Some of Berkoff's Hamlet company: from left to right; Sally Dexter, John Prior, Linda Marlow, David Auker, Matthew Scurfield, Steven Berkoff and David Meyer; on a station somewhere in Europe.

*Matthew and Katrin in Nick
Wards play, Apart From George*

A Flea in Her Ear, The Old Vic 1989

*Shakespeare's Globe, Two Gentleman of Verona, on the steps of The New Victory Theatre
New York 1997. From the back left to right: Steven Alvery, Anastasia Hille, Aicha Kossoko,
Jim Bywater, George Innes, Matthew Scurfield, Ben Walden, Jack Shepherd, Graham Brown,
Mark Rylance, Lennie James, Stephanie Roth, Amanda Orton and Maralyn Sarrington*

Shakespeare's New Globe, the where's Wally inaugural company photo 1998. I'm fourth in from the right second row with the kindly David Lear leaning on the shoulder

Ponji bottom right as scorer, with Pink Floyd Cricket team, early 70's

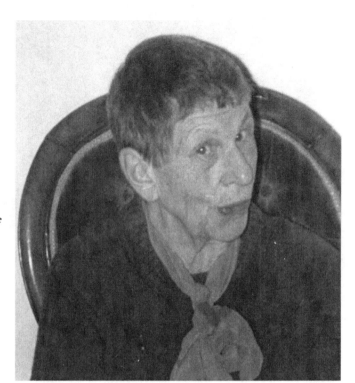

Cecilia in repose late 80's

George in his favourite recline, late 80's

Cesar Sarachu about to leave the pages for the Street of Crocodiles, 1996

Sean, Mick, Lena and Spencer, 1985

As the Duke in Two Gentleman of Verona, Shakespeare's Globe 1997

Beautiful Lena with the equally beautiful Michael George, 1986

Mick giving us his first lesson, winter 1985

46

By the time 1989 came around, nearly two and a half decades after starting out as an actor in Wales, I was married with a loving wife and a proud father of our four year old son. We were sitting comfortably in our self made idyllic home in the depths of the Shropshire countryside. I was in one of those troughs that a jobbing out-of-work actor tends to find himself in, thinking that I might never tread the boards again, when the phone rang. On answering, the voice of a clipped sounding gentleman radiating well spoken English greeted my ear.

"Hallo, am I speaking to Matthew Scurfield?"

"Yes."

"Hallo Matthew, I'm from the BBC", there was a slight but eminent pause, "I shall be directing a series for the radio and I was wondering if you would be interested in being a part of that?"

"Oh yes" I said, trying not to sound like a hungry squirrel too eager for his nuts.

"It's not a leading role".

"That's all right".

"Your place in the piece would actually only involve a small part, How do you feel about that?"

I thought for a few quick seconds and because acting work had been a little short of nothing of late, I engaged further by saying "alright". The timbre in his voice became even crisper, as he proceeded further by saying that I would only be taking part in two scenes toward the end of the piece; "would that still be of any interest to you?"

"Sounds okay" I said reassuringly.

"If I was to tell you it was only two lines in the last scene, would you still want to do it?"

Without too much hesitation the whore in me said "yes", at which point the voice changed into the all too familiar east London accent with; "Now I know how low you'll stoop".

I had fallen headlong for the bait. So convincing was his annoyingly simple act, that Steven Berkoff had caught me out like a fisherman netting an old kipper.

Once he had stopped playing the dog with the bone, he presented me with a pertinent question. Would I be interested in being in his adaptation of Kafka's *The Trial*, which he wanted to unleash on the public at the National Theatre?

Having felt a little miffed at being caught off guard, I let the question hang in the air and then said I'd think about it.

I knew from past experience what working for Steven entailed and had learnt through hard graft that if I wasn't clear and strong with the choice from the start, I could end up a demolished wreck on his dance floor. But I was also well aware that if I put across what I wanted with humour and in a direct and confident way, it could be rewarded by the extraordinary and often enlightening experience of devising a play with him. I pitched in, perhaps a little tentatively, with how I needed time to read the script and take in Kafka's painful and influential story. Without any hesitation on his part Steven allowed for my homework and said he would get back to me.

True to his word, a couple of weeks later the phone rang. Aside from some affected plummy undertones, he was more or less straightforward. What were my thoughts on *The Trial*? I was ready with a rehearsed answer and came straight in with "the lawyer; if I can play the lawyer Huld, I'll do it!" Much to my surprise he said "That's a perfect part for you, you'd be a superlative lawyer, that's a great role", then he immediately mooched in with "How do you feel about chorus and the character of Block?" I held the seat to my pants with gritty determination and made it clear that I wasn't interested unless it was THE LAWYER. Somehow I wasn't surprised when he replied by saying "I'll get onto your agent to sort the contract out". He finished the phone conversation on a more personal note. "How are Mike and Lerner?" (My wife and son, Lena and Mick) "They're well", I said, looking back over the many years we'd known each other and bemused as to why he'd never learnt their names properly. "Alright", he said; "I'll see you on the first night".

I put the phone down, feeling pleased that I'd stood up to Steven's uncertain strength and happy that I'd got a job at the National Theatre playing a major role. As soon as I started to congratulate myself, the doubting actor started to worry about what I had got myself into and whether I was really up to the job. Steven's uncanny sixth sense must have picked up on my kvetching, because a few hours later the phone rang.

"Hallo it's me again; you're having doubts aren't you? Listen, I know this is difficult, but with your power and presentation I see you as a terrific Block, that has to be the right way for you to go, you'll be more than gigantic in the part".

I waited while he continued dishing out the flattery with the heavy charm, then with an adrenalin rush emanating from my chest, I spoke out above and beyond his rhetoric; "Huld, I'll only do it if I can play Huld".

"Come on, Blocks a massive character for you!"

The thought of ending up a victim within his play of the play kept me on course to hold my ground. I managed yet again to squirt out the word "lawyer"; this prompted a note of frustration on his part and he ended the phone call somewhat abruptly, by declaring how he'd get back to me.

The next day I had a call from my agent, saying Steven had offered me Huld the lawyer and other parts, in his adaptation of *The Trial*. I felt good that I had stuck to my guns and agreed, as long as the money was right, which was another contentious point, but hardly worth going into here.

That evening, as if on cue, the phone rang with Steven on the other end again, this time presenting me with his best impersonation of Marlon Brando as Fletcher Christian. "Help me out here Matthew, I'm blown to the ground, you've got to take on the task of playing........."

I knew if I let go of the leash now, I would be sunk. So I laid it on with direct conclusiveness; "Steven, I've made up my mind and I won't be swayed, it's the lawyer or nothing". Then of course, the façade dropped and there was the usual colloquial abuse, the put downs, all the stuff about what he'd done for me and how without him I was nothing etc. Then finally, after some deliberate sarcastic humming and hawing on his part, we established the limitations and he went along with my demands. I was still prepared for the fall;

after all it wasn't unusual for him to go as far as promising a part unconditionally to whomever, then days later the actor would find out, often from a chance meeting with a colleague in the street, that the part wasn't in fact theirs.

Despite having this habit of changing his mind midstream, he kept on course with my part in *The Trial*. I'm not sure why his casting me should have proven to be so long winded. Maybe he was just testing me out; or perhaps it was to do with our last theatrical encounter, which had been some five years previously in another Kafka adaptation of his, *Metamorphosis*, when the composure between us became strained.

I was brought in to take over the part of the father in *Metamorphosis* from Steven, who had commitments elsewhere playing Hitler. As far as Steven was concerned, at that time I was the only actor on the planet good enough to step into his shoes. Brief though it was, this absolute belief in me as an actor, had come out of an involvement in three extremely successful collaborations, two of which, *Hamlet* and *Greek* I had been involved with from their very beginnings.

Tim Roth, whose star was already on the ascendant, was brought in to play the part of Gregor Samsa in *Metamorphosis*; this meant, along with Berkoff's growing popularity, that the play was packing them in at The Mermaid Theatre in London. By then I had enough professional experience, to know how going into a play, which was already up and running, could at best be a gruelling exercise, but to go into one of Steven's productions and to take over a part, which he saw as his alone, well my mind just boggled. Nevertheless I wasn't about to throw away this fortuitous opportunity and suggested with some careful wording that I would only step into his shoes if Linda Marlowe, who was playing the mother directed. He agreed, which left me both surprised and relieved.

I first crossed paths with Linda in 1973 whilst hanging out at Francesca Annis's house in Fulham. They were close friends and I remember Linda sitting in Francesca's kitchen, somewhat traumatised, declaring how she couldn't take any more insults from this nightmare of a guy she was working with at The Roundhouse. Through some careful eavesdropping I worked out that she'd made the painful decision not go further with the job. In fact she had walked out of rehearsals at the penultimate moment, leaving the director and production high and dry. The director happened to be Steven Berkoff and the play was his first public outing of *The Trial*.

Linda Marlow was a palpable tour de force; on stage and off, she came across as a power house of a woman who seemed to spit at the jaws of adversity. Between bringing up children on her own and buying and renovating a charming Victorian house in Clapham, she managed with single handed determination to map out an extraordinary path of diversity in the theatre.

My first professional outing with Linda was when she played Gertrude to Steven's Hamlet and my Claudius, so this meant we were on familiar ground when it came to my transformation into *Metamorphosis*.

Linda turned out to be the perfect director for me. Whilst working out the perimeter of the scenes in the tiny garden of her Clapham home, she gently familiarised me with the play, at the same time encouraging me to make it my own. The outcome however, wasn't quite as happy.

"That's not how Steven plays it" was whispered in my ear at the most inappropriate of times. If it hadn't been for Linda and Tim's absolute support, I would have been sorely tempted to walk off. Despite this annoying glitch, I kept at it and for the most part managed to make it my own. I say for the most part because much to my annoyance, there were odd nights, usually if I got wind that some VIP or celebrity was in, when terrible stage fright got the better of me and I'd end up resorting to a poor imitation of the main man.

Because of his other commitments, Steven only came to the last day of rehearsal, which happened to be late afternoon and on the day of my first performance. Needless to say he was profoundly upset by my attempt at wearing a costume that, I'm sure he felt, belonged only to him. If I'd been more confident, I'd have played the part to the hilt my way and then no doubt, walked away with Steven's respect. But following in the footsteps of the gaffer, well that was easier said than done. Paradoxically it was, I now feel, trying to be too much like Steven in *Metamorphosis* that dampened my professional relationship with him. Of that I'm not sure. But one thing I'm sure is that if he hadn't come to see Richard Jones's matchless production of *A Flea in Her Ear* at the Old Vic a year or so later in 1989, I don't think he would have considered me for the role of Huld in *The Trial*. With his renewed confidence in me, I think he felt I'd be interesting, if not flamboyant in the part. Once the casting was finally agreed to, the decision fired me into action.

I had six weeks before rehearsals of *The Trial* and knew from day one that Steven would expect some cracking theatre. I resolved to learn the part of Huld by heart and arrive at the first day of rehearsals with a fully fledged performance, then depending on how it went down with the maestro, work backwards or forwards from there.

As I entered the grotesque and pitiful arena of Kafka's world, which was enhanced to the full by Steven's innovative staging, I began to gain some real insight into my strengths and weaknesses as an actor.

I chose to play Huld as a man suffering from Amyotrophic Lateral Sclerosis, a disease of the motor nerve cells in the brain and spinal cord which causes progressive loss of motor control, as this would give me more than enough room for rampant bowel dysfunction, strident physical release and allow me the option of falling into the arms of the chorus if the weight of performing became too overwhelming. It turned out that Steven loved Huld's excesses unconditionally and often called on a particular scene during the rehearsal period if he was bored. He seemed to find working the play a rather dull affair. There certainly wasn't much discussion, he basically just expected the actors to be conversant with the mould and to fit in without question.

Like *Metamorphosis* this showcase of *The Trial* may at times have taken us near to an intriguing ride, but I remember thinking how this production seemed to remain on the surface, as a kind of spectacle. We may have had the absolute commitment of an ensemble, but behind the staging I felt Steven's work was beginning to bask in the glory of a former shadow. Apart from working a Berkoff play for a mainstream National Theatre audience, which in those days was still seen as risqué, I don't think we really embarked on an original journey. Despite a new cast, he was reproducing an exact copy of the production he had done some two decades previously at the Roundhouse.

Those who liked to hide behind lace curtains and wanted to experience the shit and grit without getting their fingers dirty, made sure every monitor throughout the National was turned on for the technical rehearsals of *The Trial*. It was the thought of what Steven might do next, which pulled them up to the peephole.

He could be obstinate, brilliant, subtle and terrible, all with one shot of the line. When he was at his impatient best, he found it hard to see that just maybe, some of the crew, especially the ones new to the ship, needed time to catch up. He wasn't interested in working the play from the psychological standpoint; with Steven you simply fitted in the frame and performed. It was just accepted that the actor should sort out any deep seated motivation for themselves and god forbid if you weren't ready on the day.

When the inner torment got the better of him he was unbearably intolerant and often treated the newcomer like they were nothing better than something he'd picked up on his shoe back stage. At its worst the contempt could spurt out from the depths of his ulcer ridden angst and confront the audacity of the perpetrator for entering the sanctity of his arena to perform. If he saw a fault in your performance during a show he'd often challenge the work, usually in full view of the spectators by way of mocking ones physical stance.

Actors who came in fresh from the outside were usually the ones who fell foul to his erratic manner; however, at some point everyone got a sharp reminder of how you should or should not act. It was Nah nah nah, not like that, like this, you whore you scum you south of the river rep-lagged old hag, why doest thou show thy cursed face on this side of the green, go back to Nottingham and turn the tide with the rest of those artless wankers. ......if it wasn't said it was certainly felt.

It wasn't unusual in rehearsal to see him leap to the floor in frustration and play out all the parts with full on energy and sumptuous ease; then he'd stop for breath midstream and like a heavyweight champion, wait menacingly, if not begrudgingly for the rest of the team to match him. At times the pressure became unbearable, which meant at some point the boiler would just have to blow.

Once, when I was playing Claudius to Steven's Hamlet at The Roundhouse, in full swing during the play, I called him a cunt in earshot of the auditorium; as in; "You cunt, this deed, for thine especial safety .....must send thee hence with fiery quickness". I don't know if I can really remember why I did this, but what I do remember is that there were many occasions, in this production and others, when I swallowed my anger and didn't use blunt expletives to express my outrage at his fervent displeasure at mine, or other members of his company, doing our best to row the boat the way he wanted. Looking back now my behaviour in *Hamlet* did fit the narrative of the play and was by no means a regular occurrence, but for Steven it was a very personal attack, for which I don't think he ever really forgave me.

As I remember it *Hamlet* was conceived in a hotel room in downtown Sydney, when Steven, Barry Phillips and I were in Australia performing *East*. Apart from Steven wanting to play Hamlet the idea was to get to the centre of the play without any external distractions to water the narrative down.

We opened *Hamlet* in Edinburgh in a large and empty gymnasium; there were no lighting rigs, no scenery, nothing whatsoever in the way of theatrical paraphernalia. This saw the actors completely exposed on all sides, which meant they were either in it, or out of it; in this case we were in it and it was a complete tour de force, a triumph of sharp expressionistic style. Many years later this introduction to play the play from behind an exposed mask, was to hold me in good stead for the inauguration of Shakespeare's New Globe, but ultimately it showed how powerful well written plays can be, when the actors are simply allowed to perform them without the trappings.

It was when he had allowed me in at the very beginning of devising *Greek* and *Hamlet* that I really started to see that Steven's sensibilities were a lot like mine. Surprising though this may seem to some, he is an extremely vulnerable soul, whose survival mechanisms in life, as in acting, became over the top, when he felt the critical eye came in to close, threatening his story telling.

Steven decided to forego any acting in his play *Greek*. It was one of the most relaxed and enjoyable journeys I undertook with him. Because of our collective past, Linda Marlow, Barry Phillips, Steven and I had become very close, which no doubt went a long way towards making this new play into a piece of seminal theatre.

One of Steven's finest strengths as a writer was to give actors what they needed to feel fulfilled. Like a tailor making a one-off suit, for the wearer this isn't indulgent; this is about releasing the actor, by giving them a body of words that will enable them to take their creativity to the heights.

Shakespeare and colleagues undoubtedly knew how to give their players wings. They wrote soliloquies and speeches, which were handed out to the actor so they might play their lines, much like a great musician does when they are called upon to play their instrument to the fore. Written in this vein *Greek* was allowed to grow and when we really got into its stride our physical presence on stage could be tuned to an extraordinary precision. The finesse of the staging, which had come about from a true collaboration, allowed for complete trust between the players and tremendous freedom behind the mask. Steven's writing filled every second of this inner world with a beautifully poetic journey that was spiced with humour and pathos in equal measure.

Working with Steven put me in touch with my friend Emo again. I plagiarised a lot of Emo's bells and whistles for Steven's plays. Emo's magnified intensity, his way of throwing the world back in our faces when he was on a roll, lent itself so completely to the Berkoff style. When Emo saw *Greek* he thought he'd come home; the play and the way we worked it caught him completely on the hop. It was a piece of theatre crying out for my dear friend to see. Much to Emo's amazement this hallowed tradition of the middle classes was no longer a holier than thou church. He came to the first night at an innovative fringe theatre called the Half Moon and was beside himself with recognition and laughter. Emo's enjoyment of the show was so contagious, it lifted the players, patrons and even the critics together, like supporters at a top end football match.

Thinking that Steven and Emo were virtually one and the same, I eagerly introduced them to each other after the show, but much to my disappointment the maestro's theatrical intent left Emo hanging somewhere between a bag of insecurity and a raging fire.

If I hadn't experienced the evolution of *Greek* and *Hamlet* from scratch with Steven, I might have left the canopy of his *Trial* jaded by his lead. But seen in perspective, playing the lawyer had given me more than a ruse for celebration, this and working with a loving and supportive team, overrode any conflict I and my colleagues may have endured.

Perhaps like others I came out of the run with my fingers burnt, but I'd been cooked to perfection by a part, which looking back was one of the great payoffs for the many years of play Steven had given me.

I first met and worked with Steven on *East* in 1976. By the time *The Trial* came to pass in 1991 I'd made up my mind it would be my last outing with the Master Chef. I had reached an external climax, both in the theatre and with yoga. I was flying too close to the wire and wanted a more grounded heart. The showing off in acting and yoga were beginning to take their toll. The external rewards, very easily tricked the subtlety and quickness of my mind into becoming complacent. If I can get applause, go the round, do the splits and get into the lotus position, I can continue to fool myself and the world that I'm an actor in charge of his craft, a yogi in command of the self.

He doth bestride Commercial Road like a colossus.
Etching by Anthony Sher 1991

47

I remember at a friend's fiftieth birthday party, which he chose to celebrate in grand style at the Fulham Town Hall, standing in line for the buffet and next to me was George Harrison. He was extremely friendly, but I was dumbstruck and because I was afraid of gushing, I nodded to anything he said without giving too much away. The man serving behind the table, stacked with a feast, asked me what I wanted and I said anything as long as it was vegetarian. By then George was holding a plate of meat and made it known to me that he was also a vegetarian and had taken the chicken because he needed the protein. Up until then I'd seen Mr Harrison as someone who lived the life he advocated in his songs. I said something flippant like each to their own and left his side with the thought of charlatan not far behind. That was in 1996. I never gave this incident any more thought until his death in 2001. He must have known at the time of the party that he had cancer and indeed needed the protein, as he was no doubt starting to fight for his life.

What an absurd judgement. So what if he ate what he ate. I'd wrapped him up without really seeing the whole picture. In making an instant summing up like this, I had missed an opportunity of telling this remarkable man how much love and inspiration he'd given me over the years.

In the end this chance meeting with George Harrison, a person I really held in such high regard, showed me in no uncertain terms something about the roots of real insights and how they come not from the eyes, but from the heart.

In theatre as in life, we often think that something outside our parameter is improbable; much as we humans must have done when the world was considered to be like a plate.

When embarking on a play, bringing to it the usual ingredients, there is every probability it will produce a known quantity. It may be something that we haven't seen before, but it more often than not leaves us feeling like we have. My experience has shown me that if the actors, writer, designer and director are prepared to go in from the beginning, without the usual preconceptions about end results, there is every possibility of some original art producing a great hit. This outcome requires a shared responsibility, fresh input and the courage to fall down in the loneliest place in the world, under a glaring spotlight.

It seemed like a lot of directors brushed me aside for not being internal enough. Maybe they were right, but they didn't have the inclination or the patience to take the practice forward into a real collaboration. I wasn't by any means a lost cause however; as there were some I'd met who were brave enough to work the fallow field.

Mike Alfreds taught us actors so much about how to really work a play so it is born into the world with an unsullied twist. Working with Mike was like taking the drama of a play back to the drawing board. Maybe it was because I had become more open to receive, but I learnt so much about acting during the rehearsals of Chekov's *The Seagull*. The whole idea of structure was turned inside out and on its head. The framework for the play was very much orientated towards the inner life. This meant that as long as you played the action of the piece, and remained within the confines of the play with absolute immersion in time, character and place, you could pretty much move where you liked. From the viewpoint of the audience, each night seemed to be spontaneously different from the last, but for the actors there was a highly disciplined inner choreography making this natural external world uncannily real.

We rehearsed *The Seagull* in a church hall in London's Belsize Park. On one occasion Mike told the ever engaging Sandra Voe and me to go off round the block to find the right mood and tempo for the scene. On our return to the rehearsal room the other characters would be set up ready and waiting. We left at great speed, winding ourselves up as we went. Little realizing where we were, we took a wrong turn; instead of it being minutes, it was well into the hour before we got back. We finally burst through the doors of the rehearsal room, full of keen anticipation, only to find our theatrical companions having tea. Mike said the energy was right, but the timing was a little off.

It may have been coincidental, but the constraints of how I looked at the staging of plays and indeed the physical body went through yet another radical change over this time.

The Seagull was an acclaimed cutting edge production and for anyone lucky enough to get tickets for consecutive nights, a real eye-opener. Mike Alfreds was a rare pioneer of theatre, who trusted actors with uncharted territory. He did the groundwork, cut the edge, while others who followed his lead took the acclaim. I don't think it was ever acknowledged as such, but wasn't it Mike's adaptation of Charles Dickens *Bleak House*, which paved the way for the RSC's infamous *Nicholas Nickleby* in the early eighties.

Although sitting at the front of the auditorium taking notes every night could at times make him seem more than a little pedantic, an open innocent eye pervaded Mike's persona. His innocence reminded me of time spent enjoying water as a child and the openness found in ongoing encounters with yoga. There was something as well, about the way Mike stood alone with the rest of the world that reminded me of my brother's ambiguous relationship with his soul, which around this time was seriously beginning to break.

Ponji used to say to me that we're mistaken by thinking that aloneness and loneliness are one and the same; leaving loneliness aside, he'd say we have to learn to stand together in our aloneness. Although I was just about able to see the wisdom in this, I couldn't help feeling that he was trying to turn his broken heart around, to make some kind of rational sense out of the pieces. At so many turns, it was hard not to be reminded of my brother's ongoing struggle with innocence, of how he fought for a youthful spirit, only to find it destroyed by the needs of our grandiose seed.

Initially Sant-Mat, Ponji's chosen spiritual path, seemed to replace a missing dream in his life, but in the end it failed in fulfilling that impossible role. With all the good will in the world if the foundation isn't built right, it doesn't matter how beautiful the sunrise, or how blissful the audible life stream, we won't get near to the foothold of the realisation.

In relative terms, it wasn't long after Ponji tried to move back to Cambridge that he saw his simple ambitions taunted by a proud and nagging reminder of not being good enough. After this, whichever way he tried to look, he just couldn't sit right with the world. Those self-flagellating fiends, which seemed to have dominated much of our family's heritage, finally got their way. On his return to London this sad trend continued to plague him, and after several years of ramifications he finally took his own life. He had found a surrogate love in the Master, but fell before the last turn in the road.

Upon hearing of my brother's mooted, but nevertheless shocking and untimely death, I appeared to the world as someone in control of their faculties, when in reality I was covering up a massive amount of anger and an inconsolable loss. It was to be the same when my cousin Francis died of Multiple Sclerosis, not long after Ponji had gone.

I tried to channel what seemed at times to be an inordinate amount of grief through acting, and in due course the snake would catch hold of its own tail.

~

I hadn't realized just how wrapped up I'd become in various aspects of the father, until I got involved in working on a play at the National Theatre studio with a young writer/director by the name of Nick Ward.

There was the fascist Dad in *East*, the guilty angry Dad in *Greek* and the murdering Stepdad in *Hamlet*. Then in 1986, shortly after finishing my time as the bigoted Dad in *Metamorphosis*, my services as an actor were suggested to Nick Ward by Peter Gill's assistant John Burgess, (Peter Gill was in charge of the National Studio at that time), to play yet another Dad. I can't remember John's actual wording to me, but it was something like "I've put your name forward to Nick Ward as someone he should meet with the view to embarking on a new project", then he said "but he's nervous because of your affiliation with Berkoff."

It seems that by going to the hub of Steven's wheel, I had inadvertently set myself up as an actor with a reputation, a reputation which seemed for the most part to put me down as an untouchable, unpredictable, unworkable, aggressive or whatever.

Until then I don't think I'd really taken in this judgmental predisposition, which so often sees an actor's career ending up on the cutting room floor. I had inklings of how a selected role can seriously colour how one is perceived when my parents came to see *East*. They pretty much saw everything I was in and were usually animated with their feedback, but after they had seen Steven's streetwise play they were uncharacteristically muted. And although this reaction cut hard, I still had no real idea of just how far away from mainstream channels I had come, or for that matter, how making a particular choice furrows the next idea of how a director will or won't see you on the stage.

When actors are sown in right from the seed of a play they often grow into the strongest oaks and Nick Ward's *Apart From George* was like this.

I was the first to arrive for the workshop, far too early for my own good and plagued by the usual bundle of nerves. Second in was a strikingly attractive gangly girl who introduced herself as Katrin Cartlidge. I tried to break the ice with a quip about knees and cartilages, but she immediately cut me to the quick, with a look and a squirt of words that made me feel she'd seen and heard it all before.

Then in walked Amelda Brown, a truly compassionate actor, who I had worked with in a Howard Barker play called *The Power of the Dog*. Amelda really could kick the proverbial football about the stage, so I knew if we were in together from the start, we were in for some gritty theatre. Sure enough once we got down to the basics, it became apparent that this was going to be one of those special journeys for an actor which doesn't happen very often.

Katrin had a way of being able to bring out everybody's nuances and this group of actors was no exception. She made clear from the start that she had difficulty with reading and writing, which meant that with some initial reluctance, I began to show her how I suffered with the same academic inadequacies.

It wasn't long before I found a true soul mate in Katrin, she was overtly intelligent and believe it or not, was the first actor I'd met who was out and upfront about being dyslexic. Her educational circumstances were so similar to mine it was uncanny, but she was far less ashamed than I was. Because her father was openly frank about his own difficulties with spelling and reading in the accepted way, she had kindred support at home. In fact he had invented a way of phonetic spelling, which had enabled him to gain his own unique style of writing, which I was to find out later was prolific.

When Katrin started at secondary school, they put her in a class called The Shed along with all the other head-bangers. If it hadn't been for an unusual teacher seeing into Katrin's abundant soul, enough to understand her poetic depths, no doubt she would have stayed there.

Her family is wonderfully hospitable; many a poet, actor, or friendly person could turn up at their house, for a night of heartfelt debate, good wine and copious food.

Nick Ward may have eaten from the same trough as many of the head-wise in Cambridge, but it came to our attention, mainly I think through Katrin's intervention, that he too had difficulties deciphering numbers and words. Despite his academic failings, he was refreshingly open about his struggles at school. He had no shame in telling us how being up at Cambridge had made him feel more of a distinct outsider, rather than someone elite. He told us how he had to sink or swim his own way, if there was going to be any chance of surviving his time there. While others made their theatrical début through The Footlights, The Mummers, The Marlow Society and other such clubs that paved a way for the stars through an open door, Nick had to go underground, inventing his own very distinctive style of theatre in small rooms, cellars, or any other space that might suggest a frame for his subtle innovative work.

My friendship with Katrin and Nick grew by the day and opened me up to a place of trust I hadn't known before. This was the first time in my life that I began to understand at a gut level, how difficulties with spelling, grammar, punctuation and even reading shouldn't have to hamper the creative process. As well as being a deeply imaginative actor, Katrin was a gifted poet and Nick wrote and directed exemplary plays; in both cases neither of them could spell nor punctuate in the accepted sense, but this didn't mean they weren't extremely talented. The way they were out-front with me about their strengths and weaknesses made me feel a whole lot better. In fact I had platform from which to celebrate.

Working with Nick brought vulnerability of the human spirit closer to home. *Apart from George* was born out of an intensive workshop, where Nick allowed us in, to find the foundations of the play, with an intelligent and sensitive respect for the staging. The weight and complexities of the characters were carved in granite. Here I discovered an introverted father, a man eaten up inside, tortured by chronic loneliness and suicidal depression.

In the aftermath of that initial vital work, Nick produced a superlative play, a piece of writing that was received as an acclaimed and powerful work of art.

It was purely coincidental that my father's name was the title's namesake in Nick Ward's cathartic play; nevertheless playing George was to be the beginning of a journey into a greater understanding of my father at a deeper level.

One of the spin-offs from getting to know and work with Nick was his inviting me to play Krogstad in Henrik Ibsen's *A Doll's House* at the Haymarket Theatre in Leicester. He brought a sharp company of players together including Miranda Foster, TP McKenna, Michelle Newell and Gabrielle Hamilton.

When I heard that Daniel Massey was going to take the role of Torvald I became somewhat wary of the job; for I'd heard, through the gossipy grapevine of show business, how he could be moody and difficult to work with. I had even caught word that some of stage management, who had worked with him on the musical *Follies* in the West End, put up notices when the full moon came around, warning actors and crew alike that this was a night when his head could get rattled.

At the end of the first day of rehearsal in London, I was standing next to the stage manager, when Daniel came over and asked her where we would be staying in Leicester, as he was concerned about laundry, what to pack etc. I seized this as my opportunity to come in with a mischievous jibe. Trying a shot at being superior I said, "I thought a man of your standing would have someone to organise all that for you". Everything in Daniel's commanding presence came bubbling to the surface and he quipped in with a gorgeously ripe reply, "Do you mean Rodney?" "Yes I do" say I. Within minutes we had woven an elaborate scenario around this fictitious character, which had us both in stitches of laughter. Over the evolution of the next few weeks, as well as putting Rodney to task, we developed a tremendously warm and welcome relationship.

Daniel's generosity of spirit never ceased to amaze me, he was the greatest of company, was supportive in every way towards the cast, crew and the director. For most nights he would stand in the wings to watch the second scene I was in and always had a positive word to say as soon as I stepped away from the stage.

He told me that when he was just a small boy, his father had gone off to Hollywood to pursue a thriving career in movies, which it seems he put above and beyond his family. His mother from all accounts was also excessively stage struck, and had a tendency to leave her offspring out to dry whenever the spotlight shone in her direction. Eventually Daniel was sent away to Eton; from there he won a scholarship to Kings College in Cambridge. Having been in a couple of Gabor's plays (the Hungarian who lived above the garage at Number Nine), he knew a bit about my background which delighted me. Playing debonair seemed bred into Daniel's psyche; his forthright upbringing and the little matter of being Noel Coward's godson, must have gone a long way toward cementing this persona. For many years everything went as it should, but the fact that Daniel had been left standing so often as a child, would eventually catch up with him.

By the time I came to be in his affable company, he'd burrowed into the field and came out glistening on the other side. He'd had a breakdown not that long before I worked with him, or as I have now learnt to call it a breakthrough. Although this must have been very hard going, it had made him see through the social and academic claptrap by a long mile. I am sure that the consecutive work, concerning this breach in his life, which he had done with the help of some intricate therapy, went a long way toward his wearing such an enlightened crown.

He was for me an absolute tonic, a revelation. As far as I was concerned his fall had enabled him to cross over the line of elitism and bourgeois grandeur, to a place where the heart is full and shows us its true worth.

Keeping in touch with Daniel after the play was over should have been easy. There were really no excuses for not meeting up, as he lived just over the river from the flat I stayed in when I was in London. But as time trickled by I let things pass. Then out of the blue I heard how he had contracted Non Hodgkin's Lymphoma. This was devastating news, but much to my shame I continually made up short-arsed excuses not to go and visit him. The thought of someone strong not being there for me was an impossible emotional knot for me to handle. At his memorial service my conscience caught up with me and I saw how absent I'd been. Even with this insight I still wasn't relaxed, or clued in enough to reach out to him, or for that matter any of my friends or family who had passed on from these shores before me.

There may have been some ways to go, but what Daniel did over those few months we worked together, was to mend my severed feelings for Cambridge and put the funny side of my upbringing back into more comfortable shoes. In doing so he brought me closer to my family especially my dad, who seemed to have much respect for Daniels irreverent take on our old home town.

~

As I was starting to love my dad with a more compassionate heart he became ill with prostate cancer. The first time I became directly aware of his illness was when we went on a trip to France together to see Elizabeth...

The phone call caught me on the hop, as those unexpected ones tend to do. The weather in Shropshire was wonderful, there wasn't much money in the bank, but the completion of a yoga studio at our home, which had been an ambitious yet rewarding hands on building project, was in sight and there was an acting job in the pipeline, so I was excited and content. I took the call sitting on the stairs with the afternoon sun pouring in through the adjoining window, warming the skin through the fabric of comfortable clothing.

My dad had called me to say that Elizabeth had landed up in hospital in France. He said he wasn't sure, but intimated that her illness was critical. He made it clear that he would have to go over to administer her paper work and tidy any other lose ends that she would have undoubtedly left behind in her chaotic life. The tone in George's voice seemed reticent, almost resigned, then after some pleasantries, he seemed prepared to leave it at that and put the phone down.

I was shocked by the news and taken aback by my father's continuing resolve to fix everything on his own. He was always over considerate about not burdening any of his children, but his incapacity to ask for help, especially at such an intimate level, had a tendency to leave me feeling somewhat inadequate; almost as if I had nothing to contribute.

This time I couldn't let it lie, and having discussed the ins and outs with Lena, I phoned him back to offer my help. He seemed relieved.

As my parents no longer had wheels, I supplied the car along with myself as the driver. We were a little strapped for extra cash at the time, and Lena's mum generously helped out.

Not long after midday George and I arrived in Caen. We had enjoyed the ferry crossing. As we seldom spent time on our own together; this was the first time in years that I felt a kind animated closeness between us. There was nothing better than sharing his love for simple pleasures. He was clearly concerned for the outcome of this trip, but seemed happy at this stage to reciprocate my feelings.

My cousin Rosemary, who had already been at the large efficiently run hospital for a number of days as a friend and doctor, filled us in with the details when we arrived.

She told us how Elizabeth had been driving between Paris and her cottage in Normandy, when the car ran out of petrol, at the same time my sister had collapsed with a seizure. Rosemary went on to explain, in her quiet and assured way, that Elizabeth had been taken down by an inflammation of the brain called Encephalitis. This could at worst lead to fatality, but in most cases, is cleared up with rest and care. She then added, almost as an afterthought, that the hospital had discovered from the blood tests that she was HIV positive. The news of this left me a little stunned. This was a time when HIV and Aids were viewed by much of the media and many bigoted people as an unspeakable and heinous disease, caught only by those who sinned for their supper.

Elizabeth was pleased as punch to see us and put on a great show, displaying much determination. Our visit culminated in her detaching the drip, leaping out of bed and racing straight out of the hospital with barely a thing on, with George and me following in hot awkward pursuit. We chased her across the car park, down the verge and then, to our utter horror, on to a major auto-route. She got halfway across the road before we were able to grab her by the arm. Pulling away she tried to convince us that we should all go for a meal at some terrific restaurant she knew in the city centre. Standing out in the middle of a busy thoroughfare, trying to coax her back, with the traffic whizzing past in both directions, it struck me that Elizabeth may have lost some of her marbles, but it was clear that she was far from letting go. The concerted effort, of getting her to return to the hospital, may have seen both George and I excessively wound up, but it was good to see that my sister still wanted to dance the tango.

Having got Elizabeth back to bed the nurses gave her the necessary sedative. She spent the remaining time before the lull, giving us lucid instructions about what we had to do to retrieve the necessary papers, the vital papers she needed to be cared for, for free, by the state run medical authorities in France. Getting proof of her citizenship wasn't the last word. She gave us orders to rescue a large barge she owned, which was moored somewhere on the Seine in the suburbs of Paris; the idea being that we should sell it to pay any of her outstanding bills. She told us proudly, that the barge was in the process of refurbishment and said in passing how it was home to a junky friend, who we would have to remove before we had a chance of getting rid of it. Then, having conveyed her love, she finally crashed out. We said our fond goodbyes to Rosemary, who was spending the night in the hospital to see everything through until the morning.

We didn't drive far before we found a small hotel suitable for our needs. Winding down from the day's events was spent over a meal in the gothic style restaurant attached to the hotel. The food didn't quite live up to our French dreams, but it allowed for some pleasant time with my father. Having talked through what we needed to do for the following day, we spent the rest of the evening reminiscing about Elizabeth. We agreed that she was a total handful, but through it all a gregarious and challenging soul who kept us on our toes with her love, wit and unconventional ways.

Although we were both worn out it wasn't easy to sleep as George kept going to the bathroom throughout the night. At first I thought this was down to restlessness for the day that lay ahead, but his visits were so frequent, it soon became clear that he wasn't well.

When I asked him about his piss awful night over coffee and croissant, which was a lot more in keeping with our French ideals than the meal from the night before, he remained light-hearted and distinctly philosophical.

We got to Elizabeth's cottage in good time and were surprised at how together she had kept all her files. Having ticked all the boxes, we settled in the elegant moth eaten armchairs and over tea marvelled at the setup. She had singlehandedly transformed a tumbledown wreck into a comfortable dwelling place, with some distinctly eccentric overtones. The whole place was brimming with knickknacks, her paintings, books, her guitars, music, her smell, her colourful clothes; even the mice, who popped their heads out from under the old oak door to see who we were, seemed part of her irreverent charm.

When it came to locking up, we stood outside for a while, with the sounds of the countryside filling the silence, near some little steps going up to a small mosaic covered shower room. Open to the elements on one side, this inimitable harbour for washing the body, was tiled by my sister using a concoction of tile bits, which she had skilfully woven into the walls to emulate an ornate work of art.

Getting into the car, we nodded in silent agreement, wondering if we would ever see her here again.

We headed out on the Normandy roads and took a nosedive into the busy Paris streets and although we tried to skirt the city on the ring roads we got lost. We went around the same group of roundabouts a few times looking for the right signs, with the tension in the car building to a crescendo. George kept asking if I was sure we were going the right way. I remained adamant. Not wanting to let the side down I kept on driving, telling him that I did know where we were going. Then out of nowhere, he suddenly exploded. "You and your bloody mother!" he said spitting and fuming, "you're both so bloody arrogant, always knowing what's best, just plain bloody arrogant!" I pulled into the side of the road. He stopped himself from going any further leaving me reeling backwards into the car seat, stunned with guilt and shaken to the core.

Arrogant or not, I wasn't mature enough to see the irrationality of his outburst and I felt deeply hurt. I couldn't see how it wasn't necessarily about me, but about him not being able to handle the oncoming responsibilities. I immediately put his overt aggression, as I always had done, down to my incapacity as a human being and slumped. The rest of the journey was certainly slower and continued in subdued silence.

We found the mooring place for the barge in the late afternoon. The sun was beginning to go down behind the trees, leaving long shadows across the open waterway. George was stiff with terror as we arrived at the gangplank, which went over to the barge from a concrete bank.

It was seeing him trembling as we made our way across to the deck that made me think his outburst hadn't been entirely personal to me. I realise now how George was petrified of not being able to handle the expected upshot of Elizabeth's losses, financial or otherwise; on top of that the thought of having to confront a heroin addict for the first time, filled him with a fear he was barely able to control.

The barge was exactly as Elizabeth said, in the midst of some chronic refurbishment. The so called junky friend couldn't have been nicer, but it was clear that he was going to be a difficult fish to get rid of.

In the end everything worked out. Somewhat ironically Elizabeth was much more together than we ever thought. She had more than enough assets, from various insurance policies, to cover the costs of her illness. She left the hospital and received an adequate incapacity pension from the French authorities, enough to leave her remaining years financially intact.

So my sister's barge and her junky friend were left at their mooring place, until such time that Elizabeth was well enough to sort it out herself.

This trip to France with my father remained a stark reminder of his anger, but overall this time together would be memorable for his undoubted love and as my last earth-trod time alone with him.

48

In 1987 Sue Birtwistle, who I had met and worked with in Nottingham, produced a television adaptation of Evelyn Waugh's sardonic novel about the newspaper business called *Scoop*. I enjoyed being in Sue's company, she had a great sense of humour and we seemed to get on very well, so I was delighted when out of the blue I got a phone call from her asking me if I would be into playing one of the journalists.

Because she came from a hands-on relationship with theatre Sue really knew actors, so it wasn't surprising that the cast of *Scoop* was an exceptional bunch. One of the actors was Jack Shepherd and from first meeting he slotted into my life like a blood brother.

Actors are often thrown in at the deep end and in only a few days begin to trade intimate secrets about what makes them tick. In my experience the better they are the more vulnerable and sensitive is their personality. During those few weeks filming in Morocco Jack and I came to know each other very well, so much so that by the end of the shoot, it was as if it had never been otherwise.

As well as holding him in high regard as an actor, I'd heard much talk about Jack's theatre workshops and how important they were to a great many actors; but any amount of star struck awe I might have shown him, was immediately washed away by his down-to-earth Yorkshire frankness.

In 1991 while I was playing in *The Trial*, Jack was performing, as part of the National Theatre repertoire, in the last remaining shows of a Tony Harrison epic, *The Trackers of Oxyrhynchus*. After a matinee one day he asked me if I'd be interested in playing the Duke in *Measure for Measure* at the National Studio. If I remember rightly he wanted to see how Shakespeare stood up in a confined venue. The Duke is considered to be the longest part in the canon and I balked at the idea, mainly because learning all those lines for no extra money seemed an unnecessarily unpleasant exercise. It was Don Warrington, an old mate from my days at Drama Centre, who convinced me to follow through with the idea. Don was to play the part of Angelo and the thought of his and Jack's kindred support and playing alongside them, gave me enough nerve to accept the challenge. At the last minute Don had to drop out due to other commitments, which left me floundering again. I expressed my concern to Jack and he came up with the idea of asking two great allies and co-workers from *The Trial* to come on board. With their inclusion the dream became much more manageable. Tempered by the right amount of trepidation, I began to look forward to the venture with some excitement.

Jack treated me with absolute respect, he presented me with the challenge and we went through the door together. The biggest question in the rehearsals for *Measure for Measure* was always, how we make the actor more comfortable in the role. Given the limitations of each character, this question, and the way Jack implemented it, became the backbone of the play.

I knew that Shakespeare held up without any lighting or set, because of my time in Berkoff's *Hamlet*, but overall that production had been presented to the audience in a precise style. Here there would be nothing to hide behind, no style as such, here we would merely tell the story as it is written in the book, the audience is a fly on the wall and the characters are seen in close-up like in a film, which meant we would have to be totally convincing or sink.

As Jack kept reminding us, we weren't there to prove anything, we were just telling a simple story, albeit an extraordinary one.

Sure enough, as we began to immerse ourselves behind this façade of humankind the story emerged from the page, like a duck born into a pond. When the mask of trust and betrayal, love and wisdom, began to fit our faces, tailor made, the actor's tricks just fell away.

I am often asked now, almost as a challenging afterthought; 'If you're dyslexic, how do you learn all those lines?' I could easily write a book on this alone, because it brings up a fundamental question, how do we learn anything?

I learnt to read from sharing *Tintin* comic books, whilst lying on the floor in my cousins Francis and Johnny's living room at Number Nine. Initially the pictures told the story, but bit by bit I wanted the words to make sense of a lasting desire to get to the heart of the story. Because it felt natural to do so I could ask either Francis or Johnny what so-and-so word meant without shame, how it was pronounced etc. It was the environment I was in, and I really want to emphasize this, which was so important and it still is. Shame and fear caused my brain to panic and freeze, especially if it was already highly stimulated by the surroundings, which for me always seemed to vibrate at a very high rate. If I am in a comfortable atmosphere my brain starts to relax and so do the words on the page. Although I am a relatively poor reader, give me a contented armchair and a relaxed brain, rather than the desk and an uptight seat, then I can enjoy a book as well as the next person.

There are many variations of a dyslexic mindset; mine is much more to do with writing and spelling than it is with reading. Nevertheless reading is still a hard terrain to traverse if I am put on the spot, as in a classroom or rehearsal environment.

When it came to lines in a play, more often than not I was still learning them slowly and methodically, parrot fashion, one dimensionally, then with a bit of luck the isolated words started joining up with the narrative. It usually took several weeks of playing if not months before the emotional journey and the lines really came together, especially if the play and the director didn't really click.

I believe it is now accepted in the more progressive primary schools to teach dyslexic children by way of tactile exercises. For instance so they remember the letter O, they might be given an orange to hold and explore; in doing so the roundness of the letter becomes something tangible, something they can touch in their minds eye, a sensual link with which to anchor the elusive letter. Jack taught me that this simple, yet extremely effective way of learning, is no different when learning lines for a play. I realized that the emotions could be my link to the words. By working, moulding, and kneading the emotional journey, the lines, with a little encouragement from our friends, could simply fall into place. With this in mind, the better the playwright, the more he/she is able to make the emotional truth resonate, the easier it is to learn; in my limited experience this makes Shakespeare one of the easiest of them all.

Measure for Measure did indeed play as if it were written for the close up and in my opinion very well. There were moments when fear clipped the monkey, but I realize in retrospect how Jack's sensitivity, understanding and dexterity as a teacher, had taken me to the heart of naturalism, a place in acting, which up until then had for the better part eluded me.

It was the last play my father was to see me in and for that fact alone I was tremendously proud of how well I did.

George decided quite early on that he didn't want to go down the conventional path of hospitals and radiotherapy. He gave the impression of being very philosophical about the hereafter – he certainly was an inspiration to us all. There was plenty of time for us and many of his friends to assimilate, joke and to talk things through, while he lay on the bed, like a life coach, getting ready for the departure. I can see him now holding forth, talking with rare enthusiasm about rereading novels written by Trollope, taking his final bow, and while he was about it arranging his own memorial service. The likes of poems from D H Lawrence and songs from Fats Domino through to William Blake would be part of the celebration – and that's how he wanted it, a party; for us to say our farewells, leaving behind an enhanced mood celebrating the rigours and joys of life.

George certainly made dying seem like a noble affair; he wasn't, or didn't appear to be, scared of death; it was the physical nature of pain he said that tormented him, when the morphine just didn't cut it. I only saw that stark terror tearing across his face once, but Cecilia must have seen that look in his eye on more than a few occasions and although it was hard to address, this must have made his last breath seem a welcome relief.

He died in December 1991 shortly before I finished making a film of *Apart From George* called *Dakota Road*, and the centre of our family caved in. He had been the pillar by which we set our standards. He was the rock. It was his example that we tried to emulate in our lives. Although we often seemed to share the same seat of discomfort, marking an uncomfortable distance between us, from here on in every step I would take would be a step into the unknown. So powerful was his presence in my life. His quest for truth and freedom helped me find the moral centre in yoga. His inspiration went a long way to my building our home in Shropshire and without him it just wouldn't seem the same.

Stoic to the last, I kept up a virtuous front, valiantly sidestepping an all-pervading loss, that is, until I fell on the doorstep of my father's ghost in Theatre de Complicite's *Street of Crocodiles* – a play which was to take up the better part of seven years of my life.

49

Unbeknownst to me, when I was strutting the green at the Lyttleton Theatre in *The Trial*, my actress friend Katrin had taken it upon herself to get involved in a workshop with a company called Theatre de Complicite, up the road at the National's Studio. On my way to the theatre one afternoon, I bumped into Katrin, when she had just finished a run-through of what turned out to be the embryo of *Street of Crocodiles*. She seemed profoundly enthused and said that I had to meet and work with this fantastic guy Simon McBurney, who she added eagerly was definitely one of us.

Up until then, the only contact I had with Theatre de Complicite was from receiving a letter from the directors of the company, during my turn in *A Flea in Her Ear* at The Old Vic, saying how I was now ready to meet up with them. Although it may not have been written in this vein it came across as blatantly arrogant and I chucked the letter in the bin. If it hadn't been for Katrin's undoubted enthusiasm and my sister Lucy waxing lyrical about a play of theirs she'd seen recently called *The Visit*, I'd have given it no more thought.

There were no formal meetings with Simon. It all seemed to happen on the hop, through chance encounters between venues; the first being in The Cut just around the corner from the Old Vic.

My initial impression was of someone who was far from arrogant; in fact he seemed a little wired, fascinating and very sweet. He asked me if I would be interested in a project based around the works and life of a Polish writer, Bruno Shultz. I said I knew nothing about the author and he handed me a copy of Shultz's short stories and said "Read that and see what you think". Then he told me how the play would, broadly speaking, explore a special relationship between a father and son. I felt somewhat taken aback at this, since my father had only just passed away and I said I wasn't sure if I could be responsible for any emotional waves that this recent tragedy might bring to the rehearsal room. He then shared with me the death of his own father, which had happened when he was on a punk-driven run in his late teens. The regret of not being there for his dad was a very personal admission. He also reminded me that he was Cambridge born and bred and like me came from the academic side of the fence. In fact he knew Adams Road very well and had been to Alice's house on more than a few occasions when he was a child. He also made frequent visits with his parents to my father's shop and made it known how he had gone to the same primary school, albeit a decade or so later, as I was nine years his senior. By sharing this information I became less anxious, in fact I became intrigued.

It wasn't until I went to see a spirited production of *A Winter's Tale*, which the company was performing at the Lyric Theatre in Hammersmith that I began to really blossom to the idea. The energy filled me with an excitement the theatre hadn't touched in me for ages. After the show I was swept along on a wave of Complicite euphoria to an eager house, where I saw the night out on the roof, under a sky of fireworks and talking earnestly to Simon about the intricacies of life and theatre. By the time I left I was smitten, bitten and completely woven into the tapestry.

In the cold light of day there were a couple of hurdles that had to be overcome, before I could really commit fully to Simon's project.

In 1989 The National Theatre decided to mount a small scale tour of *Apart from George* and *Macbeth* in the States. The outcome of this meant I was away from Lena and Mick for nine consecutive weeks, too long for my own good. Although the temptation to succumb to some heavy flirting, which at times dipped into philandering, was difficult to ward off, it was hearing Mick's soft innocent voice on the phone that I really couldn't handle; even after a couple of days he felt like a lifetime away. So the first condition was, wherever Theatre de Complicite goes, the family has to come too. The second was the usual money thing, which was going to be difficult since the tax man was making demands for my previous year's earnings. As with a lot of careless self-employed I had already spent their allotted money.

The company agreed unanimously to the first request, and because they wanted to encourage actors with a family, there was a slight increase in wages. Understandably they couldn't find any extra leeway for the demands from the Inland Revenue, which meant if I got on board the ship I was in for a substantial shortfall.

But the more I tried to squeeze the financial equation into not making sense, the greater the inclination to work this job became. In the end a friend of mine, who in his own words said he had more than enough, lent me the money I needed, and very graciously told me to pay it back when I won my first Oscar.

Now there was a song of the father's soul to be sung.

As I ascended the stairs in that dedicated building where Olivier made real the dream of a national theatre, I remember thinking how strongly our past dictates how we sit with the present. No doubt these insights were prompted by the posters of long gone productions, which lined the stairwell from the top to the bottom of that treasured space. Those playbills may have seduced my mind into running away with undisclosed dreams, but I think it was the spirit of my dad standing close by, who prompted me to walk through the doors of the rehearsal room on that new morning in 1992.

My first impression was of a rather dour band of gypsies and I couldn't help wondering, on that tentative day at The Old Vic, what I'd gotten myself into. Amongst them all I seemed to be the only one who cared about what they looked like. However, it turned out that they were all dressed for the occasion and it was actually I who was a little out of whack. Directly or indirectly, they had all experienced Simon McBurney's approach to the green before and their attire was not there to be looked at, but there to be worked.

It took a couple of days for the initial doubt and mistrust to role away with the dust, but once the literal ball was rolling, the embryos of our allotted characters in the play soon fell into place. It became apparent quite early on in the devising of *Street of Crocodiles* that everyone was unique; each one of us having been brought to the stall by Simon for that very reason.

As with any close-knit group there were moments when one wanted to throw in the towel, or even slam the jack at the wall, but what was remarkable about this troupe, was their ability to run with the wind when the emotional storm got rough.

At last my upbringing made some sense, my consistent struggle at the childhood table now came to good use. Big or small, the ego wasn't told to stand outside in the cold, here it was invited to come into the fray and dance; a full on challenge, which sometimes made a shy child blanch. Right through to the first night and into the years beyond, the cat was allowed to play with the mouse, or was it the mouse with the cat?

For my part in the play, this was a father who could fly, a father uncontained by the trappings of man, propelled by a love of poetry and the anarchy of nature, into a greater epiphany of human kind. On a personal note, this truly was the ghost of my father's heart. There wasn't a night, over those many years of playing, that I didn't see him staring back at me in the dressing room, rising like a clearly defined apparition through those minutes before curtain up. For those who knew George, my emersion into his physical form was so uncanny, it could bring them to their knees. Sometimes in the darkness of the wings, just before we were about to go on, I'd become transfixed by the sight of daddy looking out from a full length mirror; if I hadn't been whisked to my senses by the ever incorrigible Lilo Baur, I'd have found it difficult, if not impossible to have prised myself away from that threshold of loss. As it was, Lilo was my opening gambit for the play. Her teasing me into the right groove could at times take me into irrational proportions of anxiety, but as with the rest of the cast, it was absolutely right for the play. She beat a path to the door of our relationship on stage and off. For the story, she was the maid Adele, who took the father in hand with a turn of a fork, or the flick of a page; she ran the house her way and eventually, in exasperation for what she saw as the father's chaos, clips his wings, thus depriving him of flight.

The roots of Lilo's blood family were sown into the land and the mountains. Her own extraordinary journey brought her down from her village home in Switzerland and through an affiliation with L'École Jacques Lecoq in Paris, into the arms of Simon's vision. In life she was the real deal, the attractive gypsy girl playing with the evening shadows; flirty, straight forward, and down to earth, there were no airs or graces with Lilo, you just knew where you stood. She was quick-witted, a natural clown, in short a great actress and to be on stage with her was a joy. Like Katrin she became a confidante and a close friend. I was profoundly disappointed when I found out, that after around three years performing together, she couldn't work the last leg of the tour, which ended up for the second time in the heart of London. *Street of Crocodiles* played to packed houses every night at the Queens Theatre in Shaftsbury Avenue – who says original art can't make West End hits?

It was Bronagh Gallagher who took over from Lilo. A terrible responsibility to step into another's shoes as I well knew, especially coming into such a revered show as this. After some initial struggle she really pulled it off and in making the part her own, she brought a new lease of life to the table. The war torn trials and pain of her native home in Northern Ireland were never far away, and made the underlying disquiet in the play ever more prevalent.

I found it hard not to fall in love with Bronagh. She really could crack my nut. She touched the sixties funny bone in me and at times had me rolling on the floor with my pal mirth. Her taste in music was just sweet and suited me down to the ground, thank you. As with the spectacular goddess of soul Aretha Franklin, she got the whole shebang dancing in the aisles. Bronagh pulled all sorts of gems out of the musical bag, obscure tracks I hadn't heard for years, from Daddy Cleanhead, through to Steve Marriot. Like Lilo she had Simon eating out of the palm of her hand. Was I jealous? No, because I knew in the end just how much we really loved each other.

Annabel Arden was the almighty mother who sided with the maid, but lived for the father, discreetly encouraging his ever eager quest for the power of form and the transformation of matter to reveal it's self. Her right for the place of the matriarch was fully earned, through constant improvisations and those eager games. She could shock the father to the core with a knowing glint, at the same time rescue him from some twisted summer dream. We fell in and out of love in the class room, like a couple of kids in a game of kiss and tell; whichever way the fireworks blew, off stage or on, this fitted our characters in the play like a glove. Gradually we came to truly embrace each other, according to the parameters set down in Schultz's book. Like Simon her cerebral wheels could sometimes get ahead of themselves and nearly cause an accident; but with time, her patience, warmth and insightful dexterity, helped me to grow ever deeper into the virtue of play and the part of the father.

It was the same in my relationship with the ennobled Cesar Sarachu, whose basket of Spanish charm was so carefully woven, even the wildest candidate could pick cherries from his bowl; our kindred support for each other became paramount for the next move. His slight figure lived and breathed the spirit of Bruno Shultz and over time he became so much more than the company's adopted son.

It wasn't long into rehearsal before Annabel and I found ourselves fighting for the rights of the page, for the dialogue to have strength and meaning interwoven into the embroidery of Simon's abundant visionary skills. Because of my fear of being pigeonholed, I for one wanted more than just a physically tight shirt. Now I aspired to and would if restrained by the director, insist on giving more weight to the text.

We used school desks, the old fashioned ones with ink wells and sloping lids and matching chairs, as the fulcrum of the play. This agile furniture could hold a magnitude of props and cover a multitude of transformations. The first time I sat down at one of these desks to show Simon a piece of work, he shoved me out of the way and started to demonstrate how it should be done. A few years previously perhaps I might have allowed him that pleasure, but I was having none of it. I immediately scolded him with some catty remark about not playing that way and if he wanted me to play the part, then he would have to allow me to find it my own way. For a few seconds I waited for the row, but to my utter astonishment he didn't retaliate, he just allowed the wave to crash into the shore. A little later he came up to me all forlorn and wanted to know what had happened, he was profusely sorry for his liberty and I apologised for my outburst.

Simon was a fanatical game player. When the day tended to droop, as in first thing in the morning or after lunch, he initiated all sorts of manic playoffs to shift the malaise. I frequently found these combative jinks, for that is how they came across, tiresome; this isn't to say there weren't times when I enjoyed dodging the fast ball or skipping the long rope. It was yoga I'd say to him that really did it for me. A lot further into the run, Simon began to understand my need to practise yoga and how important that was for the play. Eventually he got me to teach the company and this was for me a major breakthrough. I'd received so much, and wanted nothing more than to give something truly affirmative back.

Whenever one had a query, or the need to untie a knot of any kind, Simon would tend to give a minute or two of his time, then spin off like a dragonfly and land on a kind of distracted plateau way above our heads. At times this preoccupation was so extreme that to all intents and purposes he'd have disappeared, leaving his body behind to do that disconcerting thing that I've only ever seen public schoolboys do; unpack their trunk and fidget with their crutch in full view of the communal eye. But because he was like an energetic urchin coming up to the surface for air in a pond, with Simon this disconcerting manner seemed practically endearing.

I noticed early on how Annabel and Lilo would just stop the flow of rehearsals if they weren't getting what they wanted and demand attention. I took my cue from them. When Simon was at his preoccupied best, I soon realised that if I or a scene needed help, stamping one's foot was often the only way to get it sorted.

Interspersed between crazy games and ongoing improvisations, in a rehearsal room increasingly filled to the brim with props, we read incessantly from Shultz's works. As the words flew off the page, we lived and breathed his world, immersing ourselves in the topsy-turvy magic, which at times bordered on complete bedlam, and whenever we thought the kite was going to be taken by the wind forever, we'd be brought down to earth by a life born on the brink of the Holocaust.

At the beginning of the run we really did have no idea what we were doing, or in which direction the play was going. For those first few weeks back stage in The Cottesloe it felt like theatrical pandemonium, a sheer unadulterated chaotic jumble. So comfortable was Simon with the evolution of the journey though, that on the evening of the opening night, he had the guts to go out front and casually tell the audience they were in for a dress rehearsal not a first night as advertised.

In spite of any doubts some might have held about this unequivocal work in progress, we ventured further out into the water and as our confidence grew with each consecutive performance, the stronger and more able seemed the ship.

For a couple of weeks the BBC came with a camera crew and a fly on the wall director, to make a documentary about Complicite devising a play. As they ran with the rehearsal right up to the opening night we kind of got used to them being around. One day Clive Mendes, a quintessential Englishman, who had the panache to fall from that grace at the drop of a clown's hat, decided to mock up a luvvies argument with me for our fellow guests. What was extraordinary was that they filmed it and put it out amongst the rest of the film on the box. Clive and I congratulated ourselves for having pulled it off – we could do naturalism. The trouble was we were so good; we gave the overall impression that this was a job fraught with discomfort and angst, which it wasn't.

As good as any method out there, these were actors who poured themselves head to toe into Shultz's world. The first time I witnessed Hayley Carmichael coming out of a tea chest full of books, she floored me with her wistful rendition of a Drohobycz refugee. There was no doubt with Joyce Henderson, as she sat patiently at the dining table waiting to be served, that war torn Europe was etched in close behind her serene Glaswegian face. I was enamoured by Stefan Metz's deft touch with a football and wept at his ability to come right in at the deep end with the violin and play like a maestro. When they were on form their timing was so tight and quick, that he and Eric Mallet could motor the show along like a rocket. Stefan's introverted mischief perfectly matched Eric's wild extrovert child.

I am ashamed to say there were times, during those many weeks of rehearsal, when I lost control of my senses. To the rest of the cast this must have been seen as a gross overreaction; for it was usually something relatively minor which triggered the explosion. Hayley could wear her heart on her sleeve as an actor, but she had a pragmatic outlook about the craft. Understandably her early reaction to my outbursts was to keep a distance between us. However, such was her nature, that once my fears had subsided and the turbulence died away, we became extremely fond of each other.

I had similar beginnings with Antonio Gil Martinez, whose surreal interpretations of character were as compelling as anything Salvador Dali might have thrown at the canvas. His perfection, timing and immersion into a character far outweighed any personal issues that might be lurking round the corner. He too just got on with the job. After some initial emotional entanglements, he and I became good friends.

I can see now how deeply moved I was by the loss of my father and how this loss, so often choked the better part of my judgment as an actor. I am embarrassed when I look back at my time on the stage, at just how much my heartache overruled my head, not just in this production but in others too. But somehow, through the rehearsal and performing of this play, Simon was able to work the hurting. He may at times have been exasperating in the extreme, willing us to play the show from every angle, but in the end it paid off. He is an astonishing master of the theatre, a one off, who's ability to go to the heart of the child without shame, meant we could take a ship of passion into uncharted seas.

Over the many years of playing, this extraordinary adventure never stopped evolving, and like an epiphany that's meant to be, this conjured dream, brought me ever closer to the blood heart of my own father.

Street of Crocodiles may have taken a company of colourful players on a matchless passage and induced much tears and laughter on the way, but ultimately it brought together a group of wonderful souls who were reaching out for their lives.

Katrin by Michelle Cartlidge

50

So much happened during those fruitful years at The Mill; as an actor I was pretty much never without work. While small parts in TV and film brought in enough readies to keep our life in Shropshire more-or-less afloat, theatre was still my main outlet.

Street of Crocodiles spanned a great deal of that time and took us all over the world, to places I'd never dreamed of going; an endless tour that helped to bring Lena, Mick and I forever closer as a family. As with every journey there were moments of great joy and a fair share of agony. While we were in Dublin I got the message that my sister Elizabeth, after another bout of illness, had died aged fifty five, making any kind of accolade or award for the show seem somewhat superfluous. Years of heavy drinking and smoking had taken their toll.

The tragedy wasn't so much about the excessive living, but more that the recognition of Elizabeth's life as an artist left with her, unrealised, except by those who knew her well.

I felt fortunate to be staying with Lena's mother who had a house in Dublin at the time, as she and her friends, allowed me to weep the rest of the night away without embarrassment. Between them they had seen enough tragic water go under the bridge to understand deeply the need for letting go.

Always, after the heady environment of performing, the hands on nature of renovating and owning a home like The Mill was a genuine tonic. I found something vital in working with earthly materials. I did my best work as an actor, when I was allowed time for reflection, to put what I was doing into perspective, and building work, hedging, planting and of course yoga were the means for me to find that space.

As Mick was growing through his early years, Lena and I patiently and lovingly, brought our home in Shropshire into the latter end of the twentieth century. We personally renovated the cottage and these same hands built a dedicated yoga studio with matching gable roof, which had a veranda and French windows that looked out past flower beds, a vegetable garden and small paddock, towards an ancient sprawling oak tree. The king of trees grew in abundant measure in this part of the world and we encouraged the surrounding land, of which four acres belonged to The Mill, to make home for more. I went some way into learning the traditional ways of working fresh oak, which can be carved, sawn and drawn with ease; with time the mortise shrinks to hold the tenon in a vice like grip, the natural tannins protect from insects and decay, while the wood hardens to such an extent, it's practically impenetrable. We found oak ties, buried in the walls for hundreds of years, still rock solid and in one piece; whereas the equivalent, used in the more recent past, made of steel, had disintegrated into a pile of rust in a hollow shell.

My father said of The Mill, which was to become our home for the good part of eighteen years that it was like paradise on earth. It was hard not to see why, especially when the early morning cry of a curlew, made way for the gurgling stream to sing out across the old apple orchard and wet meadow. If the elements fell into place and there was a job around the corner, everything certainly came up a damn sight more than rosy.

Incredibly enough, even with this new found bliss, those old demons were still lurking in the wings, waiting to turn the tide toward a horizon of gloom.

Mick was thriving and showed no signs of dyslexic fumbling, in fact, unlike his father he seemed to adapt to his primary school in Shropshire quite well. Many an afternoon I stood outside the school gates, waiting longingly for him to come out. I was aware of a powerful anxiety invading my senses then, but I hadn't as yet got any real inclination of how deeply irrational this was.

Katrin was the first friend who came to The Mill as a guest. Along with a few of our possessions, she came up from London in a van we'd hired for the move. Sitting on makeshift chairs next to the fire in the empty cottage before it was restored, we had long talks well into the nights, where thoughts and ideas leapt to the surface of our combined imaginations, like jumping fish in a dark lake.

How and why she had such a profoundly sensitive relationship with words became clear to me soon after our first meeting. Although Katrin brought me some way towards accepting dyslexia, I still found it hard not to live under a canopy of disgrace for what I continued to believe was a chronic liability.

Ashamed and embarrassed to admit to such a place, I had spent most of my grown up life covering up the fact of not being able to read or write well. With Katrin there was no such shame, she was rather proud of her dyslexia. In this context I use the word dyslexia as she would have done, to indicate something beyond our experience and our knowledge, something that is perhaps unknown in the conventional sense.

The emotional alchemy of her childhood was such that it enabled her to see with great sensitivity and clarity, the space surrounding us. When others were ensconced by the dot on the horizon, she was able to see with a peripheral vision.

Through our years of solidarity, it was mutual friends, the dialectics of families, acting and schooling that seemed to infuse most of our conversations.

It wasn't long after we settled into a way of life at The Mill, that Chris and Robin Lawrie moved into a farmhouse across a field from us, becoming our closest neighbours. To the casual observer there may not have been anything unusual in this, but for me it was to become another welcome testament to my struggles with dyslexia. Robin is a passionate gifted illustrator of children's books, who loves mountain biking and vintage cars. As well as keeping horses Chris is a skilful editor, she has an inquisitive mind and is always searching out the different curve. Together they make an industrious team and their temperament is as rugged as the Shropshire hills. They had a son, a year older than Mick, whose struggles and frustrations with the school authorities seemed to exactly mirror mine. He loved the social aspect but his means for survival in the academic arena meant the teachers and many of the pupils road rough shod over him. I thought things were supposed to have moved on, but when I looked a little closer, I saw the same old shit going down in those classrooms as had gone down in mine. I am told in earnest that things have changed, that there have been shifts in methods, the most radical being the changes in the law regarding corporal punishment. But the teacher is under such pressure that psychological manipulation is now even more insidious. As far as I can tell, playing one kid off against another in front of a packed class has become a national pastime. I believe failure is the great predator here, covering every corner of the curriculum, and the teachers are the first to be caught out by this shark, followed closely by the many children who don't fit in with the system. Is it that the fear of failure has reached endemic proportions and is driving us into a kind of desperate submission? We are shown so often that failure in school doesn't mean failure in life and the many who make something out of their lives, tell us clearly that it was often no thanks to their schooling, and we're still not convinced. For every success there are simply hundreds who end up in prisons or in some squalid drug infested doorway and we still plough on with a belief in our children's education, which is born of antiquated Edwardian roots.

I could see the challenge in my new friends and yet I felt disenfranchised, unable to help Robin and Chris's son Jamie at that time, because to all intents and purposes I was standing in the same seat as him. Extraordinary and pathetic as it may seem, I still felt like someone who couldn't tie his shoe laces up, someone who was basically still scared to death of getting on the school bus.

The Old Mill before...

51

During the beginning of Mick's last year at primary school, we received a letter from the government saying that we were invited to make, as they put it "A very important decision for our child", in choosing the right secondary school.

When we were looking round these schools, a ghastly feeling of déjà vu leapt out from the shadows and I was completely thrown back into the horrors of what education meant to me. It seems hard to believe now, but it was quite extraordinary just how much the power of these unresolved memories affected me and my family.

It wasn't a hard choice, as Mick's closest friend had decided on going to a school in Shrewsbury. We went with that same decision and then waited to see if our application had been accepted.

At the end of the last term at his primary school, Mick was brought to his knees by a terrible and extended gastric flu and he never really recovered his strength. Throughout the summer holidays he remained sick and depleted. When the doctors could find nothing wrong, my reaction was to put Mick's continuing illness down to psychological avoidance. I just assumed categorically that he was putting it on as a way of avoiding the next step in his life, exactly as I had done. As far as I was concerned it was like father like son all the way down the line; but I was forgetting what should have been an extremely obvious factor, unlike his dad, Mick in his own fashion enjoyed the specifics and did very well at school.

To make matters worse our preference for Mick's secondary school was turned down; the reason being that this particular scholastic avenue was now oversubscribed. This meant we were left with two options, both of which struck me at the time as being like the same prefabricated boot camps from bygone years that I might have endured, and I was mortified.

Due to Mick's continuing ill-health, the first term of his secondary school was to be an absolute nightmare for all of us. The more run down he became; the more frustrated and angry I became. It should have been clear from the start that this intense reaction was sown in deeply into my own past, but it wasn't. I'd succumbed to the same destructive pattern that my parents had with me. I may have kidded myself otherwise, but I was still a long way off from an even keel. I made the grave mistake of believing that school is the all important step into adulthood.

Up until then the doctors and most of the teachers seemed to encourage my feelings of doubt and mistrust for my son. We even had one doctor on a residential visit, who said the trouble is it's too nice at home for him. We ended up cajoling, willing and trying every which way to get him into the classroom. A few of the more enlightened teachers tried to be helpful, but a couple who were truly appalling in their ignorance gave him a hard time. Mick attended some of the classes, but he found the very physical process excruciatingly exhausting. Eventually Lena could no longer suffer the pain of seeing him struggling like this and pulled the plug. There was to be no more school. Although Lena had already seen the error of our ways, it wasn't until the school suggested Mick see their psychologist, a regular process when there is prolonged absenteeism, and he told us with no uncertainty to take Mick out of the classroom that I began to accept the decision. The school psychologist was able to see that the stress of trying to attend school in Mick's condition was counterproductive to any recovery. So strong was my need for adult approval I still needed the expert to tell me otherwise. Nevertheless, despite any misgivings on my part, letting go of the knot was a profound relief all round. After this, the possibility of moving on became more feasible.

Mick was eventually given home tuition and during this time, we had a visit from a child psychiatrist who suggested that he was suffering from post viral fatigue syndrome. Although this was helpful, we were never satisfied and chipped away until we discovered, through a process of elimination, that Mick had Myalgic Encephalomyelitis, M.E. This was at a time when the understanding of M.E., or Chronic Fatigue Syndrome, was still in its infancy and there had been a lot of incredulous press about it being an illness dreamt up by those who wanted an easy way out. By many it simply became known as the yuppies flu. Having a label to pin on our troubles offered some respite, but our son's lack lustre self continued to be distressing. At times other people's scepticism was so in my face that I still fell back into the trap of thinking Mick's illness was a psychosomatic wheeze, dreamt up to avoid the trappings of an adult world. Like some kind of karmic stumble, I'd fallen into the same pattern my parents had with me, only the headache wasn't dyslexia, but M.E.

In the middle of all this stomach churning turmoil, I received a phone call from Jack Shepherd, asking me if I could come down to

London with a view to working at The New Globe on the South Bank. My first reaction to the re-creation of Shakespeare's Globe was like a good many others in the profession, one of disparagement.

Jack had been invited by Mark Rylance, the appointed artistic director of the Globe, to direct *Two Gentlemen of Verona* as a tryout production, so the historians, architects, builders, writers, actors, scholars and any others involved, could see what was needed to bring the stage and the auditorium through to its completion.

With the continuing worries at home and Shakespeare goes Disney churning around inside my head, I made my way from Waterloo station along the side of the River Thames towards Southwark and the theatre, where I was to meet Mark Rylance. I came round the corner from Bankside, past the yet to be defined Tate Modern and there among the ashes of a present day building site, grown from the earth like a magnificent celestial crown, was Sam Wanamaker's dream reconstruction of Shakespeare's Globe.

I'd met Mark a few times in the past and he was always forthcoming, but nothing was to prepare me for how special he was.

Having done with the formalities, the gleam in his eye was as keen to show me around, this oncoming work of art, as I was to look.

Everything that had gone into making this timber framed amphitheatre, had love and dedication woven into its boughs. The attention to detail and the fine craftsmanship were just mind boggling. There were some finishing touches remaining, but Peter McCurdy the master carpenter and his team, were at the tail end of a supreme quest. I was swept off my feet at the sheer size and beauty of its oak grandeur. As far as I was concerned The Globe was a triumph and so much more than a mere replica. This was more like the resurrection of an eager spirit, rather than a dud copy. And as I was to find out soon enough Mark was the perfect partner, more like a shaman at the helm, than a so called artistic director. Unafraid to blow with the wind, he embraced the four elements with a cosmic grip, but Mark also stood comfortably as twenty first century man and wasn't afraid to sit round a board table and talk money. I wanted in from the beginning.

Many of the actors, who came to work at The Globe, seemed like returning souls who had come back to reclaim what was rightfully theirs from the Puritans. The feeling of equal and creative space encapsulated by this particular time at The Globe came about because of who Mark was. He was paramount in guiding us actors, especially ones new to the circle, to a centre where they found a welcome breathing space from the usual disparaging, competitive bag. It would have been hard, even for the most cynical player, not to have been won over by Mark's irreverent charm. His strength lay in the absolute belief that Shakespeare's old home was a dedicated enclave for the player's spirit to shine; a theatre which wasn't going to end up as some fag end drooping from a director's mouth. His altruistic energy made sure The Globe was funnelled precisely into a place which truly suited the action to the word, the word to the action. This was an enormously refreshing change, away from the head locked battles of how the classics should or should not be performed.

Mark seemed imbued with a playful essence which I think perfectly suited the Shakespearian throne. He loved the art of pretending, playing the play. The stage was his home from home and if you couldn't plunge right in with him it was your loss.

Some of the scholars took exception to Jack Shepherd's final decision of playing *Two Gentlemen of Verona* in modern dress; they even went as far as trying to oust him from the production, but Mark saw Jack's method through to the finish. They both understood so well how the actor's submersion into the narrative of the play is what draws the audience in.

I found it kind of ironic that Jack's subtle and intimate approach to directing, lent itself so completely to the flamboyant nature of this celebrated space.

As with *Measure for Measure* he was patient and refreshingly straightforward with the actors. He encouraged us to find the limitations of our characters and the corresponding comfort or discomfort within the scene.

Rather than impose a vision as is so often the way, Jack wasn't afraid to leave the costumes and set until the actors had found the world of the play. This left the designer on a knife edge, but as Jenny Tiramani was prepared, like all of us, to go to this front as a willing pioneer, she accepted the challenge with full on leniency. With me it was the now familiar armchair that allowed the Duke of Milan his confident stance. Once we had found the throne, a kind of Sicilian dynasty began to ensnare his world and the Armani suit becomes an obvious dress choice. Very gradually the play began to find its trappings and emotional shape. Due to limitations with the number of actors there was the little matter of the outlaws in the forest, but Jack had a trick up his sleeve for this casting conundrum in the use of grotesque masks. Up until then I had little idea of how masks really worked. They were one of Jack's passions and over those weeks in rehearsal I and many of the cast were drawn inside out by some wild and hilarious turns these coercers of change induced.

It wasn't just the actors who fitted right in on that first night; the audience, made up mostly of locals, who had been given tickets as a token gesture for all the disruption they had put up with during the rebuild, came into the arena like it was made for them. From the very first word the groundlings (Spectators in the cheap standing-room section of an Elizabethan theatre), were on board the play, like a rough diamond on a pirate ship; a truly refreshing audience. This wasn't a must see atracton for the tourists, this was a great night out for the working man. *Two Gentlemen of Verona* may be considered a difficult play for a contemporary audience, but here they got every nuance.

Having been curtailed for four hundred years the spirit lit up the Wooden O like a wild fire. Any first night is heightened, but this was something extraordinary. The Globe was like a giant conduit for raw energy, the force of which I don't think anyone in their wildest dreams could have foreseen. The quintessence of something lost and buried had been unleashed and nothing in the theatre after this night would seem the same again.

...and after.

52

I felt I had reached a definitive pinnacle by becoming part of the acting company at The Globe. Because I had such respect for Jack and Mark and held them in high regard as performers, a large part of me felt like I'd obtained an equal footing among the best in the field. On paper it read like I'd arrived, but frustratingly I still couldn't stop the old nagging feeling that sat, like some rabid dog waiting to be startled by the intruder, in the distant pit of my stomach.

Mark's leadership seemed to be a beacon of hope in a tradition that was becoming increasingly business oriented, so I was delighted when he expressed an interest in working with me again.

In the winter of 1998, after finishing a short run of *Two Gentlemen of Verona* in New York, I had the privilege of being asked back to play Exeter in *Henry V* and Yellowhammer in *A Chaste Maid in Cheapside*, which were to open The Globe officially the following year.

On returning to The South Bank I was somewhat taken aback by the buildings which had grown up around the Wooden O, as if in defence against our modern world. I realise this was all part of the package, but these plate glass windows and brick walls left a kind of stale aftertaste for how we have evolved into the present day. I guess those of us who were privy to that previous prologue season were lucky to have fallen at the feet of the uncovered swan.

Under Mark's leadership The Globe decided to line up an opening that rang the bell of tradition and it was thought the name Laurence Olivier said it all. Decades previously The National Theatre had been kicked into life largely due to the great actor's reputation and his undoubted dedication. At the tail end of World War II Olivier had pulled the ranks of the country together by directing a seminal film of

Shakespeare's *Henry V,* calling out to the nation's pride. The film's early scenes are set on Bank Side using the setting of The Globe as a backdrop, which like an imaginative storyteller lures us onward into a hardy world of real landscapes and the battle of Agincourt. Why not tap into the same pioneering spirit as the fathers for the inaugural opening of this doubted, but soon to be lauded space. And who better to strike this rich cord than Laurence Olivier's son Richard.

Richard Oliver may have had a vested interest in directing *Henry V,* not least because he was the great actor's son; but this was less than half the story. He came to The Globe with two agendas in mind; one was to rise up to the certain challenge of putting on the play and the other was to work the all-male company as he would have done had he been running one of his men's retreats. Richard wanted to merge his knowledge and experience of what is called the men's movement into the heart of *Henry V.* The hope that he might marry these two heavy weights together, took up the greater part of the rehearsals during that optimistic time before the opening in 1999.

In the recent past Richard had worked closely with Robert Bly, the author of the controversial book *Iron John,* in which Bly advocates releasing the power of a man's heart through fairy tales, mythology, poetry and storytelling. I had read *Iron John* a couple of years previously and it had touched a nerve, so I was looking forward to Richards's rendition of this man's work.

By the end of the first week of rehearsals we went away for a long weekend to a disused airbase out in the country. I think some of the company thought our time away was going to be centred on improvising and playing games relevant to the production, but Richard had a greater plan afoot. Although we did spend time in French and English camps, acting out the story, as told through Shakespeare's great play, we also went a long way toward baring our hearts and souls to each other.

Sitting or standing in a group circle and spilling the beans, became an essential part of our lives over those few days, and for most of the company an indispensable way into the play.

Before the very first gathering, an extremely accomplished actor came up to me and said that he was so scared of the prospect of acting again, he was going to end the day before it had begun by handing in his resignation.

I knew exactly how he felt and suggested something I wasn't courageous enough to do myself; that he bite the bullet and let everyone know of his fears when we all gathered in the ring. You could taste the relief when he spoke his truth, as he saw his colleagues gather to the breach with their full on support. Guided by Richard we took him through various helpful exercises and eventually landed him in a lair of trust. From that day on he became an enthusiastic team mate, who worked the play and the company, as if they were sown into his very fabric.

I found the work Richard had brought from his own life support genuinely conducive to bringing the group closer together. Drawing on the strength of his father's spirit, he encouraged us to go to the centre of grief, so it might encourage us as soldiers in arms. Most of us held little back.

The ritual of building lodges, where sweating out the toxins from another life and calling on Pan to dance, sing and weep the rendered heart full, became as familiar to us as the star studded sky under which we sat.

As we dug that bit deeper, I was no longer able to keep any emotional equilibrium together and the anguish, which had been held fast, began to pour forth. I was by no means alone in my tears which made it even more poignant.

Later there was to be some fallout due to the little matter of putting on a play, but for now it was enough to put the curtain aside and live for the challenge that lay in front of us.

Richard Olivier held no shame in revealing the impossible side of being born to parents who were committed more to their art than their children. He had nothing to hide, and indeed had written a book a few years previously called *Melting the Stone*, which gave an extremely frank and insightful description of what it was like to be the son of someone who was considered to be the greatest actor in the world. At times, he said it was as if The National Theatre and acting was his father's only child. Although he now has nothing but love and respect for his parents, from all accounts it was a tough ride. For Richard to share the heart-sleeves of his grief so openly was extraordinarily inspiring. It made the weight of my own loss seem far less of a burden.

Richard's set of circumstances may have been a long way from mine, but I think I can safely say there was a similar, if not identical longing. Yes we were grieving for the fathers who died, but we were also yearning for the father who, for lack of his own inner resolve, wasn't able to bring a much needed strength to their son. It also brought up the question of the price we pay for our work. Do we really have to sacrifice our families for our art, for our science, for our engineering? The answers, if we follow the trend, seem satisfied with leaving our children behind, to be looked after by so many strangers, while we go all-out for our career, hell bent on getting to the top no matter what.

Richard had looked into the well of his father's overriding ambitions and much to the chagrin of family solidarity he spoke openly about being brought up in an emotional vacuum. The questions that plague the king in Shakespeare's play were brought ever nearer to home by his very private admissions.

Some members of the company remained sceptical, reluctant to bring any of their personal issues into the circle – that was their prerogative and they were never pressured to do otherwise. While these few were making their point, the majority of us went along with the director's resolve, securing ourselves as a band of brothers. We made our choice and some of our deepest feelings were revealed. It was clear that due to a more committed personal involvement we became enormously trusting of each other on stage. This in the end may have been the all-important point, but I had dug that little bit too deep.

Through Richard's prompting I had opened a proverbial can of worms. But as the bottom line meant I was there to work the stage, I was told at the penultimate moment to put the lid back on my feelings.

It was agreed that we should continue the circle after Henry V had ended its run. But as many of the leading lights in the group wouldn't be able to attend, this was a bit like second-best and I felt let down. If it hadn't been for the other actors, especially my good friend Rory Edwards, who came to my side when the chips were all in and picked up the pieces, I'd have turned for the worst. A sometime troubled soul, Rory had such healing powers.

A day or so before the opening, Richard and Mark decided they'd had enough of my sorrow and shut me down for drawing the focus away from the play. By now I was so full of the pain we had been working hard to reveal; it was hard for me to contain it. However, not wanting to cause further disruption, I managed with some difficulty to stifle my feelings. Without a word leaving his lips Rory stood by me. But his standing wasn't nailed down in the normal sense. He walked like an aboriginal chief in dreamtime, transporting himself through the ether. Even though he was physically somewhere else, his towering presence filled the room I was staying in on that nerve fuelled night and reassured me until I finally went to sleep. The next day in the circle, he pulled Richard and Mark up for the way they had treated me. They then apologised for being heavy handed. What was extraordinary was that I hadn't spoken about any of this to Rory, he just had that sense, just seemed to know.

The end of that opening season at The Globe may have left me a little lost and bewildered, but I had come to a clear decision about wanting to join myself up as a father and a human being.

In working with Richard Olivier I had allowed my vulnerabilities to come much closer to the surface. Rejection and criticism are part of the actor's lot, but I was finding it harder to accept this and it was increasingly difficult not to see acting as an unforgiving art. There always seemed to be a greener side to the fence. That constant dream of a Shangri-La job somewhere out there had become more and more vivid, like a rabid distraction taking hold of my life.

The more fulfilling acting jobs I got were usually based on the director or producer knowing my work. Unfortunately the variety of plays I did manage to fit into didn't bring in enough money to keep our way of life at The Mill going, and no doubt added to the pressure. Understandably I wanted a more secure place in the world and like many of my friends I had seen success in film as a way of gaining a foothold with a bit more clout. There were ample opportunities to audition for movies and television, but unless the director knew how to work this player, I was either too star struck, or having got the job just too camera shy. On top of this, reading for the part, which had become essential in the quick fisted nineties, was beginning to trigger those major feelings of failure in me again. The demoralising nature of interviews, where I had to sight-read and sell my wares like a peacock on parade, were really taking their toll and kept bringing me back to a seemingly impenetrable question. Why?

This wasn't altogether a hard luck story, as holding down a career as an actor in the late 90s had become far blander than in previous years. All face and no trousers, was the order of the day. Money and time were the dominant considerations; the skill for the craft was being increasingly brushed aside for immediate results. It was becoming part and parcel of the actor's life, if you didn't look right or sound right in that first interview, the job wasn't yours. This brought a lot of disillusionment to me and many friends in the profession. In the aftermath of *Street of Crocodiles* and working at The Globe, most other jobs seemed to present a desert of lost opportunities. So often it was meeting some pretentious director who thought he was the next Orson Welles, or it would be an episode in some long lost soap, where the company made out like they were making some mainstream Hollywood epic. There were odd exceptions to this rule, but this, along with the fact of having to display myself with umpteen other actors for that coveted part, had seriously started to wilt my flower.

Unlike acting, yoga came back to ground me time after time. Practising with a keen eye was hard, but overall yoga was relentlessly forgiving and it certainly staved off my arrogant posturing from precipitating a desperate fall.

Through the continued practise of yoga I had begun to unlock new doors of intelligence and wisdom in the body, which for years had been driven by trepidation and willpower. Like my brother before me, was yoga unleashing something else within my subconscious, something I hadn't been able to resolve?

On the surface I still believed in that sublime state I had experienced, where the mask plays between the finite and the infinite, but for the life of me I couldn't fit it into the market place. In addition to this, the delayed grief, for all those close to me who had died, was beginning to be overwhelming, making it imperative to find where the priorities in these remaining years really lay.

One of the actors in the *Henry V* company, the sprightly young Toby Cockerel, had announced after the first read-through that he was dyslexic. There was absolutely no disgrace in this; he told us all how he enjoyed the whole process of what dyslexia did for his life and his acting. Having given a superlative rendition in French, of the Princess, he completely bowled me over by this admission and his enthusiasm. I had done my usual thing of hammering the lines home like a parrot, so that it could be seen that I might be a brilliant sight reader on that first day. The initial tentative understanding of dyslexia that Katrin Cartlidge had helped me foster was now given real fuel by Toby. What Toby had done was to put my ridiculous embarrassment into that stark question; why? Why was there a need for me to continue hiding my shame when everybody seemed absolutely accepting and even delighted as to who Toby was and how he went about his work? He informed me after the read-through that he had learnt the French from his mother phonetically, and he would use the rehearsal period to bring the emotional narrative and understanding to the words.

Along with his openness, the loving camaraderie of the company actively inspired me to take the next step.

When autumn started to roll out the winter carpet, the season at the Globe came to an end and I'd made up my mind that I would go and have myself tested for dyslexia. I needed to put to rest, once and for all, those voices in my head, which had for years been trying to tell me otherwise. Was my raging insecurity a psychological misdemeanour or a disabling reality?

As Exeter, Trying to convince Hilary Clinton and Cheri Blare not to go to war with France
Henry V, Shakespeare's Globe 1998.

53

This was a first. I had finally passed an exam with flying colours. What an extraordinary outcome. Eight out of ten marked I was seriously dyslexic.

Once the results from this comprehensive testing had sunk in, a lot of incomprehensible parts of my life came to make sense. The relief was enormous, bringing with it waves of euphoria. Then after the high came the fallout, the outrage and the anger. This anger was like nothing I'd experienced before, erupting as it did like a violent volcano. I wanted absolute revenge. I wanted, demanded, some kind of retribution for the way in which I had been treated, especially during my school years. For what happened to me and many others like me, seemed more like a war crime, than an unfortunate mistake. This isn't as farfetched as we might think.

In war, we talk with amazement at the idea of someone, held in captivity enduring specialist torture; the constant drip drip drip of water on the same spot hour after hour. Then when they are freed, very often as heroes, they are given respect and retain dignity.

It wasn't uncommon for the dyslexic to be told day in day out, (overtly or not), at home, at school and in the work environment that they wouldn't make the grade, that he or she was a lost cause, that they were too thick and would never make anything of their lives. It became perfectly normal to hear many times over; "Unfortunately you have to be left out", "I am sorry but you didn't pass", "I hope you understand this, but not you". If you don't go to the next grade, you will not get ahead. So for GOD'S sake remember the three E's; Education, Education, Education; if you don't get the result, win the competition, you cannot join the club! Day in day out, drip, drip, drip, drip.

By then it was all too easy to feel put down and left out to make or do anything worthwhile. We started out from the first day of schooling with a feeling that being a long way behind was a regular, albeit excruciating and incoherent, trait in our character makeup. With this heavy weight of failure in tow we were expected to lead a normal life, function as so called normal people do. Then if we moved to state our case, it's – you are not the only pebble on the beach, play the game, fit in, get a job and grow up!

How much has changed?

Not one to take things lying down, I spent months and months researching, searching, and trying to come to terms with this hands down result. I devoured all the books and articles about dyslexia I could find. There were tons. Most of them seemed obsessed with seeing dyslexia as a problem to correct. There were some inspiring exceptions to this rule *The Gift of Dyslexia* by Ronald D. Davis being one. But it was Thomas G West's *In the Mind's Eye* which hit the greatest cord. A different picture was beginning to emerge.

What Thomas West does so eloquently in his book, is show that there are many examples of the talents of people who flunked at school, who have become unquestionably beneficial to society; from the actress Susan Hampshire to Leonardo da Vinci, from William Butler Yeats to Winston Churchill, George S Patton and others. He underlines Einstein's incompatibility and despair with school, which becomes lost and forgotten when sized up against his glory.

Sadly these examples pale into insignificance when weighed up against the thousands who don't have the wherewithal to get out from under the heavy carpet of failure.

It has become very complicated for the educational establishment to get away from the notion that one size fits all. Our belief in how to teach has become so entrenched in dogma. There is no doubt that reading, spelling and mathematics are an integral part of life's tapestry, but they have become a prison in which the teacher and the pupil are constrained. Words and figures arranged on the page, a code, the deciphering of which will ensure our future and our life. How sad that the perception of our potential is narrowed down to this.

What are we really doing with our patronizing and missionary teaching of the misfit? We think that by teaching them to read and write we have done our bit. We flatter ourselves with newer and cleverer methods for getting through to the underachiever; if only it was this simple.

I believe that when dealing with the outsider you have to start from the basis that each individual is internally unique. Trying to teach us to fit into a frame will usually make us even more determined to break out and society is so often the loser.

I was told many times over that school was a training ground, a way of preparing us for the outside world.

If school is like a mini society, then the head teacher becomes our judge, teachers and parents become the lawyers, barristers and jury, prefects become our policemen etc. If we use this analogy and I am constantly being told that I am wrong or an oddball, it then becomes so easy to fall into the trap of feeling like the accused. And in a society where the accused is so often seen to be guilty before the trial, it becomes very hard not to lash out for one's corner no matter how shitty it seems. This is the only security we have left. The fighting becomes more and more like familiar ground and in our familiar world we feel a sense of security, even if it's harmful to ourselves and others.

We are so convinced that dyslexia is about learning in the accepted sense that we associate the word with schooling and college. But it doesn't stop when school finishes; this is important to understand. The fear of failing has followed me into the grownup world like a mangy wild animal on a scent for food.

Many people lumbered with the label of dyslexia have little clout in the broad world of institution, but they can have a profound understanding of survival that is perhaps unseen by what is readily accepted to be the standard eye – i.e. survival that stems from a state of mind, which has been told so often that it has the equation wrong, it is no longer afraid of taking an unconventional step towards a solution.

When I look back now, I can't help feeling how lucky I was to have jumped as far as I did out of the school dumb-bag; at least far enough to see how crucial it is to learn, or for that matter how important it is to want to learn.

For what it's worth, I think schools should be like public libraries and national parks, places which are open to all at any age; and when the time is right, we will walk in because we need and want to, not because we are forced or told to. It's time to turn the whole idea of schooling on its head. School as it is simply doesn't work. As it is too many of us are left out in the cold, where revenge and mayhem are so often an all too familiar guide. For all the best will in the world it becomes elitist and is therefore destructive. Don't just take a disgruntled ex-students word for it; some of our most celebrated teachers have been telling us to stop for years.

'When I was teaching in school, a man came to a parents' meeting and complained about the extraordinary amount of testing we were doing. His words went right to the heart of the matter: 'you're like a gardener who constantly pulls his plants up by the roots to see if they're growing.' – John Holt

'We are faced with the paradoxical fact that education has become one of the chief obstacles to intelligence and freedom of thought'. – Bertrand Russell

'What we want to see is the child in pursuit of knowledge, and not knowledge in pursuit of the child.' – George Bernard Shaw

'Whatever their claims, schools are training most young people to be habitually subservient.' – Chris Shute

'School is a twelve-year jail sentence where bad habits are the only curriculum truly learned. I teach school and win awards doing it. I should know.' – John Taylor Gatto

'A school, like a fascist state, is about the business of compelling people to conform to a pattern of behaviour and a way of thinking decided by the few who hold power over them.' – Chris Shute

'Imagination is more important than knowledge.' – Albert Einstein

'The aim of education is to induce the largest amount of neurosis that an individual can bear without cracking up.' – W. H. Auden

'I have never allowed schooling to interfere with my education.' – Mark Twain

'When I look back on all the crap I learned at high school it's a wonder I can think at all'. – Paul Simon

'My schooling not only failed to teach me what it professed to be teaching, but prevented me from being educated to an extent which infuriates me when I think of all I might have learned at home by myself.' – George Bernard Shaw

'Thousands of caring, humane people work in schools, as teachers, and aides and administrators, but the abstract logic of the institution overwhelms their individual contributions. Although teachers do care and do work very, very hard, the institution is psychopathic; it has no conscience. It rings a bell and the young man in the middle of writing a poem must close his notebook and move to a different cell.
– John Taylor Gatto

If that wasn't enough to turn the heart cold this should...

'The boy must be transformed into the man; in this school he must not only learn to obey, but must thereby acquire a basis for commanding later. He must learn to be silent not only when he is justly blamed, but must also learn, when necessary, to bear injustice in silence.' – Adolf Hitler

These aforementioned quotes are just a few compiled for *The Freethinkers' Guide to the Educational Universe,* by Professor Roland Meighan and there are many more. When I first came across this booklet, I found it to be immensely reassuring. But there was one quote from the renowned psychiatrist and author Alice Miller which stood out for me, because it spoke clearly of the repercussions.

'Children who are lectured to, learn how to lecture; if they are admonished, they learn how to admonish; if scolded, they learn how to scold; if ridiculed, they learn how to ridicule; if humiliated, they learn how to humiliate; if their psyche is killed, they learn how to kill – the only question is who will be killed: oneself, others or both.' – Alice Miller

So strong was the mindset of failure in my early life, I had simply been convinced that a crucial part of my wellbeing was still locked in as educationally subnormal/substandard. A great deal of my time, if not years, was wasted, plotting and scheming sweet revenge. I had reached a kind of kill or be killed boiling point and leapt at the dyslexic label, as if my whole life depended on it.

Covering up my vulnerabilities at all costs, was as normal to me as getting dressed in the morning. I had become particularly good at keeping up this subtle facade in my adult years. The only time my stark shame became apparent on the outside, was if the coordination of words or movement spontaneously caught me out. If I was made to read on the spot, or when I was asked on the hop to follow some elaborate chorography in a play, the unsuspecting director had to be prepared for some defensive flack from this dancer. Although I had started, intuitively, to address some aspects of this over the top reaction, I still couldn't stop myself from panicking when the time came to report to the drill sergeant. Unless the person giving instructions had some understanding of how I ticked, it was impossible for me not to burst into tears or to blow a fuse when put under pressure. Over the years I had become like a time-bomb waiting for one more innocent person to say, not like that like this you idiot, to trigger a monumental explosion.

There is no doubt that pinning the dyslexic label on the emotional backlog was enormously helpful to me at this critical stage. However, it is certainly not my intention to get caught up in the label, for I realise today that the negative or patronizing connotations, stigmatised by the word dyslexia, only exist if we draw excessive attention to the things a dyslexic can or cannot do.

It seems to me that the outcome, of what the label dyslexia represents in today's world, depends on whether we are fearless or fearful of asking the appropriate question to illuminate the situation. I use the word situation, because the word problem usually means it's the person who isn't able to perform the necessary function, in the purported regular sense, who ends up being the problem. This is exactly the opposite of what's needed here. Although my upbringing gave me enough bravado to jump in at the deep end, what I couldn't do when I was at school and later in the working environment, was to calmly ask for clarification, ask the appropriate questions, because I had learnt to be terrified of the repercussions; and this was where the problem lay, not in my dyslexia, nor in the nature of my intelligence or for that matter in my talent.

Whether we are outside the dyslexic or inside, the truth of the matter is we need to broaden our way of looking at what dyslexia is or isn't. For I am sure that if we allow the stumbling blocks to fall away, rather than induce havoc, it can become possible for us to arrive at a different place, where the lack of insight no longer stultifies creativity. At school or in the workplace there is no greater challenge than an unashamed dyslexic, because they move the goal posts. Their way is the non linear way; home to creativity.

Whichever way we try to pigeonhole dyslexia, here we surely have a mass of vibrant extended thought patterns, out of which can grow the greatest art, or the worst of wars.

Thankfully I now saw all this in the clear light of day, however, I had yet to accept that there might be an even deeper explanation for constantly tumbling into this pit of low self-esteem, stemming from something dishonourable, way back, far beyond the limitations of a label.

So many of my friends, and family members had been lured directly or indirectly into a mindset of intense self-doubt and even self-hatred by academic fear mongering; some of them have ended up as burdens on society, or buried in drug addiction and even death. If I cared to look, I would see that many of them had sailed through the academic requirements with flying colours, or even surpassed them. Their damaged lives had not come about from the way they took to spelling, reading, mathematics and writing, but from something more fundamental, yet much more difficult to pin down. This crucial insight was yet to come.

To begin with, having this label to hang my troubled past on offered some relief and gave me the confidence to tell the world. I set about wondering what I could do to help other adults and children, who like me, have suffered the same misfortunes of inadequacy and powerlessness. And what better ways to do this than through the medium of theatre, after all somewhere in there I was still an actor.

I come to discover that like me, many of the actors, or come to that people that I talk to who are dyslexic, live with a great deal of confusion, often entwined with huge amounts of anger. This spurs me on, channels the energy; it must become a theatrical event, something to draw people's attention towards this painful thread that is so often buried, best unseen, behind a smokescreen of unending exhausting pretence.

Mick and I had built, tinkered with and maintained computers for a few years and one of the great eureka moments that came out of this for me was the discovery of voice dictation; a nonlinear way through a linear curtain into a multidimensional world. This was a major turning point, a massive breakthrough and cannot be over emphasised.

I could finally get the words out of my head and onto the page.

Although speech recognition was in its infancy, this miracle of modern science finally made writing a distinct and powerful reality. The embryo of this book was made possible here. Up until then I had hardly written a letter. My understanding of the English language, especially the spelling thereof, was a nonstarter. All I really had at my disposal was what I had picked up from working as an actor and essential titbits from my mother and father. On discovering the personal computer and speech recognition, I now had the facility to write. I began to learn, through trial and error, how to approach a threshold that had rendered me powerless for all these years. Through asking, debating and doing, I came to realize, quite literally as I went along, the power of the pen. The house of words, like paints mixed together on the painter's pallet, each one suggesting a colour or tone, adding light and shade to the oncoming story.

Using this extraordinary tool, speaking into a quality microphone, the blank canvas began to come alive. Before I knew it, I had drawn up a cathartic essay on how dyslexia had affected my life. I then sent these pages out to various friends of mine and members of my family, who I thought deserved some kind of explanation for the backlog of irrational behaviour that might have been flying around when in my company. I then went on to combine this essay with a brief description of a theatrical workshop, centred on the exploration of dyslexia, and sent these out to various funding bodies and other professional people, one of them being my cousin Dr Robert Johnson.

As a high profile Consultant Psychiatrist, Bob Johnson seemed to be one of those people who carried a bulk of controversy around with him; a lot of his medical colleagues, along with legal and political counterparts have tried to ostracise him at every turn. Lena and I had recently seen a BBC Panorama program based around his groundbreaking work at the high security prison Parkhurst, and how the model along with Bob were dismissed by the then home secretary Michael Howard – we needed prisoners in prison, rather than men who were healed and redeemed on the outside – more people in prison meant more votes.

A few days later I had a phone call from Bob and his wife Sue, saying how they had received my essay and expressed a great deal of interest in what I was doing. Somewhere during this phone call, Bob mentioned a Conference for the James Nayler Foundation* in London and how it would be good if I could come.

*The James Nayler foundation is a charity, which was born out of the publicity surrounding Bob Johnson's work with those suffering the most extreme forms of personality disorder, on the violently dangerous men in a special unit in Parkhurst Prison. His work with this group of people was widely reported in the papers and on television and gave hope that understanding and treatment was possible. The James Nayler foundation was set up for the relief not only of violence and other severe Personality Disorders but also for other forms of Personality Disorder, which includes such distressing conditions as self-harming, anorexia, and panic attacks.

At the conference, on saying hello and after a heartfelt hug from Bob, we shared a few hasty words with each other. We touched briefly on my essay and talked fondly about our family. His mother and my mother are sisters; the family demons hold no truck for him, but he admits to their powers and to this end knows my background very well. Half way through this conversation I had the uncomfortable feeling that he was reading between the lines, especially when he interjected in his light-hearted way that he felt something other than dyslexia was going on. I cracked slightly, after all I had put so much store by what dyslexia was and what it meant for me. I was so sure that everything I had discovered was cemented in a conclusion of truth; I felt challenged.

Bob suggested that if I was interested, I could come to see him for a one on one session and explore further. I wanted to be sure that my insights into dyslexia were not like sandcastles, eventually engulfed by the sea. As he had nothing to prove to me and I had already come this far why not test the camel's back. I said yes to meeting up with him.

Back in Shropshire I called Bob up to verify what he'd said and to make sure our time of meeting was appropriate. A part of me was hoping he'd say no, but he came through with a categorical yes.

As the day drew near, a familiar worm, tucked away inside my head, started to make threatening suggestions, insisting that my dyslexia wasn't real after all. I slowly began to feel a renewed sense of powerlessness. With growing disquiet I became increasingly knotted up. Perhaps I had got it all wrong! A need to prove that I was right began to overwhelm me. Lena was away. I had no one to talk to. Welling up inside, this ferocious beast needs the valve to blow; God help anyone in its way. My mother calls. The steam ruptures the tank and she gets the works. She thinks it's all her fault, I think it's all mine, she gets angry, I get angry, I feel great, she feels like shit, she feels great, I feel terrible, on and on until the seesaw of emotional entanglement leaves us both hanging exhausted at the end of a line. My mother Cecilia is eighty three for fucks sake! The shame of this conversation propels me back into a pit of feeling helpless, hopeless and out of sorts. It is with these feelings that I turn up at Dr. Bob Johnson's office for my first session.

54

I am five minutes early. Apprehensive, but determined, I sit in the office waiting room. The time it takes is the time it is. Bob arrives; he welcomes me warmly and with no further ado we go straight to his office. The two chairs are set up opposite each other at the appropriate distance. I am reminded of a lot of interview rooms that actors frequent when going up for jobs, there is even a small camera at the ready which takes me slightly by surprise.

Having collected my thoughts I start to mumble something pitiful about dyslexia and my mother. Before I have time to complete a sentence, Bob leaps in with a leading query – "Where is your father in all this?"

I am caught off guard by this million-dollar question. It immediately propels me into feelings of how proud I am of my dad. My quick footed reaction is to become distrustful of this whole set-up. I wanted to leap to my father's defence; how dare this powerhouse of a shrink imply anything untoward.

With a great deal of unease my eyes dart across the room, trying to avoid the man sitting in the opposite chair. My mind begins racing, chattering, trying to rationalize, putting into pockets of black and white sense the reason why I had come to York in the first place.

The scattered thoughts tearing about inside my head eventually fall into a place of some order. Gradually I'm able to look into Bob's unflustered face. I start to relax, and in becoming less anxious those introverted fireworks come to rest in a field of trust. Through a daze of tears the unfocused begins to pull into focus.

When it became known to some members of my family that I was seeing Bob on a professional basis, I was greeted with a wave of scepticism. But I wasn't, as I had done with Dr R D Laing and colleagues a decade or so previously, going to let those doubting voices get the better of me again. This time I was going to trust my gut instinct.

Even though he had been dead for a number of years, somewhere inside I am panicked, if not downright defensive when challenged about my dad. Locked in a quarrel with justification, my brain tries to justify these apprehensive feelings around my father, or indeed anyone who might question his standing. I had wrestled with these feelings many times when he was alive, but as the years rolled by I assumed them to be part of my chaotic personality, like a family trait, as normal as a genetic tic.

There was no doubt that we had much love for each other, but as my father George and I grew through the years together, if ever we tried to talk in depth, to really try and tell each other about our feelings, it just seemed to stultify any empathy, leaving a mutual aftermath of sadness and frustration between us.

As my sessions with Bob evolved, I realised that even after all these years I was still obsessed with gaining my parent's approval. Did this mean that somewhere in there I was still terrified of their disapproval?

Amazing though it may seem, this was the first time in my life that I had been able to talk with someone, (I was going to say grownup but I hesitate somewhat and use the word mature) mature, about this vulnerable and sometimes painful side of my relationship with my parents.

What had become almost unnoticeable, buried beneath a crust of integrity was this barb in my side, which unbelievably was now beginning to shift loose. All I had needed was to share my truth with someone who was able to hear with an open ear, someone who wasn't scared to delve that little bit deeper, for these cumbersome restraints to fall away.

The umbilical cord is something we know becomes severed and we go on from there, needing huge amounts of physical and emotional nourishment. I started life loved, but dwarfed by my father, unable to leave his side. Within a year of my being born my mother was busy with my sister Sarah. I think what happens then is that my emotional umbilical cord is naturally transferred to my father, who has more time for bringing up their son. This time is all-important; without nurturing the baby becomes a screaming jelly.

The emotional and physical needs of the baby are primal; the baby reaches out spontaneously to those most able to give. For those early years of infancy my father filled this need. He gave love the best way he could, but George's view of the world at that time must have been saturated with shock as well as relief. It was 1949 don't forget and aside from any personal misgivings, the waves of war were still resounding with an all too powerful echo. These dark feelings and horrific shadows are surely inherited if not exhumed. This may sound dramatic, but doesn't the aftermath of any destructive event have emotional and physical ramifications. The extremes for my father and many of his generation who survived the war, must have been mind numbing. There was no mention of post-war stress in those days. It was just accepted and expected that those fortunate enough to have come through this horrendous conflict, brush any horrors aside, knuckle down and slot back into their respective lives.

Was this intelligent sensitive man innocently sharing life with atrocities locked up inside of an undisclosed self? Like all of us, my father wanted the world to be just so. Did his flashbacks of the war, along with his dreams, especially those of becoming a writer, start to go somewhere he found hard to deal with? There were times when he certainly seemed to be carrying something very taut and explosive inside.

One question seems to open up another.

What was the nature of the link between my father's experiences and my chaotic feelings? Are fears passed on, from parent to child, from the first small Neanderthal fright, gaining in largeness like a downhill snowball, picking up speed and increasing in size as it races through the generations? Was I still trying to protect the cellar of my parent's undisclosed fears? Was this the weight that so frequently sat like lead in the pit of my stomach?

George often talked about his mother but rarely about his father. What were they like? Whether it was post-war stress, or the fears passed on through his mother and father, or a combination of both, it is hard to say, but one thing is for sure; I believe now that it is inevitable that petrified feelings are transferred through the emotional vortex, unless they can be exorcised.

In further sessions I learnt how I was still terrified of my mother's rejection and how irrational this now was. I admitted that the biggest fear I had was of upsetting my mother, but in opening up to this admission I saw how infantile my rationale was. I began to see that the underlying relationship with my mother revolved around the premise that if I upset her I don't exist. While this might be understandable for a small child, I saw how ridiculous it was for a fifty-three year old man to be frightened of being put in or out of his place by a spirited old lady, even if she did happen to be his mother.

I saw how frozen in the past my relationship with my mother was and how destructive my infantile need for her had become as an adult.

Without nurturing the infant is presented with the very real prospect of not existing, or to put it bluntly dying; but I was no longer a powerless infant, and this is the crux.

Once I had swallowed the stark embarrassment at the obvious simplicity of this crucial insight, I began to grasp the compassionate key. It was then that I really saw how tough my mother's journey had been and what a remarkable and interesting woman she turned out to be. Most importantly, by looking into the very heart of Cecilia's pain, and understanding fundamentally how impossible her childhood had been, I saw how her feelings towards the child-life were disenchanted from the start.

I had identified an obvious apparition, one that had been constantly difficult to realise. My mother and father were intelligent, peace loving, people whose dark private fears had unintentionally been passed on to them like a title down the ages, and then on to me. Now it was time for the exorcism, to get rid of these intolerable fears once and for all. I could no longer tolerate them; after all I am not my father's, my grandfather's, my great grandfather's, or anyone else's ghost.

How I resolve this stark irrationality now becomes a pressing life altering question. Books are written, wars are fought and yet when all is finished, the debilitating force seems to hold no bounds; I'm drawn into it, time after time.

There is no doubt that without yoga I would have died in the water a long while back, but for my practice to really find any kind of lasting peace, I believe it was essential to start untying these psychological knots, so deeply embedded in the body/mind.

If the infantile terror isn't resolved, is carried with us into the adult world, then we become the adults who are compounding the problem not recognizing it and certainly not resolving it.

The fact of the matter is that the word dyslexia didn't really exist when I was growing up in the fifties; you were either bright and intelligent, or thick and stupid, with not much in-between. The *I know best* syndrome, like a well oiled machine, was stressed to such an extent that it ran amuck in Cambridge and certainly succeeded in placing me squarely in a place of revenge and anger. The lack of acknowledgment and disrespect, for me and my kind, forced my outlook towards the mind and what it represented into a loathsome dead-end. This separation accentuated the divide, not just on the outside, but on the inside, encouraging the body and mind to become separated, caught up in a spiralling wheel of repellent conflict and self-hatred.

I can see now that if an innocent party said the right thing at the wrong time I would lash out with an over-the-top reaction. Because of this volatile temperament it isn't hard to see how it could have led to a major criminal offence. Thankfully I had now gained enough understanding of how these provocative triggers work, to introduce some mature rationale into the equation.

The anger and constant shame in my life, so frequently hard to contain, now tells me a different story. The mask of dyslexia, or for that matter any other mask, is not the problem, but the deeply embedded fears that create anger and shame are.

In my case frozen terror appeared as fear of failure, fear of abandonment, fear of what others thought and fear of my parent's disapproval, but most of all there was the fear of a monster in me, which had latterly almost grown too big for me see.

I came to understand, through many years of yoga practice, how excessive fear creates excessive tension. However, here I have learnt that if this fear remains in an infantile mind set, I can wilfully present an asana, paint that masterpiece, present that successful role in a play, but ultimately the destructive trait will remain, a dreadful liability. I will fail to realise a true sense of worth. Unresolved, the underlying disturbance will eventually come to the brink no matter what and somewhere down the line explode or implode. The more iced up I am in these past terrors the angrier and more violent are the terrible possibilities.

Over this essential time with Bob I came to see clearly, that the burns of anger become severe when the fires of fear are stoked. By seeing that the cause of blind and inflamed rage is terror, frozen in some carefully hidden past, it becomes obvious that as adults we have the opportunity to melt this seemingly intractable terror, thus quelling the rage.

The need in me for change had to be resolved, unless society really just wanted another fuck up. To talk of terror in someone with such privileges may seem scandalous, but that is how irrational the emotional centre can become if it isn't fixed.

If you think all this sounds a bit simplistic, idealistic even, think again.

This frozen terror may seem hypothetical, but frozen terror, to the one entrenched in it, is the brink of death. That, as infant, child, or powerless person, is the enormity of the fear; the fear experienced when feeling vulnerable and unprotected, dependent on someone unable to make you emotionally and or physically safe. If I don't escape this threatened and totally unprotected vulnerability, shut down here, immediately, I will be swallowed up by the black hole of death. The shutting down can become internal or external. When the shutdown is internal it might be hard to notice until it eventually manifests as depression for example. When external it can become screaming-agitated-out of control, making enough disturbances to shut everything out. Depending on the intensity of the terror these states can manifest in varying degrees. As an adult it is quite possible to lead a so called perfectly normal life and still be carrying the underlying, cleverly guarded terror deep inside. Often this drives and informs how we live out our lives, even if they seem successful.

Admitting to and going into this mess has been embarrassing and painful in the extreme, but it has made me aware of just how much of a psychological grip these deep rooted fears had on the path I took. It may seem illogical, annoyingly absurd, but when they were in full flight these powerful mindsets held me in a grip that was so severe I could have done untold damage.

For years I had tried to keep the difficulties in my life as far away from other members of the family as possible, especially my mother, because of the hurt it might bring; but how long could I keep up this charade?

Troublesome quirks in our children are put down to being part of their character, contained and separate from us; in them alone. This was our collective family conviction. I now see how this false belief created huge emotional rifts in our family. This is absolutely not a question of fault or blame, but a lifesaving question of why? Why are these painful and destructive behaviours treated merely as passing phases, troublesome quirks, when, for a great many of us, they lay down the foundations for how we map out the bulk of our lives?

For much of his adult life my father held a lot of anger close to his chest. This anger was rarely taken out directly on those closest to him, but it could often be seen if I pressed the wrong button, or when some political injustice reared its head, then it would come raging up through his body like some red hot herring. He was extremely intelligent, but sadly in his lifetime he wasn't able to resolve or relinquish the bulk of his underlying fear. I never knew why I felt affronted if friends of mine said your father's great but he seems so angry. But now I have accepted what this anger means, I feel closer than ever to being at one with the well being of his soul.

When my son Mick was born I was told by several people that the world was now my oyster. I had someone to carry the family name forwards and the family name meant togetherness, sanity and absolute conviction that nothing can be wrong with us. Here I was still being seduced by that strictest of commandments - the family's sanctum was god. At the beginning of Mick's illness, once again I became angry with the unfairness in the world with all its high handed institutions. It wasn't long before the anger overpowered me to such an extent, I caved in. And this was when the resolve in my life really started. In a way this full stop was what I needed and had been waiting for all along, but I had never allowed this to happen to me under the umbrella of my family because of our pride.

Denial cannot be taken lightly here, it has to be dug out, revealed and looked in the face. As in my case, it often takes a collapse of some kind to be able to start the work. Arriving at a place where one feels one is giving up – this is exactly what is needed. A giving up of our own rigid defences and overly intense survival mechanisms that have built up over the years has to be achieved. In denial, the clever part of our brain rationalizes away the fact that there can be anything wrong, in a flippant or philosophical way. It becomes like the building tension in a film noir, where the protagonist is never going to find out what happened, because the truth is very cleverly and cunningly covered up at every turn. As my brother constantly told me, the intellect may be useful, but it can also be extremely fickle.

I have had so many pointers along the way that something wasn't right, which I did my best to blank out. But most of all there is my own offence, this anger, which when turned against itself, had on occasion been so severe that like my brother I could only see suicide as a way of preventing any more pain.

Devastating though it was, Ponji felt impelled to take his own life; but it's the violent way in which he did it that stands out for me now. He chose a very public arena. It surely doesn't take much imagination, to see how he could have taken many other lives with him if he'd wanted to do so. That's how dangerous and destructive these unresolved fears become, if we don't pay them the due respect they deserve. Moved to the world stage war comes as no surprise.

This isn't about holding a family to ransom; this is about having the courage to face our own demons and untie the knots, which have impelled us to hold a pistol to the heads of reason for so long.

If it hadn't been for what happened to my brother, it would have been very difficult for me to really face the humble truth in my own life. I am sure I would have gone on with the family tradition of trying to convince myself and the world, that nothing was amiss – living in a place where I buried my fear under a blanket of deception – where I became supremely clever at persuading myself and those I love of reasons to live, other than what they really are, avoiding the all important life enhancing truths.

I can understand that my family's simmering fear and anxieties are not something that might come to mind among our friends, relations and genial social circle. But for me, sailing these emotional seas has been erratic, far from secure and a daily reality.

To many of my friends and family it will seem scandalous to paint a picture of my upbringing as anything other than privileged. Some may say that in spite of everything I've managed to get this far. But I think it is more imperative to ask why, despite a seemingly successful and flamboyant life, I was still tormented by so much underlying, debilitating and in the end irrational fear. The very fact of asking this simple, yet essential question brought with it the first vital steps of realising a new maturity.

Then, once my fears were allowed to become conscious, to reveal themselves in an open mind without censorship, they lost their stranglehold, their absolute power over me and I was able to realize an inner freedom that might never otherwise have seen the light of day.

If I have offended any of my family, near or extended, by telling this story, I apologise. It was never my intention to hurt, but merely to convey how it came across from this side of the fence.

I wanted to make amends.

Only when I make the choice to reach out, does the shroud of guilt and torment become disrobed and the heart-spring of healing begin its turn. The mist of tears and pain falls away into a distant past, like so many scales from the eyes and a never ending love o'er rides my senses, like a wave sweeping way across the shore, only to come again.

The warm glow of her lantern had been shimmering across the water from the river bank all along – I had just lost touch with how to see it.

I recognize now how lucky I've been to have had Lena and Mick at such close quarters and how fortunate I was to have found enough emotional clarity through yoga – for without these saving graces there can be no doubt that I would have ended up as the butt of someone else's idea, in someone else's coffin, a pawn in someone else's game, or at best on skid row.

It seems through some quirk of providence that I was destined to take the long way round, to tread near the edge for a wiser understanding of this extraordinary life.

I realize with gratitude, tinted with a little irony, that my parents have, perhaps unwillingly and certainly unwittingly, been complicit in this story. Now that I can look into the well of the past with some humility, one thing that stands out above all else – I have their extraordinary zeal to thank for putting me well and truly on this path. There is no doubt that it was George and Cecilia's gregarious spirit, which dictated an undefined need, guiding me almost unintentionally into this new world. Their call to celebrate freedom propelled me forward and ultimately led me to beg the question as to what freedom really is.

My mother and father may have started me on a road, wracked with pain and uncertainty, but I shall leave it with their laughter spilling from my heart.

And so it came for us to move on.

The upkeep of our house in Shropshire was usually one beat ahead of our earnings. We always said that if our financial constraints came to dominate for too long then it was time to cash in our assets, free things up and live according to our means. Although it's conducive to one's practice, you don't need a studio for yoga; for if the asana is released and focused, a mat and clear clean floor is all that's required.

As I see it now acting and yoga are about connection and non-connection with the great play of consciousness. We may build our bridges, our motorways, our monumental buildings and our rocket ships to Mars; but the more I reach for the infinite, the more I see how impossible it is to hold on to the all too familiar masks of the known.

Through chipping in with our resources and dreams, Mick, Lena and I have lived for the good part of five years on an island in the Mediterranean.

We live in a beautiful house, full of light, not far from the sea and I am closer than ever to a place that has no boundaries, where bricks and mortar need do no more than provide a seat for shelter.

I have spent my days here writing, practising yoga, supervising and sharing in some building projects – trying to savour the time. There are still dreams and fantasies of being left out and even moments when I lose a sense of reason, but when these fears tug at my sleeve they are mostly familiar ones, shrunk to my own size. On the occasions when I am caught unawares by a bigger one, the insight and the recovery is thankfully quick.

With those close, in the middle distance and faraway leaving these shores in ever increasing circles, it becomes clear that the dead hold a key to our universe, to our immortality. By touching the hand of my brother, sister, my father and dear friends who have passed before me, I see how their love and the undying spirit can purge the threshold and take me all the way.

My brother said many times how the body is an illusion tempered by the wrath of time on this earth. I may not have seen it quite like that when he was alive, but I have come to believe fundamentally that the body is a gateway to heaven here on earth today.

And the dialogue continues.

This is by no means the end, but as sure as day gives way to night, the sands of the hour glass have turned. While the wind may crack its tune and the sun beat a torrent drum, I will endeavour to go to the blood heart of the undying, unfathomable now and sit at ease with my sceptre of dust and crown of stars.

Note

I have gone to fetch some lettuce and veg;
There are blue flowers in the garden,
White wine in the fridge,
Red wine on the dresser,
The feast will soon begin.

George Scurfield 1988

Acknowledgements

To all the musicians and actors, who inspired me to take this journey when the odds seemed overwhelmingly against my ever doing so, thank you.

A very particular thanks to Sarah Grenville, Lucy Scurfield, Sophie Williams, Polly Mules, Margaret Alice Stewart Liberty, Sophia Stewart Liberty, Ian Moore, Jack Shepherd, Jim and Angela Cartwright, Ira Donner, Pixie Lillas, John Summers, Jack Murray, Amy Hollingworth, all of you have helped to clarify, hone and bring into the light of day this all-important and compelling part of my life. Your truths and support, careful ear and belief, have been central in seeing this book through to the present draft, I will always be encouraged and eternally grateful for that.

I am indebted to Robin Jones, Steven Beard and Rosemary Wilton, who became welcome collaborators, easing me into the realities of editing.

Thank you to Andrew Wilde and in turn Sue Johnson, whose enthusiasm and flare gave me the confidence to take the book to the penultimate stage – the understanding and sensitivity you both brought to the work gave me the extra clarity I needed to take the good with the bad out there.

I remain forever indebted to Bellur Krishnamachar Sundararaja Iyengar in bringing me to the yogic path, without which I would have surely perished.

A big thank you to my son Mick, whose love and great company is, and always has been, a huge inspiration. I hope this book goes some way towards giving you something back. I am so proud of you.

To Sean and Spencer, who put up with the bullshit and helped me to see in those twilight hours, I am sorry if I haven't been the greatest of support.

Above all, thank you for the patience of my wife Lena, whose insights and careful ear saw this book through its unique journey. I will never forget the excitement we had as we rearranged the words on the page to make some of the more ambiguous images sing. Quite simply, without your encouragement and undying love I just wouldn't have had a chance.

Index

Author

Matthew Scurfield lives in Gozo with his wife Lena and son Mick, where he is currently conjuring up another book.

As an actor he worked extensively in the theatre: credits include: Exeter in Henry V and Yellowhammer in A Chaste Maid in Cheapside for Shakespeare's Globe, Duke of Milan in Two Gentlemen of Verona also for the Globe, London and New York, The Father in Street of crocodiles (Theatre de Complicite /Royal National Theatre), Huld in The Trial (Royal National Theatre), Frosh in DieFledermaus (English National Opera), A Flea in Her Ear (Old Vic); Krogstad in A Dolls House (Haymarket Leicester), Macduff in Shakespeare's Macbeth (Royal National Theatre and US tour), Shadowing the Conqueror (Traverse Theatre Edinburgh), Metamorphosis (Mermaid Theatre), Malvolio in Twelfth Night (Bristol Little Theatre), Edward11 (Foco Novo); War Crimes (ICA), The Seagull (Shared Experience), Apart From George (National Theatre/Royal Court), Psy-Warriors (Royal Court), Agamemnon, East, Greek, Hamlet and Metamorphosis for (Steven Berkoff's London Theatre Group), seasons at The Nottingham Playhouse, Sheffield Crucible, The Everyman Liverpool and The Bristol Little Theatre.

Television credits include: Out of Hours, Kavanagh QC, A Dance to the Music of Time, Cosmic Sucker, Dangerfield, Pity, Winthrop Investigates, Casualty, Hitchhikers Guide to the Galaxy, Tales from the Crypt, Pie in the Sky, Wycliffe, A Touch of Frost, Here Comes the Mirror Man, Karaoke, Look Me in the Eye, Time after Time, Piglet Files, Minder, Sharps Honour, Smokescreen, The Chief, Blue Heaven, The Young Indiana Jones Chronicles, Murder of Quality, Zorro, Brookside, Shelley, a Guilty Thing Surprised and Heart of the Country.

Film credits include: Amy Foster, Black Beauty, Dakota Road, Monster Maker, Wedekind, The Loss Adjuster, 1984, The Jigsaw Man, Raiders of The Lost Ark, Sweeney 2 and McVicar.